Morris Ital Owners Workshop Manual

John S Mead

Models covered

Morris Ital 1.7 L, HL, HLS and SLX Saloon; 1695 cc
Morris Ital 1.7 L, HL, HLS, SL and SLX Estate; 1695 cc
Morris Ital 2.0 HLS Saloon and Estate; 1993 cc

ISBN 1 85010 064 0

Printed in England *(714–6K1)*

ABCDE
FGHIJ
KLMNI

HAYNES PUBLISHING GROUP
SPARKFORD YEOVIL SOMERSET BA22 7JJ ENGLAND
distributed in the USA by
HAYNES PUBLICATIONS INC
861 LAWRENCE DRIVE
NEWBURY PARK
CALIFORNIA 91320
USA

D1333208

Acknowledgements

Thanks are due to BL Cars Limited and also to Vincents of Yeovil for the supply of technical information. The Champion Sparking Plug Company supplied the illustrations showing the various spark plug conditions and Sykes-Pickavant Ltd provided some of the workshop tools. Special thanks are due to all those people at Sparkford who helped in the production of this manual.

About this manual

Its aim

The aim of this manual is to help you get the best from your car. It can do so in several ways. It can help you decide what work must be done (even should you choose to get it done by a garage), provide information on routine maintenance and servicing, and give a logical course of action and diagnosis when random faults occur. However, it is hoped that you will use the manual by tackling the work yourself. On simpler jobs it may even be quicker than booking the car into a garage and going there twice to leave and collect it. Perhaps most important, a lot of money can be saved by avoiding the costs the garage must charge to cover its labour and overheads.

The manual has drawings and descriptions to show the function of the various components so that their layout can be understood. Then the tasks are described and photographed in a step-by-step sequence so that even a novice can do the work.

Its arrangement

The manual is divided into twelve Chapters, each covering a logical sub-division of the vehicle. The Chapters are each divided into Sections, numbered with single figures, eg 5; and the Sections into paragraphs (or sub-sections), with decimal numbers following on from the Section they are in, eg 5.1. 5.2, 5.3 etc.

It is freely illustrated, especially in those parts where there is a detailed sequence of operations to be carried out. There are two forms of illustration: figures and photographs. The figures are numbered in sequence with decimal numbers, according to their position in the Chapter – Fig. 6.4 is the fourth drawing/illustration in Chapter 6. Photographs carry the same number (either individually or in related groups) as the Section or sub-section to which they relate.

There is an alphabetical index at the back of the manual as well as a contents list at the front. Each Chapter is also preceded by its own individual contents list.

References to the 'left' or 'right' of the vehicle are in the sense of a person in the driver's seat facing forwards.

Unless otherwise stated, nuts and bolts are removed by turning anti-clockwise, and tightened by turning clockwise.

Vehicle manufacturers continually make changes to specifications and recommendations, and these, when notified, are incorporated into our manuals at the earliest opportunity.

Whilst every care is taken to ensure that the information in this manual is correct, no liability can be accepted by the authors or publishers for loss, damage or injury caused by any errors in, or omissions from, the information given.

Introduction to the Morris Ital 1.7 and 2.0

Introduced as a replacement for the Marina, the Ital has been extensively restyled around a proven formula, offering spacious and comfortable accommodation, lively performance and acceptable handling.

The models covered by this manual are all powered by the in-line, single overhead camshaft O-series engine, available in either 1.7 or 2.0 litre versions.

All models are equipped with dual circuit servo-assisted brakes, disc on the front wheels and drum at the rear.

Front suspension is independent by torsion bars, while at the rear a live axle is used in conjunction with leaf springs and telescopic shock absorbers. Anti-roll bars are fitted at the front and rear.

The steering gear is of the rack-and-pinion type, incorporating a segmented impact absorbing column.

A four-speed all-synchromesh manual gearbox is fitted as standard equipment to 1.7 litre models, with a three-speed automatic transmission available as an option. The 2.0 litre models are available with automatic transmission only.

The Ital is relatively simple and straightforward to work on. All the major components have been proven in use previously, so have a long development period behind them resulting in good reliability.

Contents

Morris Ital HLS Saloon

Morris Ital HL Estate

Buying spare parts and vehicle identification numbers

Buying spare parts

Spare parts are available from many sources, for example: BL dealers, other garages and accessory shops, and motor factors. Our advice regarding spare part sources is as follows:

Officially appointed BL garages – This is the best source of parts which are peculiar to your car and are otherwise not generally available (eg complete cylinder heads, internal gearbox components, badges, interior trim etc). It is also the only place at which you should have repairs carried out if your car is still under warranty – non-BL components may invalidate the warranty. To be sure of obtaining the correct parts it will always be necessary to give the storeman your car's vehicle identification number, and if possible, to take the old part along for positive identification. It obviously makes good sense to go straight to the specialists on your car for this type of part for they are best equipped to supply you.

Other garages and accessory shops – These are often very good places to buy materials and components needed for the maintenance of your car (eg spark plugs, bulbs, fan belts, oils and greases, filler paste etc). They also sell general accessories, usually have convenient opening hours, charge reasonable prices and can often be found not far from home.

Motor factors – Good factors will stock all the more important components which wear out relatively quickly (eg clutch components, pistons, valves, exhaust systems, brake cylinders/pipes/hoses/seals/shoes and pads etc). Motor factors will often provide new or reconditioned components on a part exchange basis – this can save a considerable amount of money.

Vehicle identification numbers

The car number is located on a metal plate fixed to the bonnet lock platform.

The engine number is stamped on a plate fixed to the cylinder block on the right-hand side of the engine.

The manual gearbox number is on a label attached to the right-hand side of the casing. *On automatic transmission models,* the number is stamped on the left-hand side of the casing.

The rear axle number is stamped on the outside face of the differential casing joint flange.

Jacking and towing

Jacking points

To change a wheel in an emergency, use the jack supplied with the car. Ensure that the roadwheel nuts are slackened before jacking up the car, that the handbrake is applied, and that the diagonally opposite wheel to the one being removed is suitably chocked. Make sure that the jack is standing on a firm surface and that the peg on the jack head locates in the hole of the jacking point.

The jack supplied with the car is not suitable for use when raising the car for maintenance or repair operations. For this work use a trolley, hydraulic or screw-type jack located under the front chassis members or the rear axle. Always supplement the jack with axle stands or other suitable supports before crawling under the car.

Towing

If the car is being towed, attach the tow rope to the towing eyes located forward of each front tie-bar on the chassis members. If the car is equipped with automatic transmission, the distance towed must not exceed 30 miles (48 km), nor the speed exceed 30 mph (48 km/h), otherwise serious damage to the transmission may result. If these limits are likely to be exceeded, or there are unusual noises coming from the transmission, disconnect and remove the propeller shaft.

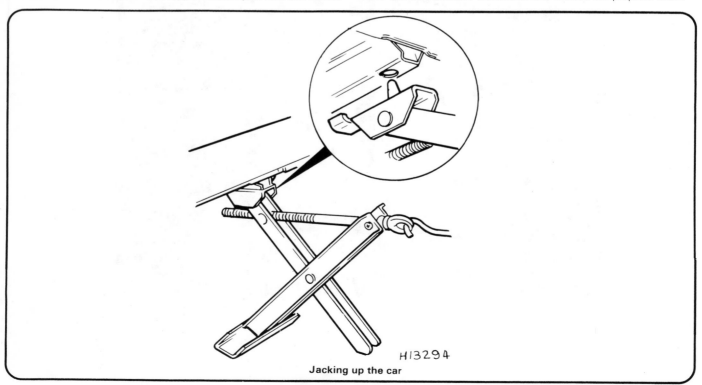

H13294

Jacking up the car

Tools and working facilities

Introduction

A selection of good tools is a fundamental requirement for anyone contemplating the maintenance and repair of a motor vehicle. For the owner who does not possess any, their purchase will prove a considerable expense, offsetting some of the savings made by doing-it-yourself. However, provided that the tools purchased are of good quality, they will last for many years and prove an extremely worthwhile investment.

To help the average owner to decide which tools are needed to carry out the various tasks detailed in this manual, we have compiled three lists of tools under the following headings: *Maintenance and minor repair, Repair and overhaul,* and *Special.* The newcomer to practical mechanics should start off with the *Maintenance and minor repair* tool kit and confine himself to the simpler jobs around the vehicle. Then, as his confidence and experience grows, he can undertake more difficult tasks, buying extra tools as, and when, they are needed. In this way, a *Maintenance and minor repair* tool kit can be built-up into a *Repair and overhaul* tool kit over a considerable period of time without any major cash outlays. The experienced do-it-yourselfer will have a tool kit good enough for most repair and overhaul procedures and will add tools from the *Special* category when he feels the expense is justified by the amount of use to which these tools will be put.

It is obviously not possible to cover the subject of tools fully here. For those who wish to learn more about tools and their use there is a book entitled *How to Choose and Use Car Tools* available from the publishers of this manual.

Maintenance and minor repair tool kit

The tools given in this list should be considered as a minimum requirement if routine maintenance, servicing and minor repair operations are to be undertaken. We recommend the purchase of combination spanners (ring one end, open-ended the other); although more expensive than open-ended ones, they do give the advantages of both types of spanner.

Combination spanners - $\frac{7}{16}$, $\frac{1}{2}$, $\frac{9}{16}$, $\frac{5}{8}$, $\frac{13}{16}$, $\frac{15}{16}$ in AF
Adjustable spanner - 9 inch
Rear axle drain plug key
Spark plug spanner (with rubber insert)
Spark plug gap adjustment tool
Set of feeler gauges
Brake bleed nipple spanner
Screwdriver - 4 in long x $\frac{1}{4}$ in dia (flat blade)
Screwdriver - 4 in long x $\frac{1}{4}$ in dia (cross blade)
Combination pliers - 6 inch
Hacksaw (junior)
Tyre pump
Tyre pressure gauge
Grease gun
Oil can
Fine emery cloth (1 sheet)
Wire brush (small)
Funnel (medium size)

Repair and overhaul tool kit

These tools are virtually essential for anyone undertaking any major repairs to a motor vehicle, and are additional to those given in the *Maintenance and minor repair* list. Included in this list is a comprehensive set of sockets. Although these are expensive they will be found invaluable as they are so versatile - particularly if various drives are included in the set. We recommend the $\frac{1}{2}$ in square-drive type, as this can be used with most proprietary torque spanners. If you cannot afford a socket set, even bought piecemeal, then inexpensive tubular box wrenches are a useful alternative.

The tools in this list will occasionally need to be supplemented by tools from the *Special* list.

Sockets (or box spanners) to cover range in previous list
Reversible ratchet drive (for use with sockets)
Extension piece, 10 inch (for use with sockets)
Universal joint (for use with sockets)
Torque wrench (for use with sockets)
'Mole' wrench — 8 inch
Ball pein hammer
Soft-faced hammer, plastic or rubber
Screwdriver - 6 in long x $\frac{5}{16}$ in dia (flat blade)
Screwdriver - 2 in long x $\frac{5}{16}$ in square (flat blade)
Screwdriver - 1$\frac{1}{2}$ in long x $\frac{1}{4}$ in (cross blade)
Screwdriver - 3 in long x $\frac{1}{8}$ in dia (electricians)
Pliers - electricians side cutters
Pliers - needle nosed
Pliers - circlip (internal and external)
Cold chisel - $\frac{1}{2}$ inch
Scriber
Scraper
Centre punch
Pin punch
Hacksaw
Valve grinding tool
Steel rule/straight-edge
Allen keys
Selection of files
Wire brush (large)
Axle-stands
Jack (strong scissor or hydraulic type)

Special tools

The tools in this list are those which are not used regularly, are expensive to buy, or which need to be used in accordance with their manufacturers' instructions. Unless relatively difficult mechanical jobs are undertaken frequently, it will not be economic to buy many of these tools. Where this is the case, you could consider clubbing together with friends (or joining a motorists' club) to make a joint purchase, or borrowing the tools against a deposit from a local garage or tool hire specialist.

The following list contains only those tools and instruments freely available to the public, and not those special tools produced by the vehicle manufacturer specifically for its dealer network. You will find occasional references to these manufacturers' special tools in the text of this manual. Generally, an alternative method of doing the job without the vehicle manufacturers' special tool is given. However, sometimes, there is no alternative to using them. Where this is the case and the relevant tool cannot be bought or borrowed you will have to entrust the work to a franchised garage.

Valve spring compressor
Piston ring compressor
Balljoint separator
Universal hub/bearing puller
Impact screwdriver
Micrometer and/or vernier gauge
Dial gauge
Stroboscopic timing light
Dwell angle meter/tachometer
Universal electrical multi-meter
Cylinder compression gauge
Lifting tackle
Trolley jack
Light with extension lead

Buying tools

For practically all tools, a tool dealer is the best source since he will have a very comprehensive range compared with the average garage or accessory shop. Having said that, accessory shops often offer excellent quality tools at discount prices, so it pays to shop around.

Remember, you don't have to buy the most expensive items on the shelf, but it is always advisable to steer clear of the very cheap tools. There are plenty of good tools around at reasonable prices, so ask the proprietor or manager of the shop for advice before making a purchase.

Care and maintenance of tools

Having purchased a reasonable tool kit, it is necessary to keep the tools in a clean serviceable condition. After use, always wipe off any dirt, grease and metal particles using a clean, dry cloth, before putting the tools away. Never leave them lying around after they have been used. A simple tool rack on the garage or workshop wall, for items such as screwdrivers and pliers is a good idea. Store all normal spanners and sockets in a metal box. Any measuring instruments, gauges, meters, etc, must be carefully stored where they cannot be damaged or become rusty.

Take a little care when tools are used. Hammer heads inevitably become marked and screwdrivers lose the keen edge on their blades from time to time. A little timely attention with emery cloth or a file will soon restore items like this to a good serviceable finish.

Working facilities

Not to be forgotten when discussing tools, is the workshop itself. If anything more than routine maintenance is to be carried out, some form of suitable working area becomes essential.

It is appreciated that many an owner mechanic is forced by circumstances to remove an engine or similar item, without the benefit of a garage or workshop. Having done this, any repairs should always be done under the cover of a roof.

Wherever possible, any dismantling should be done on a clean flat workbench or table at a suitable working height.

Any workbench needs a vice: one with a jaw opening of 4 in (100 mm) is suitable for most jobs. As mentioned previously, some clean dry storage space is also required for tools, as well as the lubricants, cleaning fluids, touch-up paints and so on which become necessary.

Another item which may be required, and which has a much more general usage, is an electric drill with a chuck capacity of at least $\frac{5}{16}$ in (8 mm). This, together with a good range of twist drills, is virtually essential for fitting accessories such as wing mirrors and reversing lights.

Last, but not least, always keep a supply of old newspapers and clean, lint-free rags available, and try to keep any working area as clean as possible.

Spanner jaw gap comparison table

Jaw gap (in)	Spanner size
0.250	$\frac{1}{4}$ in AF
0.276	7 mm
0.313	$\frac{5}{16}$ in AF
0.315	8 mm
0.344	$\frac{11}{32}$ in AF; $\frac{1}{8}$ in Whitworth
0.354	9 mm
0.375	$\frac{3}{8}$ in AF
0.394	10 mm
0.433	11 mm
0.438	$\frac{7}{16}$ in AF
0.445	$\frac{3}{16}$ in Whitworth; $\frac{1}{4}$ in BSF
0.472	12 mm
0.500	$\frac{1}{2}$ in AF
0.512	13 mm
0.525	$\frac{1}{4}$ in Whitworth; $\frac{5}{16}$ in BSF
0.551	14 mm
0.563	$\frac{9}{16}$ in AF
0.591	15 mm
0.600	$\frac{5}{16}$ in Whitworth; $\frac{3}{8}$ in BSF
0.625	$\frac{5}{8}$ in AF
0.630	16 mm
0.669	17 mm
0.686	$\frac{11}{16}$ in AF
0.709	18 mm
0.710	$\frac{3}{8}$ in Whitworth, $\frac{7}{16}$ in BSF
0.748	19 mm
0.750	$\frac{3}{4}$ in AF
0.813	$\frac{13}{16}$ in AF
0.820	$\frac{7}{16}$ in Whitworth; $\frac{1}{2}$ in BSF
0.866	22 mm
0.875	$\frac{7}{8}$ in AF
0.920	$\frac{1}{2}$ in Whitworth; $\frac{9}{16}$ in BSF
0.938	$\frac{15}{16}$ in AF
0.945	24 mm
1.000	1 in AF
1.010	$\frac{9}{16}$ in Whitworth; $\frac{5}{8}$ in BSF
1.024	26 mm
1.063	$1\frac{1}{16}$ in AF; 27 mm
1.100	$\frac{5}{8}$ in Whitworth; $\frac{11}{16}$ in BSF
1.125	$1\frac{1}{8}$ in AF
1.181	30 mm
1.200	$\frac{11}{16}$ in Whitworth; $\frac{3}{4}$ in BSF
1.250	$1\frac{1}{4}$ in AF
1.260	32 mm
1.300	$\frac{3}{4}$ in Whitworth; $\frac{7}{8}$ in BSF
1.313	$1\frac{5}{16}$ in AF
1.390	$\frac{13}{16}$ in Whitworth; $\frac{15}{16}$ in BSF
1.417	36 mm
1.438	$1\frac{7}{16}$ in AF
1.480	$\frac{7}{8}$ in Whitworth; 1 in BSF
1.500	$1\frac{1}{2}$ in AF
1.575	40 mm; $\frac{15}{16}$ in Whitworth
1.614	41 mm
1.625	$1\frac{5}{8}$ in AF
1.670	1 in Whitworth; $1\frac{1}{8}$ in BSF
1.688	$1\frac{11}{16}$ in AF
1.811	46 mm
1.813	$1\frac{13}{16}$ in AF
1.860	$1\frac{1}{8}$ in Whitworth; $1\frac{1}{4}$ in BSF
1.875	$1\frac{7}{8}$ in AF
1.969	50 mm
2.000	2 in AF
2.050	$1\frac{1}{4}$ in Whitworth; $1\frac{3}{8}$ in BSF
2.165	55 mm
2.362	60 mm

General repair procedures

Whenever servicing, repair or overhaul work is carried out on the car or its components, it is necessary to observe the following procedures and instructions. This will assist in carrying out the operation efficiently and to a professional standard of workmanship.

Joint mating faces and gaskets

Where a gasket is used between the mating faces of two components, ensure that it is renewed on reassembly, and fit it dry unless otherwise stated in the repair procedure. Make sure that the mating faces are clean and dry with all traces of old gasket removed. When cleaning a joint face, use a tool which is not likely to score or damage the face, and remove any burrs or nicks with an oilstone or fine file.

Make sure that tapped holes are cleaned with a pipe cleaner, and keep them free of jointing compound if this is being used unless specifically instructed otherwise.

Ensure that all orifices, channels or pipes are clear and blow through them, preferably using compressed air.

Oil seals

Whenever an oil seal is removed from its working location, either individually or as part of an assembly, it should be renewed.

The very fine sealing lip of the seal is easily damaged and will not seal if the surface it contacts is not completely clean and free from scratches, nicks or grooves. If the original sealing surface of the component cannot be restored, the component should be renewed.

Protect the lips of the seal from any surface which may damage them in the course of fitting. Use tape or a conical sleeve where possible. Lubricate the seal lips with oil before fitting and, on dual lipped seals, fill the space between the lips with grease.

Unless otherwise stated, oil seals must be fitted with their sealing lips toward the lubricant to be sealed.

Use a tubular drift or block of wood of the appropriate size to install the seal and, if the seal housing is shouldered, drive the seal down to the shoulder. If the seal housing is unshouldered, the seal should be fitted with its face flush with the housing top face.

Screw threads and fastenings

Always ensure that a blind tapped hole is completely free from oil, grease, water or other fluid before installing the bolt or stud. Failure to do this could cause the housing to crack due to the hydraulic action of the bolt or stud as it is screwed in.

When tightening a castellated nut to accept a split pin, tighten the nut to the specified torque, where applicable, and then tighten further to the next split pin hole. Never slacken the nut to align a split pin hole unless stated in the repair procedure.

When checking or retightening a nut or bolt to a specified torque setting, slacken the nut or bolt by a quarter of a turn, and then retighten to the specified setting.

Locknuts, locktabs and washers

Any fastening which will rotate against a component or housing in the course of tightening should always have a washer between it and the relevant component or housing.

Spring or split washers should always be renewed when they are used to lock a critical component such as a big-end bearing retaining nut or bolt.

Locktabs which are folded over to retain a nut or bolt should always be renewed.

Self-locking nuts can be reused in non-critical areas, providing resistance can be felt when the locking portion passes over the bolt or stud thread.

Split pins must always be replaced with new ones of the correct size for the hole.

Special tools

Some repair procedures in this manual entail the use of special tools such as a press, two or three-legged pullers, spring compressors etc. Wherever possible, suitable readily available alternatives to the manufacturer's special tools are described, and are shown in use. In some instances, where no alternative is possible, it has been necessary to resort to the use of a manufacturer's tool and this has been done for reasons of safety as well as the efficient completion of the repair operation. Unless you are highly skilled and have a thorough understanding of the procedure described, never attempt to bypass the use of any special tool when the procedure described specifies its use. Not only is there a very great risk of personal injury, but expensive damage could be caused to the components involved.

Recommended lubricants and fluids

Component or system	Lubricant type or specification
Engine (1)	SAE 15W/50 multigrade engine oil
Manual transmission (2)	SAE 90EP gear oil
Automatic transmission (3)	Automatic transmission fluid type G
Rear axle (4)	SAE 90EP gear oil
Grease points (5)	Multi-purpose lithium grease
Carburettor piston damper (6)	SAE 15W/50 multigrade engine oil
Brake and clutch master cylinder reservoirs (7)	Universal hydraulic fluid to specification J1703C
Cooling system (8)	Universal antifreeze to specification BS 3151 or 3152
Locks, hinges, pivots, etc (9)	General purpose light oil
Automatic transmission linkage (10)	SAE 15W/50 multigrade engine oil
Distributor (11)	SAE 15W/50 multigrade engine oil and multi-purpose lithium grease (see Chapter 4)

Note *The above are general recommendations only. Different operating territories require different lubricants. If in doubt, consult the driver's handbook or the nearest BL dealer.*

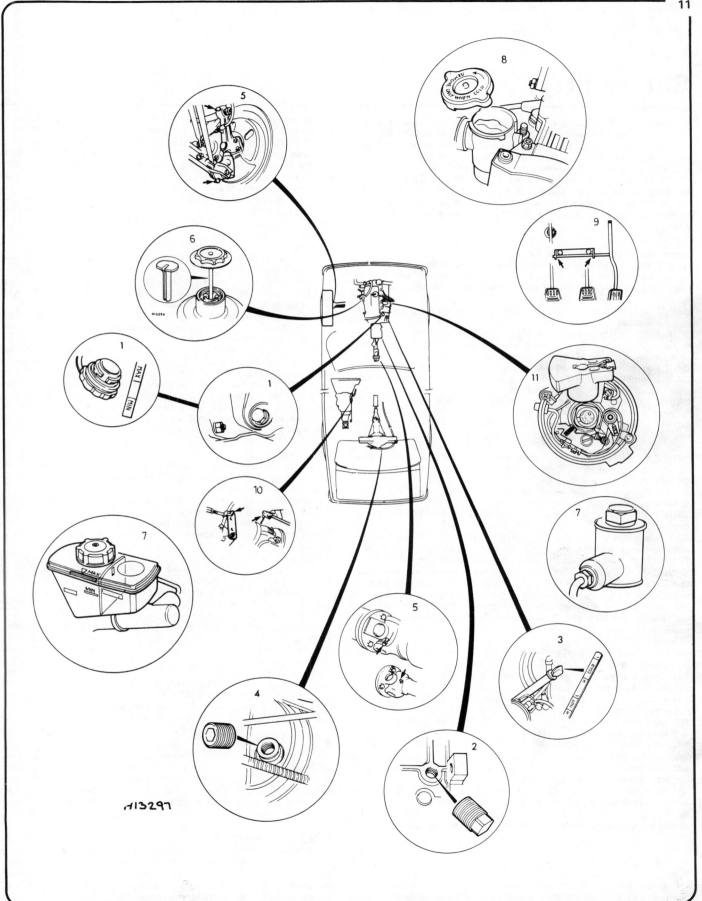

Safety first!

Professional motor mechanics are trained in safe working procedures. However enthusiastic you may be about getting on with the job in hand, do take the time to ensure that your safety is not put at risk. A moment's lack of attention can result in an accident, as can failure to observe certain elementary precautions.

There will always be new ways of having accidents, and the following points do not pretend to be a comprehensive list of all dangers; they are intended rather to make you aware of the risks and to encourage a safety-conscious approach to all work you carry out on your vehicle.

Essential DOs and DON'Ts

DON'T rely on a single jack when working underneath the vehicle. Always use reliable additional means of support, such as axle stands, securely placed under a part of the vehicle that you know will not give way.

DON'T attempt to loosen or tighten high-torque nuts (e.g. wheel hub nuts) while the vehicle is on a jack; it may be pulled off.

DON'T start the engine without first ascertaining that the transmission is in neutral (or 'Park' where applicable) and the parking brake applied.

DON'T suddenly remove the filler cap from a hot cooling system — cover it with a cloth and release the pressure gradually first, or you may get scalded by escaping coolant.

DON'T attempt to drain oil until you are sure it has cooled sufficiently to avoid scalding you.

DON'T grasp any part of the engine, exhaust or catalytic converter without first ascertaining that it is sufficiently cool to avoid burning you.

DON'T syphon toxic liquids such as fuel, brake fluid or antifreeze by mouth, or allow them to remain on your skin.

DON'T inhale brake lining dust — it is injurious to health.

DON'T allow any spilt oil or grease to remain on the floor — wipe it up straight away, before someone slips on it.

DON'T use ill-fitting spanners or other tools which may slip and cause injury.

DON'T attempt to lift a heavy component which may be beyond your capability — get assistance.

DON'T rush to finish a job, or take unverified short cuts.

DON'T allow children or animals in or around an unattended vehicle.

DO wear eye protection when using power tools such as drill, sander, bench grinder etc, and when working under the vehicle.

DO use a barrier cream on your hands prior to undertaking dirty jobs — it will protect your skin from infection as well as making the dirt easier to remove afterwards; but make sure your hands aren't left slippery.

DO keep loose clothing (cuffs, tie etc) and long hair well out of the way of moving mechanical parts.

DO remove rings, wristwatch etc, before working on the vehicle — especially the electrical system.

DO ensure that any lifting tackle used has a safe working load rating adequate for the job.

DO keep your work area tidy — it is only too easy to fall over articles left lying around.

DO get someone to check periodically that all is well, when working alone on the vehicle.

DO carry out work in a logical sequence and check that everything is correctly assembled and tightened afterwards.

DO remember that your vehicle's safety affects that of yourself and others. If in doubt on any point, get specialist advice.

IF, in spite of following these precautions, you are unfortunate enough to injure yourself, seek medical attention as soon as possible.

Fire

Remember at all times that petrol (gasoline) is highly flammable. Never smoke, or have any kind of naked flame around, when working

on the vehicle. But the risk does not end there — a spark caused by an electrical short-circuit, by two metal surfaces contacting each other, or even by static electricity built up in your body under certain conditions, can ignite petrol vapour, which in a confined space is highly explosive.

Always disconnect the battery earth (ground) terminal before working on any part of the fuel system, and never risk spilling fuel on to a hot engine or exhaust.

It is recommended that a fire extinguisher of a type suitable for fuel and electrical fires is kept handy in the garage or workplace at all times. Never try to extinguish a fuel or electrical fire with water.

Fumes

Certain fumes are highly toxic and can quickly cause unconsciousness and even death if inhaled to any extent. Petrol (gasoline) vapour comes into this category, as do the vapours from certain solvents such as trichloroethylene. Any draining or pouring of such volatile fluids should be done in a well ventilated area.

When using cleaning fluids and solvents, read the instructions carefully. Never use materials from unmarked containers — they may give off poisonous vapours.

Never run the engine of a motor vehicle in an enclosed space such as a garage. Exhaust fumes contain carbon monoxide which is extremely poisonous; if you need to run the engine, always do so in the open air or at least have the rear of the vehicle outside the workplace.

If you are fortunate enough to have the use of an inspection pit, never drain or pour petrol, and never run the engine, while the vehicle is standing over it; the fumes, being heavier than air, will concentrate in the pit with possibly lethal results.

The battery

Never cause a spark, or allow a naked light, near the vehicle's battery. It will normally be giving off a certain amount of hydrogen gas, which is highly explosive.

Always disconnect the battery earth (ground) terminal before working on the fuel or electrical systems.

If possible, loosen the filler plugs or cover when charging the battery from an external source. Do not charge at an excessive rate or the battery may burst.

Take care when topping up and when carrying the battery. The acid electrolyte, even when diluted, is very corrosive and should not be allowed to contact the eyes or skin.

If you ever need to prepare electrolyte yourself, always add the acid slowly to the water, and never the other way round. Protect against splashes by wearing rubber gloves and goggles.

When jump starting a car using a booster battery, for negative earth (ground) vehicles, connect the jump leads in the following sequence: First connect one jump lead between the positive (+) terminals of the two batteries. Then connect the other jump lead first to the negative (−) terminal of the booster battery, and then to a good earthing (ground) point on the vehicle to be started, at least 18 in (45 cm) from the battery if possible. Ensure that hands and jump leads are clear of any moving parts, and that the two vehicles do not touch. Disconnect the leads in the reverse order.

Mains electricity

When using an electric power tool, inspection light etc, which works from the mains, always ensure that the appliance is correctly connected to its plug and that, where necessary, it is properly earthed (grounded). Do not use such appliances in damp conditions and, again, beware of creating a spark or applying excessive heat in the vicinity of fuel or fuel vapour.

Ignition HT voltage

A severe electric shock can result from touching certain parts of the ignition system, such as the HT leads, when the engine is running or being cranked, particularly if components are damp or the insulation is defective. Where an electronic ignition system is fitted, the HT voltage is much higher and could prove fatal.

Routine maintenance

Maintenance is essential for ensuring safety and desirable for the purpose of getting the best in terms of performance and economy from your car. Over the years the need for periodic lubrication, oiling, greasing and so on, has been drastically reduced if not totally eliminated. This has unfortunately tended to lead some owners to think that because no such action is required, components either no longer exist, or will last forever. This is a serious delusion. It follows, therefore, that the largest initial element of maintenance is visual examination. This may lead to repairs or renewals.

The maintenace instructions are those recommended by the manufacturers. They are supplemented by additional maintenance tasks which, from practical experience, need to be carried out.

Every 250 miles (400 km) or weekly – whichever comes first

1   Remove the dipstick and check the engine oil level, which should be up to the MAX mark. Top up the oil in the sump with the recommended oil. On no account allow the oil to fall below the MIN mark on the dipstick. The distance between MAX and MIN marks corresponds to approximately 1.5 pints (0.85 litres).

2   Check the battery electrolyte level and top up as necessary with distilled water. Make sure that the top of the battery is always kept clean and free of moisture. See Chapter 10 (photo).

3   Check the level of coolant in the translucent expansion tank. This should be maintained at the required level mark by adding coolant via the cap (photo). If the expansion tank is empty, top up the cooling system via the filler cap on the thermostat housing as described in Chapter 2, and check for leaks (photo). **Note**: *If the engine is hot, place a rag over the expansion tank pressure cap and release the pressure cap slowly to avoid injury from escaping steam.*

4   Check the tyre pressures with an accurate gauge and adjust as necessary. Make sure that the tyre walls and treads are free of damage. Remember that the tyre tread should have a minimum of 1 millimetre depth across the total width of the tread.

5   Refill the windscreen washer container. Add an anti-freezing solution satchel in cold weather to prevent freezing. *(do not use ordinary antifreeze)*. Check that the jets operate correctly.

6   Remove the wheel trims and check all wheel nuts for tightness, but take care not to overtighten.

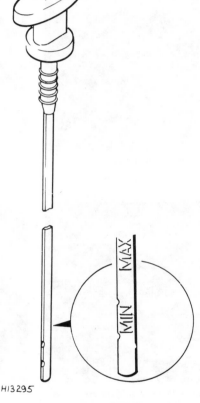

H13295

Engine oil level dipstick

Top up the battery with distilled water

Keep the expansion tank topped up to the level mark on the side of the tank

If the tank is empty, top up the system via the thermostat housing

The oil sump drain plug is on the right-hand side of the sump

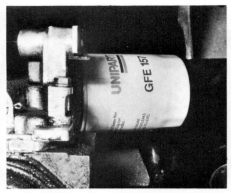

The oil filter is accessible from underneath the car

Refill the engine with the recommended grade of oil

Grease the swivel hub top...

...and bottom nipples

Lubricate the handbrake cable and linkage with engine oil

The rear axle oil level should be up to the filler plug aperture

Check the security of the exhaust mountings

Gearbox level/filler plug (A) and drain plug (B)

The oil level in the carburettor piston damper should be level with the top of the hollow piston rod

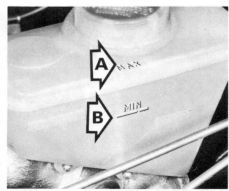

Maintain the fluid level in the brake master cylinder between the MAX (A) and MIN (B) marks

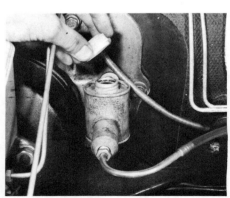

The fluid level in the clutch master cylinder should be up to the base of the filler cap threads

Every 6000 miles (10 000 km) or 6 months – whichever comes first

1   Jack up the front of the car and securely support it on axle stands.

2   Place a bowl or other suitable container beneath the engine sump drain plug which is located on the right-hand side at the rear of the sump (photo). Using a socket or ring spanner, unscrew the drain plug together with its copper sealing washer and allow the oil to drain into the container.

3   While the oil is draining, unscrew the engine oil filter canister located on the right-hand side of the engine and discard it (photo). The filter will probably be initially tight and will require a strap wrench or similar oil filter removing tool to unscrew it. Smear the rubber seal on a new canister with a little engine oil and refit it to the filter head. Screw it on and tighten it by hand only.

4   Check the sump drain plug copper sealing washer, and if damaged fit a new one. By now the oil should have finished draining, allowing the drain plug to be refitted. Refill the engine with the recommended grade and quantity of engine oil, and clean off any oil which may have been spilled over the engine or its components (photo).

5   With the front of the car still jacked up, remove the front roadwheels and carefully inspect the brake pads for wear and the discs for scoring or damage. Renew both sets of pads if any pad is worn to less than the minimum thickness given in the Specifications at the beginning of Chapter 9. Also examine the brake pipes and flexible hoses for signs of corrosion or deterioration and renew as necessary.

6   Lubricate the top and bottom grease nipples on each of the front swivel hubs with a few strokes of a grease gun filled with multi-purpose lithium grease (photos).

7   Inspect the steering rack rubber boots for signs of leakage or deterioration which, if evident, must be rectified as described in Chapter 11.

8   Inspect all the steering and front suspension components for wear or damage, and all the securing nuts and bolts for tightness. Lubricate where necessary. Refer to Chapter 11 for full information on the suspension and steering components.

9   Carefully inspect the front tyres for cuts in the fabric, exposure of the ply or cord structure, and for lumps or bulges. Make sure that there is a minimum of 1 mm depth across total width of the tread.

10   Refit the front roadwheels and lower the car to the ground. Recheck the tightness of the wheel nuts after lowering the car.

11   Now jack up the rear of the car and support it on axle stands.

12   Refer to Chapter 9 and adjust the rear brakes, and if necessary the handbrake. Lubricate the exposed mechanical linkage of the handbrake with engine oil and inspect the cable for signs of fraying (photo). Also check the hydraulic brake pipes and the rear flexible hose for corrosion or deterioration and take remedial action, if necessary, as described in Chapter 9.

13   Using a suitable Allen key unscrew the rear axle oil filler/level plug and check that the oil level is just up to the bottom of the filler aperture threads (photo). If necessary top up with the specified grade of gear oil. Refit and fully tighten the filler/level plug.

14   Inspect all the rear suspension components for any signs of wear or damage and check the retaining nuts and bolts for tightness.

15   Carry out a careful inspection of the exhaust system, making sure that all the joints and mountings are secure and that there is no sign of leakage or corrosion in the system (photo). Any small leaks may be repaired with a proprietary exhaust repair bandage, but if the leak is severe the exhaust section should be renewed as described in Chapter 3.

16   Check the propeller shaft universal joints for wear as described in Chapter 7. Lubricate the grease nipples with a few strokes of the grease gun.

17   If a manual gearbox is fitted, unscrew the oil filler plug located on the right-hand side of the casing and check that the oil level is up to the bottom of the filler aperture threads (photo). If necessary top up using the specified grade of oil and then refit the filler plug.

18   If automatic transmission is fitted, lubricate the exposed selector linkage with a few drops of engine oil.

19   Carefully inspect the condition of the rear tyres as described in paragraph 9, and then check the front and rear tyre pressures. Having done that, lower the rear of the car to the ground.

20   Working in the engine compartment, first carefully examine the cooling and heater system for signs of leaks. Make sure that all hose clips are tight and that none of the hoses have cracked or perished. Do not attempt to repair a leaking hose, always fit a new item. Generally inspect the exterior of the engine and radiator for signs of water leaks or stains. This check is particularly important before filling the cooling system with antifreeze as it has a greater searching action than pure water and is bound to find any weak spots.

21   Examine the condition of the fanbelt and renew it or adjust its tension as described in Chapter 2.

22   Unscrew the carburettor piston damper from the top of the carburettor dashpot and withdraw the damper. Top up with clean engine oil to bring the level to the top of the hollow piston rod (photo). Carefully refit the damper and screw it down firmly.

23   Wipe the top of the brake and clutch master cylinder reservoirs and unscrew the filler caps. Check the level of hydraulic fluid in the reservoirs and top up if necessary (photos). Take care not to spill any hydraulic fluid on the paintwork as it acts as a solvent. Now refit the caps. Check also the visible clutch and brake hydraulic pipes and hoses for any signs of leaks or chafing.

24   Top up the battery with distilled water and then clean the battery terminals. Apply a smear of petroleum jelly to each terminal. Never use an ordinary grease.

25   Check the water level in the windscreen washer reservoir and top up if necessary. On Estate models also check the water level in the rear window washer reservoir (photos).

26   Lubricate the throttle and choke linkages on the carburettor with a few drops of engine oil. Also lubricate the throttle pedal pivot shaft under the facia.

27   Remove the distributor cap and check the condition and gap of the contact breaker points. Lubricate the distributor spindle and advance weights with a few drops of engine oil. Remove the spark plugs and then clean them and reset the electrode gap. Full details on all these operations will be found in Chapter 4. Refit the spark plugs, distributor cap and leads on completion.

28   Start the engine and allow it to reach normal operating temperature. As the engine is warming up check the condition of the spare tyre as previously described and check its pressure. Also lubricate all locks and hinges with a few drops of light oil. **Note:** *Do not lubricate the steering lock.*

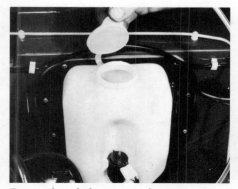

Top up the windscreen washer reservoir ...

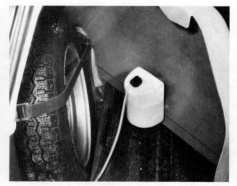

... and tailgate washer reservoir on Estate models

Top arm inner swivel shaft grease nipple (telescopic shock absorbers)

29 When the engine has reached normal operating temperature, check and if necessary, adjust the ignition timing as described in Chapter 4 and the carburettor settings as described in Chapter 3.

30 If automatic transmission is fitted check the fluid level as described in Chapter 6.

31 Generally check the operation of all lights and electrical equipment. Renew any blown bulbs with bulbs of the same wattage rating and rectify any electrical faults. See Chapter 10.

32 Check the condition of the windscreen wiper blades (and tail wiper blade on Estate models) and renew any that have split, softened or perished. Ideally they should be renewed every 12 months.

33 With the engine stopped, recheck the engine oil level and top it up until it reaches the MAX mark on the dipstick.

34 Inspect the seat belts for damage to the webbing and make sure that all anchorages are secure. Also check for correct functioning of the inertia mechanism.

35 Make sure that the rear view mirrors are secure in their mountings and are not cracked or glazed.

36 Finally have the front wheel alignment and headlight alignment checked by your BL dealer, as special equipment is needed for these operations.

Every 12 000 miles (20 000 km) or 12 months – whichever comes first

Complete the items in the 6000 mile service as applicable plus:

1 Check the condition of the rear brake shoes as described in Chapter 9 and renew all the shoes if any are worn to less than the minimum specified thickness.

2 Refer to Chapter 11 and adjust the front hub bearings.

3 Renew the air cleaner element as described in Chapter 3.

4 Inspect the ignition HT leads for cracks or deterioration and renew any that are suspect.

5 Renew the contact breaker points and the spark plugs.

Every 24 000 miles (40 000 km) or two years – whichever comes first

Complete the items in the 6000 and 12 000 mile services as applicable plus:

1 If the fanbelt has not been renewed during the past 24 000 miles (40 000 km) it must be renewed at this service. Refer to Chapter 2 for removal and refitting procedures.

2 Completely drain the brake hydraulic system, renew all system seals and refill with clean fresh hydraulic fluid. Refer to Chapter 9.

3 Remove the timing belt cover and check the condition and tension of the timing belt as described in Chapter 1. Adjust or renew as necessary.

4 Fit new rubber grommets on the timing belt cover.

Every 48 000 miles (80 000 km) or 4 years – whichever comes first

1 Refer to Chapter 1 and renew the timing belt.

2 Refer to Chapter 9 and renew the brake servo unit air filter.

Fault diagnosis

Introduction

The car owner who does his or her own maintenance according to the recommended schedules should not have to use this section of the manual very often. Modern component reliability is such that, provided those items subject to wear or deterioration are inspected or renewed at the specified intervals, sudden failure is comparatively rare. Faults do not usually just happen as a result of sudden failure, but develop over a period of time. Major mechanical failures in particular are usually preceded by characteristic symptoms over hundreds or even thousands of miles. Those components which do occasionally fail without warning are often small and easily carried in the car.

With any fault finding, the first step is to decide where to begin investigations. Sometimes this is obvious, but on other occasions a little detective work will be necessary. The owner who makes half a dozen haphazard adjustments or replacements may be successful in curing a fault (or its symptoms), but he will be none the wiser if the fault recurs and he may well have spent more time and money than was necessary. A calm and logical approach will be found to be more satisfactory in the long run. Always take into account any warning signs or abnormalities that may have been noticed in the period preceding the fault – power loss, high or low gauge readings, unusual noises or smells, etc – and remember that failure of components such as fuses or spark plugs may only be pointers to some underlying fault.

The pages which follow here are intended to help in cases of failure to start or breakdown on the road. There is also a Fault Diagnosis Section at the end of each Chapter which should be consulted if the preliminary checks prove unfruitful. Whatever the fault, certain basic principles apply. These are as follows:

Verify the fault. This is simply a matter of being sure that you know what the symptoms are before starting work. This is particularly important if you are investigating a fault for someone else who may not have described it very accurately.

Don't overlook the obvious. For example, if the car won't start, is there petrol in the tank? (Don't take anyone else's word on this particular point, and don't trust the fuel gauge either!) If an electrical fault is indicated, look for loose or broken wires before digging out the test gear.

Cure the disease, not the symptom. Substituting a flat battery with a fully charged one will get you off the hard shoulder, but if the underlying cause is not attended to, the new battery will go the same way. Similarly, changing oil-fouled spark plugs for a new set will get you moving again, but remember that the reason for the fouling (if it wasn't simply an incorrect grade of plug) will have to be established and corrected.

Don't take anything for granted. Particularly, don't forget that a 'new' component may itself be defective (especially if it's been rattling round in the boot for months), and don't leave components out of a fault diagnosis sequence just because they are new or recently fitted. When you do finally diagnose a difficult fault, you'll probably realise that all the evidence was there from the start.

Electrical faults

Electrical faults can be more puzzling than straightforward mechanical failures, but they are no less susceptible to logical analysis if the basic principles of operation are understood. Car electrical wiring exists in extremely unfavourable conditions – heat, vibration and chemical attack – and the first things to look for are loose or corroded connections and broken or chafed wires, especially where the wires pass through holes in the bodywork or are subject to vibration.

All metal-bodied cars in current production have one pole of the battery 'earthed', ie connected to the car bodywork, and in nearly all modern cars it is the negative (–) terminal. The various electrical components' motors, bulb holders etc – are also connected to earth, either by means of a lead or directly by their mountings. Electric current flows through the component and then back to the battery via the car bodywork. If the component mounting is loose or corroded, or if a good path back to the battery is not available, the circuit will be incomplete and malfunction will result. The engine and/or gearbox are also earthed by means of flexible metal straps to the body or subframe; if these straps are loose or missing, starter motor, generator and ignition trouble may result.

Assuming the earth return to be satisfactory, electrical faults will be due either to component malfunction or to defects in the current supply. Individual components are dealt with in Chapter 10. If supply wires are broken or cracked internally this results in an open-circuit, and the easiest way to check for this is to bypass the suspect wire temporarily with a length of wire having a crocodile clip or suitable connector at each end. Alternatively, a 12V test lamp can be used to verify the presence of supply voltage at various points along the wire and the break can be thus isolated.

If a bare portion of a live wire touches the car bodywork or other earthed metal part, the electricity will take the low-resistance path thus formed back to the battery: this is known as a short-circuit. Hopefully a short-circuit will blow a fuse, but otherwise it may cause burning of the insulation (and possibly further short-circuits) or even a fire. This is why it is inadvisable to bypass persistently blowing fuses with silver foil or wire.

Spares and tool kit

Most cars are only supplied with sufficient tools for wheel changing; the *Maintenance and minor repair* tool kit detailed in *Tools and working facilities*, with the addition of a hammer, is probably

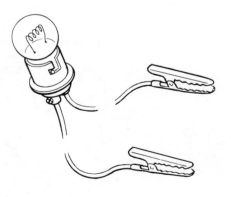

A simple test lamp is useful for tracing electrical faults

sufficient for those repairs that most motorists would consider attempting at the roadside. In addition a few items which can be fitted without too much trouble in the event of a breakdown should be carried. Experience and available space will modify the list below, but the following may save having to call on professional assistance:

Spark plugs, clean and correctly gapped
HT lead and plug cap – long enough to reach the plug furthest from the distributor
Distributor rotor, condenser and contact breaker points
Drivebelt – emergency type may suffice
Spare fuses
Set of principal light bulbs
Tin of radiator sealer and hose bandage
Exhaust bandage
Roll of insulating tape
Length of soft iron wire
Length of electrical flex
Torch or inspection lamp (can double as test lamp)
Battery jump leads
Tow-rope
Ignition waterproofing aerosol
Litre of engine oil
Sealed can of hydraulic fluid
Emergency windscreen
Worm drive hose
Tube of filler paste

If spare fuel is carried, a can designed for the purpose should be used to minimise risks of leakage and collision damage. A first aid kit and a warning triangle, whilst not at present compulsory in the UK, are obviously sensible items to carry in addition to the above.

When touring abroad it may be advisable to carry additional spares which, even if you cannot fit them yourself, could save having to wait while parts are obtained. The items below may be worth considering:

Timing belt
Throttle cable
Cylinder head gasket
Alternator brushes
Tyre valve core

One of the motoring organisations will be able to advise on availability of fuel etc in foreign countries.

Engine will not start

Engine fails to turn when starter operated

Flat battery (recharge, use jump leads, or push start)
Battery terminals loose or corroded
Battery earth to body defective
Engine earth strap loose or broken
Starter motor (or solenoid) wiring loose or broken
Automatic transmission selector in wrong position, or inhibitor switch faulty
Ignition/starter switch faulty
Major mechanical failure (seizure) or long disuse (piston rings rusted to bores)
Starter or solenoid internal fault (see Chapter 10)

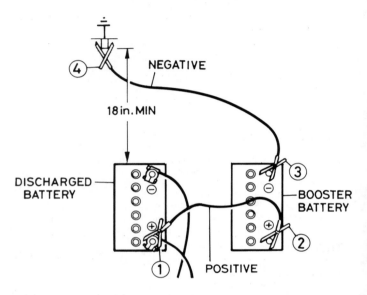

Jump start lead connections for negative earth vehicles – connect leads in order shown

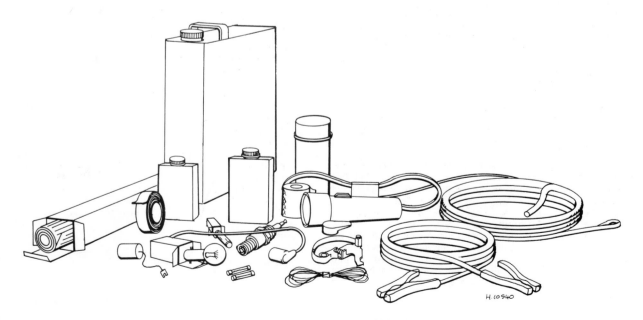

Carrying a few spares can save you a long walk!

Starter motor turns engine slowly

Partially discharged battery (recharge, use jump leads, or push start)
Battery terminals loose or corroded
Battery earth to body defective
Engine earth strap loose
Starter motor (or solenoid) wiring loose
Starter motor internal fault (see Chapter 10)

Starter motor spins without turning engine

Flat battery
Starter motor pinion sticking on sleeve
Flywheel gear teeth damaged or worn
Starter motor mounting bolts loose

Engine turns normally but fails to start

Damp or dirty HT leads and distributor cap (crank engine and check for spark)
Dirty or incorrectly gapped CB points
No fuel in tank (check for delivery at carburettor)
Excessive choke (hot engine) or insufficient choke (cold engine)
Fouled or incorrectly gapped spark plugs (remove, clean and regap)
Other ignition system fault (see Chapter 4)
Other fuel system fault (see Chapter 3)
Poor compression (see Chapter 1)
Major mechanical failure (eg camshaft drive)

Engine fires but will not run

Insufficient choke (cold engine)
Air leaks at carburettor or inlet manifold
Fuel starvation (see Chapter 3)
Other ignition fault (see Chapter 4)

Engine cuts out and will not restart

Engine cuts out suddenly — ignition fault

Loose or disconnected LT wires
Wet HT leads or distributor cap (after transversing water splash)
Coil or condenser failure (check for spark)
Other ignition fault (see Chapter 4)

Engine misfires before cutting out — fuel fault

Fuel tank empty
Fuel pump defective or filter blocked (check for delivery)
Fuel tank filler vent blocked (suction will be evident on releasing cap)
Carburettor needle valve sticking
Other fuel system fault (see Chapter 3)

Engine cuts out — other causes

Serious overheating
Major mechanical failure (eg camshaft drive)

Engine overheats

Ignition (no-charge) warning light illuminated

Slack or broken drivebelt — retension or renew (Chapter 2)

Ignition warning light not illuminated

Coolant loss due to internal or external leakage (see Chapter 2)
Thermostat defective
Low oil level
Brakes binding
Radiator clogged externally or internally
Engine waterways clogged
Ignition timing incorrect or automatic advance malfunctioning
Mixture too weak

Note: *Do not add cold water to an overheated engine or damage may result*

Low engine oil pressure

Gauge reads low or warning light illuminated with engine running

Oil level low or incorrect grade
Defective gauge or sender unit
Wire to sender unit earthed
Engine overheating
Oil filter clogged or bypass valve defective
Oil pressure relief valve defective
Oil pick-up strainer clogged
Oil pump worn or mountings loose
Worn main or big-end bearings

Note: *Low oil pressure in a high-mileage engine at tickover is not ncessarily a cause for concern. Sudden pressure loss at speed is far more significant. In any event, check the gauge or warning light sender before condemning the engine.*

Engine noises

Pre-ignition (pinking) on acceleration

Incorrect grade of fuel
Ignition timing incorrect
Distributor faulty or worn
Worn or maladjusted carburettor
Excessive carbon build-up in engine

Whistling or wheezing noises

Leaking vacuum hose
Leaking carburettor or manifold gasket
Blowing head gasket

Tapping or rattling

Incorrect valve clearances
Worn valve gear
Worn timing belt
Broken piston ring (ticking noise)

Knocking or thumping

Unintentional mechanical contact (eg fan blades)
Worn fanbelt
Peripheral component fault (generator, water pump etc)
Worn big-end bearings (regular heavy knocking, perhaps less under load)
Worn main bearings (rumbling and knocking, perhaps worsening under load)
Piston slap (most noticeable when cold)

Chapter 1 Engine

Contents

Specifications

1695 cc engine (manufacturer's type 17V)
Engine (general)

Type	17V, overhead camshaft
Number of cylinders	4
Bore	3.325 in (84.45 mm)
Stroke	2.984 in (75.8 mm)
Capacity	103.73 cu in (1695 cc)
Firing order	1 – 3 – 4 – 2
Valve operation	Overhead camshaft
Compression ratio	9.0:1
Torque at 3700 rpm	99 lbf ft (13.7 kgf m)

Crankshaft

Main journal diameter	2.1262 to 2.1270 in (54.005 to 54.026 mm)
Crankpin journal diameter	1.8754 to 1.8759 in (47.635 to 47.647 mm)
Crankshaft endthrust	Taken on thrust washers at centre bearing
Crankshaft endfloat	0.001 to 0.005 in (0.025 to 0.14 mm)

Main bearings

Number and type	5, steel-backed thin wall type
Width:	
Front, centre and rear	1.125 in (28.57 mm)
Intermediate	0.760 in (19.3 mm)
Diametrical clearance	0.001 to 0.003 in (0.025 to 0.077 mm)
Undersizes	0.010 in (0.254 mm)
	0.020 in (0.508 mm)
	0.030 in (0.762 mm)
	0.040 in (1.016 mm)

Connecting rods

Type	Horizontal, split big-end, plain small-end offset
Length between centres	5.86 in (149 mm)

Big-end bearings
Type	Steel-backed thin wall
Width	0.775 to 0.785 in (19.68 to 19.94 mm)
Diametrical clearance	0.0015 to 0.0032 in (0.038 to 0.081 mm)
Undersizes	0.010 in (0.254 mm)
	0.020 in (0.508 mm)
	0.030 in (0.762 mm)
	0.040 in (1.016 mm)

Gudgeon pin
Type	Press in connecting rod
Fit in piston	Handpush at 16°C (60°F)
Diameter	0.8125 to 0.8127 in (20.638 to 20.634 mm)

Pistons
Type	Duotherm, solid skirt with combustion chamber in crown
Clearance in cylinder:	
Below oil control groove	0.0008 to 0.0051 in (0.02 to 0.13 mm)
Bottom of skirt	0.0004 to 0.0023 (0.01 to 0.06 mm)
Number of rings	3 (2 compression, 1 oil control)
Width of ring grooves:	
Top and second	0.070 to 0.071 in (1.78 to 1.80 mm)
Oil control	0.157 to 0.158 in (4.00 to 4.02 mm)
Gudgeon pin bore	0.8128 to 0.8130 in (20.646 to 20.651 mm)
Offset from centre	0.059 in (1.5 mm)

Piston rings
Compression rings:	
Type:	
Top	Plain, chrome faced
Second	Stepped scraper
Ring-to-groove clearance	0.0015 to 0.0027 in (0.04 to 0.07 mm)
Fitted gap	0.012 to 0.020 in (0.3 to 0.5 mm)
Oil control ring:	
Type	Two chrome faced rings with butted expander
Fitted gap	0.015 to 0.055 in (0.33 to 1.4 mm)

Camshaft
Journal diameters	1.888 to 1.889 in (47.96 to 47.97 mm)
Number of bearings	3
Bearing type	Direct in cylinder head and cover
Diametrical clearance	0.0017 to 0.0037 in (0.043 to 0.094 mm)
Endthrust	Taken on rear cover
Endfloat	0.003 to 0.007 in (0.07 to 0.18 mm)
Drive	Toothed belt from crankshaft sprocket
Timing belt tension:	
New belt	13 lbf (58N)
Used belt	11 lbf (49N)

Tappets
Type	Bucket with flat base
Outside diameter	1.2491 to 1.2498 in (31.729 to 31.745 mm)
Adjustment	Selective shim

Valves
Face angle	45° 30′
Seat angle	45°
Head diameter:	
Inlet	1.575 in (40 mm)
Exhaust	1.339 in (34 mm)
Stem diameter:	
Inlet	0.2917 to 0.2921 in (7.41 to 7.42 mm)
Exhaust	0.2909 to 0.2917 in (7.39 to 7.41 mm)
Stem-to-guide clearance:	
Inlet	0.001 to 0.002 in (0.027 to 0.053 mm)
Exhaust	0.0015 to 0.0028 in (0.04 to 0.073 mm)
Cam lift	0.375 in (9.525 mm)

Valve guides
Length	1.532 in (38.90 mm)
Outside diameter	0.474 to 0.475 in (12.04 to 12.06 mm)
Inside diameter	0.293 to 0.2937 in (7.45 to 7.46 mm)
Fitted height above head	0.394 in (10 mm)
Interference fit in head	0.0015 to 0.003 in (0.04 to 0.09 mm)

Valve springs

Free length	1.646 in (41.81 mm)
Fitted length	1.375 in (34.92 mm)
Load at fitted length	44.5 lbf (20 kgf)
Number of working coils	4.5

Valve timing

Inlet valve:

Opens	15° BTDC
Closes	45° ABDC

Exhaust valve:

Opens	50° BBDC
Closes	10° ATDC
Tappet clearance (standard)	0.012 in (0.30 mm)

Lubrication system

System type	Wet sump, pressure fed

Pressure:

Running	60 to 90 lbf/in² (4.1 to 6.2 bar)
Idling	40 to 60 lbf/in² (2.8 to 4.1 bar)
Oil pump type	Eccentric rotors mounted around crankshaft

Pump operating clearances:

Outer rotor to body	0.004 in (0.10 mm)
Rotor lobe clearance	0.002 in (0.05 mm)
Outer rotor endfloat	0.003 in (0.08 mm)

Relief valve spring:

Free length	1.525 in (38.7 mm)
Fitted length	0.960 in (24.4 mm)
Load at fitted length	17.4 lbf (77N)
Oil filter type	Full-flow disposable cartridge
Lubricant type	SAE 15W/50 multigrade engine oil
Lubricant capacity (including filter)	7 pints (4 litres)

Torque wrench settings

	lbf ft	Nm
Main bearing cap bolts	75	100
Big-end bearing cup nuts	33	45
Backplate:		
8 mm bolts	22	30
10 mm bolts	37	51
Flywheel-to-crankshaft bolts	42	58
Oil pump cover bolts	2	3
Oil pump securing bolts	8	11
Oil pressure switch	9	12
Camshaft sprocket bolt	48	66
Crankshaft pulley bolt	62	85
Camshaft cover bolts	9	12
Cylinder head bolts:		
Pre-tighten	35	47
Fully tighten	60	81
Manifold-to-cylinder head bolts	18	25
Oil separator-to-block bolts	22	30
Water pump to block	8	11
Thermostat housing to cylinder head	8	11
Coolant temperature switch	5	7
Sump drain plug	27	38
Mounting bracket-to-engine bolts	38	52
Mounting bracket-to-body bolts	26 to 28	36 to 39
Mounting rubber-to-bracket nuts	38	52
Rear mounting rubber-to-crossmember nuts	20 to 22	27 to 30
Restrictor plate to mounting rubber	28 to 35	39 to 48
Rear crossmember to body	20 to 22	27 to 30
Exhaust pipe to manifold	21 to 23	29 to 32

1993 cc engine (manufacturer's type 20V)*

The specifications for the 2.0 litre engine are as for the 1.7 litre engine, except for the differences noted below:

Engine (general)

Type	20V, overhead camshaft
Stroke	3.504 in (89.0 mm)
Capacity	121.68 cu in (1993 cc)
Torque	115 lbf ft (15.9 kgf m) at 3400 rpm

Valve timing

Inlet valve:
Opens .... 19° BTDC
Closes .... 41° ABDC
Exhaust valve:
Opens .... 61° BBDC
Closes .... 15° ATDC

compiled using available information at time of writing — if in doubt, consult your dealer

---

1   General description

The BL O-series engine is fitted to all Ital models covered by this manual. This unit is a water cooled, four-cylinder four-stroke petrol engine of overhead camshaft configuration and 1700 or 1994 cc capacity.

The combined crankcase and cylinder block is of cast iron construction and houses the pistons, connecting rods and crankshaft. The solid skirt cast aluminium alloy pistons are retained on the

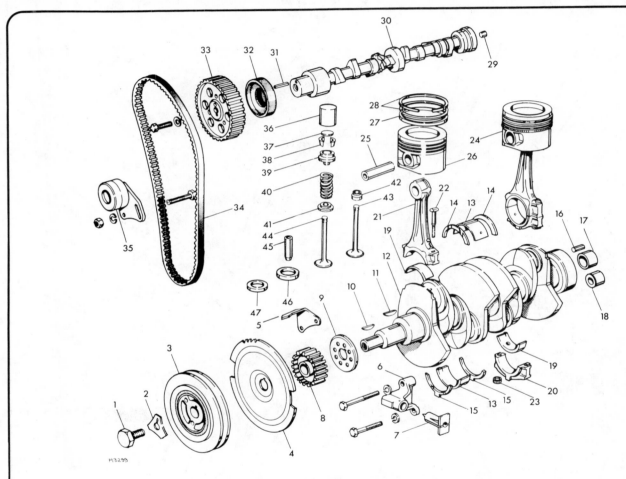

Fig. 1.1 Exploded view of engine moving components (Sec 1)

1 Crankshaft pulley bolt	17 1st motion shaft bush	33 Camshaft sprocket
2 Lockwasher	18 Converter bush	34 Timing belt
3 Pulley/vibration damper	19 Big-end bearings (half)	35 Timing belt tensioner
4 Timing disc	20 Connecting rod cap	36 Valve tappet
5 Timing pointer	21 Connecting rod (RH)	37 Shim (selective)
6 LED transducer bracket	22 Connecting rod bolt	38 Valve collets
7 Transducer bracket plug	23 Connecting rod nut	39 Valve spring cup
8 Crankshaft sprocket	24 Connecting rod and piston (LH)	40 Valve spring
9 Flange	25 Gudgeon pin	41 Valve spring seat
10 Pulley and sprocket key	26 Piston	42 Inlet valve stem seal
11 Oil pump key	27 Oil control piston rings	43 Inlet valve
12 Crankshaft	28 1st/2nd compression piston rings	44 Exhaust valve
13 Main bearings (half)	29 Camshaft plug	45 Valve guide
14 Upper crankshaft thrust washers	30 Camshaft	46 Inlet valve seat inserts
15 Lower crankshaft thrust washers	31 Camshaft sprocket roll pin	47 Exhaust valve seat inserts
16 Flywheel dowel	32 Camshaft oil seal	

I13298

Fig. 1.2 Exploded view of engine static components (Sec 1)

1 Front crankshaft main bearing cap
2 Intermediate crankshaft main bearing cap
3 Centre crankshaft main bearing cap
4 Rear crankshaft main bearing cap
5 Setscrew
6 Dowel
7 Sealing insert
8 Cylinder block and crankcase
9 Oil separator and gasket
10 Coolant drain plug
11 Oil blanking plate and gasket
12 Core plug
13 Oil gallery plug
14 Oil pump dowel
15 Cylinder head dowel
16 Oil pump and gasket
17 Plugs (with oil cooler not fitted)
18 Plug (with oil cooler fitted)
19 Oil filter cartridge and seal
20 Oil pressure relief valve split pin
21 Oil pressure relief valve plunger
22 Oil pressure relief valve spring
23 Oil pressure relief valve plug and O-seal
24 Oil pump oil seal
25 Oil pump plug
26 Oil pressure switch
27 Switch extension
28 Hot box
29 Inlet/exhaust manifold and gasket
30 Banjo connection brake servo screw
31 Distributor vacuum adaptor
32 Sealing washer
33 Cylinder head gasket
34 Cylinder head
35 Camshaft bearing cover
36 Cover-to-cylinder head ring dowel
37 Fuel pump gasket
38 Camshaft rear end cover and gasket
39 Cylinder head short bolt
40 Cylinder head long bolt
41 Washer
42 Cover-to-cylinder head bolt
43 Oil filler and breather cap
44 Timing belt cover bracket
45 Timing belt cover
46 Cover grommet
47 Spark plug (taper seat)
48 Warning label (for spark plug)
49 Coolant filler cap
50 Thermostat and O-ring seal
51 Thermostat housing and O-ring seal
52 Thermal transmitter
53 Engine oil dipstick
54 Dipstick tube
55 Water pump and gasket
56 Belt cover pillar
57 Water pump pulley
58 Cylinder head core plug

connecting rods by gudgeon pins which are an interference fit in the connecting rod small-end bore. The connecting rods are attached to the crankshaft by renewable shell type big-end bearings.

The forged steel crankshaft is carried in five main bearings also of the renewable shell type. Crankshaft endfloat is controlled by thrust washers which are located on either side of the centre main bearing.

The camshaft is located in the cylinder head and is retained in position by an aluminium cover which is bolted to the upper face of the cylinder head. The camshaft is supported by three bearing journals machined directly in the head and camshaft cover. Drive to the camshaft is via a toothed composite rubber timing belt from a sprocket on the front end of the crankshaft. A spring-loaded tensioner is fitted to eliminate backlash and prevent slackness of the belt.

Two valves per cylinder are mounted vertically in the aluminium cylinder head. The valves are operated by bucket type tappets acted upon directly by the lobes of the camshaft. Valve/tappet clearance adjustment is by selective shims.

The cylinder head is of the non-crossflow type, all eight inlet and exhaust ports being on the left-hand side.

Engine lubrication is by the conventional forced feed system and a detailed description of its operation will be found in Section 23.

2 Major operations possible with engine in car

The following major operations can be carried out on the engine with it in place in the car:

1 Removal and refitting of camshaft
2 Removal and refitting of cylinder head
3 Removal and refitting of timing belt
4 Removal and refitting of oil pump
5 Removal and refitting of oil sump
6 Removal and refitting of pistons and connecting rods and big-end bearings
7 Removal and refitting of engine mountings
8 Removal and refitting of flywheel
9 Removal and refitting of front and rear crankshaft oil seals

3 Major operations requiring engine removal

The following major operations must be carried out with the engine out of the car and on a bench or the floor:

1 Removal and refitting of the main bearings
2 Removal and refitting of the crankshaft

4 Valve tappet clearances – checking and adjusting

To retain the camshaft in position during the checking operation, BL special tools 18G1301 and 18G1302 will be required. If these tools are not available it is possible to make up suitable alternatives as described below and shown in the photos. Read through the entire section first to familiarize yourself with the procedure, and then obtain or make up the special tools before proceeding.

1   Unscrew the distributor cap securing screws, lift off the cap and place it to one side (photo).
2   Mark the relative position of the distributor mounting flange to the camshaft cover as a guide to refitting. Disconnect the vacuum pipe from the vacuum advance unit and LT lead at the wiring connector.
3   Undo and remove the two distributor securing nuts and washers and withdraw the distributor (photo).
4   Disconnect the two fuel pipes from the fuel pump (photo). Plug the pipe ends to prevent loss of fluid and dirt ingress.
5   Turn the crankshaft to the 90° BTDC position. This is achieved when the dimple on the rear face of the camshaft sprocket is opposite the pointer on the upper surface of the camshaft cover (photo). At the same time the single notch in the crankshaft timing disc is opposite the timing pointer. The crankshaft can be turned using a socket on the crankshaft pulley bolt or, on cars with manual transmission only, by engaging top gear and moving the car forward. Removal of the spark plugs will enable the crankshaft to be turned with greater ease.
6   Lift away the timing belt cover (photo).
7   Undo and remove the nut securing the clutch bleed tube support bracket and brake servo vacuum pipe retaining clip to the cylinder

4.1 Unscrew the retaining screws and lift off the distributor cap

4.3 Undo and remove the two retaining nuts and washers and withdraw the distributor.

4.4 Disconnect the fuel pipes from the fuel pump

4.5 Dimple on camshaft gear (arrowed) aligned with pointer on cover indicating 90° BTDC

4.6 Lift off the timing belt cover

4.7a Undo and remove the retaining nut and lift off the clutch bleed tube support bracket ...

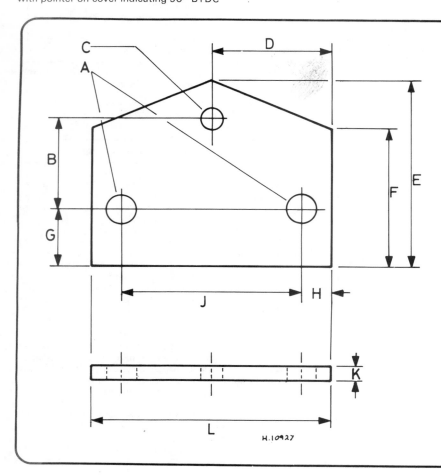

Fig. 1.3 Camshaft rear support plate dimensions (Sec 4)

A = 0.31 in (7.93 mm)
B = 1.00 in (25.4 mm)
C = 0.25 in (6.35 mm) diameter clearance for $\frac{1}{4}$ UNF nut and bolt
D = 1.25 in (31.75 mm)
E = 2.00 in (50.80 mm)
F = 1.50 in (38.10 mm)
G = 0.62 in (15.87 mm)
H = 0.31 in (7.93 mm)
J = 1.87 in (47.62 mm)
K = 0.12 in (3.17 mm)
L = 2.50 in (63.50 mm)

H.10927

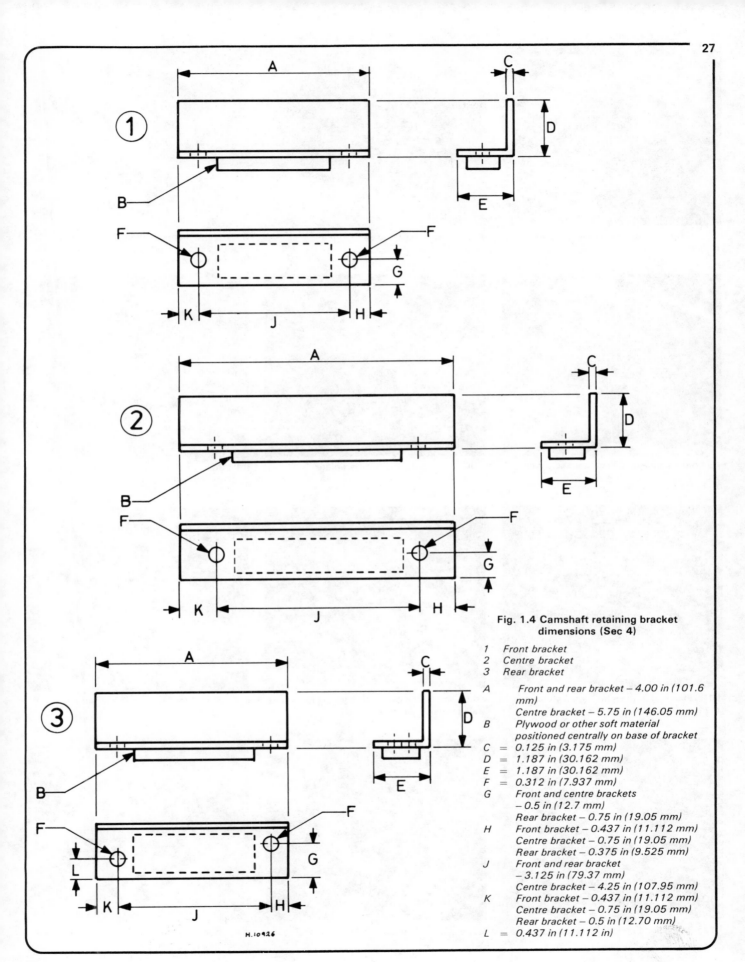

Fig. 1.4 Camshaft retaining bracket
dimensions (Sec 4)

1   Front bracket
2   Centre bracket
3   Rear bracket

A   Front and rear bracket – 4.00 in (101.6
         mm)
         Centre bracket – 5.75 in (146.05 mm)
B   Plywood or other soft material
         positioned centrally on base of bracket
C = 0.125 in (3.175 mm)
D = 1.187 in (30.162 mm)
E = 1.187 in (30.162 mm)
F = 0.312 in (7.937 mm)
G   Front and centre brackets
         – 0.5 in (12.7 mm)
         Rear bracket – 0.75 in (19.05 mm)
H   Front bracket – 0.437 in (11.112 mm)
         Centre bracket – 0.75 in (19.05 mm)
         Rear bracket – 0.375 in (9.525 mm)
J   Front and rear bracket
         – 3.125 in (79.37 mm)
         Centre bracket – 4.25 in (107.95 mm)
K   Front bracket – 0.437 in (11.112 mm)
         Centre bracket – 0.75 in (19.05 mm)
         Rear bracket – 0.5 in (12.70 mm)
L = 0.437 in (11.112 in)

H.10926

4.7b ... and the brake servo vacuum pipe retaining clip

4.8a The camshaft rear support plate ...

4.8b ... and the three camshaft retaining brackets can be made up if the special tools are not available

4.9a Remove the camshaft rear end cover ...

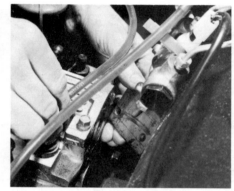

4.9b ... and fit the rear support plate

4.9c Support plate in position (shown with engine removed in this photo)

4.10 Undo and remove the camshaft cover retaining bolts and lift off the cover

4.11a Secure the camshaft with the retaining brackets using the cover bolts

4.11b The three brackets in position

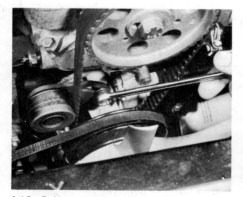

4.12a Release the timing belt tensioner ...

4.12b ... and slip the belt off the camshaft gear

4.13 Measure the valve tappet clearance with feeler gauges

head (photo). Lift off the bleed tube and bracket and move it to one side. Undo and remove the vacuum pipe banjo union on the inlet manifold, taking care not to lose the two washers. Lift the retaining clip off the cylinder head stud and position the vacuum pipe clear of the engine (photo).

8 If BL special tools 18G1301 and 18G1302 are not available, make up the three camshaft retaining brackets and a rear support plate to the dimensions shown in Figs. 1.3 and 1.4 (photos) using suitable scrap metal and angle iron.

9 Undo and remove the five bolts securing the camshaft rear end cover and lift off the cover and gasket (photo). Fit the homemade rear support plate or tool 18G1302 in position and secure with two of the rear end cover retaining bolts. Make sure that the rounded bolt head of the homemade tool, or the tapered projection of the BL tool, fits squarely into the recess at the rear of the camshaft (photos).

10 Slacken evenly, and in a side-to-side sequence, each of the nine bolts securing the camshaft cover to the cylinder head. Remove the bolts and then lift off the camshaft cover (photo).

11 Place the three clamps of BL special tool 18G1302 or the three homemade brackets in position over the camshaft bearings and secure with the camshaft cover retaining bolts (photos). When in position the clamps or brackets should be exerting a light pressure only on the camshaft bearing journals; sufficient to hold the camshaft firmly in place while still allowing it to be rotated.

12 Release the timing belt tensioner and slip the belt off the camshaft gear (photos).

13 Rotate the camshaft in the normal direction of rotation to bring each pair of cam lobes to the vertical position, ie 1 and 4, 2 and 5, 6 and 7, 3 and 8. As each pair of cam lobes reaches the vertical position measure and record the clearance between the heel of the cam lobe and the tappet using feeler gauges (photo).

14 The standard valve tappet clearance is 0.012 in (0.30 mm). Provided that the measured clearances do not exceed this figure or are not less than 0.008 in (0.20 mm), adjustment is not necessary and the camshaft cover and components can be refitted as described in paragraphs 22 to 30. If, however, adjustment is required proceed as follows.

15 Undo and remove the bolt securing the camshaft gear to the camshaft and withdraw the gear (photo).

16 Remove the camshaft rear support plate and then progressively slacken the camshaft retaining bracket bolts. When the spring tension is released, remove the bolts and lift away the brackets.

17 Lift the camshaft out of its location in the cylinder head and carefully remove the front oil seal.

18 Remove each tappet requiring adjustment in turn and extract the shim from the valve spring cup (or from inside the tappet). Measure and record the thickness of the shim with a micrometer.

19 If the measured clearance was too small, then a smaller shim is required. If the clearance was too large then a longer shim is required, ie

$A + B - C$ = shim thickness required
Where: A = Measured clearance
B = Thickness of existing shim
C = Standard tappet clearance

For example: 0.006 in (0.15 mm) + 0.105 in (2.67 mm) - 0.012 in (0.30 mm) = 0.099 in (2.52 mm). Shims are available in the following sizes:

in	mm
0.091	2.32
0.093	2.37
0.095	2.42
0.097	2.47
0.099	2.52
0.101	2.56
0.103	2.62
0.105	2.67
0.107	2.72
0.109	2.77
0.111	2.83
0.113	2.87
0.115	2.93
0.117	2.98

20 Having selected each required new shim, place it in the spring cup on top of the valve and refit the tappet in its original bore.

21 Liberally lubricate the camshaft bearing journals with engine oil and place the camshaft in position (photo). Lubricate the outer circumference and sealing lip of the oil seal and position it over the camshaft until it is in contact with the register in the cylinder head.

22 Remove all traces of old sealant from the camshaft cover and cylinder head and ensure that the mating faces are clean and dry.

23 Apply a very thin bead, $\frac{1}{16}$ in (1.5 mm) diameter, of RTV silicone sealant to the mating face of the camshaft cover. Refit the cover and timing belt cover bracket and then tighten the retaining bolts evenly and progressively to the specified torque (photo).

24 Refit the camshaft rear end cover using a new gasket if necessary.

25 Refit the camshaft gear and fully tighten the retaining bolt.

26 Ensure that the crankshaft is still at the 90°BTDC position and then turn the camshaft until the dimple on the gear is aligned with the pointer on the cover. Now refit and tension the timing belt as described in Section 11.

27 Refit the brake servo vacuum pipe banjo union to the inlet manifold. Reposition the retaining clip and clutch bleed tube support bracket over the cylinder head stud and secure with the retaining nut.

28 Refit the timing belt cover.

29 Reconnect the two fuel pipes to the fuel pump.

30 Refer to Chapter 4 and refit the distributor.

5 Methods of engine removal

The engine may be removed either on its own or in unit with the gearbox or automatic transmission. If the engine is to be removed on its own, it is lifted out from above using a crane or overhead hoist. If the engine is to be removed in unit with the gearbox or automatic transmission, it may be lifted out from above or lowered to the ground and withdrawn from under the car. However, due to the weight factor, the very steep angle and the lifting height required to remove the power unit with transmission from above, it is considered easier to lower the assembly to the ground and remove it from below. Therefore in the following Section this is the method described.

4.15 Undo and remove the camshaft gear retaining bolt

4.21 Liberally lubricate the camshaft journals

4.23 Tighten the cover retaining bolts evenly and progressively to the specified torque

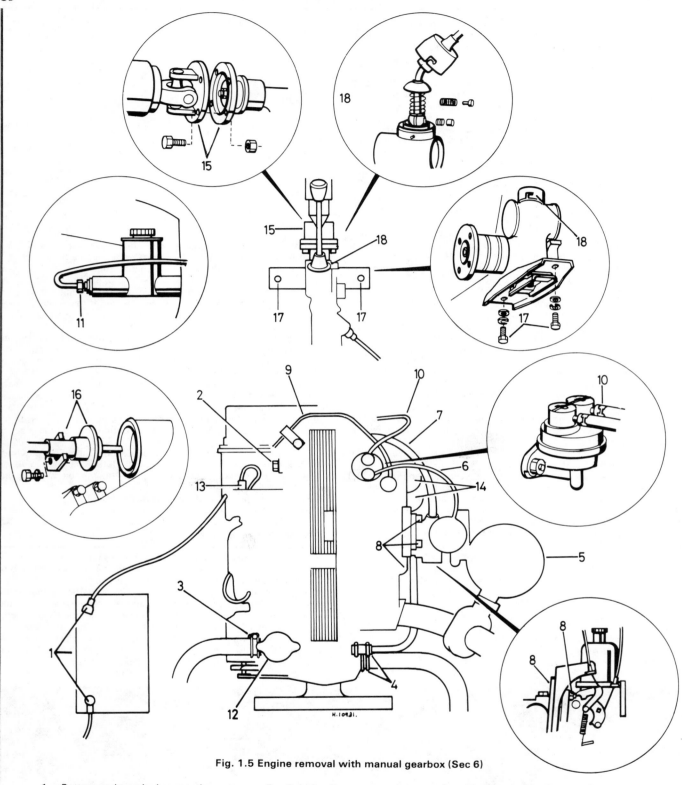

Fig. 1.5 Engine removal with manual gearbox (Sec 6)

1	Battery and terminal connections	7	Breather hose	13	Electrical leads at starter solenoid
2	Cylinder block coolant drain plug	8	Carburettor retaining nuts and heatshield	14	Exhaust front pipes
3	Temperature gauge transmitter lead	9	Brake servo vacuum pipe	15	Propeller shaft and gearbox flanges
4	Heater and bottom hose connections	10	Fuel pump inlet hose	16	Speedometer cable and clamp
5	Air cleaner	11	Clutch hydraulic pipe union	17	Gearbox crossmember retaining bolts
6	Fuel inlet hose	12	Oil pressure switch location	18	Gear lever-to-gearbox attachment

6 Engine – removal (with manual gearbox or automatic transmission)

1   The sequence of operations listed in this Section is not critical, as the position of the person undertaking the work, or the tool in his hand, will determine to a certain extent the order in which the work is tackled. Obviously the power unit cannot be removed until everything is disconnected from it and the following sequence will ensure that nothing is forgotten.

2   Begin by disconnecting the battery earth terminal.

3   Remove the bonnet as described in Chapter 12.

4   Drain the cooling system and remove the fan as described in Chapter 2.

5   Slacken the hose clips and remove the radiator top and bottom hoses. At the rear of the engine slacken the hose clips and remove the two heater hoses from the heater pipes.

6   Unscrew the wing nut and washer securing the air cleaner to the carburettor adaptor. Lift off the air cleaner body, detach the hot and cold air intake ducts and remove the air cleaner.

7   Disconnect the fuel pipe, engine breather and vacuum pipe connections from the carburettor body. Plug the fuel pipe to prevent loss of fluid and dirt ingress. On models equipped with automatic transmission disconnect the downshift cable from the carburettor linkage.

8   Undo and remove the four nuts and washers securing the carburettors to the manifold studs. Slide the carburettor off the studs and place it to one side well clear of the engine. Now remove the heat shield, support bracket and insulation block assembly.

9   Slacken the retaining clip and detach the brake servo vacuum hose from the vacuum pipe.

10   Disconnect the fuel tank feed pipe from the fuel pump. Plug the pipe to prevent fuel syphoning out.

11   Undo and remove the hydraulic fluid pipe at the union on the clutch master cylinder. Plug the pipe end and the master cylinder union to prevent loss of fluid and dirt ingress.

12   Make a note of their locations and then disconnect the electrical leads at the water temperature gauge transmitter and oil pressure switch.

13   Disconnect the wiring multi-plug from the rear of the alternator.

14   Mark the spark plug HT leads to ensure correct refitting and then pull them off the spark plugs. Undo and remove the two distributor cap retaining screws and lift away the cap and leads.

15   Make a note of the cable connections at the rear of the starter motor solenoid and disconnect them.

16   Disconnect the distributor LT lead at the wiring connector.

17   Chock the rear wheels, raise the front of the car and support it on axle stands or other suitable supports. The front of the car must be raised high enough (at least 27 in/686 mm) to allow for removal of the power unit from under the car.

18   Undo and remove the exhaust front pipe-to-manifold securing nuts and the nut and bolt securing the exhaust support bracket to the bellhousing. Tie the exhaust system to the torsion bar to keep it clear of the power unit.

19   Undo and remove the nut and washer securing the engine earth strap to the chassis member.

20   Mark the propeller shaft and gearbox/transmission drive flanges to ensure correct realignment. Undo and remove the four nuts and bolts securing the two flanges and tie the front propeller shaft to one side.

21   Undo and remove the bolt securing the speedometer cable clamp to the gearbox/transmission extension housing. Lift off the clamp and withdraw the speedometer cable.

22   If a manual gearbox is fitted, withdraw the grommet from the floor just above the speedometer cable-to-gearbox attachment and disconnect the reversing light switch wiring connector.

23   If automatic transmission is fitted disconnect the starter inhibitor/reversing light switch multi-plug connectors. Also release the retaining clip and detach the gear selector rod from the transmission selector lever.

24   Place a jack beneath the rear of the gearbox or automatic transmission and *just* take the weight of the unit.

25   Undo and remove the two bolts securing the rear crossmember to the body.

26   On cars equipped with a manual gearbox, lower the gearbox by about 3 in (75 mm). Release the gear lever from the gearbox by pressing down on the cap and turning it anti-clockwise. Release the cap, lift the gear lever out of its location and recover the anti-rattle

spring and plunger from the gear lever ball.

27   Refer to Chapter 11 and remove the front anti-roll bar.

28   Fit lifting screws or place a rope sling or chain around the engine. Attach the ropes or chain to a crane or hoist and position them so that the point of lift is at the rear of the engine. Raise the hoist and *just* take the weight of the engine.

29   Undo and remove the nuts and bolts that secure the engine mounting brackets to the chassis side members.

30   Lower the jack at the rear of the gearbox/transmission until the entire weight of the power unit is taken by the crane or hoist. Remove the jack.

31   Make a final check that all cables, pipes, hoses etc have been disconnected and are positioned out of the way.

32   Place a low trolley or a board under the power unit and carefully lower the complete assembly down through the engine compartment until it is resting on the trolley or board.

33   Detach the lifting gear from the engine and withdraw the power unit out from under the car.

7 Engine – removal (without manual gearbox or automatic transmission)

1   Begin by disconnecting the battery earth terminal.

2   Remove the bonnet as described in Chapter 12.

3   Refer to Chapter 2, drain the cooling system and then remove the radiator.

4   On models equipped with automatic transmission, refer to Chapter 6 and drain the fluid into a suitable container.

5   Unscrew the fan retaining bolts (or the fan hub retaining nut on 2.0 litre models – see Chapter 2) and lift away the fan.

6   Unscrew the wing nut and washer securing the air cleaner to the carburettor adaptor. Lift off the air cleaner body, detach the hot and cold air intake ducts and remove the air cleaner.

7   At the rear of the engine, slacken the hose clips and detach the two heater hoses from the heater pipes (photo).

8   Disconnect the throttle and choke cables from the trunnions on the carburettor linkage (photo). Release the cables from their support brackets and move them well clear of the engine. If automatic transmission is fitted, disconnect the downshift cable from the carburettor linkage.

9   Slacken the retaining clip and detach the brake servo vacuum hose from the vacuum pipe (photo).

10   Disconnect the fuel tank feed pipe from the fuel pump. Plug the pipe to prevent fuel syphoning out.

11   Undo and remove the nut securing the slave cylinder bleed tube support bracket to the cylinder head stud (photo). Position the tube and bracket well clear of the engine.

12   Mark the spark plug HT leads to ensure correct refitting and then pull them off the spark plugs. Undo and remove the two distributor cap retaining screws and lift away the cap and leads.

13   Disconnect the distributor LT lead at the wiring connector (photo).

14   Make a note of their locations and then disconnect the electrical leads at the water temperature gauge transmitter and oil pressure switch (photo).

15   Disconnect the wiring multi-plug from the rear of the alternator (photo).

16   Make a note of the cable connections at the rear of the starter motor solenoid and disconnect them (photo).

17   Jack up the front of the car and support it on axle stands.

18   From underneath the car undo and remove the nuts securing the twin exhaust front pipes to the manifold (photo). Now undo and remove the nut and bolt securing the front pipe support bracket to the bellhousing (photo). Move the exhaust system to one side and tie it to the torsion bar.

19   Undo and remove the two bolts securing the sump connecting plate to the bellhousing.

20   Undo and remove the starter motor lower retaining bolt and the four bellhousing-to-engine retaining bolts that are accessible from beneath the car. Note that the engine earth strap is also secured by one of the bolts on the right-hand side (photo).

21   Undo and remove the two nuts and bolts each side that secure the anti-roll bar bushes to the front chassis members. Release the anti-roll bar and move it down at the front to allow removal of the engine.

22   Lower the front of the car to the ground.

23   Undo and remove the starter motor upper securing bolt and the

7.7 Disconnect the heater hoses from the heater pipes

7.8 Disconnect the throttle and choke cables from the carburettor linkage

7.9 Disconnect the brake servo vacuum hose from the vacuum pipe

7.11 Undo and remove the retaining nut and lift off the clutch bleed tube and vacuum pipe clip

7.13 Disconnect the LT lead connector ...

7.14 ... the water temperature gauge lead ...

7.15 ... and the alternator wiring multi-plug

7.16 Note their position and disconnect the wires at the starter solenoid

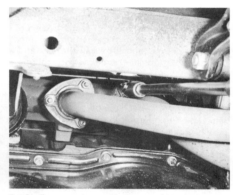

7.18a From underneath the car detach the exhaust pipes from the manifold ...

7.18b ... and the support bracket from the bellhousing

7.20 Note the location of the engine earth strap

7.27 Undo and remove the nuts securing the engine mountings to the cylinder block brackets

7.29 On the right-hand side undo and remove the nuts securing the mounting bracket to the chassis member

7.33 Check that all disconnected wires, cables, pipes etc are clear as the engine is lifted out

two rear support bolts and lift away the starter.

24 Using a suitable jack, support the weight of the gearbox or automatic transmission.

25 Fit lifting brackets or place a rope sling or chain around the engine. Attach the ropes or chain to a crane or hoist and position them so that the point of lift is at the centre of the engine.

26 Undo and remove the remaining nuts and bolts that secure the engine to the bellhousing.

27 Undo and remove the nuts securing the engine mountings to the brackets attached to the cylinder block (photo).

28 Raise the crane or hoist slightly and *just* take the weight of the engine.

29 Undo and remove the nuts and bolts securing the right-hand engine mounting bracket to the chassis side member and then remove the mounting completely (photo).

30 Make a final check that all cables, pipes, hoses etc have been disconnected and are positioned out of the way.

31 Lift the engine slightly until the left-hand bracket is clear of the engine mounting. Make sure that the jack supporting the gearbox is also raised.

32 Draw the engine forward until the gearbox/transmission input shaft is clear of the clutch assembly or torque converter. On automatic transmission models, be prepared for a quantity of automatic transmission fluid to be released from the torque converter as the engine is drawn forward. The torque converter cannot be completely drained, so place a container or some old rags under the car to catch the fluid.

33 Continue lifting the engine out of the engine compartment, keeping a careful check that everything is clear (photo). Move it forwards or push the car rearwards and lower the engine to the ground.

8 Engine – separation from manual gearbox or automatic transmission

1 If the engine and gearbox/transmission have been removed as a complete assembly, it will be necessary to separate the two units before major dismantling work on the engine can begin.

2 With the power unit out of the car and on the floor, undo and remove the retaining bolts and lift off the starter motor.

3 Undo and remove the nut securing the clutch slave cylinder bleed tube support bracket to the cylinder head stud. Lift off the bracket and tube.

4 Undo and remove the bolts securing the bellhousing to the engine, and also the two bolts securing the sump connecting plate to the bellhousing.

5 Carefully draw the gearbox or automatic transmission rearwards, detaching it from the dowel located at the top rear of the cylinder

block. **Note:** *If automatic transmission is fitted a small quantity of transmission fluid will be released from the torque converter as the transmission is removed. Have some rags handy to catch the fluid as it is released.*

9 Engine dismantling – general

1 It is best to mount the engine on a dismantling stand, but if one is not available, stand the engine on a strong bench to be at a comfortable working height. It can be dismantled on the floor but it is not easy.

2 During the dismantling process, greatest care should be taken to keep the exposed parts free from dirt. As an aid to achieving this, thoroughly clean down the outside of the engine, removing all traces of oil and congealed dirt.

3 Use paraffin or a proprietary grease solvent. The latter compound will make the job much easier, for after the solvent has been applied and allowed to stand for a time, a vigorous jet of water will wash off the solvent with all the grease and dirt. If the dirt is thick and deeply embedded, work the solvent into it with a wire brush.

4 Finally wipe down the exterior of the engine with a rag and only then, when it is quite clean, should the dismantling process begin. As the engine is stripped, clean each part in a bath of paraffin.

5 Never immerse parts with oilways (for example the crankshaft) in paraffin, but to clean, wipe down carefully with a paraffin dampened cloth. Oilways can be cleaned out with nylon pipe cleaners. If an air line is available, all parts can be blown dry and the oilways blown through as an added precaution.

6 Re-use of old engine gaskets is false economy and will lead to oil and water leaks, if nothing worse. Always use new gaskets throughout.

7 Do not throw the old gasket away, for it sometimes happens that an immediate replacement cannot be found and the old gasket is then very useful as a template. Hang up the old gaskets as they are removed.

8 To strip the engine it is best to work from the top down. The underside of the crankcase, when supported on wood blocks, acts as a firm base. When the stage is reached where the crankshaft and connecting rods have to be removed, the engine can be turned on its side and all other work carried out with it in this position.

9 Whenever possible, refit nuts, bolts and washers finger-tight from wherever they were removed. This helps avoid loss and muddle later. If they cannot be refitted lay them out in such a fashion that it is clear from whence they came.

10 Don't forget to drain the oil from the engine, if this has not already been done, before dismantling begins.

10 Engine ancillary components – removal

Before basic engine dismantling begins, it is necessary to remove the following ancillary components:

Alternator
Distributor
Spark plugs
Fuel pump
Carburettor
Inlet/exhaust manifold
Thermostat and thermostat housing
Temperature gauge transmitter
Water pump
Oil pressure switch
Oil separator
Oil filter
Clutch assembly or torque converter

Some of these items have to be removed for individual servicing or renewal periodically. Details can be found in the appropriate Chapter of this manual.

11 Timing belt – checking, removal and refitting

1   The condition and tension of the timing belt must be checked after 24 000 miles (40 000 km) or 2 years and adjusted if necessary. If defective, it must be renewed. A new timing belt must be fitted after 48 000 miles (80 000 km) or 4 years usage.
2   Remove the timing belt cover, fanbelt and fan.
3   Examine the timing belt. If the teeth are worn or show signs of uneven wear, cracking or oil contamination, it must be renewed (photo).
4   Using a spring balance connected to the timing belt at the point in-line with the water pump inlet pipe, check the pull required to align the outside face of the timing belt with the line on the inlet pipe.
5   The correct belt tension for new and used timing belts is shown in the Specifications. If the belt is in good condition but extends beyond the line on the inlet pipe it must be adjusted as follows:

   (a) *Slacken the timing belt tensioner securing nuts*
   (b) *Push the tensioner against the belt and tighten the tensioner securing nuts*
   (c) *Recheck the timing belt tension and readjust the tension further if necessary*

6   To remove the timing belt, the fanbelt must first be removed.
7   Turn the crankshaft 90° BTDC (the V-notch in the timing disc opposite the timing pointer). **Note**: *It is essential that the crankshaft is set at this position before removing the timing belt. The crankshaft*

11.3 Examine the timing belt teeth for wear

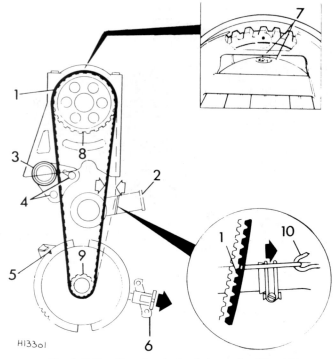

Fig. 1.6 Checking the timing belt tension (Sec 11)

1 *Timing belt*	7 *Camshaft sprocket dimple*
2 *Water pump inlet*	*and camshaft cover pointer*
3 *Timing belt tensioner*	8 *Camshaft sprocket*
4 *Tensioner securing nuts*	9 *Crankshaft sprocket*
5 *Crankshaft 90° BTDC setting*	10 *Spring balance*
6 *LED timing bracket*	

must not be turned while the camshaft is disconnected as this will result in damage to the valves and pistons.
8   Slacken the timing belt tensioner securing nuts and release the belt tension.
9   Ease the timing belt off the camshaft gear. Withdraw the plug from the LED sensor timing brackets, lift the timing pointer slightly and lift away the timing belt.
10 Refitting the timing belt is the reverse of the removal procedures but the following additional points should be noted:
11 Ensure that the crankshaft is still set at 90° BTDC and that the dimple on the rear face of the camshaft gear is opposite the pointer on the camshaft cover.
12 Adjust the belt tension, see paragraphs 4 and 5.
13 Adjust the fanbelt tension; refer to Chapter 2.

12 Cylinder head – removal (engine in car)

1   Disconnect the battery earth terminal.
2   Refer to Chapter 2 and drain the cooling system.
3   Mark the spark plug HT leads to ensure correct refitting and then detach them from the spark plugs.
4   Disconnect the distributor LT lead at the wiring connector and the temperature gauge lead at the transmitter.
5   Detach the distributor vacuum advance pipe at the union on the inlet manifold.
6   Undo and remove the air cleaner retaining nut, lift the air cleaner assembly off the carburettor adaptor and detach the intake ducting.
7   Disconnect the crankcase breather hose from the carburettor.
8   On models equipped with automatic transmission disconnect the downshift cable at the carburettor linkage.
9   Disconnect the two fuel pipes at the fuel pump and plug their ends to prevent syphoning of fuel and dirt ingress.
10 Undo and remove the four nuts securing the carburettor to the inlet manifold. Slide the carburettor off the studs and place it to one

side. Remove the insulation block, support bracket and heatshield.

11 Undo and remove the brake servo vacuum pipe banjo union on the inlet manifold. Take care not to lose the two copper washers.

12 Undo and remove the nut securing the slave cylinder bleed tube support bracket and vacuum pipe retaining clip to the cylinder head. Lift off the support bracket and vacuum pipe clip and position them both clear of the cylinder head.

13 Slacken the clip and detach the heater inlet hose from the front of the cylinder head. Slacken the clip and detach the radiator top hose from the thermostat housing.

14 Undo and remove the six nuts securing the twin exhaust front pipe flanges to the manifold.

15 Remove the timing belt cover by pulling it off its mounting spigots.

16 The crankshaft must be positioned at 90° BTDC before the timing belt is removed. Rotate the crankshaft until the V in the timing disc is in-line with the timing pointer on the crankcase and the dimple on the rear face of the camshaft gear is opposite the pointer on the camshaft cover. **Note:** *The crankshaft must not be rotated whilst the camshaft is disconnected as the pistons and valves may be damaged.*

17 Release the timing belt tensioner by slackening the securing nuts and remove the timing belt from the camshaft gear.

18 Slacken the cylinder head bolts in a progressive manner in the reverse of the tightening sequence shown in Fig. 1.7. Remove the bolts.

19 The cylinder head assembly can now be removed by lifting upwards. To break the seal, it will probably be necessary to lever under the two lugs on the right-hand side. *Do not try to prise it apart from the block by inserting a screwdriver between the faces of the cylinder head and the cylinder block, as this will result in serious damage to the cylinder head.*

20 Remove the cylinder head gasket from the cylinder block.

13 Cylinder head – removal (engine on bench)

The procedure for removing the cylinder head with the engine on the bench is the same as that for removal with the engine in the car, with the exception of disconnecting the controls and services. Refer to Section 12 and follow the operations described in paragraphs 15 to 20 inclusive.

14 Timing belt, timing belt tensioner and LED sensor timing bracket – removal

1 Remove the nuts that secure the timing belt tensioner to the cylinder block and lift away the tensioner.

2 Undo and remove the two bolts that secure the LED sensor timing bracket and lift away the bracket.

3 Remove the timing belt.

15 Flywheel, crankshaft rear oil seal and engine backplate – removal

If this operation is being carried out with the engine in the car, it will first be necessary to remove the gearbox or automatic transmission as described in Chapter 6, and then the clutch assembly or torque converter as described in Chapters 5 and 6 respectively.

1 Lock the flywheel using a suitable wedge in mesh with the starter ring gear (photo 50.2). Undo the bolts that secure the flywheel or torque converter driveplate to the crankshaft in a diagonal and progressive manner. Remove the bolts and the locking plate.

2 Mark the relative positions of the flywheel or driveplate to the crankshaft to ensure correct refitment. Lift away the flywheel or driveplate.

3 Undo and remove the bolts that secure the crankshaft rear oil seal retainer and lift away the retainer.

4 The engine backplate retaining bolts can now be removed and the backplate complete with oil seal and gasket lifted off. With the backplate removed tap out the old oil seal using a suitable drift.

16 Sump and oil strainer – removal

1 If the engine is in the car, undo and remove the two bolts each

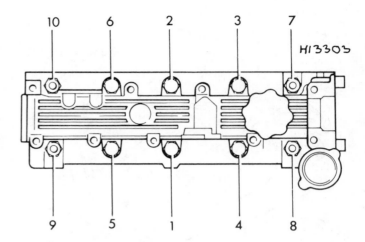

Fig. 1.7 Tightening sequence of cylinder head bolts (Secs 12 and 49)

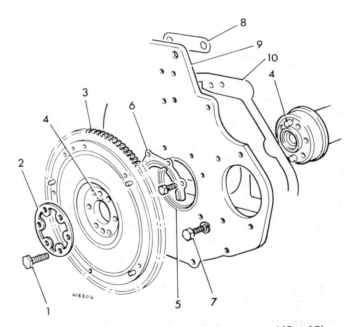

Fig. 1.8 Flywheel and engine backplate removal (Sec 15)

1	Flywheel securing bolts	7	Backplate securing bolt
2	Shaped lockwasher		and spring washer
3	Flywheel	8	Gasket (upper)
4	Mating marks	9	Engine backplate
5	Crankshaft rear oil seal	10	Gasket (lower)
6	Oil sealer retainer		

side securing the anti-roll bar bushes to the front chassis members. Lower the anti-roll bar sufficiently to allow removal of the sump. Drain the oil into a suitable container and then remove the two bolts securing the sump connecting plate to the bellhousing.

2 Undo and remove the bolts and spring washers that secure the sump in position. Note that the bolt fitted at the right-hand rear of the sump is longer than the other bolts.

3 Remove the sump and sump gasket.

4 Undo and remove the three bolts that secure the oil strainer and lift away the strainer and gasket.

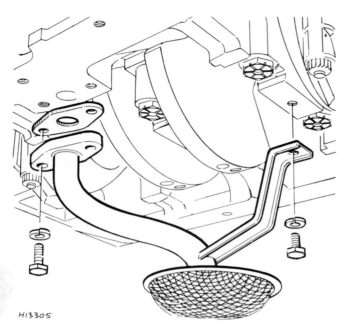

H13305

Fig. 1.9 Oil strainer removal (Sec 16)

17 Crankshaft pulley, timing disc, sprocket, flange and oil pump – removal

If this task is being carried out with the engine in the car, it will first be necessary to remove the radiator as described in Chapter 2, the timing belt as described in Section 11, and the fan.

1   Assuming the engine to be out of the car, lock the crankshaft to prevent it turning, with a block of wood placed between a crankshaft web and the crankcase. If the engine is in the car, remove the starter motor and engage a large screwdriver with the flywheel ring gear teeth.
2   Using a socket and suitable extension, undo and remove the bolt securing the crankshaft pulley and recover the lockwasher.
3   Using a large screwdriver, ease the pulley off the crankshaft, followed by the timing disc then the crankshaft sprocket and sprocket flange.
4   Remove the key from the crankshaft.
5   Slacken the nine bolts that secure the oil pump housing to the crankcase, remove the bolts and lift away the oil pump housing assembly. Remove the gasket.
6   Unscrew the oil pressure switch extension. Remove the extension and switch. Unscrew and remove the oil filter.

18 Pistons, connecting rods and big-end bearings – removal

1   Note that the pistons are marked on the top with the word FRONT, or by an arrow or a groove which must face towards the front of the engine.
2   Check that the big-end bearing caps and connecting rods have identification marks. If not, suitably mark them to ensure that the correct end caps are fitted to the correct connecting rods and the correct connecting rods are fitted in their respective cylinder bores.
3   Remove the big-end cap securing nuts and put them to one side in the order in which they were removed.
4   Remove the big-end caps, taking care to keep them in the right order. Ensure that the bearing shells are kept with their respective big-end caps unless the bearings are to be renewed.
5   If the big-end caps are difficult to remove, they may be gently tapped with a soft-faced hammer.
6   To remove the shell bearings, press the bearing opposite the groove in both the connecting rod and its cap, and the bearing shell will slide out easily.
7   Push the piston and connecting rod assemblies upwards and withdraw them from the top of the cylinder block.

19 Crankshaft and main bearings – removal

1   Note that the main bearing caps Nos 2, 3 and 4 have their numbers, together with arrows, cast on the front face of the caps.
2   Undo by one turn at a time the bolts that secure the main bearing caps.
3   Lift away each main bearing cap and the bottom half of each bearing shell, taking care to keep the bearing shell with the right cap.
4   When removing the front and rear main bearing caps, note the cork sealing joints.
5   When removing the centre main bearing cap, note the bottom semi-circular halves of the thrust washers, one half located on each side of the main bearing. Lay them, with the centre bearing cap, along the correct side.
6   Slightly rotate the crankshaft to free the upper halves of the bearing shells and thrust washers, which can be extracted and placed over the respective bearing caps.
7   Remove the crankshaft by lifting it from the crankcase.

20 Cylinder head and camshaft assembly – dismantling

1   Undo and remove the two securing nuts and washers and withdraw the distributor from the camshaft cover.
2   Remove the securing bolts and lift away the hot air box, inlet/exhaust manifold and the manifold gasket.
3   Unscrew the coolant temperature switch.
4   Undo and remove the bolt that secures the thermostat housing to the cylinder head and lift away the housing complete with thermostat. Remove the O-ring seal.
5   Undo and remove the bolt that secures the camshaft sprocket and pull the sprocket off the camshaft.
6   Undo and remove the five bolts that secure the camshaft end cover and lift away the cover and gasket.
7   Slacken the nine bolts that secure the camshaft bearing cover in a progressive and even sequence until the valve spring tension is released, then remove the bolts, release the oil filler cap and lift away the cover bracket.
8   Lift off the camshaft bearing cover.
9   Remove the camshaft complete with the front oil seal from the cylinder head. Pull the oil seal off the front of the camshaft.
10 Lift out each tappet and shim and lay them out in the correct order, 1 to 8, to ensure that they can be refitted in their original positions.
11 To remove the valves, compress each spring in turn with a universal valve spring compressor until the two halves of the collet can be removed. Release the compressor and lift away the spring top cup, valve spring, oil seal (inlet valves only), valve spring seat and the valve.
12 If, when the valve spring compressor is screwed down, the valve spring top cup refuses to free and expose the split collet, do not continue to screw down on the compressor, but gently tap the top of the tool directly over the cup with a light hammer. This should free the cup. To avoid the compressor jumping off the valve retaining cup when it is tapped, hold the compressor firmly in position.
13 It is essential that the valves are kept in their correct order unless they are so badly worn or burnt that they are to be renewed. If they are going to be refitted, place them in their correct sequences along with the tappets and shims previously removed. Also keep the valve springs, cups and collets in the same order.

21 Gudgeon pins – removal and refitting

The gudgeon pins are a press fit in the connecting rod and it is important that no damage is caused during removal and refitting. Because of this, should it be necessary to fit new pistons or connecting rods, take the parts along to the local BL garage who will have the special equipment required to carry out this work.

22 Piston rings – removal

1   To remove the piston rings, slide them carefully over the top of the piston, taking care not to scratch the aluminium alloy of the piston. Never slide them off the bottom of the piston skirt. It is very easy to

break piston rings if they are pulled off roughly so this operation should be done with extreme caution. It is helpful to use an old 0.020 in (0.5 mm) feeler gauge to facilitate their removal as follows.

2   Lift one end of the piston ring to be removed out of its groove and insert the end of the feeler gauge under it.

3   Turn the feeler gauge slowly round the piston; as the ring comes out of its groove it rests on the land above. It can then be eased off the piston with the feeler gauge stopping it from slipping into any empty grooves.

23 Lubrication system – description

The pressed steel oil sump is attached to the underside of the crankcase and acts as a reservoir for the engine oil. The oil pump draws oil through a strainer located under the oil surface, passes it along a short passage and into the full-flow oil filter which is screwed onto the oil pump housing. The freshly filtered oil flows from the filter and enters the main gallery. Five small drillings connect the main gallery to the five main bearings. The oil passes from the main bearings through drillings in the crankshaft to the big-end bearings.

When the crankshaft is rotating, oil is thrown from the hole in each big-end of the connecting rod and splashes the thrust side of the piston and bore.

Further drillings connect the main oil gallery to the overhead

25.2a Remove the oil pump backplate securing screws ...

25.2b ... and lift off the backplate

camshaft in order to lubricate the bearings, cams and tappets. The oil then drains back to the sump via large drillings in the cylinder head and cylinder block.

A pressure relief valve is incorporated in the oil pump housing to keep the oil pressure within the specified limit.

24 Oil filter – removal and refitting

1   The oil filter is a throw-away cartridge type screwed into the left-hand side of the oil pump housing.

2   Simply unscrew the old unit; if it is very tight use a strap wrench to slacken it.

3   Fit a new sealing ring in position and smear it with engine oil, then screw the new filter on, *hand-tight only*.

4   Run the engine and check for oil leaks.

25 Oil pump – dismantling, inspection and reassembly

Note: *The oil pump is not repairable and if defective it must be renewed.*

1   Scribe an alignment mark on the pump housing and pump backplate to ensure that the backplate is refitted in its original position at reassembly.

2   Using a 3 mm Allen key, remove the backplate securing screws and lift off the backplate (photos).

3   Remove the outer and inner rotors.

4   Remove the split pin that retains the pressure relief valve, then remove the plug from the housing by pushing down on the relief valve spring with a screwdriver through the oil return hole. Collect the spring and valve plunger. Discard the plug O-ring seal.

5   Remove the front crankshaft oil seal from the oil pump housing.

6   Thoroughly clean all the component parts then check the rotor endfloat and lobe clearance.

7   Fit the outer rotor in the housing and, using a feeler gauge, check the clearance between the outer rotor and the pump body A in Fig. 1.10.

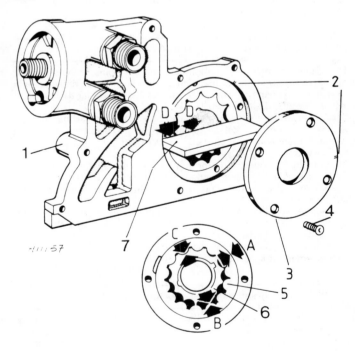

Fig. 1.10 Checking the oil pump clearance – see text
(Sec 25)

1	Oil pump housing	5	Outer rotor
2	Alignment marks	6	Inner rotor
3	Backplate	7	Straight edge
4	Screw		

25.8 Measure the lobe clearance with a feeler gauge

25.12a Fitting a new seal in the oil pump housing

25.12b The seal must be flush with the housing when fitted

8   Fit the inner rotor and measure the lobe clearance B and C in Fig. 1.10 (photo).
9   Measure the outer rotor to housing face clearance D in Fig. 1.10.
10 If any of these clearances exceed the limits shown in the Specifications, the pump must be renewed.
11 Check the free length of the pressure relief valve spring. If its length differs from the dimension shown in the Specifications, renew the spring.
12 Reassembly is the reverse of the dismantling procedure. Liberally lubricate the oil pump components with engine oil, fit a new O-ring on the pressure relief valve plug and a new crankshaft front oil seal in the pump housing (photos).

26 Engine components – examination and renovation (general)

With the engine stripped down and all parts thoroughly cleaned, it is now time to examine every component for wear. The components listed in the following Sections should be inspected and, where necessary, renovated or renewed.

27 Crankshaft – examination and renovation

1   Inspect the main bearing journals and crankpins. If there are any scratches or score marks then the shaft will need regrinding. Such conditions will nearly always be accompanied by similar deterioration in the matching bearings shells.
2   Each bearing journal should also be round and can be checked with a micrometer or caliper gauge around the periphery at several points. If there is more than 0.001 in (0.25 mm) of ovality, regrinding is necessary.
3   A main BL agent or motor engineering specialist will be able to decide to what extent regrinding is necessary, and also supply the special undersize shell bearing to match whatever may need grinding off.
4   Before taking the crankshaft for regrinding, also check the cylinder bores and pistons, as it may be advantageous to have the whole engine done at the same time.
5   Check the condition of the spigot bush in the crankshaft rear flange. Renew it if necessary.

28 Main and big-end bearings – examination and renovation

1   With careful servicing and regular oil and filter changes, bearings will last for a very long time, but they can still fail for unforeseen reasons. With big-end bearings the indication is a regular rhythmic loud knocking from the crankcase. The frequency depends on engine speed and is particulatly noticeable when the engine is under load. This symptom is accompanied by a fall in oil pressure, although this is not normally noticeable unless an oil pressure gauge is fitted. Main bearing failure is usually indicated by serious vibration, particularly at higher engine revolutions, accompanied by a more significant drop in oil pressure and a rumbling noise.
2   Bearing shells in good condition have bearing surfaces with a smooth even matt silver/grey colour all over. Worn bearings will show patches of a different colour where the bearing metal has worn away and exposed the underlay. Damaged bearings will be pitted or scored. It is always well worthwhile fitting new shells as their cost is relatively low. If the crankshaft is in good condition it is merely a question of obtaining another set of standard size. A reground crankshaft will need new bearing shells as a matter of course.

29 Cylinder bores – examination and renovation

1   A new cylinder is perfectly round and the walls parallel throughout its length. The action of the piston tends to wear the walls at right angles to the gudgeon pin due to side thrust. This wear takes place principally on that section of the cylinder swept by the piston rings.
2   It is possible to get an indication of bore wear by removing the cylinder head with the engine still in the car. With the piston down in the bore, first signs of wear can be seen and felt just below the top of the bore where the top piston ring reaches, and there will be a noticeable lip. If there is no lip it is fairly reasonable to assume that bore wear is not severe and any lack of compression or excessive oil consumption is due to worn or broken piston rings or pistons.
3   If it is possible to obtain a bore measuring micrometer, measure the bore in the thrust plane below the lip and again at the bottom of the cylinder in the same plane. If the difference is more than 0.006 in (0.15 mm), a rebore is necessary. Similarly, a difference of 0.006 in (0.15 mm) or more between two measurements of the bore diameter taken at right angles to each other is a sign of excessive ovality, calling for a rebore.
4   Any bore which is significantly scratched or scored will need reboring. This symptom usually indicates that the piston or rings are also damaged. Even in the event of only one cylinder being in need of reboring, it will still be necessary for all four to be bored and fitted with new oversize pistons and rings. A motor engineering specialist will be able to rebore the cylinders and supply the necessary matched pistons. If the crankshaft is also undergoing regrinding, it is a good idea to let the same firm renovate and reassemble the crankshaft and pistons to the block. A reputable firm normally gives a guarantee for such work.
5   If reboring is not necessary and new standard size pistons and/or piston rings are to be fitted, it will be necessary to remove the hard surface finish glaze of the cylinder walls. If this is not done the new piston rings will not bed in adequately and oil consumption is likely to be excessive.
6   To carry out the de-glazing operation, soak a suitable piece of medium grade emery paper in paraffin and rub it up and down the inside of the cylinder bores. Use a twisting action at the same time so that a criss-cross pattern is achieved in the bore. Continue this operation until all the shine in the cylinder bore is removed and a dull grey surface finish appears around the entire bore. On completion thoroughly clean the bores and ensure that all traces of emery grit are removed.

30 Pistons and piston rings – examination and renovation

1   If the old pistons are to be refitted, carefully remove the piston rings and then thoroughly clean them. Take particular care to clean out

the piston ring grooves. Do not scratch the aluminium in any way. If new rings are to be fitted to the old pistons, then the top ring should be of the stepped type so as to clear the ridge left above the previous top ring. If a normal but oversize new ring is fitted, it will hit the ridge and break, because the new ring will not have worn in the same way as the old.

2   Before fitting the rings on the pistons, each should be inserted approximately 3 in (76 mm) down the cylinder bore and the gap measured with a feeler gauge. This should be between the limits given in the Specifications at the beginning of this Chapter. It is essential that the gap is measured at the bottom of the ring travel, for if it is measured at the top of a worn bore and gives a perfect fit, it could easily seize at the bottom. If the ring gap is too small, rub down the ends of the ring with a very fine file until the gap is correct when fitted. To keep the rings square in the bore for measurement, line each one up in turn with an old piston inserted in the bore upside down, and use the piston to push the ring down about 3 in (76 mm). Remove the piston and measure the piston ring gap.

3   The groove clearance of the new rings in old pistons should be within the tolerance given in the Specifications. If it is not enough, the rings could stick in the piston grooves causing loss of compression. The ring grooves in the piston in this case will need machining out to accept the new rings.

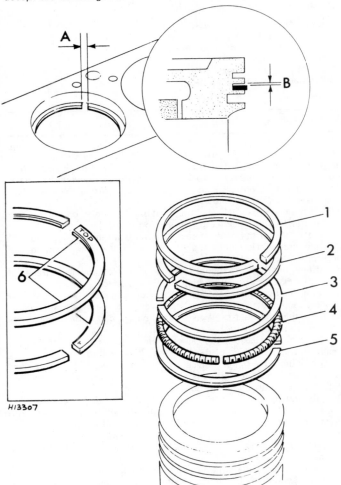

H13307

Fig. 1.11 Piston ring measurement and assembly details (Secs 30 and 39)

A	Piston ring gap	3	Control ring top rail
B	Ring side clearance	4	Control ring expander
1	Top compression ring	5	Control ring bottom rail
2	Stepped compression ring	6	The compression rings are marked TOP or T

4   Before fitting new rings onto an old piston, clean out the grooves with a piece of broken ring.

5   If new pistons are obtained, the rings will be included, so it must be emphasised that the top ring be stepped if fitted to a cylinder bore that has not been rebored or has not had the top ridge removed.

31 Tappets – examination

1   The faces of the tappets in contact with the lobes on the camshaft should show no signs of pitting, scoring or other forms of wear. They should not be a loose fit in the cylinder head.

2   Tappets with any of these defects must be renewed.

32 Valves, valve seats and valve guides – examination and renovation

1   With the valves removed from the cylinder head, scrape away all traces of carbon from the valves and the combustion chambers and ports in the cylinder head using a knife and suitable scraper.

2   Examine the heads of the valves for signs of cracking, burning away or pitting of the valve face or the edge of the valve head. The valve seats in the cylinder head should also be examined for the same signs. Usually it is the valve that deteriorates first, but if a bad valve is not rectified the seat will suffer, and this is more difficult to repair. If the valve face and seat are deeply pitted, or if the valve face is concave where it contacts the seat, it will be necessary to have the valve refaced and the seat recut by a BL dealer or motor engineering specialist. It is worth considering having this work done in any case if the engine has covered a high mileage. A little extra time and money spent ensuring that the cylinder head and valves are in first class condition will make a tremendous difference to the performance and economy of the engine after overhaul. If any of the valves are cracked or burnt away they must be renewed. Any similar damage that may have occurred to the valve seats can be repaired by renewing the seat. However, this is a job that can only be carried out by a specialist.

3   Another form of valve wear can occur on the stem where it runs in the guide in the cylinder head. This can be detected by trying to rock the valve from side to side. If there is any movement at all it is an indication that the valve stem or guide is worn. Check the stem first with a micrometer at points along and around its length. If they are not within the specified size, new valves will probably solve the problem. If the guides are worn, however, they will need renewing. The valve seats will also need recutting to ensure they are concentric with the stems. This work should be given to your BL dealer or local engineering works.

4   Assuming that the valve faces and seats are only lightly pitted, or that new valves are to be fitted, the valves should be lapped into their seats. This may be done by placing a smear of fine carborundum paste on the edge of the valve and, using a suction type valve holder, lapping the valve in situ. This is done with a semi-rotary action, rotating the handle of the valve holder between the hands and lifting it occasionally to redistribute the traces of paste. As soon as a matt grey unbroken line appears on both the valve face and seat, the valve is 'ground in'.

5   When all work on the cylinder head and valves is complete, it is essential that all traces of carbon dust and grinding paste is removed. This should be done by thoroughly washing the components in paraffin or a suitable engine cleaner and blowing out with a jet of air. If particles of carbon or grinding paste should work their way into the engine, they would cause havoc with bearings or cylinder walls.

33 Camshaft and camshaft bearings – examination and renovation

1   Check the camshaft journals and cams for scoring and wear. If there are very slight scoring marks, these can be removed with emery cloth or a fine oil stone. The greatest care must be taken to keep the cam profiles smooth.

2   Examine the ignition distributor drivegear for wear or chipping of the gear teeth.

3   Examine the camshaft bearing surfaces in the cylinder head and camshaft bearing cover, if they are scored and worn it means a new cylinder head and camshaft cover will be required.

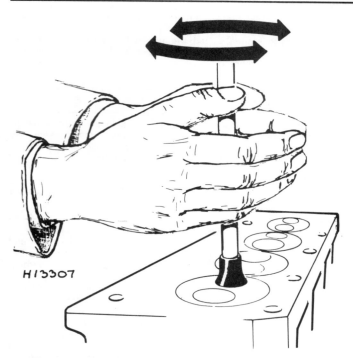

H13307

Fig. 1.12 Valve grinding using hand suction tool (Sec 32)

mask off the adjacent cylinder bores and all surrounding water jacket orifices with paper and adhesive tape. Press grease into the gap all round the piston to keep carbon particles out and then scrape all carbon away by hand. Do not use a power drill and wire brush when the engine is in the car, as it will be virtually impossible to keep all the carbon dust clear of the engine. When completed, carefully clear out the grease around the rim of the piston with a matchstick or something similar – bringing any carbon particles with it. Repeat the process on the other piston crown, then turn the engine over until the remaining two pistons are at the top of their stroke. It is not recommended that a ring of carbon is left round the edge of the piston on the theory that it will aid oil consumption. This was valid in the early days of long stroke low revving engines, but modern engines, fuels and lubricants cause less carbon deposits anyway, and any left behind tend merely to cause hot spots.

36 Engine reassembly – general

Before reassembly begins, all components of the engine must be cleaned of oil, sludge and old gaskets, and the working area should also be cleared and clean. In addition to the normal range of good quality socket spanners and general tools which are essential, the following must also be available:

Complete set of new gaskets
Supply of clean rags
Clean oil can full of clean engine oil
Torque wrench
Suitable jointing compound
All new parts as necessary

34 Flywheel starter ring gear – examination and renovation

1   If the teeth on the flywheel starter ring gear are badly worn, or if some are missing, then it will be necessary to remove the ring. This is achieved by splitting the old ring using a cold chisel. Care must be taken not to damage the flywheel during this process. Take suitable precautions to avoid injury caused by flying fragments.
2   To fit a new ring gear, it will be necessary to heat it gently and evenly with an oxy-acetylene flame until a temperature of approximately 350°C is reached. This is indicated by a grey/brown surface colour. With the ring gear at this temperature, fit it to the flywheel with the bevelled edge of the teeth facing the engine facing end of the flywheel. The ring gear should be either pressed or lightly tapped onto its register and left to cool naturally, when the contraction of the metal on cooling will ensure that it is a secure and permanent fit. Great care must be taken not to overheat the ring gear, for if this happens the temper of the ring gear will be lost.
3   An alternative method is to use a high temperature oven to heat the ring.
4   Because of the need of oxy-acetylene equipment or a special oven it is not normally practical for refitment to take place at home. Take the flywheel and new starter ring to an engineering works willing to do the job.

35 Cylinder head and pistons – decarbonisation

1   When the cylinder head is removed, either in the course of an overhaul or for an inspection of bores or valve condition when the engine is in the car, it is normal to remove all carbon deposits from the piston crowns and head.
2   This is best done with a cup shaped wire brush and an electric drill, and is fairly straightforward when the engine is dismantled and the pistons removed. Sometimes hard spots of carbon are not easily removed except by a scraper. When cleaning the pistons with a scraper, take care not to damage the surface of the piston in any way.
3   When the engine is in the car certain precautions must be taken when decarbonising the piston crowns in order to prevent dislodged pieces of carbon falling into the interior of the engine which could cause damage to the cylinder bores, pistons and rings – or if allowed into the water passages – damage to the water pump. Turn the engine so that the piston being worked on is at the top of its stroke, and then

37 Crankshaft – refitting

Ensure that the crankcase is thoroughly clean and that all the oilways are clear. A thin twist drill is useful for cleaning them out. If possible, blow them out with compressed air. Treat the crankshaft in the same fashion and then inject engine oil into the crankshaft oilways. Commence work on rebuilding the engine by refitting the crankshaft and main bearings as follows:
1   Fit the five upper halves of the main bearing shells to their location in the crankcase after wiping the location clean.
2   Note that on the back of each bearing is a tab which engages in locating grooves in either the crankcase or the main bearing cap housings (photo).
3   If new bearings are being fitted, carefully clean away all traces of the protective grease with which they are coated.
4   With the five upper bearing shells securely in place, wipe the lower bearing cap housings and fit the five lower shell bearings to their caps, ensuring that the right shell goes into the right cap if the old bearings are being refitted (photo).
5   Wipe the recesses either side of the centre main bearing which locate the upper halves of the thrust washers (photo).
6   Introduce the upper halves of the thrust washers (the halves without tabs) into their grooves either side of the centre main bearing with their oil grooves facing outwards (photo).
7   Generously lubricate the crankshaft journals and the upper and lower main bearing shells and carefully lower the crankshaft into position. Make sure that it is the right way round (photos).
8   Fit the main bearing caps into position, ensuring that they locate properly. The mating surfaces must be spotlessly clean or the caps will not seat correctly.
9   When refitting the centre main bearing cap, ensure that the thrust washers, generously lubricated, are fitted with their oil grooves facing outwards and the locating tab of each washer is in the slot in the bearing cap (photo).
10   Refit the main bearing cap bolts and screw them up finger-tight (photo).
11   Test the crankshaft for freedom of rotation. Should it be very stiff to turn or possess high spots, a most careful inspection must be made, preferably by a skilled mechanic with a micrometer to trace the cause of the trouble. It is very seldom that any trouble of this nature will be experienced when fitting the crankshaft.
12   Tighten the main bearing cap bolts to the specified torque and recheck the crankshaft for freedom of rotation (photo).

37.2 Ensure the tab on the bearing shell locates in the groove

37.4 Fit the bearing shells in the crankcase

37.5 The centre main bearing is recessed on each side to accept the thrust washers

37.6 The thrust washers are fitted with the oil grooves facing outward

37.7a Lubricate the main bearings ...

37.7b ... and lower the crankshaft into position

37.9 Fit the main bearing caps ...

37.10 ... screw-in the bearing cap retaining bolts ...

37.12 ... and tighten them to the specified torque

13 Using a screwdriver between one crankshaft web and main bearing cap, lever the crankshaft forwards and check the endfloat using feeler gauges. This should be as shown in the Specifications. If excessive, new thrust washers must be fitted.

38 Pistons and connecting rods – reassembly

As the gudgeon pin is a press fit in the connecting rod, this operation must be carried out by a BL dealer or motor engineering specialist.

39 Piston rings – refitting

1   Check that the piston ring grooves and oilways are thoroughly clean and unblocked. Piston rings must always be fitted over the head of the piston and *never* from the bottom.

2   The easiest method to use when fitting rings is to position two 0.015 in (0.38 mm) feeler blades on either side of the piston and slide the rings down over the blades. This will stop the rings from dropping into a vacant ring groove. When the ring is adjacent to its correct grove, slide out the feeler blades and the ring will drop in.

3   The procedure for fitting the rings is as follows. Start by sliding the bottom rail of the oil control ring down the piston and position it below the bottom piston ring groove. Fit the oil control expander into the bottom ring groove and then move the bottom oil control ring rail into the bottom groove. Now fit the top oil control ring rail into the bottom groove. Make sure that the ends of the expander are butting together and not overlapping. Position the gaps of the two rails and the expander at 90° to each other.

4   Fit the second compression ring to its groove with the step towards the gudgeon pin and the word TOP or the letter T facing the top of the piston.

5   Fit the chrome plated top compression ring to its groove with the word TOP or the letter T facing the top of the piston.

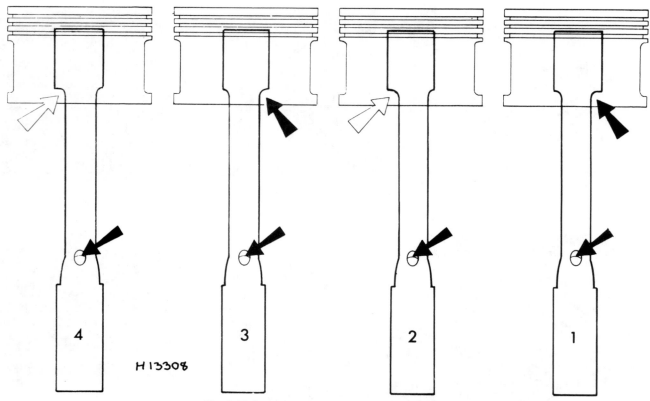

Fig. 1.13 Details of connecting rod small-end offset
(Sec 40)

6   When all the piston rings are in place, set the ring gaps of the compression rings at 90° to each other and away from the thrust side of the piston.

40 Pistons – refitting

1   Wipe the cylinder bores clean with a clean rag.
2   The pistons, complete with connecting rods, must be fitted to their bores from the top of the block.
3   Check that the two upper piston ring gaps are spaced at 90° to each other.
4   Check that the piston is the correct one for the cylinder bore and that the small-end offset of the connecting rod is correct for the bore; see Fig. 1.13.
5   Lubricate the cylinder bore and piston with clean engine oil.
6   Fit a universal piston ring compressor over the rings. A large diameter worm-drive hose clip will serve as a ring compressor if the proper tool is not available.
7   Insert the first piston into its bore making sure that the front of the piston (marked on top with the word FRONT or an arrow) is towards the front of the engine (photo).
8   Slide the piston connecting rod assembly down the bore until the bottom of the piston ring compressor rests on the cylinder block face. Now gently but firmly tap the piston through the compressor using a block of wood or the handle of a mallet (photo).

41 Connecting rods to crankshaft – reassembly

1   Wipe the connecting rod half of the big-end bearing location and the underside of the shell bearing clean (as for the main bearing shells) and fit the shell in position with its locating tab engaged with the corresponding groove in the connecting rod. Always fit new shells (photo).
2   Generously lubricate the crankpin journals with engine oil and turn the crankshaft so that the crankpin is in the most advantageous position for the connecting rod to be drawn onto it.
3   Fit the bearing shell to the connecting rod cap in the same way as

with the connecting rod itself.
4   Generously lubricate the shell bearing and offer up the connecting rod bearing cap to the connecting rod. Note that the bearing shell grooves in the connecting rod and cap must both be on the same side (photo).
5   Refit the connecting rod cap retaining nuts and tighten them to the specified torque (photo).

42 Oil strainer and sump – refitting

1   Refit the oil strainer. Always use a new flange gasket. Fit the two bolts that secure the oil strainer flange to the crankcase and the bolt that secures the support stay (photo).
2   Ensure that all traces of the old gasket have been removed from the mating faces of the sump and crankcase.
3   Apply a jointing compound to the joint faces of the front and rear main bearing caps and fit new cork seals to the caps (photo).
4   Place a new sump gasket on the crankcase. Use a little grease to keep the gasket in position and then fit the oil sump (photo).
5   Refit the sump securing bolts and spring washers; the longer bolt is fitted at the rear right-hand location. Tighten the bolts to the specified torque.

43 Oil pump, timing pointer and LED sensor timing bracket – refitting

1   Ensure that the joint faces of the crankcase and oil pump housing are clean. Position a new gasket on the oil pump.
2   Fit the oil pump drive key in the crankshaft (photo).
3   Fit a protective sleeve over the end of the crankshaft (photo). Line-up the keyway in the pump with the drive key on the crankshaft and fit the oil pump. Take care not to damage the oil seal.
4   Fit the securing bolts, timing pointer and LED sensor bracket. The long bolt is fitted adjacent to the core plug. Tighten the bolts to the specified torque (photos).
5   Prime the oil pump by removing the bottom plug and injecting oil into the pump.

40.7 The piston is marked with the word FRONT or an arrow

40.8 Carefully tap the piston into the cylinder bore

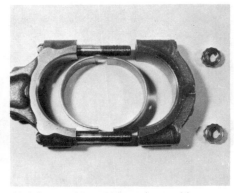
41.1 Connecting rod big-end assembly

41.4 Fit the connecting rod big-end cap ...

41.5 ... and tighten the bolts to the specified torque

42.1 Fitting the oil strainer

42.3 Use jointing compound when fitting the cork seals (arrowed)

42.4 Fitting the oil sump

43.2 Ensure the oil pump drive key is correctly located in the crankshaft

43.3 Wrap some tape around the end of the crankshaft to prevent damage to the oil seal

43.4a Fit the oil pump securing bolts ...

43.4b ... and the LED sensor bracket

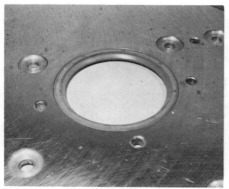
44.2 With a new oil seal in position ...

44.3 ... fit the engine backplate ...

44.4 ... and tighten the bolts to the specified torque

45.1 Screw the oil pressure switch and extension into the pump housing

46.2 Place a new gasket on the water pump

46.4a Fit the water pump to the block ...

46.4b ... and secure with the retaining bolts and nuts. Make sure the timing belt tensioner bolts are in position

47.1 Fit the key in the crankshaft ...

47.2a ... slide on the sprocket flange and sprocket ...

47.2b ... followed by the timing disc and pulley

47.4 Tighten the pulley retaining bolt to the specified torque

48.2 Insert the valve in the valve guide

44 Engine backplate – refitting

1   Lubricate a new seal with SAE 90EP oil and fit the seal in the backplate with the tip of the seal facing to the front of the engine.
2   Ensure that the seal is pressed in square, with the front of the seal flush with the front face of the backplate (photo).
3   Locate the rear oil seal retainer, then fit the retainer and backplate securing bolts (photo).
4   Tighten the oil seal retainer securing bolts and the backplate securing bolts to the specified torque (photo).

45 Oil pressure switch – refitting

Screw the oil pressure switch into the extension and then screw the extension into the oil pump housing (photo). Fully tighten the switch and the switch extension.

46 Water pump – refitting

1   Ensure that the mating faces of the water pump and cylinder block are free of old gasket or jointing compound.
2   Smear a little grease on the joint face of the water pump and place a new gasket on the pump (photo).
3   Locate the two bolts that secure the timing belt tensioner in the water pump housing. Use some grease to retain them in the housing while fitting the water pump.
4   Fit the water pump to the cylinder block and secure it in position with the five bolts and the stud. Tighten the stud and five bolts to the specified torque (photos).

47 Crankshaft sprocket, timing disc and pulley – refitting

1   Fit the drive key on the crankshaft (photo).
2   Fit the sprocket flange followed by the sprocket, then the timing disc and the crankshaft pulley (photos).
3   Using a new lockwasher, fit the crankshaft pulley securing bolt.
4   Fit two bolts temporarily in the rear flange of the crankshaft, and use a lever between them to prevent the crankshaft from turning whilst tightening the crankshaft pulley bolt to the specified torque (photo).
5   Lock the bolt by bending over two tabs of the lockwasher.

48 Valves – refitting

1   With the valves and valve seats suitably prepared (see Section 32) and in their correct order, start with No 1 cylinder.
2   Lubricate the valve stem with oil and insert the valve into its guide (photo).
3   On inlet valves, fit a new oil seal well-lubricated with engine oil.
4   Fit the valve spring seat, valve spring and valve spring cup over the valve stem (photos).
5   Using a valve spring compressor tool, compress the valve spring

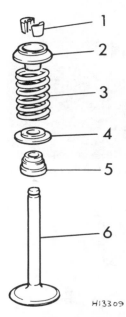

Fig. 1.14 Inlet valve and spring assembly (Sec 48)

1   Split collet
2   Valve spring cup
3   Spring
4   Valve spring seat
5   Oil seal (not fitted on exhaust valves)
6   Valve

until the split collets can be slid into position, then carefully release the valve spring compressor in order not to displace the collets (photo).
6   Refit the other valves in the same way. When they are all fitted, tap the end of each valve stem using a plastic-faced hammer or a hammer with a block of hardwood interposed. This will settle the valve components ready for checking the valve clearances.

49 Cylinder head, camshaft and camshaft cover – refitting

1   Ensure that the mating faces of the cylinder block and cylinder head are perfectly clean and dry.
2   Position a new cylinder head gasket on the cylinder block, locating it over the dowels in the block (photo). The gasket is pre-coated and must be fitted dry. Do not use grease or jointing compound on the gasket.
3   Check that the crankshaft is positioned at 90° BTDC as described in Section 4 paragraph 5 (photo).
4   Lower the cylinder head into position, locating it over the dowels. Ensure that the retaining bolt threads are clean and dry, and then screw them in finger tight. Progressively tighten the bolts in the sequence shown in Fig. 1.7 to the specified torque (photos).

48.4a Fit the valve spring and seat ...

48.4b ... then the valve spring and spring cup

48.5 Compress the valve spring and fit the split collets

49.2 Position a new gasket on the cylinder block

49.3 Set the crankshaft at 90° BTDC with the single notch in the timing disc opposite the timing pointer

49.4a Lower the cylinder head onto the block ...

49.4b ... fit the cylinder head retaining bolts ...

49.4c ... and tighten them to the specified torque

49.5 Fit the valve shims and tappets

50.1 Position the flywheel on the crankshaft flange

50.2 Lock the flywheel with a wedge and tighten the retaining bolts to the specified torque

51.1a Fit the inlet/exhaust manifold ...

51.1b ... hot air box ...

51.1c ... oil separator ...

51.1d ... and heatshield

5   Place the valve clearance adjusting shims into their original valve spring cap recesses. Lubricate the valve tappets and place them over the top of each valve spring cap in their original positions (photo).
6   Liberally lubricate the camshaft journals and place the camshaft in position on the cylinder head.
7   Using BL special tool 18G 1301 or the alternative brackets described in Section 4, secure the camshaft in position in the cylinder head. When in position the clamps or brackets should be exerting a light pressure only on the camshaft bearing journals; sufficient to hold the camshaft firmly in place while still allowing it to be rotated.
8   Again refer to Section 4 paragraphs 13 to 26 and check/adjust the valve tappet clearances.
9   If the engine is in the car, reverse the operations described in Section 12 paragraphs 1 to 14.
10   After refitting the cylinder head, run the engine at a fast idle for 15 minutes, then switch off and allow it to cool. Now slacken each cylinder head bolt individually in the correct sequence, half a turn, and then retighten to the specified torque.

50 Flywheel and clutch – refitting

1   Clean the mating faces of the crankshaft and flywheel. Fit the flywheel, locating it on the dowel in the end of the crankshaft flange,

51.3 Fit the thermostat housing ...

51.5 ... and the fuel pump

and with the alignment marks made at removal correctly matched (photo).
2   Refit the locking plate and the six securing bolts. Using a suitable wedge, lock the flywheel and tighten the securing bolts in a diagonal and progressive manner to the specified torque (photo).
3   Lock the bolts by bending over the locking plate.
4   Refit the clutch assembly as described in Chapter 5, or the torque converter as described in Chapter 6.

51 Final assembly

1   Using a new gasket, refit the inlet/exhaust manifold, the hot air box, the oil separator and the heatshield (photos).
2   Refit the coolant temperature switch.
3   Refer to Chapter 2 and refit the thermostat housing, complete with thermostat (photo).
4   Refit the distributor as described in Chapter 4.
5   Refit the fuel pump as described in Chapter 3 (photo).
6   Refit the alternator as described in Chapter 10.
7   Refit the carburettor as described in Chapter 3.
8   Refit the spark plugs.
9   Fit a new oil filter cartridge as described in Section 24.

52 Engine – reconnecting to manual gearbox or automatic transmission

1   If the engine was removed in unit with the gearbox or automatic transmission, it may be reattached in the following manner.
2   Place the engine on the floor and suitably support it on blocks. If a manual gearbox is fitted make sure that the clutch disc is correctly centralised as described in Chapter 5. If automatic transmission is fitted align the torque converter front pump driving dogs and slots horizontally. Similarly align the driving dogs on the transmission input shaft.
3   Lift up the gearbox or automatic transmission and insert the input shaft through the centre of the clutch or torque converter. Push the unit fully home until the bellhousing abuts the engine backplate. It may be necessary to move the gearbox or transmission from side to side or up and down slightly to align the input shaft. *On no account allow the weight of the gearbox or transmission to hang unsupported on the input shaft.*
4   Once the gearbox or transmission is in place, support its weight on blocks and then refit the bellhousing-to-engine securing bolts.
5   Refit the starter motor and ensure that any other pipes or hoses are correctly located in their brackets or clips where applicable.
6   The power unit is now ready for refitting into the car.

53 Engine – refitting in car

1   Refitting the engine either with or without manual gearbox or automatic transmission is a reversal of the removal procedure. Assuming the gearbox or automatic transmission to still be in position in the car, a little trouble taken in getting the engine properly slung (so it takes up a suspended angle similar to its final position) will pay off when it comes to locating it on the engine mountings.
2   Ensure that all loose leads, cables, hoses etc are tucked out of the way. If not, it is easy to trap one and cause additional work after the engine is refitted to the car.
3   If a manual gearbox is fitted, make sure that the clutch disc is correctly centralised as described in Chapter 5. If automatic transmission is fitted, align the torque converter front pump driving dogs and slots horizontally. Similarly align the driving dogs on the transmission input shaft.
4   The engine is likely to be stiff to turn over initially if new bearings or pistons and rings have been fitted, and it will save a lot of frustration if the battery is well charged. After a rebore the stiffness may initially be more than the battery can cope with, so be prepared to connect another battery in parallel with jump leads.
5   The following check list should ensure the engine starts safely and with the minimum of delay:

  (a) Fuel lines connected and tightened
  (b) Water hoses connected and all clips tightened

(c)   Coolant drain plug fitted and tightened
(d)   Cooling system replenished
(e)   Sump drain plug fitted and tight
(f)   Oil in engine
(g)   LT wiring connected to distributor and coil
(h)   Temperature gauge and oil pressure warning light wires
        connected
(i)   Timing belt correctly fitted and ignition timing set statically
(j)   Distributor rotor arm, cap and HT leads fitted
(k)   Throttle and choke cables connected
(l)   Earth strap connected
(m) Alternator and starter motor leads connected
(n)   Battery fully charged and leads connected
(o)   Oil or fluid in gearbox or automatic transmission
(p)   Clutch hydraulic system bled (where applicable)

54 Engine – initial start-up after overhaul or major repair

1   Make sure the battery is fully charged and all lubricants, coolant
and fuel are replenished.
2   If the fuel system has been dismantled, it will require several
revolutions of the engine on the starter motor to pump the petrol up
to the carburettor, so be prepared for this.
3   As soon as the engine fires and runs, keep it going at a fast idle
only and bring it up to normal working temperature.
4   As the engine warms up there will be odd smells and some smoke
from parts getting hot and burning off oil deposits. Look for leaks of
petrol, water or oil, which will be obvious if serious. Check also the
exhaust pipe-to-manifold joints, as these do not always find their exact
gas-tight positions until the heat and vibration have acted upon them,
and it is almost certain that they will require further tightening. This
should be done, of course, with the engine stopped.
5   When normal running temperature has been reached, adjust the
carburettor settings as described in Chapter 3.
6   Stop the engine and wait a few minutes to see if any lubricant or
coolant is dripping out when the engine is stationary.
7   After the engine has run for fifteen minutes, switch if off and
retorque the cylinder head as described in Section 49. Also check the
tightness of the manifold and sump bolts.
8   Road test the car to check that the ignition and carburettor
settings are correct and that the engine is delivering the necessary
smoothness and power. Do not race the engine – if new bearings
and/or pistons have been fitted, it should be treated as a new engine
and run in at reduced speed for the first 1000 miles (1610 km).

55 Fault diagnosis – engine

Symptom	Reason(s)
Engine turns over but will not start	Ignition system damp or wet
	Ignition leads to spark plugs loose
	Shorted or disconnected low tension leads
	Dirty, incorrectly set ot pitted contact breaker points
	Faulty condenser
	Defective ignition switch
	Ignition LT leads connected wrong way round
	Faulty coil
	Contact breaker point spring earthed or broken
	No petrol in petrol tank
	Vapour lock in fuel line (in hot conditions or at high altitude)
	Blocked float chamber needle valve
	Faulty fuel pump
	Too much choke allowing too rich a mixture to wet plugs
	Float damaged or leaking or needle not seating
	Float lever incorrectly adjusted
Engine stalls and will not start	Ignition failure – sudden
	Ignition failure – misfiring precludes total stoppage
	Ignition failure – in severe rain or after traversing water splash
	No petrol in petrol tank
	Petrol tank breather choked
	Sudden obstruction in carburettor
	Water in fuel system
Engine misfires or idles unevenly	Ignition leads loose
	Battery earth strap loose on body attachment point
	Engine earth lead loose
	Low tension leads to terminals on coil loose
	Low tension lead from coil to distributor loose
	Dirty or incorrectly gapped spark plugs
	Dirty, incorrectly set or pitted contact breaker points
	Tracking across distributor cap
	Ignition too retarded
	Faulty coil
	Mixture too weak
	Air leak in carburettor
	Air leak at inlet manifold to cylinder head, or inlet manifold to carburettor
	Burnt out exhaust valves
	Sticking or leaking valves
	Weak or broken valve springs
	Worn valve guides or stems
	Worn pistons and pistons rings

Symptom	Reason(s)
Lack of power and poor compression	Burnt out exhaust valves
	Sticking or leaking valves
	Worn valve guides and stems
	Weak or broken valve springs
	Blown cylinder head gasket (accompanied by increase in noise)
	Worn pistons and piston rings
	Worn or scored cylinder bores
	Ignition timing wrongly set; too advanced or retarded
	Contact breaker points incorrectly gapped
	Valve timing incorrect
	Incorrectly set spark plugs
	Carburettor too rich or too weak
	Dirty contact breaker points
	Distributor automatic balance weights or vacuum advance and retard mechanisms not functioning correctly
	Faulty fuel pump giving top end fuel starvation
Excessive oil consumption	Badly worn, perished or missing valve stem oil seals
	Excessively worn valve stems and valve guides
	Worn piston rings
	Worn pistons and cylinder bores
	Excessive piston ring gap allowing blow-by
	Piston oil return holes choked
Oil being lost due to leaks	Leaking oil filter gasket
	Leaking rocker cover gasket
	Leaking timing cover gasket
	Leaking sump gasket
	Loose sump plug
Unusual noises from engine	Worn valve gear (noisy tapping from rocker covers)
	Worn big-end bearing (regular heavy knocking)
	Worn main bearings (rumbling and vibration)
	Worn crankshaft (knocking, rumbling and vibration)

Chapter 2 Cooling system

Contents

Specifications

Type .... Pressurised system with expansion tank

Thermostat
Type .... Wax
Opening temperature:
    Standard .... 180°F (82°C)
    Cold climate .... 190°F (88°C)

Expansion tank
Filler cap relief pressure .... 15 lbf/in² (1.0 bar)

Fanbelt tension .... 0.16 in (4 mm) deflection on shortest run

Cooling system capacity (including heater) .... 10 pints (5.6 litres)

Torque wrench settings

	lbf ft	Nm
Water pump retaining bolts	8	11
Pulley and fan-to-pump flange	9	12
Thermostat housing to cylinder head	8	11
Cylinder block drain plug	27	37

1 General description

The engine cooling water is circulated by a thermo-syphon, water pump assisted system, with the coolant pressurised. This is primarily to prevent premature boiling in adverse conditions and to allow the engine to operate at its most efficient running temperature, this being just under the boiling point of water. The overflow pipe from the radiator is connected to an expansion chamber which makes topping-up virtually unnecessary. The coolant expands when hot, and instead of being forced down an overflow pipe and lost, it flows into the expansion chamber. As the engine cools, the coolant contracts, and because of the pressure differential, flows back into the radiator.

The cap on the expansion chamber is set to a pressure of 15 lbf/in² (1.0 bar) which increases the boiling point of the coolant to 230°F. If the coolant temperature exceeds this figure and the coolant boils, the pressure in the system forces the internal valve of the cap off its seat, thus exposing the expansion tank overflow pipe, down which the steam from the boiling coolant escapes and so relieves the pressure. It is therefore important to check that the expansion chamber cap is in good condition and that the spring behind the sealing washers has not weakened. Check that the rubber seal has not perished and its seating in the neck is clean to ensure a good seal. A special tool which enables a cap to be pressure tested is available at some garages.

The cooling system comprises the radiator, top and bottom hoses, heater hoses, the water pump (mounted on the front of the engine, it carries the fan blades and is driven by the fanbelt) and the thermostat. On 2.0 litre models the cooling fan incorporates a viscous drive hub which allows the fan blades to rotate at pulley speed at low engine speed, and at a speed slower than that of the pulley at high engine speed. This has the effect of reducing the power-consuming drag of the fan blades at high speed when sufficient cooling air is provided by the forward motion of the vehicle.

The system functions as follows: Cold coolant from the radiator circulates up the lower radiator hose to the water pump where it is pushed round the water passages in the cylinder block, helping to keep the cylinder bores and pistons cool.

The coolant then travels up into the cylinder head and circulates round the combustion spaces and valve seats, absorbing more heat. Then, when the engine is at its normal operating temperature, the coolant travels out of the cylinder head, past the now open thermostat into the upper radiator hose and so into the radiator. The coolant passes along the radiator from one side to the other where it is rapidly cooled by the rush of cold air through the horizontal radiator core. The coolant, now cool, reaches the bottom hose when the cycle is repeated.

When the engine is cold the thermostat (a valve which opens and closes according to the temperature of the coolant) maintains the circulation of the same coolant in the engine, and only when the correct minimum operating temperature has been reached, as shown in the Specifications, does the thermostat begin to open thus allowing the coolant to return to the radiator.

2 Cooling system – draining

1 If the engine is cold, remove the pressure relief cap from the expansion tank. If the engine is hot, then turn the cap very slightly to release the pressure in the system. Use a rag over the cap to protect your hands from escaping steam. If the engine is hot and the cap is released suddenly, the drop in pressure can result in the coolant boiling.

2 Place a suitable container beneath the radiator bottom hose connection, slacken the hose clip and slowly pull off the hose. Allow the coolant to drain into the container.

3 The cylinder block may be drained completely by removing the drain plug located on the right-hand side of the cylinder block.

4 When the coolant has finished draining out of the cylinder block drain hole, probe the orifice with a short piece of wire to dislodge any particles of rust or sediment which may be causing a blockage, thus preventing complete draining.

Note: Vehicles from VIN 17V 647AHH 95669 are not equipped with a cylinder block drain plug. Draining is achieved simply by removing the lower radiator hose.

3 Cooling system – flushing

1 In time, the cooling system will gradually lose its efficiency as the radiator becomes choked with rust, scale deposits from the water, and other sediment. To clean the system out, remove the coolant filler cap from the thermostat housing and lift out the thermostat.

2 Disconnect the bottom radiator hose and remove the cylinder block drain plug, then leave a hose running in the thermostat housing for ten to fifteen minutes.

3 In very bad cases, the radiator should be reversed flushed. This can be done with the radiator in position. Disconnect the top and bottom hoses from the radiator and connect a supply of running water to the bottom hose connection on the radiator.

4 When flushing the cooling system, it is recommended that some polythene sheeting is placed over the engine to prevent water finding its way into the electrical system.

4 Cooling system – filling

1 Refit the cylinder block drain plug and reconnect the bottom hose.

2 Remove the coolant filler cap on the thermostat housing and lift out the thermostat.

3 Fill the system slowly to ensure that no air-locks develop. Check that the heater control is set at hot, otherwise an air-lock may form in the heater.

4 Use an anti-freeze solution (see Section 12) and keep filling the system until the coolant flows into the expansion tank, then refit the coolant filler cap.

5 Now top up the expansion tank to the level marked on the tank. Refit the expansion tank cap.

6 Start the engine and run it for half a minute at a fast idle, then switch off.

7 Remove the filler cap and top up the cooling system through the thermostat housing, then refit the thermostat in the thermostat housing (see Section 7) and refit the filler cap.

8 Run the engine until it has reached its normal operating temperature. Stop the engine and allow it to cool.

9 Top up the expansion tank to the level marked.

5 Radiator – removal and refitting

1 Drain the cooling system as described in Section 2.

2 Slacken the clip that secures the expansion tank hose to the radiator. Carefully ease the hose from the union pipe on the radiator (photo).

3 Slacken the clips that secure the radiator top and bottom hoses to the radiator inlet pipes and carefully ease the two hoses from these pipes (photos).

4 Undo and remove the nuts with spring and plain washers, that secure the two top radiator mounting brackets to the front panel. Lift away these two brackets (photo).

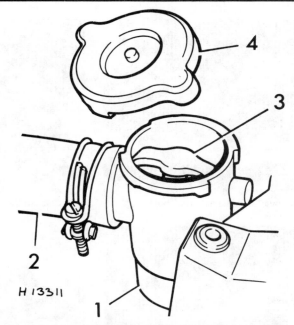

Fig. 2.1 The cooling system is filled through the thermostat housing (Sec 4)

1 Thermostat housing   3 Thermostat
2 Top hose   4 Filler cap

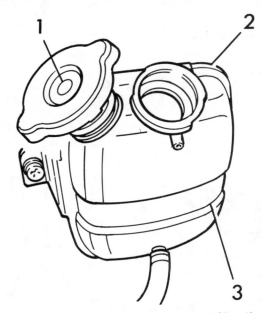

Fig. 2.2 Cooling system expansion tank (Sec 4)

1 Expansion tank cap   3 Coolant level
2 Expansion tank

5 The radiator may now be lifted up from its lowest mountings and away from the front of the car (photo).

6 Refitting the radiator is the reverse sequence to removal. Refill the cooling system as described in Section 4. Carefully check to ensure that all hose joints are water tight.

6 Radiator – inspection and cleaning

1 With the radiator out of the car, carefully inspect the core and side tanks for damage or signs of leaks. If the radiator requires repair, it is

5.2 Remove the expansion tank hose

5.3a Slacken the radiator tank hose retaining clip ...

5.3b ... and bottom hose retaining clip, then pull off the hoses

5.4 Undo and remove the upper mounting retaining nuts and lift away the mounting brackets

5.5 Carefully lift out the radiator

7.2 Removing the thermostat

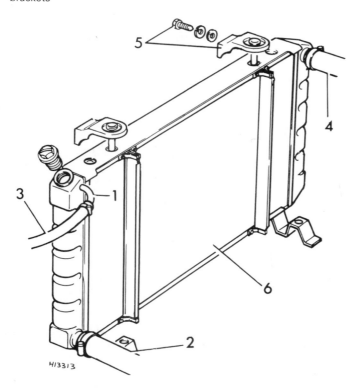
Fig. 2.3 Radiator assembly (Sec 5)

1 Outlet elbow
2 Bottom hose
3 Expansion tank hose
4 Top hose
5 Securing bolts and bracket
6 Radiator

advisable to fit an exchange radiator or have the repair done by a specialist.

2   Assuming the radiator to be in good condition, clean the exterior by hosing down the matrix with a strong jet of water to clean away road dirt, dead flies etc. Turn the radiator upside down and leave a hose running in the bottom outlet for ten or fifteen minutes.

3   Inspect the hoses for cracks or damage resulting from over-tightening the clips and fit new hoses if the old ones have deteriorated. Also renew the hose clips if the old ones are damaged or corroded.

7   Thermostat – removal, testing and refitting

1   Carefully remove the filler cap from the expansion tank. If the engine is hot, place a rag over the cap to protect your hands and then turn the cap very slightly to release the pressure in the system. When the pressure is released remove the cap.

2   Remove the filler cap on the thermostat housing and lift out the thermostat (photo). It may be necessary to use a pair of pliers to pull the thermostat from its seating in the housing.

3   Test the thermostat for correct functioning by suspending it, together with a thermometer on a string, in a container of cold water. Heat the water and note the temperature at which the thermostat begins to open. This should be 82°C (180°F) for a standard thermostat. It is advantageous in winter to fit a thermostat that does not open until 88°C (190°F). Discard the thermostat if it opens too early. Continue heating the water until the thermostat is fully open. Then let it cool down naturally. If the thermostat does not fully open in boiling water, or does not close down as the water cools, then it must be discarded and a new one fitted. If the thermostat is stuck open when cold, this will be apparent when removing it from the housing.

4   When refitting the thermostat, ensure that the inside of the thermostat housing is clean and then fit a new O-ring seal in the housing.

5   Check that it is the correct thermostat. The temperature is stamped in degrees centigrade on the bottom of the thermostat.

6   Fit the thermostat in the housing. Top up the cooling system and refit the coolant filler cap.

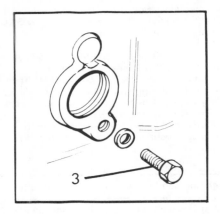

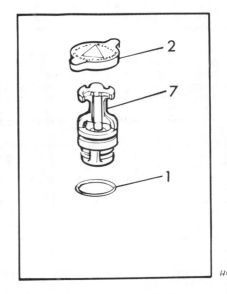

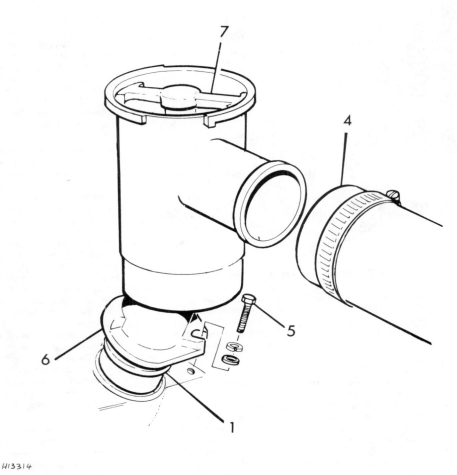

H13314

Fig. 2.4 Thermostat housing removal (Sec 8)

1	O-ring seals	3 Drain plug	5 Housing securing bolt	7 Thermostat
2	Filler cap	4 Top hose	6 Thermostat housing	

8 Thermostat housing – removal and refitting

1 Remove the thermostat as described in the previous Section.
2 Remove the drain plug from the cylinder block and partially drain the cooling system; approximately 4 pints (2.2 litres) is enough.
3 Refit the drain plug.
4 Slacken the securing clip and disconnect the top hose from the thermostat housing.
5 Undo and remove the bolt that secures the housing to the cylinder head and lift away the thermostat housing complete with thermostat. Remove the O-ring seal.
6 Refitting is the reverse or the removal procedure. Ensure that the seating in the cylinder head is clean and fit a new O-ring seal. Tighten the housing securing bolt to the specified torque.
7 Refit the thermostat when refilling the cooling system as described in Section 7.

9 Water pump – removal and refitting

1 Drain the cooling system as described in Section 2.
2 Remove the radiator as described in Section 5.
3 Slacken the alternator pivot and adjusting link bolts and remove the fanbelt.
4 On 1.7 litre models, undo and remove the securing bolts and lift off the fan and water pump pulley.

5 On 2.0 litre models undo and remove the four bolts securing the fan to the viscous drive coupling and lift away the fan. Now unscrew the large nut at the rear of the viscous drive coupling that secures the coupling to the water pump hub. Note that this nut has a left-hand thread. To prevent the water pump hub turning as the nut is unscrewed, feed an old fanbelt over the pulley and insert the loop of the belt through a tube of suitable length and diameter. With the tube in contact with the pulley, the free end of the belt should protrude through the end of the tube just sufficiently to enable a screwdriver or bar to be inserted through the loop of the belt. The tube will tension the belt and prevent the pulley turning. With the nut undone, lift away the coupling and then undo and remove the four bolts securing the pulley to the hub flange. Withdraw the pulley.
6 Remove the timing belt cover by pulling it off its mounting spigots.
7 Slacken the securing clip and disconnect the bottom hose from the water pump inlet.
8 Undo and remove the two nuts that secure the timing belt tensioner and lift away the tensioner.
9 Undo the five bolts and the stud that secures the water pump to the cylinder block. Lift away the pump.
10 Remove the water pump gasket.
11 Collect the two bolts on which the timing belt tensioner is located from the rear of the water pump body.
12 If the water pump leaks, shows signs of excessive movement of the spindle, or is noisy during operation, it is recommended that a service exchange reconditioned pump is fitted.
13 Refitting is the reverse of the removal procedure, but the following

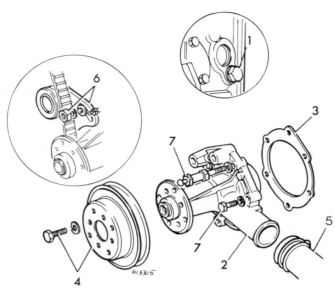

Fig. 2.5 Water pump removal (Sec 9)

1 Drain plug	5 Bottom hose
2 Water pump	6 Timing belt tensioner
3 Gasket	securing nuts
4 Drivebelt pulley and	7 Water pump securing
securing bolt	stud and bolts

additional points should be noted:

(a)   Ensure the mating faces of the pump body and cylinder block
are clean. Always use a new gasket
(b)   Do not forget to fit the timing belt tensioner bolts in the pump
body; use grease to keep them in their location
(c)   Tighten the pump securing bolts to the specified torque
(d)   Adjust the timing belt tension as described in Chapter 1
(e)   Refer to Section 1⅓ and adjust the fanbelt tension
(f)   Refill the cooling system as described in Section 4

10 Fanbelt – removal, refitting and tensioning

1   If the fanbelt is worn or has overstretched, it should be renewed.
The most common reason for renewal is that the belt has broken in
service. It is therefore recommended that a spare belt and the
necessary tools to fit it, are always carried in the car.
2   To remove the existing fanbelt, slacken the two alternator mounting nuts and bolts, and the nut that secures the adjustment arm to the
stud on the cylinder block.
3   Move the alternator towards the engine and slip the belt off the
crankshaft, water pump and alternator pulleys.
4   Before refitting, examine the fanbelt for cracks or deterioration,
and if at all suspicious, renew the belt.
5   Pass the new belt around the crankshaft and water pump pulleys,
then ease it over the alternator pulley.

6   Carefully lever the alternator away from the engine until it is
possible to deflect the belt, using moderate finger pressure, by 0.16 in
(4 mm) at a point midway between the alternator and water pump
pulleys.
7   With the alternator held in this position, tighten the adjustment
arm nut and the two mountings, then recheck the tension.
8   It is most important to maintain correct fanbelt tension. The belt
being too slack will result in its slipping and reducing the efficiency of
the alternator and cooling system. A belt too tight will place excessive
strain on the alternator and water pump bearings.
9   Always recheck the tension of a new belt after approximately 250
miles, as slight stretching will probably have taken place and further
adjustment may be required.

11 Temperature gauge and sender unit – removal and refitting

1   If the temperature gauge fails to work, either the gauge, the
sender unit or the wiring and connections are at fault.
2   It is not possible to repair either the gauge or the sender unit, as
they are both sealed assemblies and must be replaced by new units if
at fault.
3   A quick check can be made when attempting to isolate a possible
fault, by removing the electrical lead from the sender unit and earthing
it on a suitable, non-painted engine bolt or component. With the
ignition switched on the temperature gauge should read maximum. If
this is the case the sender unit is at fault. If no reading is shown on the
gauge, the gauge or wiring are faulty.
4   Removal and refitting of the temperature gauge is described in
Chapter 10.
5   To remove the sender unit, first partially drain the cooling system
as described in Section 2 (approximately 4 pints/2.2 litres is enough).
6   Detach the electrical lead from the sender unit and unscrew it
from its location on the right-hand side of the cylinder head, below the
thermostat housing.
7   Screw the new unit into the cylinder head, refit the electrical lead
and refill the cooling system.

12 Antifreeze mixture

1   Prior to anticipated freezing conditions, it is essential that antifreeze is added to the cooling system.
2   Any antifreeze which conforms with specification BS 3151 or BS
3152 can be used. Never use an antifreeze with an alcohol base as the
evaporation rate is too high.
3   Antifreeze with an anti-corrosion additive can be left in the cooling
system for up to two years, but after six months it is advisable to have
the specific gravity of the coolant checked at your local garage, and
thereafter, every three months.
4   The amounts of antifreeze which should be added to ensure
adequate protection down to the temperature given are as follows:

Amount of antifreeze	Protection to
33% mixture – 4 pints (2.3 litres)	-2°F (-19°C)
50% mixture – 5.5 pints (3.1 litres)	-33°F (-36°C)

5   When adding antifreeze to the cooling system, also add 0.25 pint
(0.15 litre) of neat antifreeze to the expansion tank. **Note**: *Never use
antifreeze in the windscreen washer reservoir as it will cause damage
to the paintwork.*

13 Fault diagnosis – cooling system

Symptom	Reason(s)
Overheating	Insuffficient water in cooling system
	Fanbelt slipping (accompanied by a shrieking noise on rapid engine acceleration)
	Radiator core blocked or radiator grille restricted
	Bottom water hose collapsed impeding flow
	Thermostat not opening properly
	Ignition advance and retard incorrectly set (accompanied by loss of power and perhaps misfiring)
	Carburettor incorrectly adjusted (mixture too weak)
	Exhaust system partially blocked
	Oil level in sump too low
	Blown cylinder head gasket
	Engine not yet run-in
	Brakes binding
Overcooling	Thermostat jammed open
	Incorrect grade of thermostat fitted allowing premature opening of valve
	Thermostat missing
Loss of coolant	Loose clips on water hoses
	Hoses perished and leaking
	Radiator core leaking
	Thermostat housing O-ring leaking
	Pressure cap spring worn or seal ineffective
	Blown cylinder head gasket
	Cylinder wall or head cracked
	Heater matrix leaking

Chapter 3 Fuel and exhaust systems

Contents

Specifications

Air cleaner
Type .... Renewable paper element, with air temperature control valve

Fuel pump
Make and type .... SU mechanical AUF800
Delivery pressure (minimum) .... 6.0 lbf/in^2 (0.4 bar)

Carburettor

	1.7 litre	2.0 litre
Make and type	SU HIF 6	SU HIF 44
Piston spring colour	Red	Yellow
Jet size	0.100 in	0.100 in
Needle	BEK	BFB
Float level setting (see text)	0.02 to 0.06 in (0.5 to 1.5 mm)	0.02 to 0.06 in (0.5 to 1.5 mm)
Exhaust CO content	1.5 to 3.5%	1.5 to 3.5%
Idling speed:		
Manual transmission	750 rpm	–
Automatic transmission	850 rpm	650 rpm
Fast idle speed	1100 rpm	1100 rpm

Fuel tank
Capacity .... 11.5 gallons (52 litres)

Torque wrench settings

	lbf ft	Nm
Carburettor to manifold	19	25
Exhaust front pipes to manifold	21 to 23	29 to 32

1 General description

The fuel system comprises a fuel tank at the rear of the car, a mechanical pump located on the left-hand side of the camshaft cover, and a single horizontally mounted SU carburettor.

A renewable paper element air cleaner is fitted which must be renewed at the recommended mileages. Operation of the individual components is described elsewhere in this Chapter.

2 Fuel pump – general description

The mechanically operated fuel pump is mounted on the left-hand side of the camshaft cover and is operated by a separate lobe on the camshaft.

As the camshaft rotates the rocker lever is actuated, one end of which is connected to the diaphragm operating rod. When the rocker arm is moved by the cam lobe the diaphragm, via a rocker arm, moves downwards causing fuel to be drawn in through the filter, past the inlet valve flap and into the diaphragm chamber. As the cam lobe moves round, the diaphragm moves upwards under the action of the spring, and fuel flows via the large outlet valve to the carburettor float chamber.

When the float chamber has the requisite amount of fuel in it, the needle valve in the top delivery valve line closes and holds the diaphragm down against the action of the diaphragm spring until the needle valve in the float chamber opens to admit more fuel.

3 Fuel pump – testing on engine

Assuming that the fuel lines and unions are in good condition and that there are no leaks anywhere, check the performance of the fuel pump in the following manner. Disconnect the fuel pipe at the carburettor inlet union, and the high tension lead to the coil, and with a suitable container or large rag in position to catch the ejected fuel, turn the engine over. A good spurt of petrol should emerge from the end of the pipe every second revolution.

4 Fuel pump – removal and refitting

1   Remove the fuel inlet and outlet connections from the fuel pump. Plug the ends of the pipes to stop loss of fuel or dirt ingress.
2   Unscrew and remove the two pump mounting flange nuts and washers. Carefully slide the pump off the two studs followed by the insulating block assembly and gasket.
3   Refitting is the reverse sequence to removal. Inspect the gaskets on either side of the insulating block, and if damaged, obtain and fit new ones.

5 Fuel pump – testing dry

If the pump is suspect, it may be dry tested by holding a finger over the inlet union and operating the rocker lever through three complete strokes. When the finger is released, a suction noise should be heard. Next, hold a finger over the outlet nozzle and press the rocker arm fully, The pressure generated should hold for a minimum of fifteen seconds.

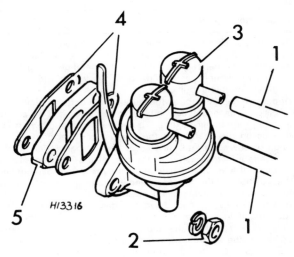

H13316

Fig. 3.1 Fuel pump removal (Sec 4)

1	Fuel pipes	4	Gaskets
2	Retaining nut	5	Insulating block
3	Fuel pump		

6.1a Unscrew the air cleaner wing nut ...

6.1b ... and lift away the cover and element

6 Air cleaner element – renewal

1   Unscrew the wing nut and lift away the cover and element (photos).
2   Clean out the body of the air cleaner and fit a new element. Refit the cover.
3   Ensure that the sealing ring between the air cleaner and carburettor adaptor is not damaged or perished.
4   Refit the air cleaner to the adaptor and secure it with the fibre washer and wing nut.
5   To check the operation of the air temperature control valve, rotate and disconnect the air intake ducts from the control valve. Depress the valve plate and check that when released, it returns to its original position; if not, it must be renewed. Refit the air intake ducts.

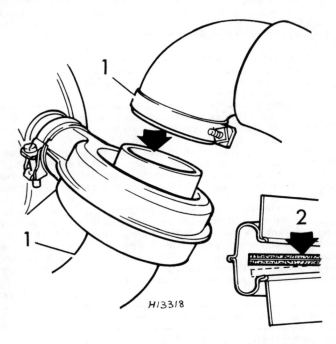

H13318

Fig. 3.2 Checking the air temperature control valve (Sec 6)

1 Intake ducts	2 Valve plate

7 Carburettor – general description

The variable choke SU carburettor is a relatively simple instrument, and is basically the same irrespective of its size and type. It differs from most other carburettors in that instead of having a number of fixed jets for different conditions, only one variable jet is fitted to deal with all possible conditions.

Air passing rapidly through the carburettor creates a slight vacuum or depression over the jet, causing fuel to be drawn into the airstream, thus forming the fuel/air mixture. The amount of fuel drawn from the jet depends on the position of the tapered carburettor needle. This moves up or down the jet orifice according to engine load or throttle opening, thus effectively altering the size of the jet. This allows the right amount of fuel to be delivered for the prevailing road conditions.

The position of the tapered needle in the jet is determined by engine vacuum. The shank of the needle is held at its top end in a piston which slides up and down the dashpot in response to the degree of manifold vacuum. This is directly controlled by the throttle. The piston is necessary so that the depression over the jet, needed to draw fuel into the airstream, can be kept approximately constant. At slow engine speeds, the air entering the carburettor would not be travelling fast enough to create sufficient vacuum to drawn fuel from the jet. By allowing the piston to partially restrict the opening through the carburettor, the incoming air is speeded up, causing an adequate depression over the jet.

With the throttle fully open, the full effect of inlet manifold vacuum is felt by the piston, which has an air bleed into the carburettor venturi on the outside of the throttle. This causes the piston to rise fully bringing the needle with it. With the throttle partially closed, only slight inlet manifold vacuum is felt by the piston (although on the engine side of the throttle, the vacuum is now greater), and the piston only rises slightly.

To prevent piston flutter and to give a richer mixture when the accelerator is suddenly depressed, an oil damper and light spring are located inside the dashpot.

The only portion of the piston assembly to come into contact with the piston chamber or dashpot is the actual piston rod. All other parts of the piston assembly, including the lower choke portion, have sufficient clearance to prevent any direct metal-to-metal contact which is essential if the carburettor is to function correctly.

The jet is held in place by a horizontal arm. This is made of a bi-metallic material, so will vary the jet height to give compensation for temperature changes. These would otherwise give mixture variation due to fuel viscosity changes. This jet mounting arm is connected through a pivot to a lever. The lever is moved by a screw in the side of the carburettor body to adjust the mixture. The screw head may be hidden under a seal.

The rich mixture needed for cold starting is provided by a special jet. This has a progressive control to allow partial enrichment, and is worked by turning a cam lever on the carburettor side opposite to that having the mixture control screw. When the cam lever is moved to enrich the mixture, the cam will push up the fast idle screw to open the throttle. The valve that controls this cold start mixture is a hollow inner core that is rotated within a cylindrical sleeve to bring a hole in it in line with one in the sleeve.

An emulsion bypass passage runs from the jet bridge to the throttle. At small throttle openings, unevaporated fuel droplets will be drawn along this passage and will be mixed with the faster travelling air. To match this passage there is a slot cut out of the base of the piston.

The correct level of the petrol in the carburettor is determined by the level of the float chamber. When the level is correct the float rises and, by means of a lever, closes the needle valve in the float chamber. This closes off the supply of fuel from the pump. When the level in the float chamber drops, as fuel is used in the carburettor, the float drops. As it does, the float needle is unseated, so allowing more fuel to enter the float chamber and restore the correct level.

8 Carburettor – removal and refitting

1   Detach the air intake ducts from the air cleaner.
2   Undo the securing bolts and remove the air intake adaptor and air cleaner assembly from the carburettor.
3   Disconnect the fuel pipe from the carburettor. Plug the end to

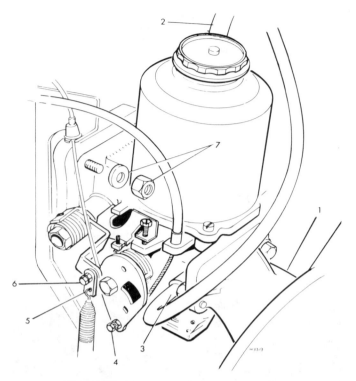

Fig. 3.3 Carburettor removal – typical (Sec 8)

1   Air cleaner adaptor
2   Breather hose
3   Fuel pipe
4   Choke cable trunnion
5   Throttle return spring
6   Throttle cable trunnion
7   Securing nut and washer

prevent the ingress of dirt.
4   Slacken the clip and ease off the engine breather pipe from the union on the carburettor body.
5   Disconnect both the throttle and choke cables from the carburettor.
6   Unhook the throttle return spring.
7   On automatic transmission models, disconnect the downshift cable from the carburettor linkage.
8   Undo and remove the four nuts and washers that secure the carburettor to the manifold studs. Withdraw the heater tube support bracket from the two bottom studs and lift away the carburettor.
9   Refitting is the reverse of the removal procedure. If necessary fit new gaskets to the inlet manifold flange and insulator block. Adjust the throttle and choke cables as described in Sections 11 and 12 respectively.

9 Carburettor – dismantling, inspection and reassembly

1   Assuming that you have the carburettor on the workbench, start by cleaning the exterior thoroughly with paraffin or a degreasing solvent, using a stiff brush where necessary.
2   Undo the cap at the top of the carburettor and withdraw it complete with the small damper piston and retainer. Empty the oil from the dashpot.
3   Mark the position of the bottom cover relative to the body and remove it by unscrewing the four screws that hold it down. Empty out any fuel still in the float chamber and recover the seal.
4   The float is held to the body by a pivot having a screw head on it. Unscrew and remove the pivot with its sealing washer, remove the float, unscrew the needle valve socket and remove it and the needle.
5   Dismantle the various control linkages, being sure by studying Figs. 3.4 and 3.7 that you know how they fit together. It is an easy matter to sort this out before you take them apart, but much more difficult when they are dismantled.

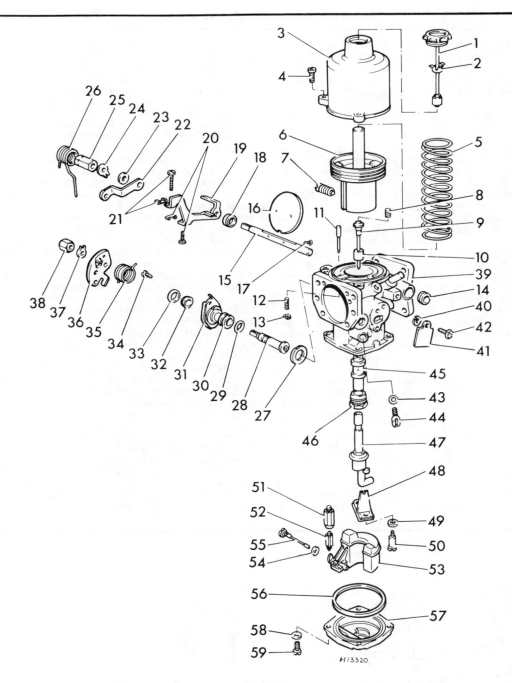

Fig. 3.4 Exploded view of typical carburettor (Sec 9)

1   Piston damper
2   Damper retainer
3   Suction chamber
4   Screw (3)
5   Piston spring
6   Piston
7   Needle retaining screw
8   Needle spring
9   Jet needle
10 Needle guide
11 Lifting pin
12 Lifting pin spring
13 Circlip
14 Throttle spindle seal
15 Throttle spindle
16 Throttle disc

17 Throttle disc screw
18 Throttle spindle seal
19 Throttle actuating lever
20 Fast idle adjustment
    screw
21 Throttle adjustment
    screw (idle)
22 Throttle lever
23 Spacing washer
24 Tab washer
25 Nut
26 Throttle spring
27 Cold start seal
28 Cold start spindle
29 O-ring
30 Cold start body

31 Retaining plate
32 Spindle seat
33 End cover
34 Retaining screw
35 Cold start spring
36 Fast idle cam
37 Tab washer
38 Retaining nut
39 Body
40 Spring washer
41 Identification tab
42 Retaining screw
43 Adjusting screw seal
44 Jet adjusting screw
    (mixture)
45 Jet bearing

46 Jet bearing nut
47 Jet assembly
48 Bi-metal jet lever
49 Jet spring
50 Jet retaining screw
51 Float needle seat
52 Float needle
53 Float
54 Pivot seal
55 Float pivot
56 Float chamber cover
    seal
57 Float chamber cover
58 Spring washer
59 Screw (4)

6   Unscrew the nut that holds the fast idle cam, having first straightened its tab washer; take off the cam, and the spring which is contained in a small housing behind it. Undo the two screws that hold down this housing and pull on the spindle which held the fast idle cam. The whole cold start assembly will now come out of the body.

7   Undo the screws that hold the throttle disc into its shaft, being careful not to put too much pressure on the shaft in the process (support it with the other hand). Remove the disc and withdraw the throttle shaft.

8   Mark the flanges and remove the dashpot (suction chamber) and the piston. Be careful of the needle on the end of the piston. A good idea is to stand the piston on a narrow-necked jar with the needle hanging inside it.

9   Unscrew the jet retaining (pivot) screw and remove the bi-metal assembly holding the jet.

10   The carburettor is now sufficiently dismantled for inspection to be carried out. One or two adjusting screws and the like have been left in the body, but it is recommended that these are only removed when you are actually ensuring that the various channels are clear. Generally speaking, the SU carburettor is very reliable, but even so it may develop faults which are not readily apparent unless a careful inspection is carried out, yet may nevertheless affect engine performance. So it is well worthwhile giving the carburettor a good look over when dismantled.

11   Inspect the carburettor needle for ridging. If this is apparent, you will probably find corresponding wear on the inside of the jet. If the needle is ridged, it must be renewed. Do not attempt to rub it down with abrasive paper, as carburettor needles are made to very fine tolerances.

12   When fitting the needle, locate it carefully in the piston. The shoulder should be flush with the piston face and the engraved line should point directly away from the channel in the piston sidewall. Note that this makes the needle incline in the direction of the carburettor air cleaner flange when the piston is fitted.

13   Inspect the jet for wear. Wear inside the jet will accompany wear on the needle. If any wear is apparent on the jet, renew it. It may be unhooked from the bi-metal spring and this may be used again.

14   Inspect the piston and the carburettor body (suction chamber) carefully for signs that these have been in contact. When the carburettor is operating, the main piston should not come into contact with the carburettor body. The whole assembly is supported by the rod

of the piston which slides in the centre bearings, this rod being attached to the cap in the top of the carburettor body. It is possible for wear in the centre bearing to allow the piston to touch the wall of the body. Check for this by assembling the piston in the suction chamber and spinning it whilst horizontal. If contact occurs and the cause is worn parts, renew them. In no circumstances try to correct piston sticking by altering the tension of the return spring, although very slight contact with the body may be cured (as a temporary measure) by polishing the offending portion of the body wall with metal polish or extremely fine emery cloth.

15   The fit of the piston in the suction chamber can be checked by plugging the air hole, assembling the piston in the chamber without its return spring and fitting the damper piston without filling the dashpot with oil. If the assembly is now turned upside down, the chamber should fall to the bottom in 5 to 7 seconds. If the time is appreciably less than this, the piston and suction chamber should both be renewed since they are matched to each other.

16   Check for wear on the throttle shaft and bushes through which it passes. Apart from the nuisance of a sticking throttle, excessive wear here can cause air leaks in the induction system, thus adversely affecting engine performance. Worn bushes can be extracted and new bushes fitted if necessary. The cold start device can be dismantled for cleaning and new parts used where necessary, when reassembling.

17   Reassembly is a straightforward reversal of the dismantling process. During reassembly, the float level can be checked and adjusted if necessary by inverting the carburettor body so that the needle valve is held shut by the weight of the float. Using a straight edge across the face of the float chamber measure the gap at the point arrowed (Fig. 3.6). It should be as shown in the Specifications. The arm can be bent carefully, if necessary, to obtain the dimensions.

18   When assembling the jet, position the adjusting screw so that the upper edge of the jet comes level with the bridge. This gives the initial position for jet adjustment.

19   When the carburettor is assembled, the dashpot should be filled with engine oil as described in Routine Maintenance. Check that the piston is operating properly by lifting it with the lifting pin and letting it fall. It should hit the bridge of the carburettor with an audible metallic click. If it does not, perhaps the needle is fouling the jet (it is supposed to touch it lightly). This should not occur with careful assembly; there is no provision for centering the jet, but if it is properly assembled, this is not necessary.

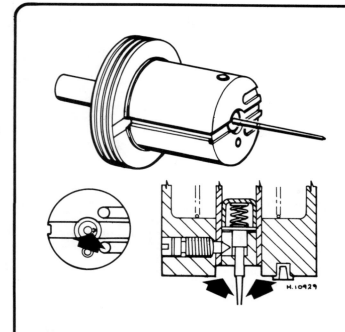

Fig. 3.5 Correct assembly of carburettor needle components (Sec 9)

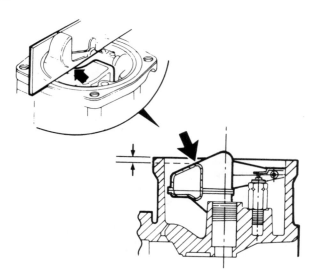

Fig. 3.6 Float level setting (Sec 9)

10 Carburettor – tuning

1   Before tuning the carburettor, ensure that the following are correctly adjusted:

  (a) *Ignition timing*
  (b) *Contact breaker points gap*
  (c) *Spark plugs gap*
  (d) *Valve clearances*

2   Carburettor tuning is limited to setting the idle and fast idle speeds and the mixture setting at idle speed. The carburettor is adjusted correctly for the whole of its engine revolution range when the idling mixture strength is correct.

3   To tune the carburettor accurately, a tachometer will be required which should be connected to the engine following the manufacturer's instructions. It is possible to manage without one, but you will have to guess the idling and fast idling speeds and listen very carefully for slight changes in engine speed as the adjustments are carried out.

4   First make sure that the carburettor piston damper in the dashpot is filled with engine oil as described in Routine Maintenance. Also check that the fast idle adjustment screw is close to, but not touching, the cam on the choke mechanism when the choke control is pushed fully in.

5   If the idling speed and mixture adjustment screws have not been previously adjusted, they will still have the tamperproof seals in place over the screw heads. If so, hook these small metal sealing caps out of the adjustment screw recesses and discard them.

6   Start the engine and allow it to warm up to normal operating temperature. Once the engine has warmed up adjust the idling speed adjustment screw if necessary to obtain the specified idling speed.

7   Rev the engine to approximately 2500 rpm and maintain this speed for 30 seconds. This will clear the inlet manifold of excess fuel. Repeat this procedure every three minutes if the mixture adjustment cannot be completed within this period of time.

8   Slowly turn the mixture adjustment screw, a quarter of a turn at a time, clockwise to richen or anti-clockwise to weaken the mixture until the fastest possible engine speed is obtained. Now turn the screw anti-clockwise until the engine speed just commences to fall.

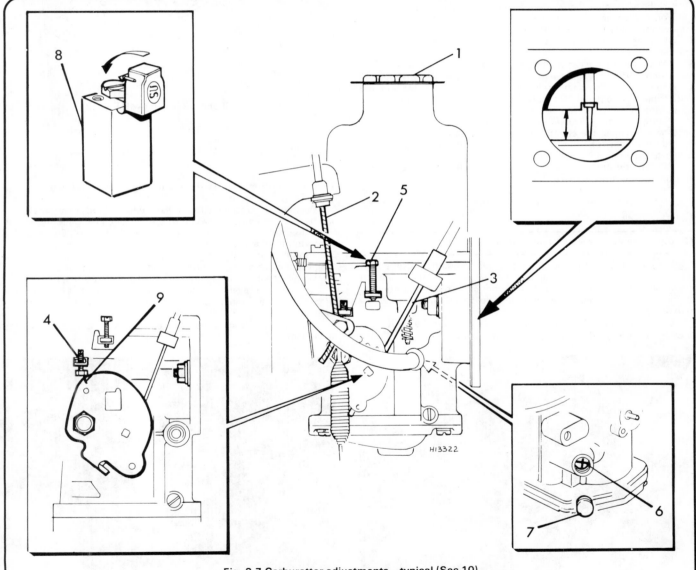

Fig. 3.7 Carburettor adjustments – typical (Sec 10)

1 *Piston damper*	4 *Fast idle adjusting screw*	6 *Mixture adjustment screw*	8 *Tamperproof cover (idling speed)*
2 *Throttle cable*	5 *Idling speed adjustment screw*	7 *Tamperproof seal (mixture)*	9 *Fast idle cam and arrow*
3 *Choke cable*			

9   Readjust the engine idling speed to return the engine to the specified idling speed.

10 With the engine idling speed and mixture strength correctly set, pull out the choke control slightly until the arrow on the fast idle cam is aligned with the fast idle adjusting screw. Lock the choke control in this position.

11 Turn the fast idle adjusting screw until the specified fast idle speed is obtained. Release the choke control.

12 It is now advisable to road test the car and carry out any minute adjustments to the mixture strength, that may be necessary, on the road. As a rough guide, if the engine tends to stall when coming down to idling speed the mixture is too weak. if the engine idles with a rhythmic unevenness or tends to roughen at high engine speed the mixture is too rich. Only make small corrections of the mixture screw, a quarter of a turn at a time, and test the car between each adjustment.

11 Throttle cable – removal and refitting

1   Using two thin open-ended spanners, slacken off the cable trunnion nut, securing the inner cable to the carburettor linkage, and remove the cable from the trunnion.

2   Slide the outer cable out of the slot in the carburettor abutment bracket.

3   Working inside the car, release the retainers and withdraw the trim panel from under the dashboard.

4   Slip off the cable retaining clip and detach the inner cable from the end of the throttle pedal. Withdraw the cable through into the engine compartment.

5   Refitting is the reverse sequence to removal, but it is now necessary to adjust the effective length of the cable.

6   Pull the inner cable through the trunnion until all free movement of the throttle pedal is eliminated.

7   Hold the throttle linkage on the carburettor in the closed position and tighten the trunnion nut.

8   Depress the throttle pedal and make sure that the cable has $\frac{1}{16}$ in (1.6 mm) of free movement before the throttle linkage begins to move.

12 Choke cable – removal and refitting

1   Disconnect the battery earth terminal. Using two thin open-ended spanners, slacken the cable trunnion nut securing the inner cable to the carburettor fast idle cam. Slide the inner cable out of the trunnion and release the outer cable from the guide on the side of the carburettor (photo).

2   Undo and remove the retaining screw and lift off the right-hand cowl from the side of the steering column (photo).

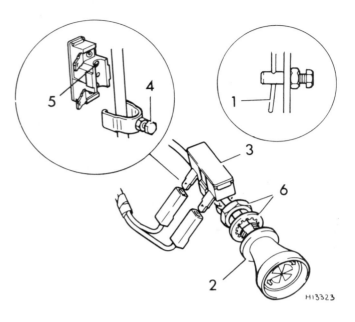

Fig. 3.8 Choke cable removal (Sec 12)

1 Choke inner cable	4 Warning switch clamp
2 Choke cable knob	screw
3 Warning lamp switch	5 Locating peg
	6 Nut and washer

3   Undo and remove the three retaining screws and withdraw the left-hand cowl (photos).

4   When fitted, loosen the locknut and unscrew the clamp screw that retains the warning light switch to the choke cable. Slide the switch along the cable and disconnect the electrical leads. Separate the clamp from the switch and remove the switch from the cable.

5   Carefully pull the cable through the body grommet and then unscrew the cable locknut from behind the left-hand cowl.

6   Extract the choke cable from the cowl and recover the lockwasher.

7   Refitting is a reversal of the removal procedure, but note that the large peg on the switch body locates in the hole nearest the control knob.

8   The choke cable must be adjusted to give 0.06 in (1.5 mm) free movement.

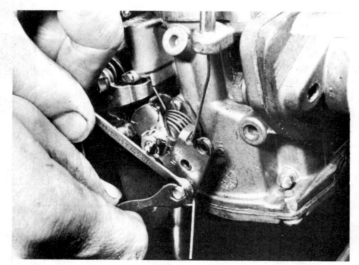

12.1 Remove the choke inner cable from the trunnion on the fast idle cam

12.2 Undo the single retaining screw and lift off the right-hand cowl

12.3a Unscrew the two inner screws ...

12.3b ... the single outer screw ...

12.3c ... then lift off the left-hand cowl to provide access to the choke outer cable

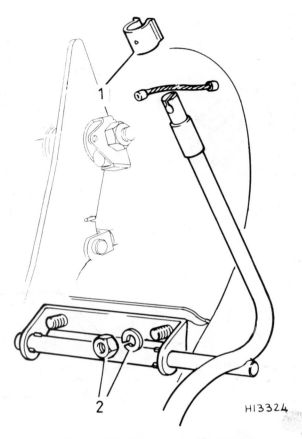

Fig. 3.9 Throttle pedal components (Sec 12)

1   Retaining clip   2   Nut and washer

13 Throttle pedal – removal and refitting

1   Release the retainers and withdraw the trim panel from beneath the dashboard.
2   Slip off the cable retainer and detach the throttle cable from the end of the pedal arm.
3   Undo and remove the two nuts and spring washers that secure the pedal bracket to the bulkhead panel.
4   Lift the pedal assembly off the mounting studs.
5   Refitting the throttle pedal is the reverse of the removal procedure.

14 Fuel tank – removal and refitting

1   For safety reasons, disconnect the battery.
2   Chock the front wheels, raise the rear of the car and support it on axle-stands located under the rear axle.
3   Unscrew the drain plug on the front of the tank and drain the fuel into a suitable container (photo).
4   Unscrew and remove the retaining screw. Detach the filler neck clamp from the body, then slacken the filler neck clamp screw. Turn the clamp clear of the body.
5   Unscrew and remove the retaining screws and withdraw the pipe protective cover into the boot (saloon models only).
6   Disconnect the vent pipe from the filler neck.
7   Detach the cable terminal from the fuel tank sender unit (photo).
8   Using a pair of pliers, compress the retaining clip that secures the fuel hose to the tank and ease off the hose.
9   Undo and remove the screws, spring washers and support plates that secure the fuel tank. Lower the tank from the body.
10 Refitting the fuel tank is the reverse of the removal procedure.

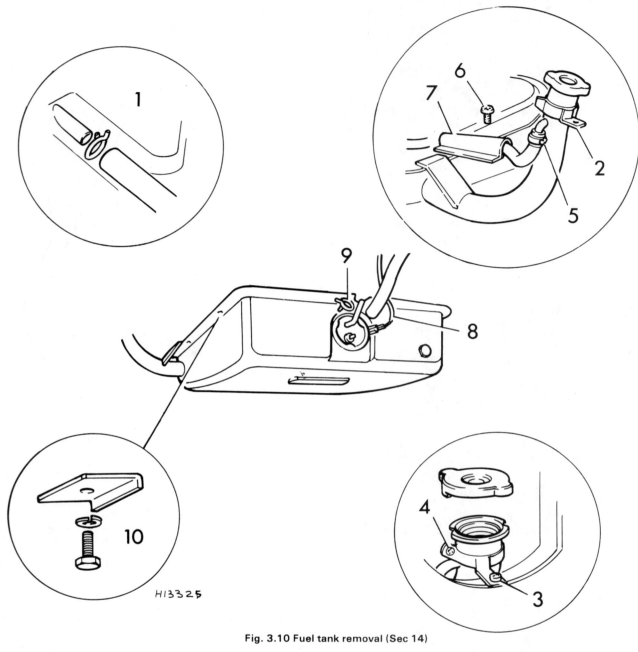

Fig. 3.10 Fuel tank removal (Sec 14)

1	Fuel pipe-to-tank connection	3	Clamp screw
2	Filler neck clamp	4	Clamp screw
		5	Vent pipe

6	Self-tapping screw	9	Hose clip
7	Cover	10	Support plate
8	Sender unit supply lead		

15 Fuel tank – cleaning

1   With time, it is likely that sediment will collect in the bottom of the fuel tank. Condensation, resulting in rust and other impurities, will usually be found in the fuel tank of any car more than three or four years old.

2   When the tank is removed, it should be vigorously flushed out and turned upside down. If facilities are available at the local garage, the tank may be steam cleaned and the exterior repainted with a lead based paint.

3   *Never weld or bring a naked light close to an empty fuel tank until it has been steam cleaned out for at least two hours or washed internally with boiling water and detergent and allowed to stand for at least three hours.*

16 Fuel tank sender unit – removal and refitting

1   For safety reasons disconnect the battery.

2   Chock the front wheels, jack up the rear of the car and support it on axle stands placed under the rear axle.

3   Unscrew the drain plug on the front of the tank and drain the fuel into a suitable container.

4   Disconnect the fuel gauge sender unit lead.

5   Using a pair of pliers, compress the retaining clip that secures the fuel hose to the tank and ease off the hose.

6   Release the sender unit locking ring by tapping it round with a brass drift. Unscrew the locking ring and lift out the tank unit assembly. Take care not to bend the float rod.

7   If the sender unit is faulty it must be renewed. The unit is a sealed

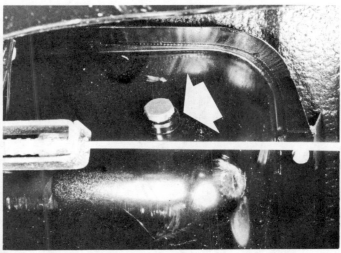

14.3 The fuel tank drain plug is located on the front of the tank

14.7 Fuel tank sender unit electrical lead and fuel outlet hose connection on the front of the tank

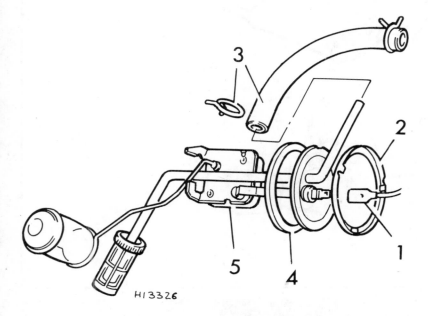

H13326

Fig. 3.11 Fuel tank sender unit (Sec 16)

1   Sender unit supply lead
2   Lock ring
3   Fuel pipe and clip
4   Sealing washer
5   Tank sender unit

assembly and cannot be repaired.

8   Refitting is the reverse of the removal procedure. Always fit a new sealing washer between the tank unit and the tank.

17 Exhaust system – general description

The exhaust system consists of a cast iron manifold, a front pipe and silencer, and a rear pipe and resonator. The system is attached to the floor pan by two brackets and flexible support straps.

At regular intervals the system should be checked for corrosion, joint leakage, the condition and security of the flexible mountings and the tightness of the joints.

18 Exhaust system – removal and refitting

1   To remove the complete system, chock the wheels on the right-hand side of the car, jack up the left-hand side and support the body on axle stands.
2   Using a length of wire or rope, support the front pipe.
3   Undo and remove the nuts that secure the twin flanges of the front pipe to the manifold.

4   Detach the left-hand rear shock absorber lower mounting and push it inwards.
5   Slacken the clips securing the front pipe to the gearbox steady bracket and slide it off the bracket.
6   Undo and remove the bolts securing the exhaust system to the flexible support straps (photos).
7   Lift the system clear of the rear axle and withdraw it from under the car.
8   After removal, the front and rear pipes can be separated after removing the securing clamp. Use liberal amounts of penetrating oil on the joint and allow time for it to soak in before attempting to separate the pipes.
9   If the tailpipe only is to be removed, chock the front wheels, jack up the rear of the car and support it on axle stands.
10 Slacken the clamp that secures the tailpipe to the front pipe and apply liberal amounts of penetrating oil to the joint.
11 Undo and remove the bolt securing the tailpipe to the rear flexible support strap.
12 Using a twisting action, release the tailpipe-to-front pipe joint, lift the pipe over the rear axle and remove it from under the car.
13 In both cases refitting is the reverse of the removal procedure. Do not tighten any of the clamps until the complete system is fitted, and then tighten them ensuring that the system is not under stress.

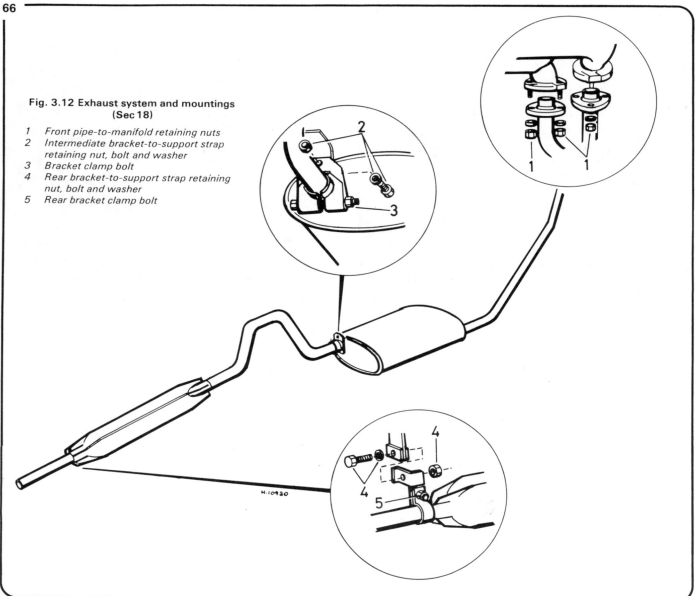

Fig. 3.12 Exhaust system and mountings (Sec 18)

1   Front pipe-to-manifold retaining nuts
2   Intermediate bracket-to-support strap retaining nut, bolt and washer
3   Bracket clamp bolt
4   Rear bracket-to-support strap retaining nut, bolt and washer
5   Rear bracket clamp bolt

H.10920

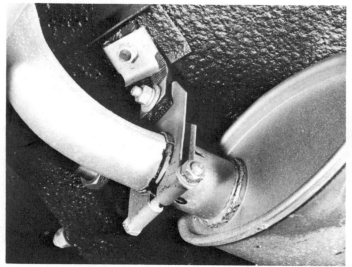

18.6a Exhaust system centre ...

18.6b ... and rear flexible support straps

19 Fault diagnosis – fuel and exhaust systems

Symptom	Reason(s)
Engine difficult to start when cold	Choke mechanism not functioning Insufficient fuel in float chamber Carburettor piston sticking *See also 'Fault diagnosis – ignition system' (Chapter 4)*
Engine difficult to start when hot	Choke mechanism not releasing Air cleaner dirty or choked Carburettor piston sticking Insufficient fuel in float chamber Float chamber flooding *See also 'Fault diagnosis – ignition system' (Chapter 4)*
Engine will not idle or idles erratically	Air cleaner dirty or choked Carburettor idle speed and/or mixture setting incorrect Carburettor piston sticking Air leaks at carburettor or manifold joint faces Generally worn carburettor
Engine performance poor, accompanied by hesitation, missing and/or cutting out	Insufficient oil in carburettor piston damper Carburettor piston sticking Carburettor mixture setting incorrect Float level incorrect Fuel pump faulty Fuel tank vent restricted Fuel lines restricted Air leak at carburettor or manifold joint faces Engine internal components worn, broken or out of adjustment *See also 'Fault diagnosis – engine' (Chapter 1) and 'Fault diagnosis – ignition system' (Chapter 4).*
Fuel consumption excessive	Air cleaner dirty or choked Carburettor mixture setting incorrect Fuel leaking from carburettor, fuel pump or fuel line Float chamber flooding Generally worn carburettor Tyre under-inflated Brakes binding
Excessive noise from exhaust system	Leaking exhaust or manifold joints Leaking, corroded or damaged silencer, pipe or resonator

Chapter 4 Ignition system

Contents

Specifications

Spark plugs
Type .... Unipart GSP 361 or 362 or equivalent (fit in sets of 4)
Electrode gap .... 0.035 in (0.90 mm)

Firing order .... 1–3–4–2 (No 1 nearest radiator)

Ignition coil
Type:
  1.7 litre .... Lucas 16C6 or AC Delco 9977230
  2.0 litre .... Lucas 15C6 or AC Delco 7992190
Primary resistance at 68°F (20°C) .... 1.1 to 1.45 ohms (1.7 litre) or 1.2 to 1.5 ohms (2.0 litre)
Ballast resistance .... 1.3 to 1.5 ohms

Distributor
Type .... Lucas 48D4
Direction of rotation .... Anti-clockwise
Contact breaker gap .... 0.014 to 0.016 in (0.35 to 0.40 mm)
Dwell angle .... 57° ± 5°

Ignition timing
Static ignition timing .... 8° BTDC (for setting-up purposes only)
Stroboscopic ignition timing (vacuum pipe disconnected) ..... 14° BTDC at 1500 rpm (1.7 litre)
                                       18° BTDC at 1500 rpm (2.0 litre)
Timing marks .... Notches on timing disc, pointer on crankcase

Torque wrench settings

	lbf ft	Nm
Distributor securing nuts	18	25
Spark plugs	7	10

---

1 General description

In order that the engine can run correctly, it is necessary for an electrical spark to ignite the fuel/air mixture in the combustion chamber at exactly the right moment in relation to engine speed and load.

The ignition system is divided into two circuits, low tension and high tension. The low tension (LT), or primary circuit, consists of the battery, ignition switch, low tension or primary coil windings, and the contact breaker points and condenser, both located at the distributor. The high tension (HT), or secondary circuit, consists of the high tension or secondary coil winding, the heavy ignition lead from the centre of the coil to the distributor cap, the rotor arm and the spark plug leads. The ignition system is based on feeding low tension voltage from the battery to the coil where it is converted to high tension voltage. The high tension voltage is powerful enough to jump the spark plug gap in the cylinders many times a second under high compression pressures, providing the system is in good condition and all adjustments are correct.

The wiring harness includes a high resistance wire in the ignition coil feed circuit and it is very important that only a 'ballast resistor' type ignition coil is used. During starting this 'ballast resistor' wire is bypassed, allowing the full battery voltage to be fed to the coil. This ensures that during cold starting, when the starter motor current draw would be high, sufficient voltage is still available at the coil to produce a powerful spark. It is therefore essential that only the correct type of coil is used. Under normal running the 12 volt supply is directed through the ballast resistor before reaching the coil.

The ignition advance is controlled both mechanically and by vacuum, to ensure that the spark occurs at just the right instant for the particular engine load and speed. The mechanical governor comprises two lead weights, which move out from the distributor shafts as the engine speed rises, due to centrifugal force. The vacuum control consists of a diaphragm, one side of which is connected via a small bore tube to the carburettor, and the other side to the contact breaker plate. Depression in the inlet manifold and carburettor, which varies with engine speed and throttle opening, causes the diaphragm to move, so moving the contact breaker plate, and advancing or retarding the spark.

2 Contact breaker points – adjustment

1   To adjust the contact breaker points so that the correct gap is obtained, first undo the two screws that secure the distributor cap to the distributor body, and lift away the cap (photo). Clean the inside and outside of the cap with a dry cloth. It is unlikely that the four segments will be badly burned or scored, but if they are, the cap must be renewed. If only a small deposit is on the segments, it may be scraped away using a small screwdriver.

2   Push in the carbon bush located in the top of the cap several times to ensure that it moves freely. The bush should protrude at least $\frac{1}{4}$ in (6.35 mm).

3   Gently prise the contact breaker points open to examine the condition of their faces. If they are rough, pitted or dirty it will be necessary to remove them to enable new points to be fitted.

4   Assuming that the points are in a satisfactory condition, or that they have been renewed, the gap between the two faces should be measured using feeler gauges. To do this, turn the engine over until the heel of the contact breaker arm is on the peak of one of the four cam lobes. A feeler gauge equal to the contact breaker points gap, as shown in the Specifications, should now just fit between the contact faces (photo).

5   If the gap varies from this amount, slacken the contact breaker plate securing screw and adjust the contact gap by inserting a

2.1 Distributor with cap and rotor removed

2.4 Measuring the points gap with a feeler gauge

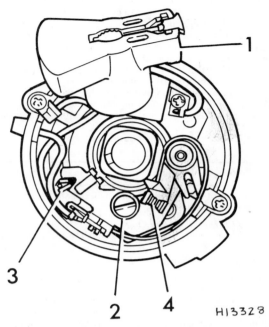

Fig. 4.1 Contact breaker points gap adjustment (Sec 2)

1 Rotor arm	3 Adjustment notch
2 Contact set securing screw	4 Contact points

screwdriver in the notched hole at the end of the plate. Move the plate in the desired direction to increase or decrease the gap.

6   Tighten the securing screw and recheck the gap again.

7   With the points correctly adjusted, refit the distributor cap and securing screws.

8   If a dwell meter is available, a far more accurate method of setting the contact breaker points gap is by measuring and setting the distributor dwell angle.

9   The dwell angle is the number of degrees of distributor cam rotation during which the contact breaker points are closed; ie the period from when the points close after being opened by one cam lobe, until they are opened again by the next cam lobe. The advantages of setting the points by this method are that any wear of the distributor shaft or cam lobes is taken into account, and also the inaccuracies of using a feeler gauge are eliminated. In general, a dwell meter should be used in accordance with the manufacturer's instructions. However, the use of one type of meter is outlined as follows.

10 To set the dwell angle, remove the distributor cap and rotor arm, and connect one lead of the dwell meter to the '+' terminal on the ignition coil, and the other lead to the '–' coil terminal.

11 Whilst an assistant turns on the ignition and operates the starter, observe the reading on the dwell meter scale. With the engine turning over on the starter, the reading should be as stated in the Specifications. **Note**: *Fluctuation of the dwell meter needle indicates that the engine is not turning over fast enough to give a steady reading. If this is the case, remove the spark plugs and repeat the checks.*

12 If the dwell angle is too small, the contact breaker points gap is too wide, and if the dwell angle is excessive, the gap is too small.

13 Adjust the contact breaker points gap, while the engine is cranking using the method described in paragraph 5, until the correct dwell angle is obtained.

14 When the dwell angle is satisfactory, disconnect the meter and refit the rotor arm and distributor cap.

3 Contact breaker points – removal and refitting

1   If the contact breaker points are burned, pitted or badly worn, they must be renewed.

2   Undo the distributor cap securing screws and lift off the cap.

3   Pull the rotor arm off the cam spindle.

4   Undo the screw that secures the contact set to the moving plate, then lift up the contact set. Press the contact set spring and release the terminal plate from the spring.

5   Lift away the contact set assembly.

6   To refit the contact set, connect the terminal plate, with the black lead uppermost, into the end of the contact spring.

7   Locate the contact set securing screw, spring and plain washer in the slot in the contact breaker adjustable plate.

8   Locate the baseplate peg in the fork of the contact set, then press the pivot post into the plate and tighten the securing screw.

9   Check and adjust the contact breaker points gap as described in Section 2.

10   Refit the rotor arm and distributor cap.

---

4   Distributor – lubrication

1   It is important that the distributor is lubricated every 6000 miles (10 000 km) as follows:

   (a) Smear the cam lightly with grease
   (b) Put a few drops of oil on the pad in the top of the cam spindle
   (c) Lubricate the advance mechanism by adding one or two drops of oil through the gap in the baseplate

2   Every 24 000 miles (40 000 km), lubricate the moving plate bearing groove with one drop of oil.

3   Great care should be taken not to use too much lubricant, as any excess that might find its way onto the contact breaker points could cause burning and misfiring. Clean off any surplus lubricant and make sure that the breaker points are dry.

---

5   Condenser – removal and refitting

1   The purpose of the condenser (sometimes known as a capacitor) is to ensure that when the contact breaker points open, there is no sparking across them, which would cause rapid wear of their faces and prevent the rapid collapse of the magnetic field in the coil. This would cause a reduction in coil HT voltage and ultimately lead to engine misfire.

2   If the engine becomes very difficult to start, or begins to miss after several miles of running, and the contact breaker points show signs of excessive burning, the condition of the condenser must be suspect. A further test can be made by separating the points by hand with the ignition switched on. If this is accompanied by a *strong* bright flash, it is indicative that the condenser has failed.

3   Without special test equipment, the only sure way to diagnose condenser trouble is to substitute a suspect unit with a new one and note if there is any improvement.

4   To remove the condenser from the distributor, undo and remove the distributor cap retaining screws and then lift off the cap and rotor arm.

5   Undo and remove the condenser retaining screw, noting the earth lead fitted under the screw head.

6   Release the contact set spring arm from the insulator and withdraw the terminal containing the condenser and low tension leads from the end of the arm.

7   Disconnect the distributor low tension lead at the wiring connector, push the lead complete with grommet through the hole in the side of the distributor, and then lift away the condenser and low tension lead assembly.

8   Refitting is the reverse sequence to removal. Make sure that the terminal containing the condenser and low tension lead is fitted to the tensioning arm of the contact breaker points with the black lead uppermost.

---

6   Distributor – removal and refitting

1   Undo and remove the two distributor cap securing screws and lift off the cap.

2   Disconnect the distributor LT lead at the connector and detach the vacuum pipe from the vacuum advance unit.

3   Turn the crankshaft in a clockwise direction until the rotor arm is in approximately the 2 o'clock position. Observe the timing disc on the front of the crankshaft and continue turning the crankshaft slowly until

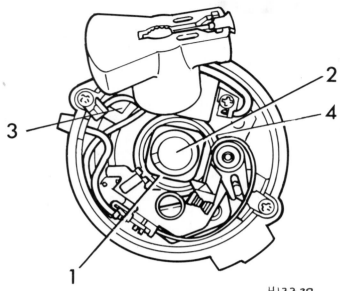

Fig. 4.2 Distributor lubrication points (Sec 4)

1	*Spindle cam*	4	*Moving plate bearing*
2	*Felt pad*		*groove*
3	*Advance mechanism*		
	lubrication point		

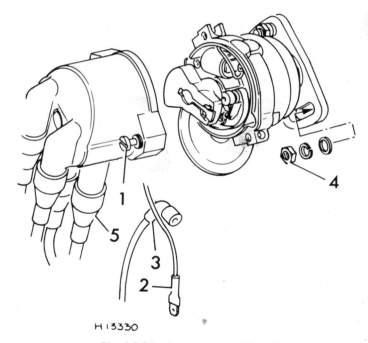

Fig. 4.3 Distributor removal (Sec 6)

1	*Distributor cap securing*	3	*Vacuum pipe*
	screw	4	*Securing nut*
2	*LT lead*	5	*HT leads*

the 8° BTDC notch on the disc is in line with the pointer on the crankcase. The rotor arm should now be in approximately the 3 o'clock position.

4   Undo and remove the two nuts securing the distributor to the camshaft cover (photo). Lift out the distributor and recover the O-ring seal from the distributor body.

5   When refitting the distributor, always fit a new O-ring seal to the distributor body.

6.4 Remove the distributor flange securing nuts

6.7 With the crankshaft at 90° BTDC the dimple on the camshaft gear is opposite the pointer

6.9 Fitting the distributor

6   Check that the contact breaker points gap is correctly set as described in Section 2.

7   Ensure that the crankshaft is still at 8° BTDC on the compression stroke for No 1 cylinder. If it has been inadvertently moved and its position lost, turn it back until the 90° BTDC notch on the timing disc is in line with the pointer. Now check that the dimple on the camshaft gear is opposite the pointer when viewed through the access hole in the rear of the camshaft cover (photo). Then rotate the crankshaft clockwise to 8° BTDC.

8   Position the rotor arm so that it is pointing towards the 1 o'clock position.

9   Hold the distributor so that the vacuum unit is 45° below horizontal and to the left. With the rotor arm still at 1 o'clock, insert the distributor into the camshaft cover and push it fully home (photo). Note that as the distributor gear engages the gear on the camshaft, the rotor arm will turn to approximately the 3 o'clock position.

10   Fit the distributor retaining nuts and washers finger tight only at this stage.

11   Slowly turn the distributor body until the points *just* begin to open, then tighten the two retaining nuts.

12   Refit the distributor cap and retaining screws, the vacuum advance pipe, and LT lead at the connector.

13   Run the engine and then accurately reset the ignition timing using a stroboscopic timing light as described in Section 10.

7   Distributor – dismantling

1   With the distributor removed from the engine and on the bench, remove the distributor cap securing screws and lift off the cap. Pull off the rotor arm.

2   Remove the felt lubricating pad from the top of the shaft.

3   Undo and remove the two screws that secure the vacuum unit, then disengage the operating arm and lift away the vacuum unit.

4   Undo the securing screw and remove the earth lead and condenser.

5   Ease the LT lead rubber grommet out of its location and push it to the inside of the distributor body.

6   Remove the two screws that secure the baseplate assembly and lift out the assembly.

7   Push the contact set spring inwards and remove the LT connector from the spring loop.

8   Undo the securing screw and remove the contact breaker set from the baseplate assembly.

9   Remove the advance control springs, taking care not to overstretch them.

10   If the drivegear has to be renewed, drive out the roll pin that secures the drivegear on the distributor shaft and remove the drivegear and thrust washer.

11   The distributor shaft can now be removed complete with the advance mechanism, spacer and plain washer.

12   The component parts of the distributor are now ready for inspection.

8   Distributor – inspection

1   Thoroughly wash all mechanical parts in paraffin and wipe dry using a clean non-fluffy rag.

2   Check the contact breaker points as described in Section 2. Check the distributor cap for signs of tracking, indicated by a thin black line between the segments. Renew the cap if evident.

3   If the metal portion of the rotor arm is badly burned or loose, renew the arm. If slightly burnt, clean the arm with a fine file. Check that the carbon brush moves freely in the centre of the distributor cover.

4   Check that the plates of the baseplate assembly move freely and that the springs are in good condition. If defective, the baseplate assembly must be renewed complete.

5   The advance mechanism must now be dismantled except for the removal of the control springs. If any of the pads are worn, the complete shaft assembly must be renewed.

6   If the shaft is a loose fit in the bush in the distributor body, then a new distributor assembly will be required.

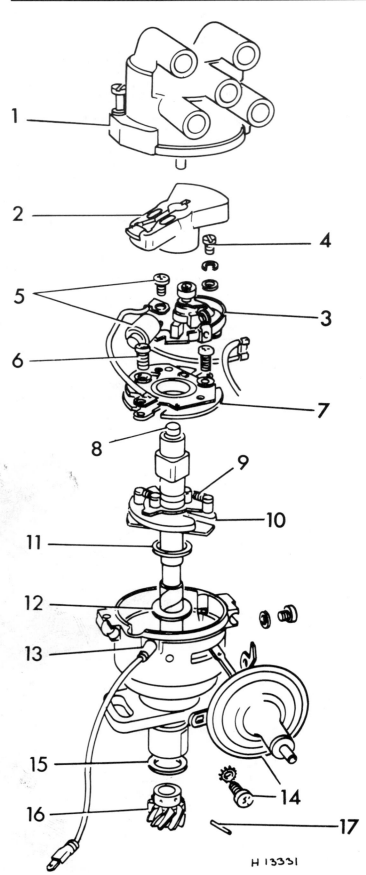

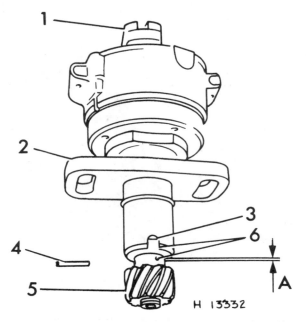

Fig. 4.5 Fitting the drivegear on a new shaft (Sec 9)

1 Rotor arm
2 Distributor flange
3 Thrust washer tab
   slot
4 Roll pin

5 Drivegear
6 Hole aligned with edge
   of slot
Dimension A - 0.005 in
(0.13 mm)

9 Distributor – reassembly

1   Reassembly is a straightforward reversal of the dismantling procedure. In addition, however, note the following:
2   Ensure that the spacer is fitted with the chamfer towards the plain washer.
3   Grease the pivots of the weights and spring and the shaft bearing area with a little Rocol MP (Molypad).
4   If the original shaft and drivegear is being refitted, slide the thrust washer and gear onto the shaft, then align the rotor keyway in the shaft with the hole in the drivegear. Drive in the roll pin to secure the gear in position.
5   When fitting a new shaft, slide on the thrust washer and drivegear. Fit the rotor arm. Position it at right-angles to the mounting flange and with its rear end towards the thrust washer tab slot in the distributor body (Fig. 4.5).
6   To set the endfloat of the shaft, insert a 0.005 in (0.13 mm) feeler gauge between the thrust washer and drivegear.
7   Align the hole in the drivegear with the edge of the thrust washer tab slot and, holding the shaft and gear tightly together, drill a $\frac{1}{8}$ in (3.2 mm) hole through the shaft.
8   Remove the feeler gauge and drive in the roll pin to secure the drivegear in position.
9   Proceed with the remainder of the reassembly.
10   Lubricate the distributor as described in Section 4.
11   Adjust the contact breaker points gap as described in Section 2.

Fig. 4.4 Exploded view of the distributor (Sec 7)

1   Distributor cap
2   Rotor arm
3   Contact set
4   Contact set securing
    screw
5   Condenser and securing
    screw
6   Baseplate securing
    screw
7   Baseplate assembly
8   Felt oil pad

9   Control springs
10 Shaft assembly
11 Spacer
12 Plain washer
13 Grommet
14 Vacuum unit and
    securing screw
15 Thrust washer
16 Drivegear
17 Roll pin

H 13331

Measuring plug gap. A feeler gauge of the correct size (see ignition system specifications) should have a slight 'drag' when slid between the electrodes. Adjust gap if necessary

Adjusting plug gap. The plug gap is adjusted by bending the earth electrode inwards, or outwards, as necessary until the correct clearance is obtained. Note the use of the correct tool

Normal. Grey-brown deposits, lightly coated core nose. Gap increasing by around 0.001 in (0.025 mm) per 1000 miles (1600 km). Plugs ideally suited to engine, and engine in good condition

Carbon fouling. Dry, black, sooty deposits. Will cause weak spark and eventually misfire. Fault: over-rich fuel mixture. Check: carburettor mixture settings, float level and jet sizes; choke operation and cleanliness of air filter. Plugs can be re-used after cleaning

Oil fouling. Wet, oily deposits. Will cause weak spark and eventually misfire. Fault: worn bores/piston rings or valve guides; sometimes occurs (temporarily) during running-in period. Plugs can be re-used after thorough cleaning

Overheating. Electrodes have glazed appearance, core nose very white – few deposits. Fault: plug overheating. Check: plug value, ignition timing, fuel octane rating (too low) and fuel mixture (too weak). Discard plugs and cure fault immediately

Electrode damage. Electrodes burned away; core nose has burned, glazed appearance. Fault: pre-ignition. Check: as for 'Overheating' but may be more severe. Discard plugs and remedy fault before piston or valve damage occurs

Split core nose (may appear initially as a crack). Damage is self-evident, but cracks will only show after cleaning. Fault: pre-ignition or wrong gap-setting technique. Check: ignition timing, cooling system, fuel octane rating (too low) and fuel mixture (too weak). Discard plugs, rectify fault immediately

10 Ignition timing – adjustment

1   For prolonged engine life, efficient running performance and
economy, it is essential for the fuel/air mixture in the combustion
chambers to be ignited by the spark plugs at precisely the right
moment in relation to engine speed and load. For this to occur, the
ignition timing must be set accurately, and should be checked at
regular intervals, or whenever the position of the distributor has been
altered. To make an accurate check of the ignition timing, it is
necessary to use a stroboscopic timing light, whereby the timing is
checked with the engine running at a specified speed.
2   Before making any adjustments to the ignition timing make sure
that the contact breaker points are correctly adjusted as described in
Section 2. If the distributor has been removed, or if for any reason its
position on the engine has been altered, obtain an initial static timing
setting, to enable the engine to be run, as described in Section 6.
3   Paint the specified notch on the timing disc and the pointer on the
crankcase with quick drying white paint (or white chalk) to highlight
these points – see Fig. 4.6. Some vehicles have more timing mark
notches on the crankshaft pulley than shown in Fig. 4.6. The peaks and
troughs of the notched section are still spaced at 2° intervals.
4   Connect the timing light between No 1 spark plug and No 1 spark
plug HT lead following the manufacturer's instructions. It will also be
necessary to connect a tachometer (if one is not fitted to the car),
between the coil '–' terminal and earth or as specified by the
manufacturer.
5   Detach the vacuum advance pipe from the distributor vacuum
unit.
6   Start the engine and turn the idle speed adjustment screw on the
carburettor until the engine is running at the specified speed for
ignition timing.
7   Point the timing light at the timing disc. The appropriate notch on
the disc will appear stationary and, if the timing is correct, will be
adjacent to the pointer on the front of the crankcase.
8   If the timing marks are not aligned, slacken the distributor flange
retaining nuts slightly and turn the distributor one way or the other
until the marks line up. Tighten the retaining nuts and recheck the
timing.
9   Reconnect the vacuum advance pipe to the distributor while
observing the timing marks. If the vacuum unit is working correctly the
timing should advance as the pipe is connected. The timing should
also advance as the engine speed is increased, indicating that the
centrifugal advance mechanism is working correctly.
10 With the timing correctly adjusted, reset the engine idling speed to
the specified setting, switch off the engine and disconnect the
instruments.

11 Spark plugs and HT leads

1   The correct functioning of the spark plugs is vital for the proper
running and efficient operation of the engine.
2   At intervals of 6000 miles (10 000 km) the plugs should be
removed, examined, cleaned, and if worn excessively, renewed. The
condition of the spark plug can also tell much about the general
condition of the engine.
3   If the insulator nose of the spark plug is clean and white with no
deposits, this is indicative of a weak mixture or too hot a plug (a hot
plug transfers heat away from the electrode slowly – a cold plug
transfers heat away quickly).
4   If the insulator nose is covered with hard black deposits, then this
is indicative that the mixture is too rich. Should the plug be black and
oily, then it is likely that the engine is fairly worn as well as the mixture
being too rich.
5   If the insulator nose is covered with light tan to greyish brown
deposits, then the mixture is correct and it is likely that the engine is
in good condition.
6   If there are any traces of long brown tapering stains on the outside
of the white portion of the plug, then the plug will have to be renewed
as this shows that there is a faulty joint between the plug body and the
insulator and compression is being allowed to leak away.
7   Plugs should be cleaned by a sand blasting machine, which will
free them from carbon more than by cleaning by hand. The machine
will also test the condition of the plugs under compression. Any plug
that fails to spark at the recommended pressure should be renewed.

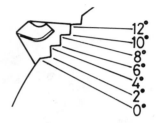

Fig. 4.6 Timing mark representation (Sec 10)

8   The spark plug gap is of considerable importance as, if it is too
large or too small the size of the spark and its efficiency will be
seriously impaired. The spark plug gap should be set to the figure given
in the Specifications at the beginning of this Chapter.
9   To set the gap, measure it with a feeler gauge and then bend open,
or close, the outer plug electrode until the correct gap is achieved. The
centre electrode should never be bent, as this may crack the insulation
and cause plug failure, if nothing worse.
10 When refitting the spark plugs, make sure that they are tightened
to the specified torque and that the leads are refitted in the correct
firing order.
11 The plug leads require no maintenance other than being kept clean
and wiped over regularly. At intervals of 6000 miles (10 000 km)
however, pull each lead off the plug in turn and remove them from the
distributor cap. Water can seep down these joints giving rise to a white
corrosive deposit which must be carefully removed from the end of
each cable.

12 Fault diagnosis – ignition system

By far the majority of breakdowns and running troubles are caused
by faults in the ignition system, either in the low tension or high
tension circuits.
There are two main symptoms indicating faults. Either the engine
will not start or fire, or the engine is difficult to start and misfires. If it
is a regular misfire (ie the engine is running on only 2 or 3 cylinders),
the fault is almost sure to be in the secondary or high tension circuit.
If the misfiring is intermittent, the fault could be in either the high or
low tension circuits. If the car stops suddenly or will not start at all, it
is likely that the fault is in the low tension circuit. Loss of power and
overheating, apart from faulty carburation settings, are normally due to
faults in the distributor or to incorrect ignition timing.

Engine fails to start
Note that on engines fitted with a ballast resistor in the ignition
system (see Specifications), should the resistor become defective or
disconnected, then the engine will fire but not run.
If the engine fails to start and the car was running normally when
it was last used, first check there is fuel in the petrol tank. If the engine
turns over normally on the starter motor and the battery is evidently
well charged, then the fault may be in either the high or low tension
circuits. First check the HT circuit. **Note**: *If the battery is known to be
fully charged, the ignition light comes on and the starter motor fails to
turn the engine, check the tightness of the leads on the battery
terminals and the secureness of the earth lead to its connection to the
body. It is quite common for the leads to have worked loose, even if
they look and feel secure. If one of the battery terminal posts gets very
hot when trying to work the starter motor, this is a sure indication of
a faulty connection to that terminal.*
One of the commonest reasons for bad starting is wet or damp
spark plug leads and distributor. Remove the distributor cap. If
condensation is visible internally, dry the cap with a rag and wipe over
the leads. Refit the cap.
If the engine still fails to start, check that voltage is reaching the
plugs by disconnecting each plug lead in turn at the spark plug end and
holding the end of the cable about $\frac{3}{16}$ in (5 mm) away from the cylinder
block. Spin the engine on the starter motor.
Sparking between the end of the cable and the block should be
fairly strong with a strong regular blue spark. Hold the lead with rubber

to avoid electric shocks. If voltage is reaching the plugs, then remove them and clean and regap them. The engine should now start.

If there is no spark at the plug leads, take off the HT lead from the centre of the distributor cap and hold it to the block as before. Spin the engine on the starter once more. A rapid succession of blue sparks between the end of the lead and the block indicate that the coil is in order and that the distributor cap is cracked, the rotor arm is faulty, or the carbon brush in the top of the distributor cap is not making good contact with the spring on the rotor arm. Possibly, the points are in bad condition. Clean and reset them as described in this Chapter, Section 3.

If there are no sparks from the end of the lead from the coil, check the connections at the coil end of the lead. If it is in order, start checking the low tension circuit.

Use a 12v voltmeter or a 12v bulb and two lengths of wire. With the ignition switched on and the points open, test between the low tension wire to the coil (it is marked '+') and earth. No reading indicates a break in the supply from the ignition switch. Check the connections at the switch to see if any are loose. Refit them and the engine should run. A reading shows a faulty coil or condenser, or broken lead between the coil and the distributor.

Remove the condenser from the distributor and with the points open, test between the moving point and earth. If there now is a reading, then the fault is in the condenser. Fit a new one and the fault is cleared.

With no reading from the moving point to earth, take a reading between earth and the '−' terminal of the coil. A reading here shows a broken wire which will need to be renewed between the coil and distributor. No reading confirms that the coil has failed and must be renewed, after which the engine will run once more. Remember to refit the condenser to the baseplate. For these tests it is sufficient to separate the points with a piece of dry paper whilst testing with the points open.

Engine misfires

If the engine misfires regularly, run it at a fast idling speed. Pull off each of the plug caps in turn and listen to the note of the engine. Hold the plug cap in a dry cloth or with a rubber glove as additional protection against a shock from the HT supply.

No difference in engine running will be noticed when the lead from the defective circuit is removed. Removing the lead from one of the good cylinders will accentuate the misfire.

Remove the plug lead from the end of the defective plug and hold it about $\frac{3}{16}$ in (5 mm) away from the block. Restart the engine. If sparking is fairly strong and regular the fault must lie in the spark plug.

The plug may be loose, the insulation may be cracked, or the points may have burnt away giving too wide a gap for the spark to jump. Worse still, one of the points may have broken off. Either renew the plug or clean it, reset the gap and then test the plug.

If there is no spark at the end of the plug lead, or if it is weak and intermittent, check the ignition lead from the distributor to the plug. If the insulation is cracked or perished, renew the lead. Check the connections at the distributor cap.

If there is still no spark, examine the distributor cap carefully for tracking. This can be recognised by a very thin black line running between two or more electrodes, or between an electrode and some other part of the distributor. These lines are paths which now conduct electricity across the cap, thus letting it run to earth. The only answer is a new distributor cap.

Apart from the ignition timing being incorrect, other causes of misfiring have already been dealt with under the Section dealing with the failure of the engine to start.

If the ignition timing is too far retarded, it should be noted that the engine will tend to overheat and there will be quite a noticeable drop in power. If the engine is overheating and power is down, and the ignition is correct, then the carburettor should be checked, as it is likely that this is where the fault lies. See Chapter 3 for details.

Chapter 5 Clutch

Contents

Specifications

Type .... Single dry plate, diaphragm spring, hydraulically operated

Make .... Borg and Beck or Laycock

Clutch disc diameter .... 8.5 in (216 mm)

Master cylinder bore .... 0.5 in (12.70 mm)

Slave cylinder bore .... 0.87 in (22.22 mm)

Hydraulic fluid .... Universal brake and clutch fluid to specification FMVSS 116 DOT 3 or SAE J1703c

Torque wrench setting

	lbf ft	Nm
Clutch-to-flywheel bolts	17	23

1 General description

The Morris Ital 1.7 and 2.0 models are equipped with an 8.5 in (216 mm) diameter diaphragm spring clutch, operated hydraulically by a master and slave cylinder.

The clutch assembly comprises a steel cover, which is bolted and dowelled to the rear face of the flywheel, and contains the pressure plate and clutch disc or driven plate.

The pressure plate, diaphragm spring and release plate are all attached to the clutch cover.

The clutch disc is free to slide along the splined gearbox input shaft and is held in position between the flywheel and pressure plate by the pressure of the diaphragm spring.

Friction lining material is riveted to the clutch disc, which has a spring-cushioned hub to absorb transmission shocks and to help ensure a smooth take-up of the drive.

The pendant clutch pedal is connected to the clutch master cylinder by a short pushrod. The combined master cylinder and hydraulic fluid reservoir are mounted on the engine side of the bulkhead in front of the driver.

Depressing the clutch pedal moves the piston in the master cylinder forwards, so forcing hydraulic fluid through the clutch hydraulic pipe to the slave cylinder.

The piston in the slave cylinder moves forward on the entry of the fluid and actuates the clutch release arm by means of a short pushrod. The opposite end of the release arm is forked and is located behind the release bearing.

As this pivoted clutch release arm moves backwards, it bears against the release bearing, pushing it forwards to bear against the release plate, so moving the centre of the diaphragm spring inwards. The spring is sandwiched between two annular rings which act as fulcrum points. The centre of the spring is pushed out, so moving the

pressure plate backwards and disengaging the pressure plate from the clutch disc.

When the clutch pedal is released, the diaphragm spring forces the pressure plate into contact with the high friction linings on the clutch disc, and at the same time pushes the clutch disc a fraction of an inch forwards on its splines, so engaging the clutch disc with the flywheel. The clutch disc is now firmly sandwiched between the pressure plate and the flywheel so the drive is taken up.

As the friction linings on the clutch disc wear, the pressure plate automatically moves closer to the disc to compensate. There is therefore no need to adjust the clutch periodically.

2 Clutch hydraulic system – bleeding

1 Gather together a clear glass jar, a length of rubber tubing which fits tightly over the bleed screw, a tin of the specified hydraulic fluid, and an assistant. On closer inspection it will be seen that the small bleed screw is located at the end of an extension tube, one end of which is attached to a bracket on the camshaft cover and the other end screwed into the slave cylinder.

2 Check that the master cylinder reservoir is full. If it is not, fill it. Also cover the bottom 2 in (5 cm) of the glass jar with fluid.

3 Place one end of the rubber tube securely over the bleed screw and insert the other end in the glass jar so that the tube orifice is below the level of the fluid.

4 Using a suitable spanner, open the bleed screw approximately three quarters of a turn. Have your assistant depress the clutch pedal and hold it down at the end of its stroke. Close the bleed screw and allow the pedal to return to its normal position.

5 Continue this series of operations until clean hydraulic fluid, without any trace of air bubbles, emerges from the end of the tubing. Make sure that the fluid reservoir is checked frequently, to ensure that

the level does not drop too far, thus letting further air into the system.

6 When no more air bubbles appear, tighten the bleed screw at the end of a downstroke and remove the rubber tubing. Discard the expelled fluid in the glass jar, as it is unsuitable for further use in the hydraulic system.

3 Clutch release bearing – removal and refitting

1 Wear of the clutch release bearing is indicated by a squealing noise, or roughness felt through the clutch pedal when the pedal is depressed with the engine running.

2 To gain access to the release bearing, the gearbox must be removed from the engine as described in Chapter 6.

3 With the gearbox removed from the car, lift out the slave cylinder pushrod, disengage the release arm from the bearing and from the fulcrum pin, then slide the release bearing off the input shaft front end cover (photos).

4 The release bearing should feel smooth and be quiet when turned. If any evidence of roughness is felt or heard, the bearing must be renewed. To do this the bearing must be removed from the bearing carrier using a large bench vice or press and suitable packing. When refitting the bearing to the carrier ensure that the load is applied only to the inner race.

5 Before refitting the release bearing and arm assembly to the gearbox, apply a trace of graphite-based grease to the input shaft front end cover, the release arm dowels and the fulcrum pin.

6 Slide the bearing onto the gearbox input shaft front end cover.

3.3a Disengage the release arm from the bearing ...

3.3b ... and fulcrum pin ...

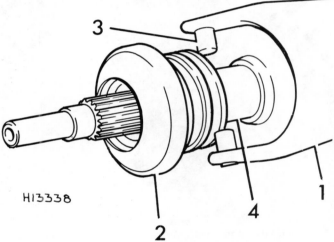

Fig. 5.1 Clutch release mechanism (Sec 3)

1 Release arm
2 Release bearing
3 Release arm dowels
4 First motion shaft front end cover

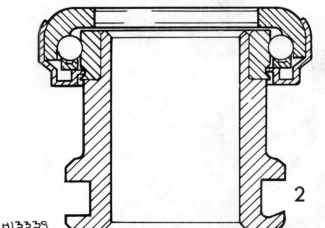

Fig. 5.2 Sectional view of clutch release bearing (Sec 3)

1 Bearing assembly   2 Bearing carrier

3.3c ... then slide the bearing off the input shaft cover

Engage the release arm dowels into the groove in the release bearing, and at the same time engage the arm retaining spring clip over the rear of the fulcrum pin in the bellhousing. Push the release arm fully into position.

7   Refit the slave cylinder pushrod ensuring that the end in contact with the release arm is well greased.

8   The gearbox can now be refitted as described in Chapter 6.

4   Clutch assembly – removal and refitting

1   Remove the gearbox as described in Chapter 6.

2   Using a scriber or file, mark the relative position of the clutch cover and flywheel to ensure correct refitting should the original parts be re-used.

3   Undo and remove the six bolts that secure the cover to the rear face of the flywheel. Unscrew the bolts diagonally half a turn at a time to prevent distortion of the cover flange.

4   With the bolts and spring washers removed, ease the clutch cover off the locating dowels. The clutch disc will drop out at this stage as it is not attached to either the clutch cover assembly or the flywheel.

5   It is important to ensure that no oil or grease is allowed to come into contact with the clutch disc friction linings or the pressure plate and flywheel faces. It is advisable to handle the parts with clean hands and to wipe down the pressure plate and flywheel faces with a clean dry rag before inspection or refitting commences.

6   To refit the clutch assembly, place the clutch disc in position with the spring housing facing outwards away from the flywheel. The words 'FLYWHEEL SIDE' will also usually be found on the other side of the disc that faces the flywheel (photo). On no account should the clutch disc be refitted the wrong way round as it will be found quite impossible to operate the clutch with the disc incorrectly fitted.

7   Refit the clutch cover assembly loosely on the dowels. Refit the six bolts and spring washers and tighten them finger tight so that the clutch disc is gripped but can still be moved (photo).

8   The clutch disc must now be centralised so that when the engine and gearbox are mated, the gearbox input shaft splines will pass through the splines in the centre of the hub.

9   Centralisation can be carried out quite easily by inserting a round bar or long screwdriver through the hole in the centre of the clutch, so that the end of the bar rests in the small hole in the end of the crankshaft containing the input shaft spigot bearing. Moving the bar sideways, or up and down, will move the clutch disc in whichever direction is necessary to achieve centralisation (photo).

10   Centralisation is easily judged by removing the bar and viewing the clutch disc hub in relation to the crankshaft spigot bearing and the hole in the centre of the diaphragm spring. When the hub appears exactly in the centre, all is correct. Alternatively, if an old input shaft, or a universal clutch aligning tool (photo), can be obtained, this will eliminate all the guesswork, obviating the need for visual alignment.

11   Tighten the cover retaining bolts gradually in a diagonal sequence to ensure the cover plate is pulled down evenly without distortion of the flange. Tighten the bolts to the torque setting given in the Specifications.

12   The gearbox can now be refitted as described in Chapter 6.

4.6 The clutch disc is stamped 'FLYWHEEL SIDE' on the centre hub

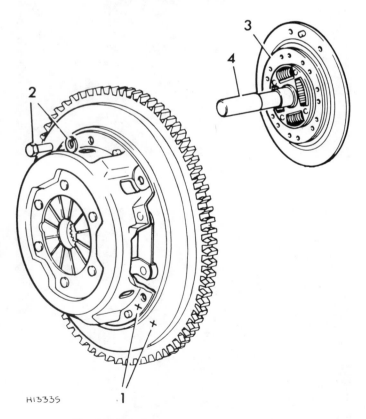

H13335

Fig. 5.3 Clutch assembly components (Sec 4)

1	Alignment marks	3	Clutch disc
2	Retaining bolt and spring washer	4	Aligning tool

4.7 Refitting the clutch disc and cover

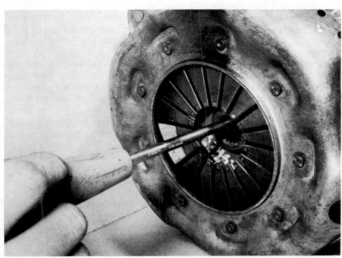

4.9 The clutch disc can be centralised using a screwdriver or bar ...

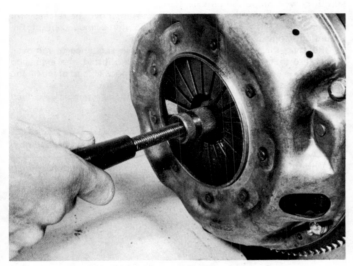

4.10 ... or preferably with a universal aligning tool

5 Clutch assembly – inspection

1   With the clutch disc and pressure plate removed from the flywheel, clean off all traces of asbestos dust using a dry cloth. This is best done outside or in a well ventilated area; *asbestos dust is harmful and must not be inhaled.*

2   Examine the clutch disc friction linings for wear and loose rivets, and the disc for rim distortion, cracks, broken hub springs and worn splines. The surface of the friction linings may be highly glazed, but as long as the friction material pattern can be clearly seen, this is satisfactory. If the friction material is worn down to the level of the rivet heads, the disc must be renewed.

3   Check the machined faces of the flywheel and pressure plate. If either is grooved or heavily scored, it should be machined until smooth, or preferably, renewed.

4   If the pressure plate is cracked or split, or if the diaphragm spring is damaged or its pressure suspect, a new unit must be fitted.

5   Check the release bearing for smoothness of operation. There should be no harshness or slackness in it. It should spin reasonably freely, bearing in mind it has been pre-packed with grease.

6   When considering renewing clutch components individually, bear in mind that new parts (or parts from different manufacturers) do not always bed into old ones satisfactorily. A clutch pressure plate or disc

renewed separately may sometimes cause judder or snatch. Although expensive, the clutch pressure plate, disc and release bearing should be renewed together, as a complete assembly, wherever possible.

6 Clutch master cylinder – removal and refitting

1   Working inside the car, release the locking buttons and lift out the trim panel beneath the dashboard to provide access to the clutch pedal.

2   Extract the split pin and withdraw the clevis pin that secures the clutch master cylinder pushrod to the pedal.

3   From inside the engine compartment, unscrew the clutch hydraulic pipe union from the end of the master cylinder and carefully pull the pipe clear. Plug the master cylinder to prevent loss of fluid and suitably protect the pipe union to prevent dirt ingress.

4   Undo and remove the two nuts and spring washers securing the master cylinder to the bulkhead and lift the cylinder away. Take care not to allow any hydraulic fluid to come into contact with the paintwork, as it acts as a solvent.

5   Refitting the master cylinder is the reverse sequence to removal. On completion, bleed the clutch hydraulic system as described in Section 2.

7 Clutch master cylinder – dismantling, inspection and re-assembly

1   With the master cylinder removed from the car, unscrew the filler cap and drain the hydraulic fluid from the reservoir.

2   Ease back the rubber dust cover from the pushrod end and then, using circlip pliers, release the circlip that retains the pushrod assembly. Lift out the pushrod complete with rubber dust cover, circlip and plain washer.

3   Tap the end of the master cylinder on a block of wood to release the piston with its seal, dished washer, main cup seal and spring retainer. Also lift out the piston return spring, noting which way round it is fitted.

4   Carefully ease the secondary cup seal from the piston, noting which way round it is fitted.

5   Thoroughly clean all components in methylated spirit or clean

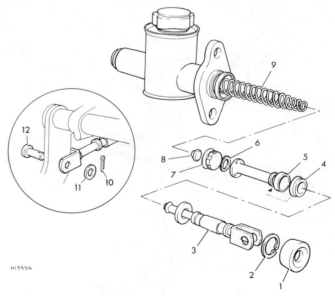

Fig. 5.4 Clutch master cylinder components (Sec 7)

1	Rubber dust cover	8	Spring retainer
2	Circlip	9	Spring
3	Pushrod		Inset: Pushrod attachments
4	Secondary cup seal	10	Split pin
5	Piston	11	Plain washer
6	Dished washer	12	Clevis pin
7	Main cup seal		

hydraulic fluid, and lay them out in the order in which they were removed, ready for inspection.

6   Carefully examine the internal cylinder bore and piston for scoring or wear, and all components for damage or distortion. In order that the seals may adequately maintain hydraulic fluid pressure without leakage, the condition of the piston and cylinder bore must be perfect. If in any doubt whatsoever about the condition of the components, renew the complete master cylinder.

7   If the master cylinder is in a satisfactory condition, a new set of seals must be obtained before reassembly. These are available in the form of a master cylinder repair kit, obtainable from your local dealer or brake and clutch factor.

8   Before reassembly begins, lubricate all the internal parts and the master cylinder bore with clean hydraulic fluid, and make sure that they are assembled wet.

9   Refit the secondary cup seal onto the piston with the lip of the seal toward the return spring end.

10 Place the spring retainer into the small end of the return spring and insert the spring into the cylinder bore, large end first.

11 Insert the main cup seal into the bore with the lip of the seal towards the spring.

12 Refit the dished washer and then carefully insert the piston assembly into the cylinder bore. Make sure that the end of the piston containing the secondary cup seal is toward the open end of the bore.

13 Smear a little rubber grease onto the ball end of the pushrod and refit the pushrod assembly. Slide down the plain washer and secure it in position with the circlip.

14 Liberally lubricate the inside of the rubber dust cover with rubber grease and place it over the end of the master cylinder.

15 The assembled cylinder can now be refitted to the car as described in Section 6.

8   Clutch slave cylinder – removal and refitting

1   Unscrew the clutch master cylinder reservoir filler cap, and if necessary top up the reservoir. Place a piece of polythene over the filler neck and refit the cap. This will minimise the loss of hydraulic fluid during subsequent operations.

2   Wipe the area around the hydraulic pipe and extension bleed tube unions on the slave cylinder and then unscrew the two pipes. Suitably protect the pipe ends against dirt ingress.

3   Push the slave cylinder pushrod into the cylinder until it clears the clutch release arm, and then withdraw the pushrod. Take great care not to drop it into the bellhousing. Note that during this operation a quantity of hydraulic fluid will be ejected from the disconnected unions on the rear of the slave cylinder. Make sure that a suitable container is in position to catch the fluid or place some old rags around the end of the cylinder. Do not allow the hydraulic fluid to come into contact with the paintwork.

4   Release the spring clip securing the slave cylinder in position in its mounting flange.

5   It is now necessary to move the clutch release arm rearwards against the pressure of the clutch diaphragm spring to provide sufficient clearance for withdrawal of the slave cylinder. It is recommended that if possible BL special tool 18G1213 should be used to do this. If suitable facilities are available a similar tool can easily be made up, or as a last resort the release arm can be moved rearwards by levering against it with a stout metal bar. If this method is being used, take great care as it is quite easy to fracture the slave cylinder mounting flange. Depending on the tool being used it may be beneficial to jack up the car and work from underneath. If so, make sure it is well supported on axle stands.

6   Using whichever method has been chosen, move the release arm rearward until it is just possible to slide the cylinder out of the mounting flange and remove it from the car.

7   Refitting the slave cylinder is the reverse sequence to removal. Make sure that when the hydraulic pipes are refitted, the extension bleed tube is uppermost, otherwise it will be impossible to bleed all the air from the system.

8   After refitting the cylinder bleed the hydraulic system as described in Section 2.

9   Clutch slave cylinder – dismantling, inspection and reassembly

1   With the slave cylinder removed from the car, thoroughly clean it externally before dismantling.

2   Withdraw the rubber dust cover and then tap the cylinder on a block of wood to release the piston, piston seal, cup filler and spring from the cylinder bore.

3   Wash all the parts in clean hydraulic fluid or methylated spirit and

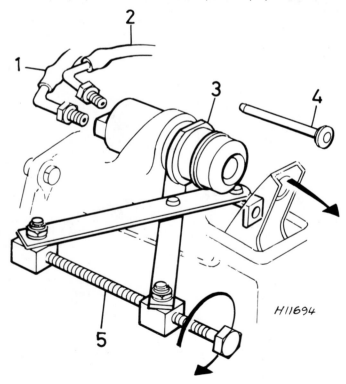

Fig. 5.5 Clutch slave cylinder removal (Sec 8)

1	Hydraulic fluid pipe	4	Pushrod
2	Extension bleed tube	5	Special tool 18G1213
3	Slave cylinder		

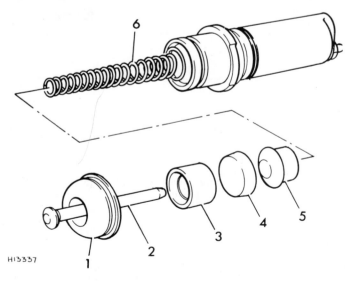

Fig. 5.6 Clutch slave cylinder components (Sec 9)

1	Rubber dust cover	4	Seal
2	Pushrod	5	Cup filler
3	Piston	6	Spring

dry them with a lint-free cloth.

4   Carefully examine the internal cylinder bore and piston for signs of scoring or wear, and if evident renew the complete slave cylinder. If the slave cylinder is in a satisfactory condition, obtain a new set of rubber seals before reassembling. Never re-use the old seals as they will have deteriorated with use even though this may not be apparent during a visual inspection.

5   Before reassembly begins, lubricate all the internal parts and the slave cylinder bore with clean hydraulic fluid and make sure that they are assembled wet.

6   Insert the spring into the cylinder bore, large end first, followed by the cup filler, piston seal and piston. The lip of the piston seal must be toward the spring.

7   Smear the inside of the rubber dust cover with rubber grease and place it in position over the cylinder bore. Ensure that the lips on the dust cover engage with the groove in the cylinder body.

8   The assembled cylinder can now be refitted to the car as described in Section 8.

10 Clutch pedal – removal and refitting

1   Release the retaining buttons and lift out the trim panel from under the dashboard.

2   Detach and withdraw the face level vent air supply tube.

3   Extract the split pin and remove the clevis pin securing the clutch master cylinder pushrod to the pedal.

4   Extract the split pin and slide the large flat washer off the clutch pedal end of the cross-shaft.

5   Release the return spring from the pedal and slide the pedal off the cross-shaft.

6   Inspect the pedal bushes for signs of wear and renew them if necessary.

7   Refitting the clutch pedal is the reverse sequence to removal.

11 Fault diagnosis – clutch

There are four main faults to which the clutch and release mechanism are prone. They may occur by themselves, or in conjunction with any of the other faults. They are clutch squeal, slip, spin and judder.

Clutch squeal

If on taking up the drive or when changing gear the clutch squeals, this is indicative of a badly worn clutch release bearing.

As well as regular wear due to normal use, wear of the clutch release bearing is much accentuated if the clutch is ridden or held down for long periods in gear with the engine running. To minimise wear of this component, the car should always be taken out of gear at traffic lights and for similar hold ups.

The clutch release bearing is not an expensive item but difficult to get at.

Clutch slip

Clutch slip is a self-evident condition which occurs when the clutch friction plate is badly worn, oil or grease have got onto the flywheel or pressure plate faces, or the pressure plate itself is faulty.

The reason for clutch slip is that due to one of the faults above, there is either insufficient pressure from the pressure plate, or insufficient friction from the friction plate to ensure solid drive.

If small amounts of oil get onto the clutch, they will be burnt off under the heat of the clutch engagement and in the process, gradually darken the linings. Excessive oil on the clutch will burn off leaving a carbon deposit which can cause quite bad slip, or fierceness, spin and judder.

If clutch slip is suspected, and confirmation of this condition is required, there are several tests which can be made.

With the engine in second or third gear and pulling lightly, sudden depression of the accelerator pedal may cause the engine to increase its speed without any increase in road speed. Easing off on the accelerator will then give a definite drop in engine speed without the car slowing.

In extreme cases of clutch slip, the engine will race under normal

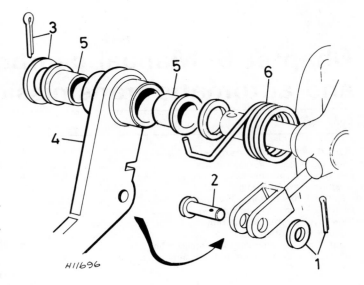

Fig. 5.7 Clutch pedal assembly (Sec 10)

1	Pushrod retaining	4	Clutch pedal
	split pin and washer	5	Pedal bushes
2	Clevis pin	6	Return spring
3	Pedal retaining split		
	pin and washer		

acceleration conditions.

If slip is due to oil or grease on the linings, a temporary cure can sometimes be effected by squirting carbon tetrachloride into the clutch. The permanent cure is of course to renew the clutch driven plate and trace and rectify the oil leak.

Clutch spin

Clutch spin is a condition which occurs when there is a leak in the clutch hydraulic actuating mechanism, there is an obstruction in the clutch, either in the first motion shaft or in the operating lever itself, or the oil may have partially burnt off the clutch lining and have left a resinous deposit, which is causing the clutch disc to stick to the pressure plate or flywheel.

The reason for clutch spin is that due to any, or a combination of, the faults just listed, the clutch pressure plate is not completely freeing from the centre plate even with the clutch pedal fully depressed.

If clutch spin is suspected, the condition can be confirmed by extreme difficulty in engaging first or reverse gear from rest, difficulty in changing gear, and very sudden take up of the clutch drive at the fully depressed end of the clutch pedal travel as the clutch is released.

Check the clutch master cylinder and slave cylinder and the connecting hydraulic pipe for leaks. Fluid in one of the rubber dust covers fitted over the end of either the master or slave cylinder is a sure sign of a leaking piston seal.

If these points are checked and found to be in order, then the fault lies internally in the clutch and it will be necessary to remove the clutch for examination.

Clutch judder

Clutch judder is a self-evident condition which occurs when the gearbox or engine mountings have become soft or worn, when there is oil on the face of the clutch linings, or when there is excessive run-out of the flywheel.

The reason for clutch judder is that due to one or more of the faults just listed, the clutch pressure plate is not freeing smoothly from the friction disc and is snatching. Clutch judder normally occurs when the clutch pedal is released in first or reverse gears and the whole car shudders as it moves off from rest.

Chapter 6 Manual gearbox and automatic transmission

Contents

Specifications

Manual gearbox
Type .... Four forward speeds, one reverse; synchromesh fitted to all forward speeds

Gear ratios
Fourth (top) 1.00:1
Third 1.30:1
Second 1.92:1
First 3.11:1
Reverse 3.42:1

Lubricant
Type .... SAE 90EP hypoid gear oil
Capacity .... 1.5 pints (0.85 litres)

Tolerances
2nd and 3rd gear endfloat on bushes .... 0.002 to 0.006 in (0.050 to 0.152 mm)
Endfloat of bushes on mainshaft .... 0.004 to 0.006 in (0.101 to 0.152 mm)
Laygear needle roller retaining rings fitted depth:
   Inner .... 0.840 to 0.850 in (21.336 to 21.590 mm)
   Outer .... 0.010 to 0.015 in (0.254 to 0.381 mm)
Centre bearing-to-circlip endfloat .... 0.000 to 0.002 in (0.000 to 0.050 mm)
Reverse idler gear bush fitted depth .... Flush to 0.010 in (0.254 mm) below gear face

Torque wrench settings

	lbf ft	Nm
Bellhousing-to-gearbox retaining bolts	28 to 30	37 to 40
Rear extension-to-gearbox retaining bolts	18 to 20	24 to 27
Drive flange nut	90 to 100	122 to 135

Automatic transmission
Type .... Borg Warner model 65

Gear ratios
First 2.39:1
Second 1.45:1
Third 1.00:1
Reverse 2.09:1

Torque converter
Diameter .... 9.5 in (240 mm)
Ratio range .... 1:1 to 2.3:1

Automatic transmission fluid

Type	Automatic transmission fluid type G
Capacity:	
Total	11.5 pints (6.5 litres)
Refill after draining	5 pints (3 litres)

Torque wrench settings

	lbf ft	Nm
Converter-to-driveplate bolts	28	37
Oil pan-to-transmission case bolts	7	9.4
Starter inhibitor switch retaining bolt	5	6

PART A – MANUAL GEARBOX

1 General description

The manual gearbox contains four forward and one reverse gear. Synchromesh is fitted to all four forward gears.

The gearchange lever is mounted on the extension housing and operates the selector mechanism in the gearbox by a long shaft. When the gearchange lever is moved sideways, the shaft is rotated so that the pins in the gearbox end of the shaft locate in the appropriate selector fork. Forward or rearward movement of the gearchange lever moves the selector fork, which in turn moves the synchromesh unit outer sleeve until the gear is firmly engaged. When reverse gear is selected, a pin on the selector shaft engages with a lever, and this in turn moves the reverse idler gear into mesh with the laygear reverse gear and mainshaft. The direction of rotation of the mainshaft is thereby reversed.

The gearbox input shaft is splined and it is onto these splines that the clutch driven plate is located. The gearbox end of the input shaft is in constant mesh with the laygear cluster, and the gears formed on the laygear are in constant mesh with the gears on the mainshaft with the exception of the reverse gear. The gears on the mainshaft are able to rotate freely which means that when the neutral position is selected the mainshaft does not rotate.

When the gearchange lever moves the synchromesh unit outer sleeve via the selector fork, the baulk ring first moves and friction caused by the conical surfaces meeting takes up initial rotational movement until the mainshaft and gear are both rotating at the same speed. This condition achieved, the sleeve is able to slide over the dog teeth of the selected gear and thereby gives a firm drive. The synchromesh unit inner hub is splined to the mainshaft, and because the outer sleeve is splined to the inner hub, engine torque is passed to the mainshaft and propeller shaft.

2 Gearbox – removal and refitting

1   The gearbox can be removed in unit with the engine as described in Chapter 1, or removed separately from under the car as described in the following paragraphs.

2   Disconnect the battery earth terminal.

3   Jack up the front of the car and support it on axle stands if a ramp or pit is not available. The higher the car is off the ground, the easier it will be to work underneath.

4   If the gearbox is being removed for repair or overhaul, it is advisable to drain the oil at this stage. Undo and remove the gearbox drain plug and allow the oil to drain into a suitable container. When all the oil has drained, refit the drain plug.

5   Remove the clutch master cylinder filler cap, place a thin piece of polythene over the filler neck and refit the cap. This will prevent loss of hydraulic fluid during subsequent operations.

6   Undo and remove the clutch hydraulic pipe and extension bleed tube from their unions at the rear of the slave cylinder.

7   Undo and remove the six nuts, and washers securing each exhaust front pipe flange to the manifold.

8   From underneath the car, undo and remove the nut and bolt securing the exhaust front pipe steady bracket to the bellhousing (photo). Move the exhaust pipes to one side and tie them out of the way.

9   Undo and remove the four nuts and bolts securing the gearbox and propeller shaft drive flanges. Move the front of the propeller shaft to one side and tie it to the torsion bar.

10 Undo and remove the bolt and spring washer that secure the

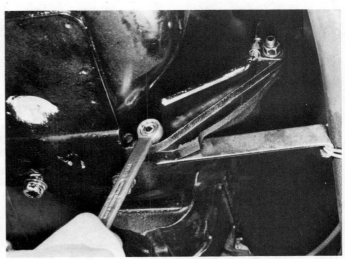

2.8 Release the exhaust pipe steady bracket from the bellhousing

2.10 Undo the retaining bolt and withdraw the speedometer cable clamp and cable

speedometer cable retaining clamp to the side of the gearbox extension (photo). Note that the bolt also retains the reversing light switch wiring support clip. Lift away the speedometer cable retaining clamp and carefully withdraw the cable.

11 Release the grommet in the floor pan above the gearbox extension and detach the reversing light switch wires at the connector.

12 Make a note of the electrical cable connections to the starter motor solenoid, detach the cables and undo and remove the two bolts and spring washers that secure the starter motor. Carefully lift away the starter.

H13541

Fig. 6.1 Sectional view of the manual gearbox (Sec 1)

1 Input shaft	26 O-ring	41 Seal	56 Gear bush
2 Circlip	27 Yoke pin	42 End ball-bearing	57 3rd speed gear
3 Front ball-bearing	28 Gear lever yoke	43 Thrust washer	58 Gear bush
4 Snap ring	29 Seat	44 Mainshaft	59 2nd speed gear
5 Gear selector shaft	30 Dust cover	45 Gearbox rear extension	60 Thrust washer
6 Gearbox case	31 Lower gear lever	46 Speedometer wheel	61 Circlip
7 Top cover	32 Seal	47 Circlip	62 Drain plug
8 Spacer	33 Upper gear lever	48 Selective washer	63 Baulk ring
9 Top cover bolt	34 Bush	49 Snap ring	64 Retaining ring
10 3rd and 4th speed synchromesh hub	35 Anti-rattle spring	50 Centre ball-bearing	65 Needle roller bearing
11 Spring	36 Anti-rattle plunger	51 Layshaft dowel	66 Laygear preload springs
12 Ball	37 End cover	52 Retaining ring	67 Layshaft
13 3rd and 4th speed operating sleeve	38 Self-locking nut	53 Rear thrust washer	68 Thrust washer
14 Selector shaft pin	39 Flange washer	54 Split collar	69 Needle roller bearing
15 Interlock spool plate	40 Flange and stone-guard assembly	55 Thrust washer	70 Circlip backing washer
16 Selective washer			
17 Interlock spool			
18 Reverse operating lever			
19 Selector shaft roll pin			
20 Mainshaft reverse gear and 1st/2nd operating sleeve			
21 Baulk ring			
22 1st speed gear			
23 Thrust washer			
24 Detent plunger			
25 Plug			

2.14 Undo and remove the two bolts securing the sump connecting plate to the bellhousing

2.15 Undo and remove the rear crossmember-to-bodyframe retaining bolts

13 Using a jack support the weight of the engine and gearbox. Position the jack under the rear of the sump with a piece of wood between jack and sump.

14 Undo and remove the two bolts, plain and spring washers that secure the sump connecting plate to the underside of the gearbox bellhousing (photo).

15 Undo and remove the two bolts and washers that secure the gearbox rear crossmember to the underside of the bodyframe (photo).

16 Place the gear lever in the neutral position and then lower the engine and gearbox assembly until the gear lever retaining cover can be reached from beneath the car. Press down the cover and turn it anti-clockwise to release its bayonet fixing. Lift the gear lever up until it is clear of the housing and allow it to lie to one side. Watch out for the anti-rattle plunger and spring which may fly out of the gear lever ball as the lever is lifted out. If the plunger stays in place, remove it, otherwise it may drop out and get lost. Undo and remove the oil separator from the engine (see Fig. 1.2, item 9). Also remove the servo vacuum pipe from the inlet manifold and remove the retaining clip from the cylinder head.

17 Undo and remove the nuts, bolts and spring washers that secure the bellhousing to the engine endplate. Note that the engine earth strap is retained by one of the nuts and bolts on the right-hand side of the bellhousing. Before removing all the retaining nuts and bolts, make sure that the gearbox is supported to avoid straining the input shaft.

H 13342

Fig. 6.2 Exploded view of the manual gearbox (Sec 3)

1 Gearbox case
2 Oil filler/level plug
3 Spacer
4 Gaskets
5 Top cover
6 Top cover bolt
7 Gasket
8 Plug
9 Detent plunger
10 Detent spring
11 Rear extension
12 End cover
13 Reversing light switch
14 Reverse lift plate
15 Oil seal
16 Interlock spool
17 Selector shaft roll pin
18 Reverse operating lever pin
19 Reverse operating lever
20 Gear selector shaft
21 Magnet
22 Interlock spool plate

23 Retaining clip
24 Seal
25 Housing
26 O-ring
27 Speedometer pinion
28 Gear lever yoke
29 Seat
30 Spring
31 Anti-rattle plunger
32 Lower gear lever
33 Upper gear lever
34 Dust cover washer
35 Dust cover
36 Knob
37 Drain plug
38 Reverse idler spindle
      locating screw
39 Reverse idler spindle
40 Reverse idler gear bush
41 Reverse idler gear
42 Reverse idler distance-
      piece

43 3rd/4th speed selector
      forks
44 1st/2nd speed selector
      forks
45 Selector fork shaft
46 Circlip
47 Backing washer
48 Snap ring
49 Ball-bearing
50 Baulk ring
51 Ball
52 Spring
53 3rd/4th speed synchromesh
      sleeve
54 3rd/4th speed operating
      sleeve
55 Baulk ring
56 Mainshaft circlip
57 3rd speed gear thrust
      washer
58 3rd speed gear

59 Gear bush
60 Selector washer
61 Gear bush
62 2nd speed gear
63 Thrust washer
64 Baulk ring
65 Ball
66 Spring
67 1st/2nd speed operating
      sleeve
68 Mainshaft reverse gear
69 Baulk ring
70 Split collar
71 1st speed gear
72 Thrust washer
73 Mainshaft centre bearing
74 Snap ring
75 Selective washer
76 Circlip
77 Speedometer wheel
78 Oil flinger

79 Front thrust washer
80 Bearing outer retaining
      ring
81 1st motion shaft
      (input shaft)
82 Needle roller bearing
83 Mainshaft
84 Washer
85 Ball-bearing
86 Drive flange
87 Washer
88 Self-locking nut
89 Laygear cluster
90 Bearing retaining
      inner ring
91 Needle rollers
92 Rear thrust washer
93 Layshaft
94 Layshaft dowel
95 Laygear preload
      springs

2.18 After removing the bellhousing bolts, withdraw the gearbox from the engine

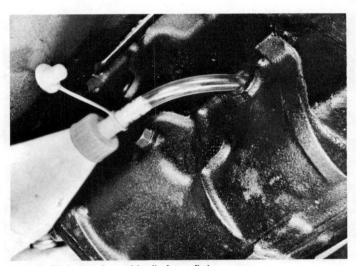

2.19 Refill the gearbox with oil after refitting

18 Lower the rear of the engine until there is sufficient clearance between the top of the bellhousing and the underside of the body. Slide the gearbox rearwards until the input shaft is clear of the clutch assembly and then lower it to the ground (photo).

19 Refitting the gearbox is the reverse sequence to removal, bearing in mind the following points:

(a) Smear a trace of high melting point grease on the gearbox input shaft splines before refitting
(b) Refill the gearbox with the specified type and quantity of oil (photo)
(c) Bleed the clutch hydraulic system as described in Chapter 5

---

3 Gearbox – dismantling

1 Before commencing work, clean the exterior of the gearbox thoroughly with a water soluble degreasing solvent or paraffin. After the solvent has been applied and allowed to stand for a time, a vigorous jet of water will wash off the solvent together with all the oil, grease and dirt. Finally wipe down the exterior of the unit with a dry lint-free cloth.

2 Begin dismantling by removing the pushrod from the clutch slave cylinder (photo).

3 Using a screwdriver or a pair of pliers, release the slave cylinder retaining wire clips from the flange on the bellhousing and slide out the slave cylinder (photos).

3.2 Remove the pushrod from the slave cylinder

3.3a Release the retaining wire clip ...

3.3b ... and slide out the cylinder

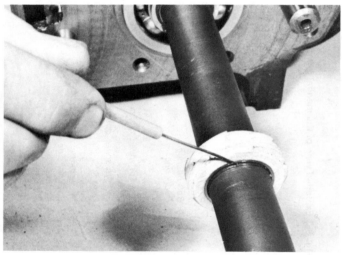

3.25 Mark the speedometer gear position on the mainshaft

4   Disengage the clutch release arm from the release bearing and from the fulcrum pin on the bellhousing. Slide the release bearing off the input shaft front end cover and lift away the release lever.

5   Undo and remove the two nuts and washers that secure the rubber mounting on the rear crossmember to the gearbox extension housing. Lift away the crossmember assembly.

6   Undo and remove the five bolts that secure the bellhousing to the gearbox casing. Note that on early gearboxes the lowermost bolt has a plain copper washer whereas the remaining bolts have spring washers.

7   Lift away the bellhousing. Collect the three laygear preload springs and the paper gasket from the front of the gearbox casing.

8   Undo and remove the nine bolts and spring washers that secure the top cover to the main casing.

9   Lift off the top cover and remove the paper gasket.

10   Note which way up the interlock spool plate is fitted and lift it from the top of the main casing.

11   Undo and remove the one bolt and spring washer that secure the reverse lift plate to the rear extension. Lift away the lift plate. Also unscrew the reversing light switch.

12   Using a screwdriver, carefully remove the rear extension end cover.

13   Hold the mainshaft drive flange in a vice and, using a socket wrench, undo and remove the locknut and washer.

14   Tap the driveflange from the end of the mainshaft.

15   Lift out the speedometer drive pinion and housing assembly from the rear extension.

16   Make a special note of the location of the selector shaft pegs and interlock spool so that there will be no mistakes on reassembly.

17   Using a suitable diameter parallel pin punch, carefully remove the roll pin from the bellhousing end of the selector shaft. Lift off the selector shaft rubber boot.

18   Undo and remove the eight bolts and spring washers that secure the rear extension to the gearbox casing.

19   Draw the rear extension rearwards whilst at the same time feeding the interlock spool from the selector shaft.

20   With the rear extension and selector shaft away from the gearbox casing, lift out the interlock spool.

21   Recover the paper gasket from the rear face of the gearbox casing.

22   If oil was leaking from the end of the rear extension, or the bearing requires renewal, the oil seal must be removed and discarded. It must never be refitted but always renewed. Ease it out with a screwdriver, noting which way round the lip is fitted.

23   To remove the bearing, obtain a long metal drift and tap it out working from inside the rear extension. Note which way round the bearing is fitted as indicated by the lettering.

24   Slide the washer from over the end of the mainshaft.

25   Mark the position of the speedometer drivegear by scribing a line on the mainshaft (photo).

26   Using a tapered but blunt drift, drive the speedometer drivegear

from the mainshaft. **Caution:** *Beware, because it is very tight and can break.*

27 Using a suitable diameter drift, tap out the selector fork shaft towards the front of the gearbox casing.

28 Note the location of the two forward gear selector forks and lift these from the synchromesh sleeve.

29 Using a suitable diameter drift, tap out the layshaft working from the front of the gearbox casing. This is because there is a layshaft restraining pin at the rear to stop it rotating.

30 Locate the gearbox to allow the laygear cluster to drop into the bottom of the casing.

31 Using a small drift placed on the bearing outer track, tap out the gearbox input shaft. If necessary, recover the caged needle roller bearing from the end of the shaft. Also recover the 4th gear baulk ring.

32 The mainshaft may now be drifted rearwards slightly, sufficiently to move the bearing and locating circlip. Using a screwdriver between the circlip and casing, ease the bearing out of its bore and from its locating shoulder on the mainshaft. Lift away the bearing from the end of the mainshaft.

33 The complete mainshaft may now be lifted away through the top of the gearbox main casing.

34 Unscrew the dowel bolt that locks the reverse idler shaft to the gearbox casing. Lift away the bolt and spring washer.

35 Using a small drift, tap the reverse idler shaft rearwards, noting the hole in the shaft into which the dowel bolt locates.

36 Note which way round the reverse idler is fitted and lift it along with its distance sleeve from the casing.

37 Lift out the laygear cluster, noting that the larger gear is toward the front of the casing.

38 Recover the two thrust washers, noting that the tags locate in grooves in the gearbox casing.

4 Gearbox – examination

1 The gearbox has been stripped, presumably, because of wear or malfunction, possibly excessive noise, ineffective synchromesh or failure to stay in a selected gear. The cause of most gearbox ailments is failure of the ball-bearings on the input or mainshaft and wear on the baulk rings, both the cone surfaces and dogs. The nose of the mainshaft which runs in the needle roller bearing in the input shaft is also subject to wear. This can prove very expensive as the mainshaft would need replacement and this represents about 20% of the total cost of a new gearbox.

2 Examine the teeth of all gears for signs of uneven or excessive wear and, of course, chipping. If a gear on the mainshaft requires renewal check that the corresponding laygear is not equally damaged. If it is, the whole laygear may need to be renewed.

3 All gears should be a good running fit on the shaft with no signs of rocking. The hubs should not be a sloppy fit on the splines.

4 Selector forks should be examined for signs of wear or ridging on the faces which are in contact with the operating sleeve.

5 Check for wear on the selector rod and interlock spool.

6 The ball-bearings may not be obviously worn, but if one has gone to the trouble of dismantling the gearbox it would be short sighted not to renew them. The same applies to the four baulk rings, although for these the mainshaft has to be completely dismantled for the new ones to be fitted.

7 The input shaft bearing retainer is fitted with an oil seal and this should be removed if there are any signs that oil has leaked past it into the clutch housing or, of course, if it is obviously damaged. The rear extension has an oil seal at the rear as well as a ball-bearing race. If either have worn or oil has leaked past the seal the parts should be renewed.

8 Check for wear, scoring or pitting of the layshaft needle roller bearings. Also check the layshaft for ridging or deterioration of the surface hardening.

9 Before finally deciding to dismantle the mainshaft and replace parts, it is advisable to make enquiries regarding the availability of parts and their cost. It may still be worth considering an exchange gearbox even at this stage. The gearbox should be reassembled before exchange.

5 Input shaft – dismantling and reassembly

1 Place the input shaft in a vice, splined end upwards, and with a pair of circlip pliers, remove the circlip which retains the ball-bearing in place. Lift away the spacer.

2 With the bearing resting on the top of the open jaws of the vice and with the splined end upwards, tap the shaft through the bearing with a soft-faced hammer. Note that the offset circlip groove in the outer track of the bearing is towards the front of the input shaft.

3 Lift away the oil flinger.

4 Remove the circlip from the old bearing outer track and transfer it to the new bearing.

5 Refit the oil flinger and, with the aid of a block of wood and vice, tap the bearing into place. Make sure it is the right way round.

6 Finally refit the spacer and bearing retaining circlip (photo).

6 Mainshaft – dismantling and reassembly

1 The component parts of the mainshaft are shown in Fig. 6.3.

2 Lift the 3rd and 4th gear synchromesh hub and operating sleeve

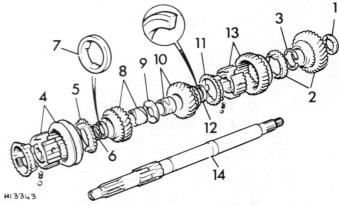

Fig. 6.3 Exploded view of the mainshaft assembly (Sec 6)

1	Thrust washer	8	3rd speed gear and bush
2	1st speed gear and baulk ring	9	Selective washer
3	Split collar	10	2nd speed gear and bush
4	3rd and 4th speed synchro unit	11	Baulk ring
5	Baulk ring	12	Thrust washer
6	Mainshaft circlip	13	1st/2nd speed synchro unit
7	3rd speed gear thrust washer	14	Mainshaft

5.6 Correct fitting of input shaft bearing, outer track circlip and retaining circlip

assembly from the end of the mainshaft.

3   Remove the 3rd gear baulk ring.

4   Using a small screwdriver, ease the 3rd gear retaining circlip from its groove in the mainshaft. Lift away the circlip.

5   Lift away the 3rd gear thrust washer.

6   Slide the 3rd gear and bush from the mainshaft, followed by the thrust washer. Note this is a selective thrust washer.

7   Slide the 2nd gear and bush from the mainshaft followed by the grooved washer. Note which way round it is fitted.

8   Detach the 2nd gear baulk ring from inside the 2nd and 1st gear synchromesh hub and lift away.

9   Slide the 2nd gear and 1st gear synchromesh hub and reverse gear sleeve assembly from the mainshaft. Recover the 1st gear baulk ring.

10 Using a small electrician's screwdriver, lift out the two split collars from their groove in the mainshaft.

11 Slide the 1st gear mainshaft washer from the mainshaft and follow this with the 1st gear.

12 The mainshaft is now completely dismantled.

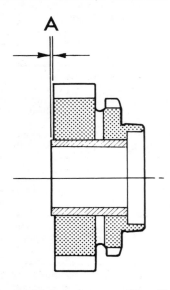

Fig. 6.4 Mainshaft gear endfloat (Sec 6)

A = 0.002 to 0.006 in (0.050 to 0.152 mm)

13 Before reassembling, refer to Fig. 6.4 and measure the endfloat of the 2nd and 3rd gears on their respective bushes. The endfloat should be within the limits quoted in the Specifications. Obtain a new bush, if necessary, to achieve the correct endfloat.

14 Temporarily refit the 2nd gear washer, oil grooved face away from the mainshaft shoulder, to the mainshaft. Assemble to the mainshaft the 3rd gear bush, selective washer, 2nd gear bush, 3rd gear thrust washer with its oil grooved face to the bush, and fit the 3rd gear mainshaft circlip. Measure the endfloat of the bushes on the mainshaft, which should be within the limits quoted in the Specifications. Obtain a new selective washer to obtain the correct endfloat. Remove the parts from the mainshaft.

15 To reassemble, slide the 1st gear onto the mainshaft followed by the washer (photo).

16 Fit the two halves of the split collar into the groove in the mainshaft and push the 1st gear hard up against the collar (photo). If the split collars are marked on one side with orange dye (as is the case on some gearboxes), then the orange marked side must face away from the 1st speed gear.

17 Fit the baulk ring onto the cone of the 1st gear (photo).

18 Slide the 1st and 2nd gear synchromesh hub and reverse gear sleeve on the mainshaft and engage it with the baulk ring (photo).

19 Fit the 2nd gear baulk ring to the synchromesh hub (photo).

20 Fit the 2nd gear washer onto the end of the mainshaft splines so that the oil grooved face is towards the front of the mainshaft (photo).

21 Slide the 2nd gear bush onto the mainshaft (photo).

22 Fit the 2nd gear onto the bush on the mainshaft and engage the taper with the internal taper of the baulk ring (photo).

23 Fit the 2nd and 3rd gear selective washer (photo).

24 Slide the 3rd gear bush onto the mainshaft (photo).

25 Fit the 3rd gear onto the bush on the mainshaft, the cone facing the front of the mainshaft (photo).

26 Slide the 3rd gear thrustwasher onto the mainshaft splines (photo).

27 Ease the 3rd gear retaining circlip into its groove in the mainshaft. Make quite sure it is fully seated (photo).

28 Fit the 3rd gear baulk ring onto the cone of the 3rd gear (photo).

29 Finally slide on the 3rd and 4th gear synchromesh hub and operating sleeve assembly and engage it with the baulk ring (photo). Fit the remaining baulk ring to the other side of the synchromesh hub (photo).

30 To keep the component parts of the mainshaft together during gearbox reassembly, it is advisable to hook a couple of rubber bands around the gears (photo), or tie them in place with string.

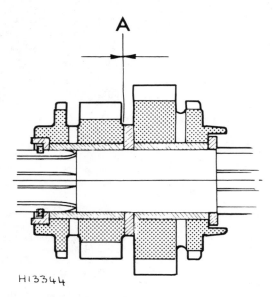

Fig. 6.5 Mainshaft bush endfloat (Sec 6)

A = 0.004 to 0.006 in (0.101 to 0.152 mm)

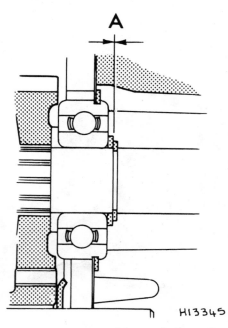

Fig. 6.6 Mainshaft centre bearing-to-circlip endfloat (Sec 6)

A = 0.000 to 0.002 in (0.000 to 0.050 mm)

6.15 Slide the 1st gear and thrust washer onto the mainshaft

6.16 Fit the two halves of the split collar into the mainshaft groove and slide 1st gear over them

6.17 Fit the baulk ring onto the cone of 1st gear

6.18 Slide on the 1st and 2nd speed synchro hub ...

6.19 ... followed by the baulk ring

6.20 Position the 2nd gear washer on the mainshaft with the oil groove facing the front of the shaft

6.21 Slide on the 2nd gear bush ...

6.22 ... followed by 2nd gear

6.23 Fit the 2nd and 3rd gear selective washer

6.24 Slide on the 3rd gear bush ...

6.25 ... followed by 3rd gear

6.26 Place the 3rd gear thrust washer onto the mainshaft splines ...

6.28 Fit the baulk ring onto the 3rd gear cone ...

6.27 ... and then ease the retaining circlip into its groove

6.29a ... and then slide on the 3rd and 4th synchro hub

6.29b ... and baulk ring

6.30 Secure the assembled mainshaft with rubber bands or string to retain the components in position

7   Gearbox − reassembly

1   Check that the magnet is in position in the gearbox casing (photo).
2   Position the laygear needle roller bearing inner retainers into the laygear bore. Apply multi-purpose grease to the ends of the laygear and fit the needle rollers. Retain the needle rollers in position with the outer retainers (photos).
3   Make up a piece of tube the same diameter as the layshaft, and the length of the laygear plus thrust washers. Slide the tube into the laygear. This will retain the needle rollers in position. Apply grease to the thrust washers and fit to the ends of the laygear. The tags must face outwards (photos).
4   Carefully lower the laygear into the bottom of the gearbox casing (photo).
5   Fit the reverse gear operating lever to the operating lever pivot. Hold the reverse idler in its approximate fitted position and slide in the idler shaft, drilled end first (photo).
6   Carefully line up the drilled hole in the idler shaft and gearbox casing and refit the dowel bolt and spring washer (photo).
7   The assembled mainshaft may now be fitted into the gearbox casing (photo).
8   Ease the mainshaft bearing up the mainshaft, circlip offset on the outer track towards the rear (photo).
9   Place a metal lever in the position shown in the photo, so

7.1 Ensure that the magnet (arrowed) is in place before reassembly

7.2a Retain the laygear needle rollers with grease ...

7.2b ... and refit the outer retainers

7.3a Slide a dummy layshaft into the laygear to retain the needle rollers ...

7.3b ... and then position the thrust washers on the laygear with the tags facing outwards

7.4 Carefully lower the laygear into the gearbox casing

7.5 Fit the reverse gear lever to the pivot, engage the idler gear with the lever and slide in the shaft

7.6 Line up the hole in the reverse idler shaft and refit the dowel bolt

7.7 Carefully insert the mainshaft into the casing

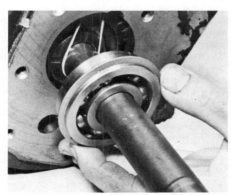

7.8 Slide the bearing up the mainshaft, circlip toward the rear

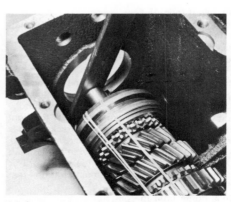

7.9 Support the mainshaft with a metal bar and drive the bearing fully home

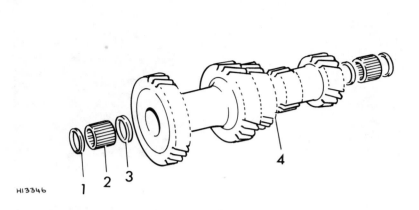

Fig. 6.7 Laygear and bearing assemblies (Sec 7)

1   Bearing outer retaining ring
2   Needle rollers
3   Bearing inner retaining ring
4   Laygear

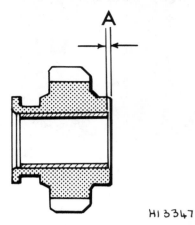

Fig. 6.8 Reverse idler gear bush location (Sec 7)

A = 0.000 to 0.010 in (0.000 to 0.254 mm)

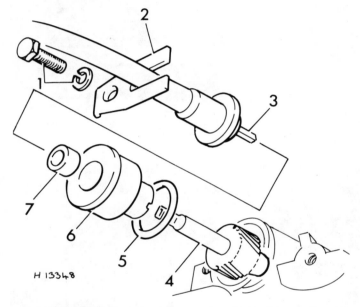

Fig. 6.9 Speedometer drive assembly (Secs 2, 3 and 7)

1   Bolt and spring washer
2   Retaining clip
3   Inner cable
4   Speedometer pinion
5   O-ring
6   Housing
7   Seal

supporting the mainshaft spigot (photo).

10 Using a suitable diameter tube, carefully drift the mainshaft bearing into position in the rear casing.

11 Fit the hexagon spacer onto the end of the mainshaft (photo).

12 Lubricate the needle roller bearing and slide it onto the end of the mainshaft (photo).

13 Fit the input shaft to the front of the gearbox casing, taking care to engage the baulk ring with the synchromesh hub. Remove the string or rubber bands used to keep the mainshaft gears together (photo).

14 Tap the input bearing until the circlip is hard up against the front gearbox casing. Check that the mainshaft bearing outer track circlip is hard up against the rear casing. Refit the washer and circlip (photos).

15 Invert the gearbox. Fit the pin into the drilled hole in the layshaft and carefully insert the layshaft from the rear of the main casing. This will push out the previously inserted tube. The pin must be to the rear of the main casing (photo).

16 Push the layshaft fully home until the pin contacts the gearbox casing. Turn the layshaft so that the pin is in a vertical position.

17 Fit the 1st and 2nd gear selector fork to the synchromesh sleeve.

18 Fit the 3rd and 4th gear selector fork to the synchromesh sleeve (photo).

19 Slide the selector fork shaft from the front through the two selector forks and into the rear of the main casing (photo).

20 Place the speedometer drivegear onto the mainshaft, and using a tube, drive the gears into its previously noted position (photo).

21 Slide the washer onto the mainshaft until it contacts the shoulder (photo).

22 Position the distance sleeve onto the reverse idler shaft (photo).

23 Fit a new gasket to the rear face of the gearbox casing and retain it in position with a little grease (photo).

24 Place the extension housing bearing into its bore, letters facing outwards, and tap it into position using a tube or socket of suitable diameter.

25 Fit a new rear extension oil seal and tap it into position with the previously used socket. The lip must face inwards.

26 Slide the interlock spool onto the selector shaft, making sure it is the correct way round. This is to give an idea of the final fitted position. Remove the interlock spool again.

27 Place the interlock spool on the selector forks with the flanges correctly engaged (photo).

28 Offer up the gearbox rear extension to the rear of the main casing at the same time feeding the selector shaft through the interlock spool. It will be found necessary to rotate the selector shaft to obtain correct engagement (photos).

29 Secure the rear extension with the eight bolts and spring washers (photo).

30 Refit the spring pin into the end of the selector shaft, ensuring that the ends are equidistant from the shaft (photo).

31 Insert the speedometer driven gear and housing into the rear extension (photo).

32 Refit the reverse lift plate and secure it with the bolt and spring washer.

33 Refit the rear extension end cover and tap it into position with the end of the lip flush with the end of the casing.

34 Fit the drive flange onto the mainshaft splines (photo). Hold the drive flange in a vice and tighten the retaining nut and washer to the specified torque (photo).

35 Refit the reversing light switch to the extension housing (photo).

36 Refit the interlock spool plate in the same position as was noted before removal.

37 Fit a new gasket to the top of the gearbox casing and refit the top cover (photo).

38 Secure the top cover with the nine bolts and spring washers. These should be progressively tightened in a diagonal manner.

39 Fit a new O-ring to the input shaft retainer and refit the retainer (photo).

40 Fit the three layshaft preload springs in their locations on the front of the gearbox casing (photo).

41 Invert the gearbox and support it clear of the bench on blocks (photo). Place a new gasket on the front face and offer up the bellhousing.

42 Refit the five bolts that secure the bellhousing to the main casing.

7.11 Fit the spacer to the front of the mainshaft ...

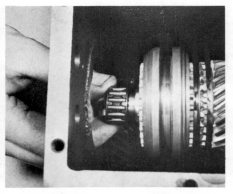

7.12 ... followed by the needle roller bearing

7.13 Insert the input shaft into the front of the casing

7.14a Refit the mainshaft rear bearing washer ...

7.14b ... and circlip

7.15 Insert the layshaft into the casing with the roll pin to the rear and vertical

7.18 Fit the selector forks to the synchromesh sleeves ...

7.19 ... and slide in the selector shaft from front to rear

7.20 Drift the speedometer gear to its previously noted position using a suitable tube

7.21 Slide the washer onto the mainshaft ...

7.22 ... and the distance sleeve onto the reverse idler shaft

7.23 Position a new gasket on the rear of the casing

7.27 Place the interlock spool on the selector forks

7.28a Carefully fit the selector shaft and rear extension ...

7.28b ... rotating the shaft and interlock spool as necessary to obtain correct engagement

7.29 Secure the rear extension with the bolts and washers

7.30 Refit the selector shaft pin ensuring that the ends are equidistant from the shaft

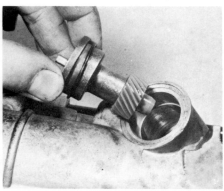

7.31 Insert the speedometer driven gear assembly into the rear extension

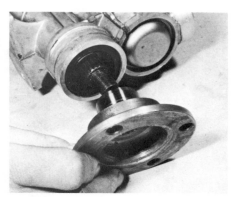

7.34a Fit the drive flange onto the mainshaft ...

7.34b ... and secure with the retaining nut

7.35 Refit the reversing light switch to the rear extension

7.36 Place the interlock spool plate in position ...

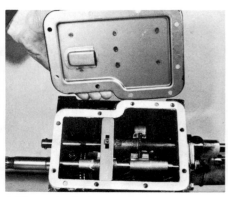

7.37 ... and refit the top cover

7.39 With a new O-ring in place, fit the input shaft retainer into the bellhousing

7.40 Place the three laygear preload springs in their locations ...

7.41 ... and offer up the bellhousing

7.44 Refit the selector shaft rubber boot

7.45 Refit the rear crossmember noting the word 'FRONT' on the mounting

8.2 Lift off the gear lever rubber boot and retaining plate ...

8.3 ... followed by the foam sound proofing

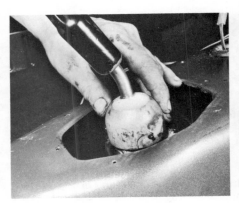

8.4a Press down and turn the cap anti-clockwise ...

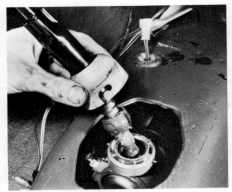

8.4b ... then lift away the gear lever

8.5 Take care not to lose the anti-rattle plunger and spring

Note that on early gearboxes the lowermost bolt has a copper washer. Tighten the bolts to the specified torque.
43 Slide the clutch release bearing assembly onto its guide, at the same time engaging the release lever.
44 Refit the gear selector shaft rubber boot (photo).
45 Refit the gearbox rear crossmember, noting that the rubber mounting is stamped with the word 'FRONT' on its top face (photo).
46 Refit the slave cylinder, retaining wire clip and pushrod.

8 Gear lever – removal and refitting

1 Remove the centre console as described in Chapter 12.

2 Unscrew the self-tapping screws securing the gear lever boot retaining plate to the transmission tunnel. Lift the rubber boot and retaining plate up and off the gear lever (photo).

3 Withdraw the foam soundproofing (photo).

4 Press down and turn the gear lever cap anti-clockwise to release the bayonet fixing and lift out the gear lever assembly (photos).

5 Recover the small anti-rattle spring and plunger from the gear lever ball (photo).

6 Refitting is the reverse sequence to removal. Lubricate the gear lever ball and selector finger with general purpose grease before fitting.

9 Fault diagnosis – manual gearbox

Symptom	Reason(s)
Gearbox noisy in neutral	Input shaft bearings worn Layshaft bearings worn Insufficient oil in gearbox Chipped or broken gear teeth
Gearbox noisy in all gears	Any of the above reasons or, mainshaft bearings worn
Gearbox noisy in one particular gear	Worn, damaged or chipped gear teeth or laygear teeth
Gearbox jumps out of gear	Worn synchromesh hubs or baulk rings Worn detent springs or selector forks Excessive mainshaft endfloat
Ineffective synchromesh	Worn baulk rings or synchromesh hubs
Difficulty in engaging gears	Clutch not releasing fully Gearbox input shaft seized or partially seized in crankshaft spigot bearing Excessive mainshaft endfloat Worn synchromesh hubs

PART B – AUTOMATIC TRANSMISSION

10 General description

The Borg Warner automatic transmission system comprises two main components: A three-element hydrokinetic torque converter coupling capable of torque multiplication at an infinitely variable ratio between 2:1 and 1:1, and a torque speed responsive and hydraulically operated epicyclic gearbox, comprising a planetary gear set providing three forward ratios and reverse gear.

Due to the complexity of the automatic transmission unit, if performance is not up to standard, or overhaul is necessary, it is imperative that this is undertaken by BL main agents who will have special equipment for accurate fault diagnosis and rectification.

The contents of the following Sections are therefore solely general and servicing information.

11 Automatic transmission fluid level – checking

1   Every 3000 miles (5000 km) the automatic transmission fluid level should be checked with the engine and transmission at normal operating temperatures. A road journey of at least half an hour's duration will achieve this.
2   With the vehicle standing on level ground and the engine idling, depress the foot brake and move the selector lever through all gear positions two or three times.
3   Return the selector lever to the P position.
4   Withdraw the transmission dipstick, wipe it clean, re-insert it, withdraw it a second time and read off the level.
5   If necessary add fuid of the specified type to bring the level up to the H mark of the 'HOT' scale. The difference between the L and H marks on the dipstick is $\frac{3}{4}$ pint (0.43 litre). *Do not overfill the transmission.*
6   After topping up, recheck the fluid level.
7   Always keep the area around the dipstick/filler tube clean; dirt particles entering the transmission could cause severe malfunctions.

12 Automatic transmission fluid – draining and refilling

1   It is not normally necessary to drain and refill the automatic transmission fluid unless the unit is being removed from the car for repair, overhaul or exchange.
2   Place the selector lever in the P position and place a suitable container beneath the drain plug located on the transmission oil pan.
3   Undo and remove the drain plug and allow the fluid to drain into

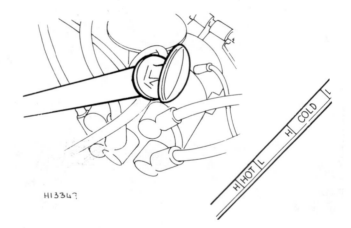

H13347

Fig. 6.10 Automatic transmission dipstick and filler tube (Sec 11)

the container. When all the fluid has drained, refit the drain plug. **Note:** *On certain transmissions a drain plug is not fitted. If this is the case it will be necessary to undo the retaining bolts and remove the oil pan to drain the fluid. Thoroughly clean the exterior of the oil pan before doing this. Absolute cleanliness is essential.*
4   To refill the transmission, withdraw the dipstick and fill the transmission with the specified fluid, through the dipstick/filler tube, until the level reaches the H mark of the 'COLD' scale on the dipstick. A quantity of fluid will remain in the torque converter and valve block and only approximately 5 pints (3 litres) will be required to fill the transmission.
5   After filling, and with the car standing on level ground, start the engine and run it at idling speed.
6   Move the selector lever through all the gear positions two or three times and then return it to the P position.
7   Withdraw the dipstick, wipe it clean, re-insert it, withdraw it a second time and read off the level.
8   If necessary top up until the fluid level reaches the H mark of the 'COLD' scale.
9   After the car has been driven for a journey of at least half an hour's duration, the level should be rechecked as described in Section 11.

13 Automatic transmission – removal and refitting

1   Any suspected faults must be referred to the main agent before unit removal, as with this type of transmission its fault must be confirmed using special equipment before it is removed from the car.
2   As the automatic transmission is relatively heavy, it is best if the car is raised from the ground on ramps, but it is possible to remove the unit if the car is placed on high axle-stands.
3   Disconnect the battery.
4   Disconnect the downshift cable from the throttle linkage at the side of the carburettor.
5   Remove the dipstick from its guide tube.
6   Disconnect the breather pipe from the guide tube.
7   Remove the dipstick guide tube after removing the securing bolt.
8   Detach the exhaust pipe from the manifold.
9   Drain the automatic transmission fluid as described in Section 12.

10 Disconnect the manual selector rod from both the transmission lever and gearchange lever. Lift away the manual selector rod.
11 Disconnect the inhibitor/reversing lamp switch at the multi-connector plugs.
12 Using a scriber or file, mark the propeller shaft and transmission flanges so that they may be refitted in their original positions.
13 Undo and remove the four locknuts and bolts that secure the two flanges together.
14 Lift the front end of the propeller shaft away from the rear of the transmission and tie it to the torsion bar with wire or strong string.
15 Undo and remove the speedometer cable clamp bolt and spring washer on the transmission extension. Lift away the clamp and withdraw the cable.
16 Using a hoist, take the weight of the complete power unit, or alternatively, position a hydraulic jack under the torque converter housing to take the weight of the unit.
17 Undo and remove the two bolts, spring and plain washers that

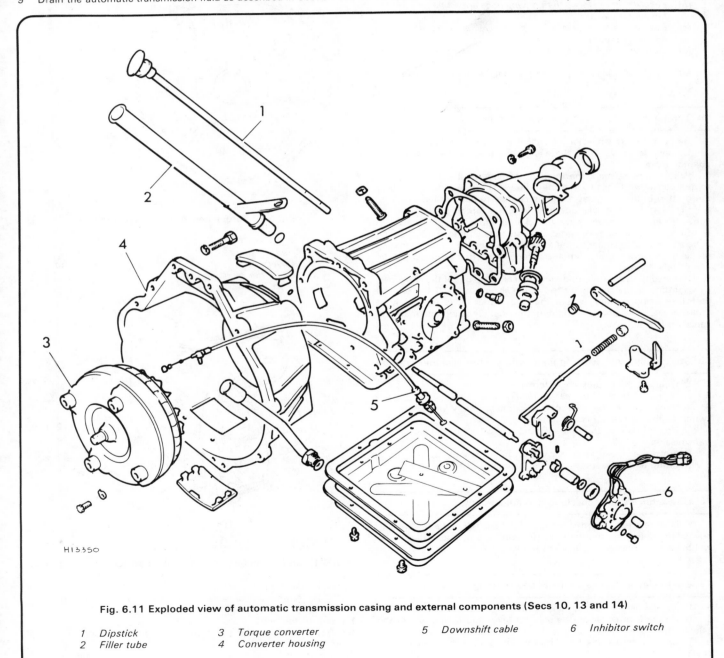

H13350

Fig. 6.11 Exploded view of automatic transmission casing and external components (Secs 10, 13 and 14)

1 Dipstick	3 Torque converter	5 Downshift cable	6 Inhibitor switch
2 Filler tube	4 Converter housing		

secure the rear mounting crossmember to the underside of the body.

18 Carefully lower the transmission so as to provide access to the top.

19 Using a second jack, support the weight of the transmission.

20 Undo and remove the two bolts that secure the sump connecting plate to the converter housing.

21 Undo and remove the remaining nine bolts that secure the converter housing to the transmission adaptor plate.

22 Very carefully withdraw the transmission rearwards until it is clear of the torque converter, and then lift it away from under the car. It is very important that the weight of the transmission is not allowed to hang on the input shaft as the shaft may become damaged.

23 Refitting is the reverse of the removal procedure, but note the following additional points:

(a) Carefully align the converter and front pump driving dogs and slots in the horizontal plane

(b) Ensure that the input shaft driving dogs are also aligned in the horizontal plane

(c) Ensure that the marks on the propeller shaft and transmission flanges are correctly aligned

(d) Observe the specified torque wrench settings where applicable

(e) Refill the transmission with the specified fluid as described in Section 12

14 Torque converter – removal and refitting

1 Remove the transmission as described in Section 13.

2 Remove the cover from the access aperture on the transmission adaptor plate.

3 With a scriber, mark the relative positions of the driveplate and torque converter if these are to be refitted. This will ensure that they are refitted in their original positions relative to each other.

4 Working through the aperture in the adaptor plate, turn the converter and then progressively slacken the four securing bolts.

5 Support the torque converter and completely remove the securing bolts and washers. Lift away the torque converter. Be prepared to mop up fluid that will issue from the torque converter as it cannot be completely drained.

6 Remove the abutment ring from the centre spigot of the converter.

7 Refitting is the reverse of the removal procedure. If the original parts are being refitted, ensure that the marks made previously at removal are in alignment. Tighten the four securing bolts to the specified torque.

15 Starter inhibitor/reversing light switch – removal and refitting

1 Disconnect the battery earth terminal.

2 Jack up the front of the car and support it on axle stands.

3 Working underneath the car, disconnect the wiring from the switch at the multi-plug connectors.

4 Undo and remove the bolt securing the switch to the side of the transmission.

5 Remove the thread protector cap and lift away the switch.

6 Refitting is the reverse sequence to removal.

16 Downshift cable – checking and adjustment

Special test equipment is required for checking and adjusting the downshift cable. This should be carried out by a BL main agent who will have the necessary equipment required.

17 Gear selector lever – removal and refitting

1 Refer to Chapter 12 and remove the centre console.

2 Undo the lock collar on the selector lever and then unscrew the selector lever knob.

3 Undo and remove the three screws that secure the selector gate cover.

4 Remove the selector gate cover and then the carpet.

5 Undo and remove the screws that secure the selector gate

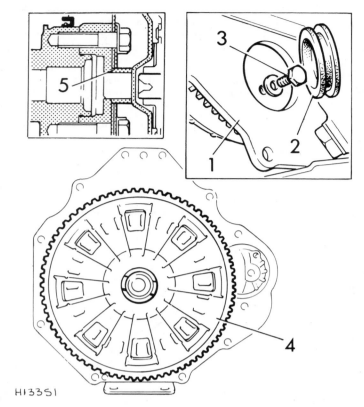

H13351

Fig. 6.12 Torque converter removal (Sec 14)

1 *Adaptor plate*   4 *Converter*
2 *Cover*   5 *Abutment ring*
3 *Converter retaining bolt*

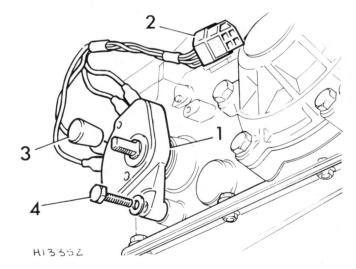

H13352

Fig. 6.13 Starter inhibitor/reversing light switch removal (Sec 15)

1 *Switch*   3 *Protector cap*
2 *Multi-plug connector*   4 *Retaining bolt*

housing to the floor.

6 Disconnect the wiring from the selector gate housing at the push-in connectors.

7 Lift the selector gate housing and release the selector rod-to-selector lever retaining clip. Disconnect the selector lever from the selector rod. Remove the gear selector lever.

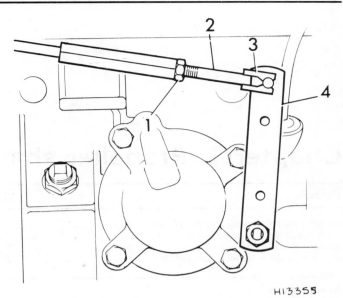

Fig. 6.15 Selector linkage adjustment (Sec 18)

1   Locknut   3   Clip
2   Threaded rod   4   Transmission selector lever

18 Selector linkage – adjustment

1   Jack up the front of the car and support it on axle stands.
2   Move the selector lever to the N position.
3   From underneath the car, slacken the selector rod locknut.
4   Release the clip that secures the selector rod to the transmission selector lever and separate the rod from the lever.
5   Ensure that the transmission selector lever is in the N position, which is the third detent back from the fully forward position.
6   The length of the selector rod is adjusted by screwing the threaded part of the selector rod in or out until the rod can be connected to the selector lever without any tension on the rod.
7   Secure the selector rod to the lever with the retaining clip and tighten the locknut on the rod.
8   Lower the car to the ground and then check the operation of the selector linkage.

19 Fault diagnosis – automatic transmission

Faults in these units are nearly always the result of incorrect adjustment of the selector linkage or downshift cable, or low fluid level. Internal faults can only be diagnosed using special test equipment and with the transmission still in position in the car. This work should be entrusted to a BL main agent or automatic transmission specialist who will have the necessary equipment to test and diagnose a fault in the transmission.

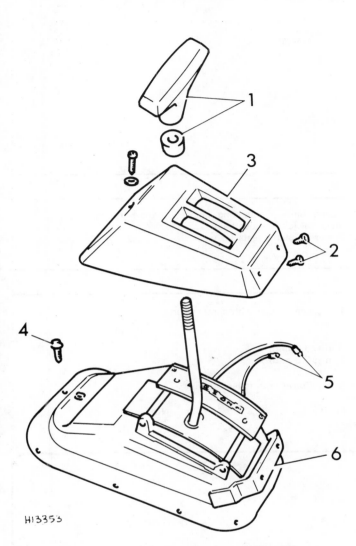

Fig. 6.14 Gear selection lever removal (Sec 17)

1   Gear lever knob and lock   4   Screw
    collar   5   Lamp leads
2   Screws   6   Selector gate housing
3   Selector gate cover

8   Refitting is the reverse of the removal procedure. Check the operation of the gear selector lever and if necessary, adjust the selector linkage as described in Section 18.

Chapter 7 Propeller shaft

Contents

Specifications

Type .... Two-piece tubular with centre bearing

Diameter
Front .... 3 in (76.2 mm)
Rear .... 2 in (50.8 mm)

Universal joints .... Hardy-Spicer with roller bearings

Torque wrench settings

	lbf ft	Nm
Centre bearing mounting bolts	22	29
Front and rear flange bolts	28	37

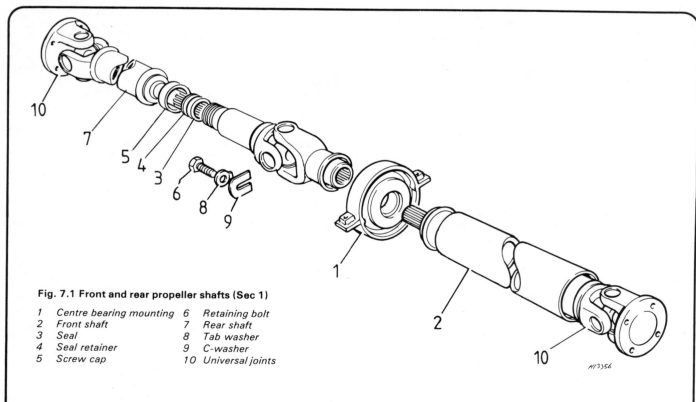

Fig. 7.1 Front and rear propeller shafts (Sec 1)

1	Centre bearing mounting	6	Retaining bolt
2	Front shaft	7	Rear shaft
3	Seal	8	Tab washer
4	Seal retainer	9	C-washer
5	Screw cap	10	Universal joints

H13356

1 General description

Drive is transmitted from the gearbox to the rear axle by means of a finely balanced Hardy-Spicer tubular propeller shaft, split into two halves and supported at the centre by a rubber mounted bearing.

Fitted to the front, centre and rear of the propeller shaft assembly are universal joints which allow for vertical movement of the rear axle and slight movement of the complete power unit on its rubber mountings. Each universal joint comprises a four-legged centre spider, four needle roller bearings and two yokes.

Fore-and-aft movement of the rear axle is absorbed by a sliding spline incorporated in the rear half of the propeller shaft assembly.

The yoke flange of the front universal joint is fitted to the gearbox mainshaft flange with four bolts, spring washers and nuts. The yoke flange on the rear universal joint is secured to the pinion flange on the rear axle in the same way.

2 Propeller shaft – removal and refitting

1 Jack up the rear of the car and support it on firmly based axle stands.

2 The propeller shaft is carefully balanced to fine limits, and it is important that it is refitted in exactly the same position as fitted prior to its removal. Scratch marks on the gearbox, differential pinion and propeller driveshaft flanges for correct realignment when refitting.

3 Support the weight of the front propeller shaft. Undo and remove the four gearbox end flange nuts and bolts (photo).

4 Support the weight of the rear propeller shaft. Undo and remove the four axle end flange nuts and bolts (photo).

5 Undo and remove the two bolts with spring and plain washers that retain the centre bearing mounting to the body brackets (photo).

6 Lift away the propeller shaft assembly from the underside of the car (photo).

7 To separate the two halves of the propeller shaft assembly, first suitably mark the two halves in relation to each other to ensure correct refitting.

8 Bend back the locking washer tab and undo and remove the retaining bolt located in the universal joint yoke adjacent to the centre support bearing. Lift away the C-washer and locking washer.

9 Draw the front propeller shaft away from the rear propeller shaft universal joint splines.

10 Reconnection and refitting the two propeller shaft halves is the reverse sequence to removal, but the following additional points should be noted:

(a) Ensure that the previously made mating marks are aligned when reassembling the two propeller shaft halves, and when refitting the assembly to the car

(b) Tighten the centre bearing and front and rear flange retaining bolts to the specified torque

2.3 Undo and remove the gearbox end flange ...

2.4 ... axle end flange ...

2.5 ... and centre bearing retaining nuts and bolts ...

2.6 ... then lift away the propeller shaft

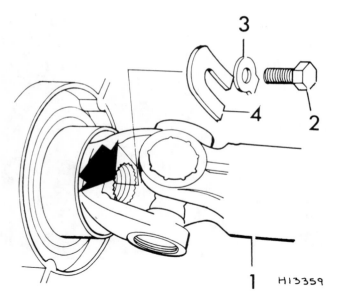

Fig. 7.2 Rear propeller shaft-to-centre bearing attachment (Sec 2)

1   Rear propeller shaft   3   Lockwasher
2   Bolt   4   C-washer

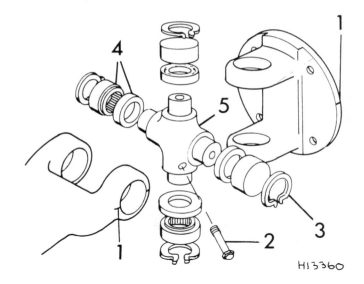

Fig. 7.3 Exploded view of universal joint (Sec 4)

1   Alignment marks on yokes   4   Needle roller bearing
2   Grease nipple (front joint   (complete with seal)
    only)   5   Spider
3   Circlip

3   Universal joints – tests for wear

1   Wear in the needle roller bearings is characterised by vibration in the transmission, clonks on taking up the drive, and in extreme cases of lack of lubrication, metallic squeaking and ultimately grating and shrieking sounds as the bearings break up.

2   To test the universal joints for wear, jack up the rear of the car and securely support it on axle stands.

3   Working under the car, apply leverage between the universal joint yokes using a large screwdriver or flat metal bar. Wear is indicated by movement between the shaft yoke and coupling flange yoke. Check all three universal joints in this way, and if any are worn renew them as described in Section 4.

4   To check the sliding spline on the rear half of the propeller shaft, grip the shaft on either side of the splined sleeve and attempt to turn the shaft in opposite directions. Any excessive movement indicates wear in the spline, which should be investigated as described in Section 6.

5   The centre bearing is a little more difficult to test for wear when mounted on the car. Undo and remove the two support securing bolts, spring and plain washers and allow the propeller shaft centre to hang down. Test the centre bearing for wear by gripping the support and rocking it. If movement is evident the bearing is worn and should be renewed as described in Section 5.

4   Universal joints – overhaul

1   Remove the propeller shaft from the car as described in Section 2.

2   Clean away all traces of dirt and grease from the circlips located on the ends of the spiders. Using a pair of circlip pliers, compress the circlips and hook them out with the aid of a screwdriver. If they are difficult to remove, place a drift between the circlip and tap the top of the bearing cup to relieve the pressure on the circlip. Remove the grease nipple if working on the front universal joint.

3   Support the shaft in a vice with the flange yoke in a vertical plane. Tap the flange downward using a large socket or tube of suitable diameter until the uppermost bearing cup protrudes by approximately $\frac{1}{4}$ in (6 mm) (photo).

4   Using a self-gripping wrench remove the exposed bearing cup from the yoke (photo).

5   Turn the shaft over so that the other flange yoke bearing cup is uppermost and repeat the above procedure. The flange can now be

lifted off the bearing spider (photo).

6   The remaining two bearing cups and the bearing spider can now be removed in the previously described manner.

7   With the universal joint dismantled, carefully examine the needle rollers, bearing cups and spider for wear, scoring or pitting of the surface finish. If any wear is detected, a new universal joint must be obtained (photo).

8   Before fitting the new bearing cups and spider, check that the bearing cups are $\frac{1}{3}$ full of fresh grease and that all the needle rollers are properly positioned.

9   Insert the new spider into the flange yoke. Partially insert one of the bearing cups into the yoke and enter the spider trunnion into the cup taking care not to dislodge the needle rollers (photos).

10   Using a socket or tube which is small enough to fit inside the yoke, press the bearing cup in just far enough to allow the circlip to be fitted (photo). Repeat this operation with the other bearing cup.

11   Insert the spider into the yokes of the propeller shaft and partially insert one of the remaining cups into the yoke. Hold the spider trunnion in place in the cup and tap the cup into position. Assemble the other bearing cup in the same way and then press both cups fully home in the previously described manner (photos).

12   Finally refit the two remaining circlips, and also the grease nipple if working on the front universal joint.

13   The propeller shaft can now be refitted to the car as described in Section 2.

5   Centre bearing – removal and refitting

1   Refer to Section 2 and remove the propeller shaft from the car. Separate the two halves.

2   Using a universal puller and suitable thrust block (a bolt screwed into the end of the shaft will do), draw the centre bearing complete with mounting from the end of the front propeller shaft. Note the direction of fitting of the bearing and mounting as an aid to reassembly.

3   If necessary the centre bearing can be removed from the mounting using a press or hammer and tubular drift. A new bearing is refitted in the same way.

4   To fit the assembly to the propeller shaft, place it in position on the end of the front shaft with the flanged lip facing away from the shaft. Tap it fully home with a hammer and tube of suitable diameter.

5   Refit the propeller shaft assembly as described in Section 2.

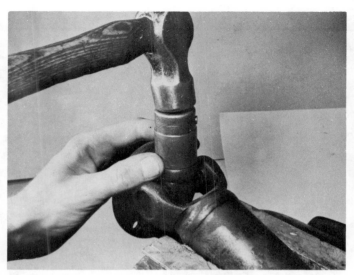

4.3 Tap the flange downward until the bearing cup protrudes ...

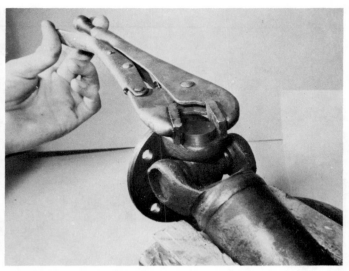

4.4 ... and then remove the cup

4.5 With both bearing cups removed, the flange can be lifted off

4.7 Component parts of the new universal joint ready for fitting

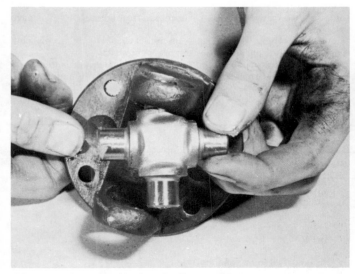

4.9a Insert the new spider into the flange yoke ...

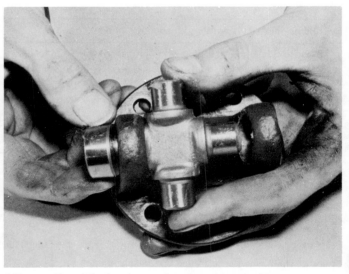

4.9b ... and insert the bearing cup into the yoke and spider

4.10 Press in the bearing cups using a small socket or tube

4.11a Insert the spider into the propeller shaft yoke and tap in one of the remaining bearing cups

4.11b Install the other bearing cup ...

4.11c ... and press both fully home

6   Sliding joint – dismantling, inspection and reassembly

1   Refer to Section 2 and remove the propeller shaft assembly.

2   Unscrew the dust cap from the sleeve and then slide the sleeve from the shaft. Take off the steel washer and cork washer.

3   With the sleeve separated from the shaft assembly, the splines can be inspected. If worn, it will be necessary to purchase a new sleeve assembly.

4   To reassemble, fit the dust cap, steel washer and a new cork gasket over the splined part of the propeller shaft.

5   Grease the splines, line up the arrow on the sleeve assembly with the arrow on the splined portion of the propeller shaft, and push the sleeve over the splines. Fit the washers to the sleeve and screw up dust cap.

7   Fault diagnosis – propeller shaft

Symptom	Reason(s)
Vibration	Worn universal joint bearings
	Wear in centre support bearing
	Wear in sliding joint splines
	Propeller shaft out of balance
	Propeller shaft distorted
Knock or clunk when accelerating and decelerating	Worn universal joint bearings
	Wear in sliding sleeve splines
	Loose drive flange bolts
	See also 'Fault diagnosis – rear axle' Chapter 8

Chapter 8 Rear axle

Contents

Specifications

Type .... Hypoid, semi-floating

Axle ratio .... 3.63 : 1

Lubricant
Type .... SAE 90 EP hypoid gear oil
Capacity .... 1.25 pints (0.71 litres)

Torque wrench settings

	lbf ft	Nm
Brake backplate securing nuts	18	24
Axleshaft nut	100 to 110	135 to 149
Differential casing-to-axle retaining nuts	20	27
Pinion drive flange nut	90	122
Axle-to-spring U-bolt nuts	15 to 18	20 to 24
Propeller shaft flange retaining nuts	28	37

1 General description

The rear axle is of the semi-floating type and is held in place by semi-elliptic springs. These springs provide the necessary lateral and longitudinal location of the axle. The rear axle incorporates a hypoid crownwheel and pinion and a two-pinion differential. All repairs can be carried out to the component parts of the rear axle without removing the axle casing from the car.

The crownwheel and pinion, together with the differential gears, are mounted on the differential unit, which is bolted to the front face of the banjo type axle casing.

The axleshafts (halfshafts) are splined at their inner ends to locate into the splines in the differential gears. The wheel bearings are mounted on the outer ends of the axleshafts and are retained by the oil seal housings to the rear axle casing.

The overhaul and repair of a differential assembly is a highly skilled task requiring special tools and equipment, and it is not recommended that the DIY mechanic should attempt this job. The best policy, in the event of mechanical failure or excessive noise, is to obtain a factory exchange reconditioned unit, or a complete axle assembly from a reputable vehicle dismantler.

2 Rear axle – removal and refitting

1 Chock the front wheels, jack up the rear of the car, and support it on firmly based axle stands located under the body and forward of the rear axle.
2 Using a scriber or file, mark the differential pinion and propeller shaft drive flanges so that they may be refitted in their original positions.
3 Undo and remove the four nuts and bolts that secure the rear propeller shaft flange to the pinion flange. Lower the rear half of the propeller shaft onto a block of wood or tie it up out of the way. Avoid

placing excessive strain on the propeller shaft centre support bearing.
4 Remove the wheel trims, undo and remove the wheel nuts and lift away the rear wheels.
5 Wipe the top of the brake master cylinder reservoir and unscrew the filler cap. Place a piece of polythene over the filler neck and refit the cap. This will prevent hydraulic fluid syphoning out during subsequent operations. Alternatively clamp the rear brake hydraulic hose with a brake hose clamp or a self-gripping wrench with its jaws suitably protected.
6 Wipe the area around the brake hydraulic pipe-to-hose union nut at the bracket on the rear axle. Unscrew the nut and carefully pull the pipe clear. Now unscrew the nut and washer securing the flexible hose to the bracket and lift away the hose. Suitably protect the ends of the pipe and hose against dirt ingress.
7 Extract the split pin and remove the washer and clevis pin securing the forked ends of the handbrake cable to the operating levers on each brake backplate.
8 Undo and remove the bolt and spring washer that secures the handbrake cable retaining strap and small support strap to the axle casing. Lower the disconnected cable assembly to the ground.
9 Using axle stands or other suitable means, support the weight of the rear axle.
10 Undo and remove the eight U-bolt locknuts that secure the rear axle to the rear springs. Tap the four U-bolts upward until they can be withdrawn from the top of the axle complete with the rubber bump stops.
11 Ease the shock absorber mounting brackets downwards and move them to one side.
12 Remove the lower spring mounting plates and rubber pads.
13 Undo and remove the securing nuts and bolts and detach the clamps securing the anti-roll bar to each side of the axle casing.
14 The rear axle may now be lifted over the rear springs and drawn away from one side of the car. Make a special note of the location of the spring packing wedge (if fitted), upper mounting plates and rubber pads.
15 Refitting the rear axle is the reverse sequence to removal bearing

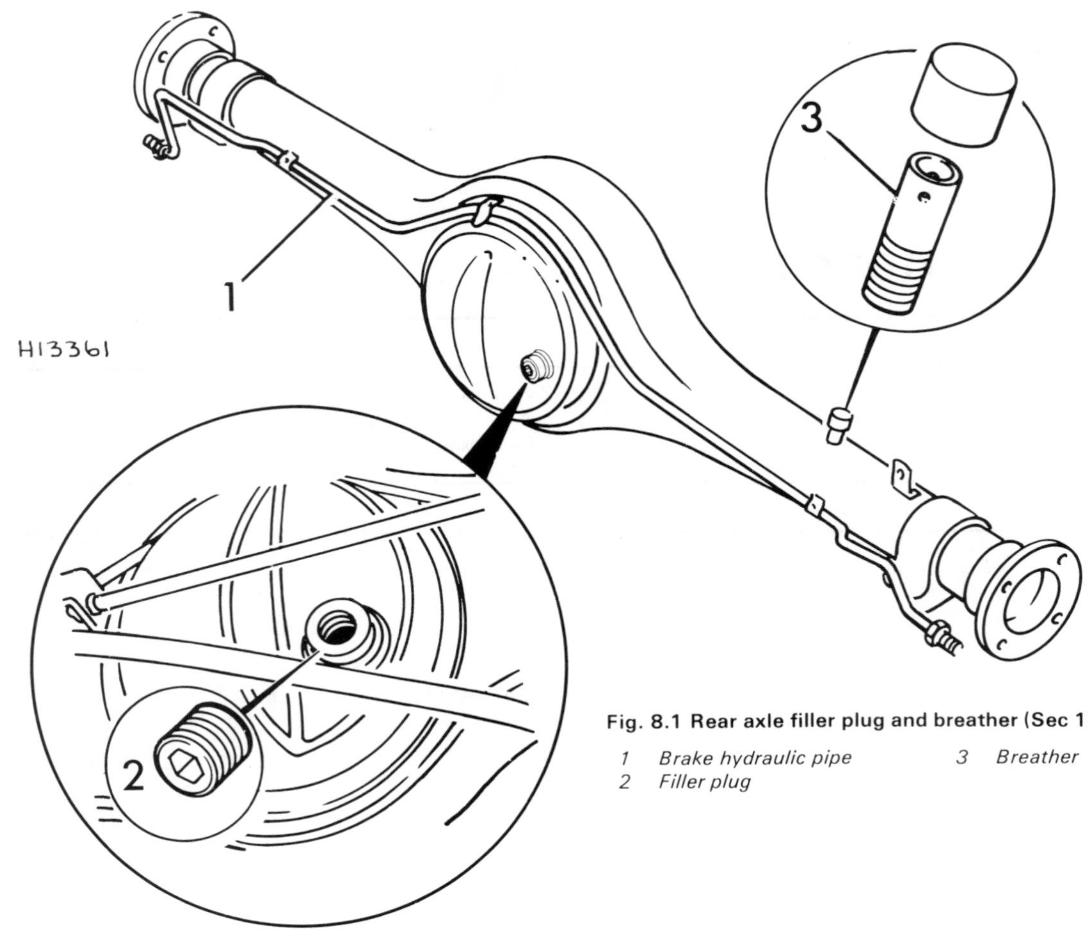

H13361

Fig. 8.1 Rear axle filler plug and breather (Sec 1)

1 Brake hydraulic pipe   3 Breather
2 Filler plug

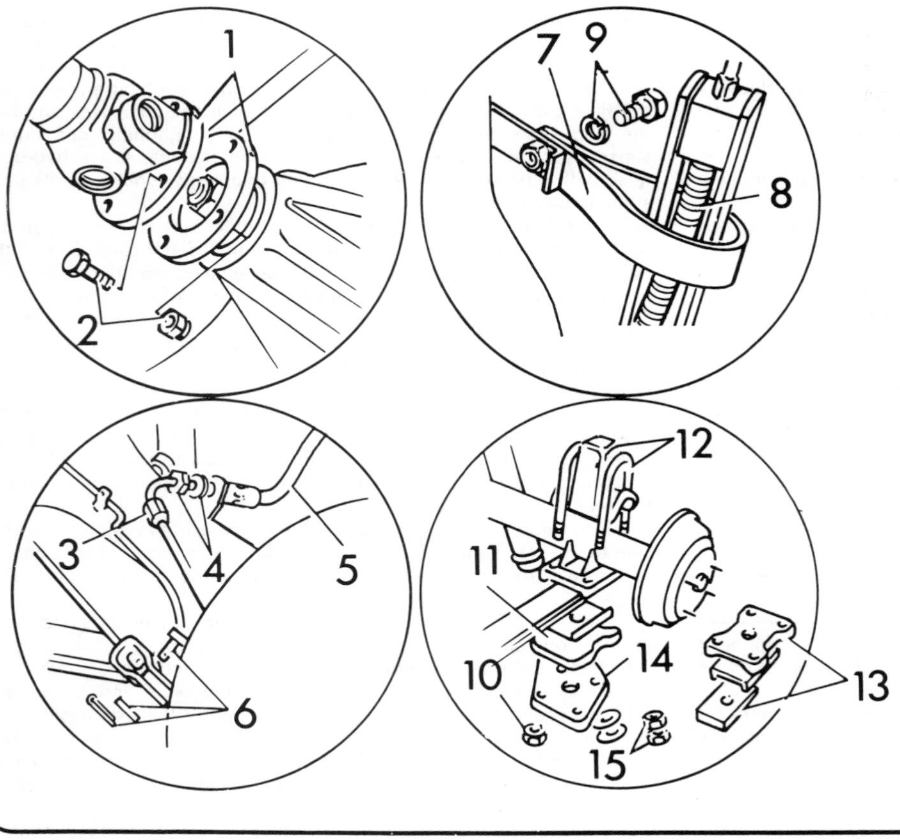

Fig. 8.2 Rear axle removal (Sec 2)

1 Propeller shaft and pinion
drive flange mating marks
2 Bolt and locknut
3 Brake hydraulic pipe union nut
4 Brake hydraulic flexible
hose locknut and washer
5 Brake hydraulic flexible hose
6 Handbrake cable clevis pin,
plain washer and split pin
7 Securing strap
8 Handbrake cable
9 Securing strap bolt and
spring washer
10 U-bolt locknuts
11 Rubber pad
12 U-bolts and rubber bump stops
13 Spring packing wedge upper
locating plate rubber pad
14 Shock absorber mounting plate
15 Shock absorber retaining nut
and locknut

in mind the following points:

(a) *Make sure that the spring packing wedges are refitted in their original positions (where applicable)*
(b) *Renew the rubber mounting pads if any sign of deterioration is evident*
(c) *Tighten the U-bolt locknuts to the specified torque wrench setting*
(d) *On completion bleed the brake hydraulic system as described in Chapter 9*

3 Axleshaft, bearing and oil seal – removal and refitting

The following procedure entails the use of BL special tool S356B, or alternatively a heavy duty universal hub puller, to remove the rear hub from the axleshaft. The hub is a taper fit on the axleshaft and considerable force is required to release it. An ordinary two or three-legged puller is unlikely to be sufficient.

1 Chock the front wheels, jack up the rear of the car and support it on firmly based axle stands. Remove the appropriate rear roadwheel.
2 Firmly apply the handbrake, and then undo and remove the axleshaft nut and plain washer. Release the handbrake.
3 Undo and remove the two screws securing the brake drum to the hub flange and lift away the drum. If it is tight, back off the brake adjuster, and using a soft-faced mallet, tap outwards on the circumference of the drum.
4 Using BL special tool S356B or similar alternative puller, draw the rear hub off the axleshaft. When doing this make sure that the centre screw of the puller bears against a thrust block, not directly against the threaded end of the axleshaft.
5 Extract the split pin, washer and clevis pin securing the handbrake cable to the lever at the rear of the brake backplate.
6 Wipe the top of the brake master cylinder reservoir and unscrew the filler cap. Place a piece of polythene over the filler neck and refit the cap. This will prevent hydraulic fluid syphoning out during subsequent operations. Alternatively, clamp the rear flexible hydraulic hose with a brake hose clamp or self-gripping wrench with suitably protected jaws.
7 Wipe the area around the hydraulic pipe union(s) at the rear of the wheel cylinder and unscrew the union(s) from the cylinder. Suitably protect the pipe end(s) against dirt ingress.
8 Undo and remove the four nuts, bolts and spring washers that secure the brake backplate to the axle casing.
9 Make a note of the fitted position of the oil catcher drip lip relative to the wheel cylinder and lift away the oil catcher.
10 The brake backplate assembly may now be lifted off.
11 Remove the rear hub oil seal and retainer assembly: the seal should be renewed if there is any sign of oil leaking past it. To remove the old seal, carefully ease it out of the retainer using a screwdriver. Once removed a new seal must always be refitted.
12 Place a suitable container under the end of the axle casing to catch any oil that will issue from the end.
13 Using a screwdriver or a pair of pliers, remove the Woodruff key from the end of the axleshaft. Put the key in a safe place where it will not be lost.
14 Using a slide hammer, draw the axleshaft and bearing out of the casing. If a slide hammer is not available, refit the rear hub and screw on the nut just sufficiently to hold the hub in place. Using a soft-faced mallet, tap the hub outwards around its circumference until the bearing is clear of the casing. The axleshaft can now be withdrawn the rest of the way by hand.
15 The inner oil seal may be removed from the casing using a flat strip of metal with one end shaped to form a hook. Pull on the seal and withdraw it from the recess in the axle casing.
16 Removal of the bearing from the axleshaft requires the use of a press. If the bearing is in need of renewal, it is advisable to take the axleshaft to your dealer and have him remove the old bearing and fit a new one for you.
17 Refitting the oil seals, bearing and axleshaft is the reverse sequence to removal, bearing in mind the following points:

(a) *Pack the bearing with a lithium based grease, and ensure that its fitted position is 2.84 in (72.14 mm) from the threaded end of the axleshaft*
(b) *Lubricate the lips of the oil seals with clean engine oil before*

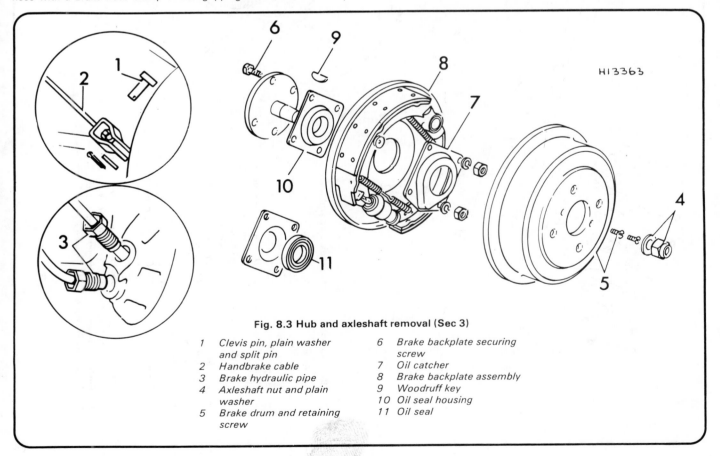

Fig. 8.3 Hub and axleshaft removal (Sec 3)

1 Clevis pin, plain washer and split pin
2 Handbrake cable
3 Brake hydraulic pipe
4 Axleshaft nut and plain washer
5 Brake drum and retaining screw
6 Brake backplate securing screw
7 Oil catcher
8 Brake backplate assembly
9 Woodruff key
10 Oil seal housing
11 Oil seal

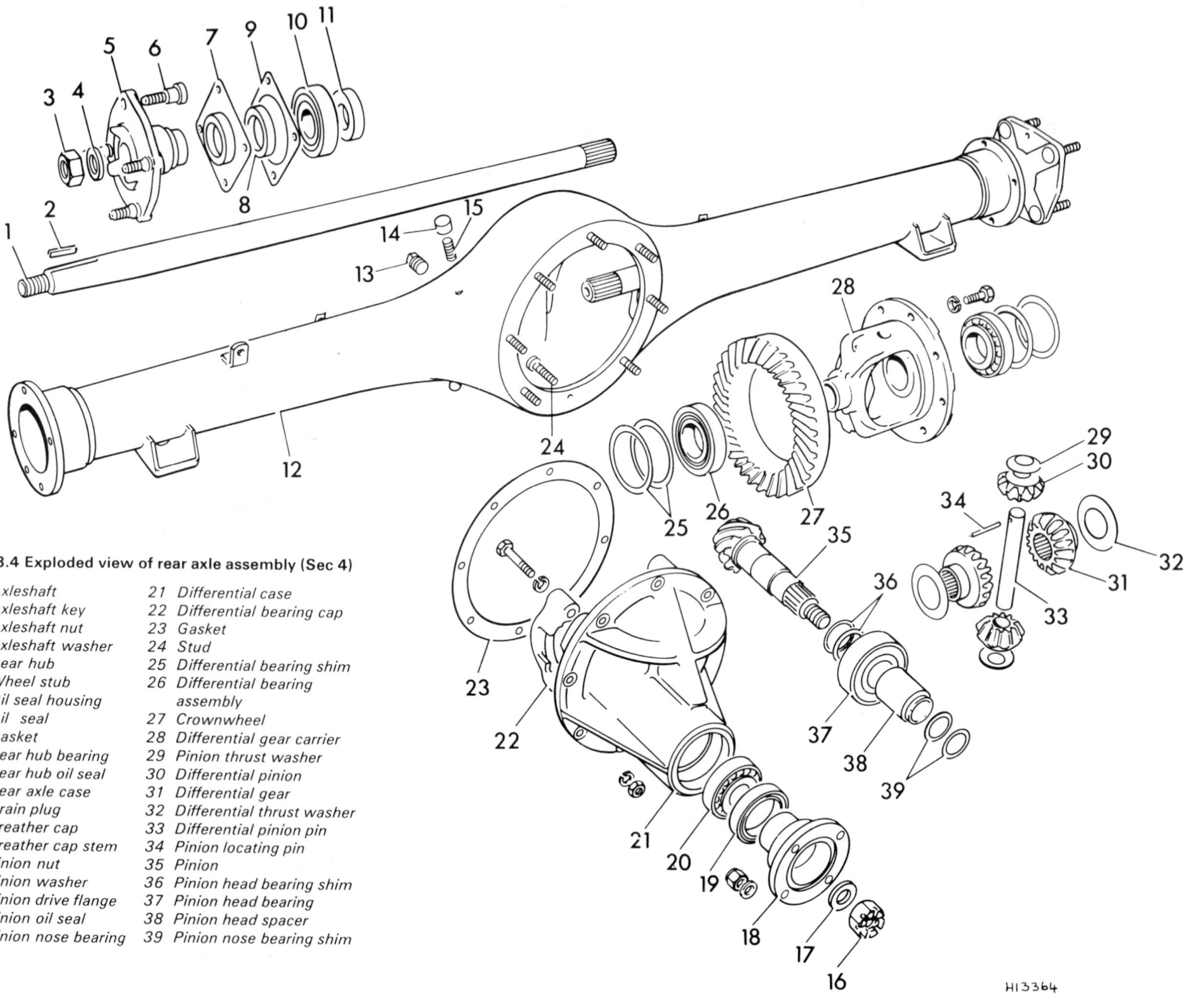

HI3364

Fig. 8.4 Exploded view of rear axle assembly (Sec 4)

1 Axleshaft
2 Axleshaft key
3 Axleshaft nut
4 Axleshaft washer
5 Rear hub
6 Wheel stub
7 Oil seal housing
8 Oil seal
9 Gasket
10 Rear hub bearing
11 Rear hub oil seal
12 Rear axle case
13 Drain plug
14 Breather cap
15 Breather cap stem
16 Pinion nut
17 Pinion washer
18 Pinion drive flange
19 Pinion oil seal
20 Pinion nose bearing
21 Differential case
22 Differential bearing cap
23 Gasket
24 Stud
25 Differential bearing shim
26 Differential bearing
      assembly
27 Crownwheel
28 Differential gear carrier
29 Pinion thrust washer
30 Differential pinion
31 Differential gear
32 Differential thrust washer
33 Differential pinion pin
34 Pinion locating pin
35 Pinion
36 Pinion head bearing shim
37 Pinion head bearing
38 Pinion head spacer
39 Pinion nose bearing shim

refitting, and ensure that they are installed with their lips facing inwards

(c) Always use a new gasket when refitting the backplate and oil seal retainer assembly

(d) Tighten the backplate and axleshaft retaining nuts to the specified torque wrench settings, and use a thread-locking compound on the axleshaft nut

(e) On completion bleed the brake hydraulic system as described in Chapter 9, and don't forget to top up the rear axle oil level

4 Differential pinion oil seal – removal and refitting

1 Chock the front wheels, jack up the rear of the car and support it on firmly based axle stands.

2 With a scriber or file mark the propeller shaft and pinion flanges so that they may be refitted correctly in their original positions.

3 Undo and remove the four nuts, bolts and spring washers that secure the pinion flange to the propeller shaft flange. Lower the propeller shaft to the floor.

4 Apply the handbrake firmly. Using a pair of pliers, extract the flange nut locking split pin.

5 With a socket wrench, undo the flange nut. Lift away the nut and plain washer.

6 Place a container under the pinion end of the rear axle to catch any oil that seeps out.

7 Using a universal puller and suitable thrust block, draw the pinion flange from the pinion.

8 The old oil seal may now be prised out using a screwdriver or thin piece of metal bar with a small hook on one end.

9 Refitting the new oil seal is the reverse sequence to removal, but

the following additional points should be noted:

(a) Soak the new oil seal in engine oil for 1 hour prior to fitting

(b) Fit the new seal with the lip facing inwards using a tubular drift

(c) Tighten the pinion flange nut to the specified torque wrench setting and lock with a new split pin

(d) Top up the rear axle oil level as necessary

5 Differential unit – removal and refitting

1 Begin by removing the axleshafts as described in Section 3.

2 Mark the propeller shaft and pinion flanges to ensure their refitment in the same relative position.

3 Undo and remove the four nuts and bolts from the flanges. Separate the two parts and lower the propeller shaft to the ground.

4 Place a container under the differential unit assembly to catch oil that will drain out during subsequent operations.

5 Undo and remove the nuts and spring washers that secure the differential unit assembly to the axle casing.

6 Draw the assembly forwards from over the studs on the axle casing. Lift away from under the car. Remove the paper joint washer.

7 Refitting the differential assembly is the reverse sequence to removal. The following additional points should be noted:

(a) Always use a new joint washer and make sure the mating faces are clean, then apply a non-setting jointing compound

(b) Tighten the differential retaining nuts to the specified torque wrench setting

(c) Refill the rear axle with the specified grade and quantity of oil

6 Fault diagnosis – rear axle

Symptom	Reason(s)
Oil leakage	Defective pinion oil seal Defective axleshaft oil seals Defective differential housing gasket Axle breather blocked
Noise	Lack of lubricant Worn bearings General wear
Clonk on acceleration and deceleration	Incorrectly tightened pinion flange nut Worn axleshaft splines Incorrect crownwheel and pinion mesh See also 'Fault diagnosis – propeller shaft' Chapter 7

Chapter 9 Braking system

Contents

Specifications

Front disc brakes
Disc diameter .... 9.785 in (248.5 mm)
Disc run-out .... 0.006 in (0.152 mm)
Minimum pad thickness .... 0.125 in (3 mm)

Rear drum brakes
Drum diameter .... 8.0 in (203.2 mm)
Minimum brake lining thickness .... 0.062 in (1.5 mm)

Torque wrench settings

	lbf ft	Nm
Master cylinder retaining nuts	15 to 19	20 to 25
Caliper retaining bolts	50	67
Wheel cylinder retaining bolts	4 to 5	5.4 to 6.7
Brake disc to hub	38 to 45	51 to 61
Caliper bracket to swivel hub	35 to 42	47 to 56
Servo to mounting bracket	8 to 10	10 to 13
Master cylinder to servo	17 to 19	23 to 25
PDWA endplug	38	50
PDWA electrical switch	3.5	4.7

1 General description

The dual circuit hydraulic system is of the split front/rear type. A pressure failure warning light is located on the facia.

Disc brakes are fitted to the front and drum brakes to the rear. They are operated by the hydraulic pressure created in the master cylinder when the brake pedal is depressed. This pressure is transferred to the wheel and caliper cylinders by a system of metal pipes and flexible hoses.

The rear drum brakes are of the internally expanding type whereby the shoes and linings are moved outwards into contact with the rotating brake drum. One wheel cylinder is fitted to each rear brake.

The handbrake operates on the rear brakes only, using a system of links and cables.

The front disc brakes are of the conventional fixed caliper design. Each half of the caliper contains a piston which operates in a bore, both being interconnected so that under hydraulic pressure their pistons move towards each other. By this action they clamp the rotating disc between two friction pads to slow rotational movement of the disc. Special seals are fitted between the piston and bore and these seals are able to stretch slightly when the piston moves to apply the brake. When the hydraulic pressure is released, the seals return to their natural shape and draw the pistons back slightly, so giving a running clearance between the pads and disc. As the pads wear, the piston is able to slide through the seal allowing wear to be taken up.

The front disc brakes are self-adjusting; the rear drum brakes are of the manually adjusted type.

A brake servo unit is fitted between the brake pedal and master cylinder to add pressure on the master cylinder pushrod when the brake pedal is being depressed.

2 Rear drum brakes – adjustment

1 Chock the front wheels, release the handbrake completely, jack up the rear of the car and support it on firmly based stands.
2 A single adjuster for each side is located on the rear of the backplate near the top. The surrounding area should be cleaned of all dirt and a small amount of engine oil smeared onto the adjuster threads.
3 Turn the adjuster clockwise (as viewed from the centre of the rear axle), preferably with a square adjuster spanner, until the brake drum is locked. Then back off the adjuster until the drum rotates without any signs of binding. About two clicks is normal (photo).
4 Repeat the procedure given in paragraph 3 for the remaining wheel.
5 Finally lower the car to the ground.

2.3 Using a brake adjuster spanner to adjust the rear drum brakes

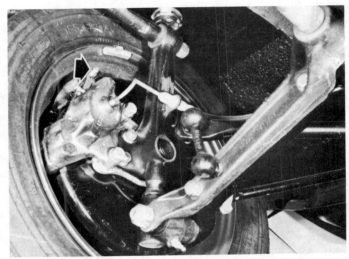

3.7a Location of the left-hand front ...

3.7b ... and left-hand rear brake bleed screws (arrowed)

3   Hydraulic system – bleeding

1   If any of the hydraulic components in the braking system have been removed or disconnected, or if the fluid level in the master cylinder reservoir has been allowed to fall appreciably, it is inevitable that air will have been introduced into the system. The removal of this air is essential if the brakes are to function correctly, and the process of removing it is known as bleeding.

2   There are a number of one-man, do-it-yourself, brake bleeding kits currently available from motor accessory shops. It is recommended that these kits should be used wherever possible, as they greatly simplify the bleeding operation and also reduce the risk of expelled air and fluid being drawn back into the system.

3   If brake bleeding kits are not available then it will be necessary to gather together two clean glass jars, and two suitable lengths of plastic or rubber tubing which are a tight fit over the bleed screws. The help of an assistant will also be required.

4   Before commencing the bleeding operation, check that all rigid pipes and flexible hoses are in good condition and that all hydraulic unions are tight. Take care not to allow hydraulic fluid to come into contact with the vehicle paintwork, otherwise the finish will be seriously damaged. Wash off any spilled fluid immediately with cold water.

5   If hydraulic fluid has been lost from the master cylinder, due to a leak in the system, ensure that the cause is traced and rectified before proceeding further or a serious malfunction of the braking system may occur.

6   To bleed the system first remove the master cylinder filler cap and top up the reservoir. Periodically check the fluid level during the following operations and top up as necessary.

7   If the one-man brake bleeding kits are being used, connect the outlet tube of one of the kits to the bleed screw at the left-hand front brake and the outlet tube of a second kit to the bleed screw at the left-hand rear brake (photos). Note that both the front and rear brake circuits must be bled at the same time and that the left-hand rear bleed screw controls the bleeding operation for both rear brakes.

8   Using a suitable spanner, open the two bleed screws approximately half a turn. If possible position the kits so that they can be viewed from the car, then depress the brake pedal firmly to the floor and release it fully. The one-way valve in the kits will prevent expelled air and fluid from returning to the system at the end of each stroke. Repeat this operation until clean hydraulic fluid, free from air bubbles, can be seen coming through the tube. Now tighten the bleed screws and remove the outlet tubes. The right-hand front brake can now be bled on its own using one of the kits.

9   If one-man brake bleeding kits are not available connect one of the plastic or rubber tubes to the bleed screw at the left-hand front brake. Connect the other tube to the bleed screw at the left-hand rear brake. Immerse the other end of the tubes in the glass jars containing sufficient clean hydraulic fluid to keep the ends of the tubes submerged. Open the bleed screws approximately half a turn and have your assistant depress the brake pedal to the floor and slowly release it. Tighten both bleed screws at the end of each downstroke to prevent expelled air and fluid from being drawn back into the system. Repeat this operation until clean hydraulic fluid, free from air bubbles, can be seen coming through the tubes. Now tighten the bleed screws and remove the tubes. The right-hand front brake can now be bled on its own in the same way.

10   When completed, recheck the fluid level in the master cylinder, top up if necessary and refit the cap. Check the 'feel' of the brake pedal, which should be firm and free from any sponginess which would indicate air still present in the system. Also check that the brake failure warning light does not glow when the brake pedal is depressed. If it does this indicates that the system is unbalanced and further bleeding is required.

11   Discard any expelled hydraulic fluid, as it is likely to be contaminated with moisture, air and dirt which makes it unsuitable for further use.

4   Front disc brake pads – removal and refitting

1   Chock the rear wheels, apply the handbrake, jack up the front of the car and support it on axle stands. Remove the front roadwheel.

2   Using a pair of pliers, extract the two pad retaining pin spring clips.

3   Withdraw the two pad retaining pins and recover the wire anti-rattle clips.

4   With the retaining pins removed, withdraw the brake pads, one at a time, from the caliper. If they are initially tight, use a screwdriver inserted in the slot on the brake pad and lever against the edge of the caliper. Lift out the anti-rattle shims, if not already removed with the pads.

5   Inspect the thickness of the brake pad friction material, and if it is less than the minimum thickness shown in the Specifications the pads must be renewed. The pads must also be renewed if there is any sign of oil or hydraulic fluid contamination of the friction material, or if any heavy scoring or cracking is visible on the pad face.

6   When renewing brake pads, they should always be renewed as a complete set (four pads); uneven braking or pulling to one side may otherwise occur.

7   With the pads removed, carefully inspect the surface of the brake disc. Concentric scores up to 0.015 in (0.4 mm) deep are acceptable; however if deeper scores are found or if the surface finish is in any other way damaged the disc must either be skimmed or, preferably, renewed.

8   To refit the pads, first ensure that the brake caliper pistons and pad seating areas are clean and free from dust and corrosion. Using a flat bar as a lever, gently push the caliper pistons back into their cylinders as far as they will go. This operation will cause a quantity of hydraulic fluid to be returned to the master cylinder via the hydraulic pipes. Place absorbent rags around the master cylinder reservoir to collect any fluid that may overflow, or preferably, drain off a small quantity of fluid from the master cylinder reservoir before retracting the caliper pistons.

9   Fit the new friction pads and anti-rattle shims with the arrow on the shims pointing upward (photo).

10   Insert the pad retaining pins while at the same time engaging the wire anti-rattle clips. Note that the looped end of one of the clips engages with the upper pin, and the looped end of the other clip engages with the lower pin. Secure the pad retaining pins with the spring clips (photos).

11   With the brake pads correctly fitted, fully depress the brake pedal

4.9 Fit the front brake pads and anti-rattle shims with the arrow on the shims pointing upward

4.10a With the pads in place fit the upper retaining pin ...

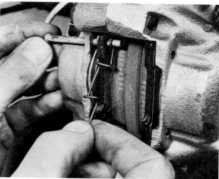

4.10b ... and engage the looped end of the anti-rattle clip over the pin

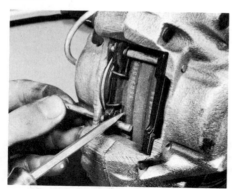

4.10c Fit the lower pin over the anti-rattle clip and then engage it with the looped end of the other clip

4.10d With the pins in position refit the spring clips

5.2 Using a self-gripping wrench with protected jaws to clamp the front flexible hose

5.3 Unscrew the metal pipe-to-flexible hose union nut ...

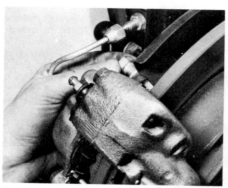

5.4a ... undo and remove the two caliper retaining bolts ...

5.4b ... and lift off the caliper complete with brake pads

several times to bring the caliper pistons into contact with the friction pads.

12 Check the hydraulic fluid level in the brake master cylinder reservoir, and top up if necessary.

13 Refit the roadwheel and lower the car to the ground.

14 New brake pads should be bedded in slowly, over a period of roughly 100 miles. During this time avoid unnecessary panic stops or prolonged heavy breaking applications.

5 Front disc brake caliper – removal and refitting

1 Apply the handbrake, chock the rear wheels, jack up the front of the car and support it on axle stands.

2 Using a brake hose clamp or a self-gripping wrench with their jaws suitably protected, clamp the front flexible brake hose (photo). This will prevent loss of hydraulic fluid during subsequent operations.

3 Wipe the area around the caliper metal brake pipe-to-flexible hose union and then unscrew the metal pipe union nut (photo).

4 Undo and remove the two bolts securing the caliper to the swivel hub. Carefully slide the caliper complete with friction pads off the swivel hub and brake disc (photos).

5 Refitting the caliper is the reverse sequence to removal bearing in mind the following points:

   (a) Tighten the caliper retaining bolts to the specified torque
   (b) Bleed the hydraulic system after refitting as described in Section 3. If precautions were taken to prevent excessive loss of fluid, it should only be necessary to bleed the brake caliper that was removed

6 Front brake disc – removal and refitting

1 Remove the appropriate brake caliper as described in the previous Section.

2 By judicious tapping and levering, remove the grease cap from the centre of the hub.

3 Extract the split pin and nut retainer, then undo and remove the hub retaining nut and splined thrust washer.

4 The front hub and brake disc can now be withdrawn taking care to hold the outer wheel bearing inner race in position as the hub assembly is lifted off the stub axle.

5 To separate the disc from the hub, first mark the relative position of the hub and disc. Undo and remove the four bolts that secure the hub to the disc and separate the two parts.

6 Carefully inspect the surface of the disc. Concentric scores up to 0.015 in (0.4 mm) are acceptable. Also, minute surface cracks due to localised surface heating are to be expected. However, if the disc is severely grooved (or if larger cracks are evident), the disc must be renewed. **Note:** *In order to maintain uniform braking, both front discs must exhibit the same surface characteristics with respect to depth of grooving and surface finish. For this reason, front disc brakes should always be renewed in pairs.*

7 Refitting the brake disc is the reverse sequence to removal, bearing in mind the following points:

   (a) *When refitting the brake disc to the hub, ensure that the mating faces are perfectly clean and free from corrosion. Tighten the securing bolts to the torque setting given in the Specifications*
   (b) *Adjust the front wheel bearings to give the correct hub endfloat, as described in Chapter 11*
   (c) *With the front wheel bearings correctly adjusted, check the brake disc run-out using a dial indicator, or feeler gauges inserted between the edge of the caliper and the disc surface, while slowly rotating the disc. Compare the figures obtained with those given in the Specifications. Excess run-out can lead to brake and steering judder, and is caused by wear or distortion of the disc, hub, or disc-to-hub mating face*

7 Rear drum brake shoes – inspection, removal and refitting

1 Chock the front wheels, jack up the rear of the car and support it

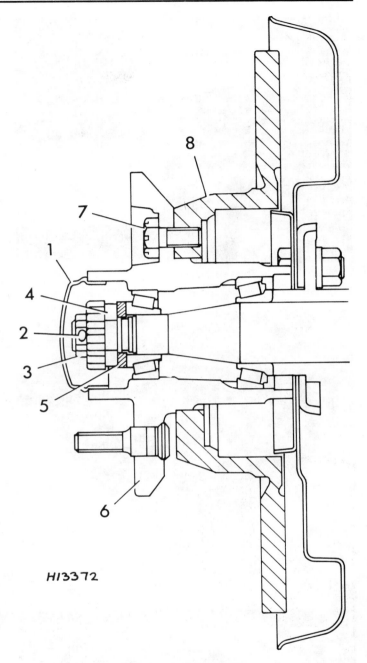

H13372

Fig. 9.1 Sectional view of front brake disc and hub (Sec 6)

1	Grease cap	5	Splined thrust washer
2	Split pin	6	Hub
3	Nut retainer	7	Disc securing bolt
4	Nut	8	Disc

on axle stands. Remove the rear roadwheel and then release the handbrake.

2 Back off the brake adjuster from the rear of the backplate until the shoes offer no resistance to the drum (photo).

3 Undo and remove the two screws securing the drum to the axle flange and withdraw the brake drum (photo). If it is initially tight, tap its circumference using a soft-faced mallet.

4 Before dismantling the brake shoes, observe the components in their assembled condition (photo). Make a note of the location of the pull-off springs, noting also which way round the various parts are fitted. Check for any hydraulic fluid leaks from the wheel cylinder or oil

7.2 Back off the rear brake adjuster ...

7.3 ... then remove the two screws and withdraw the drum

7.4 The correct fitted position of the rear brake components prior to removal (right-hand side shown)

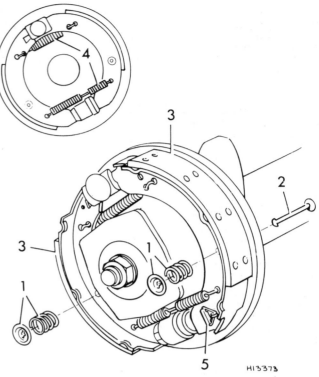

Fig. 9.2 Rear drum brake assembly – left-hand side (Sec 7)

1   Shoe retaining spring
    and retainer
2   Retainer pin
3   Brake shoe
4   Brake shoe pull-off
    springs
5   Support plate and
    retaining spring

leaks from the axleshaft oil seal. Have an assistant slowly depress the brake pedal, and observe the action of the wheel cylinder pistons. See that they are both free to operate and that they return under the action of the brake shoe pull-off springs when the pedal is released. The condition of the brake shoe friction linings and drum can also be inspected at this time. The brake shoes must be renewed if they are so worn that the rivet heads are nearly flush with the surface of the linings. If bonded linings are fitted, they must be renewed when the lining material has worn down to $\frac{1}{16}$ in (1.6 mm) at its thinnest point. The brake shoes must also be renewed if there is any sign of oil or grease contamination of the linings. Always renew brake shoes in complete axle sets (four shoes) even if only one shoe is worn; uneven braking and imbalance may otherwise occur.

5   To remove the brake shoes, begin by removing the shoe retaining springs in the centre of each brake shoe. Use a pair of pliers to release the spring retainers, rotating them through 90° (photo). Lift away the springs. retainers and pins from each brake shoe web.

6   Carefully lift the trailing shoe out of its location in the brake adjuster and wheel cylinder pivot. Detach the pull-off springs and lift away the shoe. The leading shoe can now be removed from the brake adjuster pivot, wheel cylinder and handbrake operating lever. Withdraw the retaining spring and support plate from the slot in the leading shoe (photos).

7   Thoroughly clean all traces of dust from the brake shoes, backplate and drum, using a cloth and stiff brush. *Ensure the working area is well ventilated during this operation; asbestos dust is harmful and should not be inhaled.* Brake dust is the prime cause of judder and squeal, and therefore it is important to clean away all traces.

8   Check that the brake backplate is secure and that the brake adjuster is free to turn. If any hydraulic fluid or oil leaks are apparent (or if any defects were noticed during the initial inspection), they should now be rectified before refitting the brake shoes.

9   Refitting the brake shoes is the reverse sequence to removal. Smear a trace of brake grease to the brake adjuster and wheel cylinder piston locations before fitting the shoes. *Do not allow grease to come into contact with the friction material.*

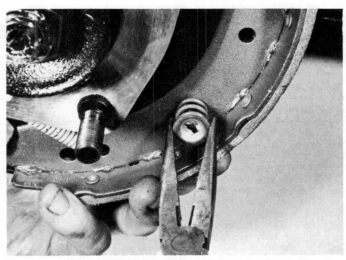

7.5 To remove the rear brake shoes first release the spring retainers by turning them through 90°

7.6a Lift the trailing shoe off the brake adjuster location and wheel cylinder pivot

7.6b Detach the pull-off springs and lift off the two shoes

7.6c With the brake shoes removed withdraw the retaining spring ...

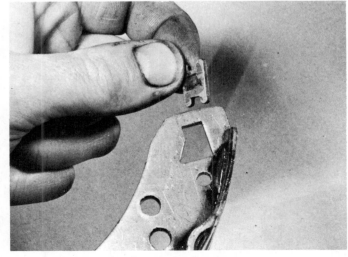

7.6d ... and support plate from the leading shoe

10 With the brake shoes reassembled and the drum in position, pump the brake pedal once or twice to centralise the shoes, then adjust the rear brakes, as described in Section 2. Refit the roadwheel in its original position and lower the car to the ground.

8 Rear brake backplate – removal and refitting

For full information refer to Chapter 8, which describes the removal of the axleshaft and hub assembly and includes the removal of the backplate.

9 Master cylinder – removal and refitting

1 Wipe the area around the hydraulic pipe unions on the master cylinder. Place a rag under the cylinder to catch any spilled hydraulic fluid, and then undo the hydraulic pipe unions. Carefully pull the pipes out of the master cylinder body. Suitably plug the master cylinder unions and the ends of the pipes to prevent loss of fluid and dirt ingress.

2 Undo and remove the two nuts and spring washers that secure the master cylinder to the servo unit.

3 Lift away the master cylinder, taking care not to allow any

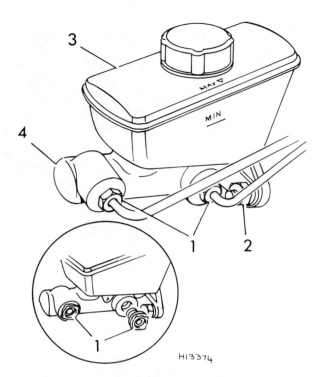

Fig. 9.3 Master cylinder removal (Sec 9)

1 Hydraulic pipe unions (inset shows unions in master cylinder plugged after pipe removal)	2 Securing nut 3 Fluid reservoir 4 Master cylinder

hydraulic fluid to drip on the paintwork. Recover the O-ring seal.
4   Refitting is the reverse sequence to removal, bearing in mind the following additional points:

(a)   Always fit a new O-ring seal
(b)   Tighten the retaining nuts to the specified torque
(c)   Bleed the hydraulic system as described in Section 3

10   Master cylinder – dismantling and reassembly

1   With the master cylinder removed from the car, unscrew the filler cap, invert the master cylinder and drain the fluid from the reservoir.
2   Extract the hairpin retaining clips and withdraw the two fluid reservoir securing pins, then lift the reservoir off the master cylinder.
3   Note the fitted position of the two reservoir seals and then extract them from the master cylinder body.
4   With the master cylinder mounted in a soft-jawed vice, use a suitable diameter rod to push the plunger fully down the cylinder bore, and then extract the secondary plunger stop pin.
5   Using a pair of circlip pliers, extract the circlip from the end of the master cylinder bore and then remove the primary plunger assembly. Place each item on a clean surface in the exact order of removal, noting which way round the seals are fitted.
6   Shake out, or alternatively blow out with a tyre pump or air line, the secondary plunger assembly; apply air pressure to the secondary outlet port.
7   Withdraw the two vacuum seals and spacers from the primary plunger tube end and detach the spring, retainer, seal and washer from the inner end of the primary plunger.
8   Similarly remove the spring and seals from the secondary plunger, again noting their fitted position.
9   Examine the bore of the cylinder carefully for any signs of scores or ridges. If this is found to be smooth all over, new seals can be fitted. If, however, there is any doubt of the condition of the bore, then a new cylinder must be fitted.
10   If the master cylinder is in a satisfactory condition, a new set of seals must be obtained before reassembly. These are available in the form of a master cylinder repair kit available from your local dealer.

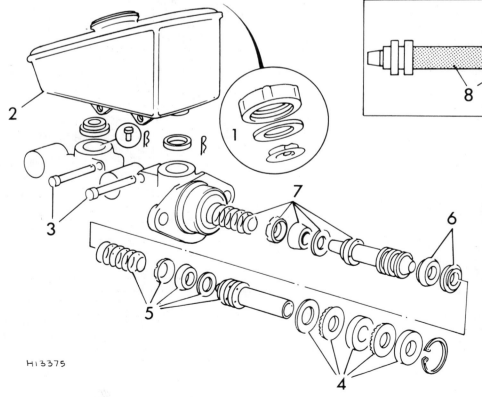

Fig. 9.4 Exploded view of brake master cylinder (Sec 10)

1   Filler cap assembly
2   Reservoir
3   Reservoir retaining pins
4   Primary plunger vacuum seals and spacers
5   Primary plunger and fluid seal assembly
6   Intermediate seals (later models have only one)
7   Secondary plunger assembly
8   Lubrication points (shaded)

H13375

11 Thoroughly clean all parts in methylated spirit or clean hydraulic fluid. Ensure that the bypass ports in the cylinder body are clear.

12 All seals should be assembled wet by dipping them in clean hydraulic fluid. Using the fingers only, fit the new seals to the primary and secondary plungers ensuring that they are the correct way round.

13 Reassembly is a reversal of the dismantling procedure, but the following additional points should be noted:

(a) *The secondary plunger return spring is larger than the primary plunger return spring*

(b) *The master cylinder bore should be smeared with clean hydraulic fluid before inserting the plunger assemblies*

(c) *The primary plunger, vacuum seals and spacers should be lubricated at the friction areas shown in Fig. 9.4 using grease supplied with the overhaul kit*

11 Rear drum brake wheel cylinder – removal and refitting

1 Remove the brake drum and brake shoes as described in Section 7.

2 Using a brake hose clamp or a self-gripping wrench with its jaws suitably protected, clamp the rear hydraulic brake hose just in front of the rear axle. Alternatively, remove the master cylinder filler cap, place a piece of polythene over the filler neck and refit the cap. This will reduce hydraulic fluid loss during subsequent operations.

3 Using an open-ended spanner, carefully unscrew the hydraulic pipe union connections at the rear of the wheel cylinder. If working on the left-hand cylinder, unscrew the bridge feed pipe union from the lower connection and the bleed screw from the upper connection. If working on the right-hand cylinder, unscrew the bridge feed pipe union from the lower connection and the hydraulic feed pipe from the upper connection.

4 Extract the split pin and lift away the washer and clevis pin that connects the handbrake cable yoke to the wheel cylinder operating lever.

5 Ease off the rubber boot from the rear of the wheel cylinder.

6 Using a screwdriver, carefully draw off the retaining plate and spring plate from the rear of the wheel cylinder.

7 The wheel cylinder may now be lifted away from the brake backplate. Detach the handbrake lever from the wheel cylinder.

8 To refit the wheel cylinder, first smear the backplate where the wheel cylinder slides with a little brake grease. Refit the handbrake lever on the wheel cylinder, ensuring that it is the correct way round. The spindles of the lever must engage in the recess on the cylinder arms.

9 Slide the spring plate between the wheel cylinder and backplate. The retaining plate may now be inserted between the spring plate and wheel cylinder, taking care the pips of the spring plate engage in the holes of the retaining plate.

10 Refit the rubber boot and reconnect the handbrake cable yoke to the handbrake lever. Insert the clevis pin, head upwards, and plain washer. Lock with a new split pin.

11 Refitting the brake shoes and drum is the reverse sequence to removal. Adjust the brakes as described in Section 2, and finally bleed the hydraulic system following the instructions in Section 3.

12 Rear drum brake wheel cylinder – overhaul

1 Ease off the rubber dust cover that protects the open end of the cylinder bore.

2 Withdraw the piston from the wheel cylinder body.

3 Using fingers only, carefully remove the piston seal from the piston, noting which way round it is fitted. Do not use a screwdriver as this could scratch the piston.

4 Thoroughly clean all the parts in clean hydraulic fluid or methylated spirit. Carefully examine the piston and cylinder for wear or scoring, and if evident, renew the complete wheel cylinder. If the components are in a satisfactory condition, a new set of seals, available in the form of a wheel cylinder kit, must be obtained. *Never re-use old seals.*

5 Smear the new rubber seal with hydraulic fluid and fit it to the piston, so that the small diameter is towards the piston.

6 Carefully insert the piston and seal into the bore, making sure the fine edge lip does not roll or become trapped.

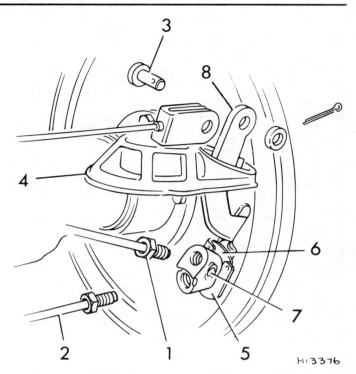

Fig. 9.5 Rear drum brake wheel cylinder removal (Sec 11)

1 Main hydraulic feed pipe
2 Bridge feed pipe
3 Clevis pin with plain washer and split pin
4 Rubber boot
5 Retaining plate
6 Spring plate
7 Wheel cylinder
8 Wheel cylinder operating lever

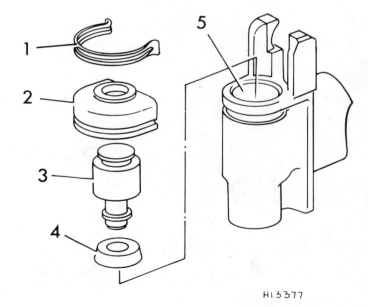

H13377

Fig. 9.6 Rear drum brake wheel cylinder components (Sec 12)

1 Clip
2 Dust cover
3 Piston
4 Seal
5 Wheel cylinder body

7 Refit the dust cover, engaging the lip with the groove in the outer surface of the wheel cylinder body. Refit the retaining ring.

13 Front disc brake caliper – overhaul

1   Remove the brake caliper, as described in Section 5.
2   Withdraw the circlip and protective rubber dust cover fitted over the ends of the pistons and edges of the caliper.
3   Place a thin, flat block of wood over one piston and hold the block and piston in place, using a small G-clamp.
4   The unclamped piston may now be forced out of the caliper, using a compressed air jet or the nozzle of a car foot pump held firmly against the metal hydraulic pipe attached to the caliper.
5   With the first piston removed, use the block of wood and the G-clamp to seal off the cylinder opening on the caliper, and repeat the above procedure to remove the remaining piston.
6   Thoroughly clean the caliper and pistons, using clean hydraulic fluid or methylated spirit. *Under no circumstances should the two halves of the caliper be separated.*
7   With all components thoroughly cleaned, the two caliper seals can be removed using a thin blunt instrument, such as a plastic knitting needle.
8   Inspect the dismantled components carefully for corrosion, scratches or wear. New seals are available in the form of a brake caliper repair kit, and should be renewed as a matter of course. If severe corrosion, scoring, or wear is apparent on the pistons or caliper cylinders, the complete caliper will have to be renewed, as these parts are not available separately.
9   To reassemble the caliper, first wet a new fluid seal with hydraulic fluid and carefully insert it into its groove in the rim half of the caliper

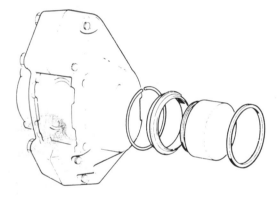

Fig. 9.7 Front brake caliper body and one piston assembly (Sec 13)

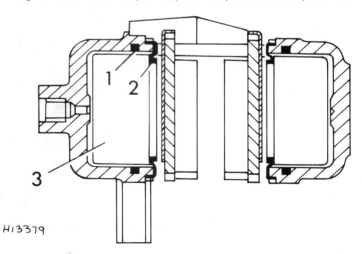

H13379

Fig. 9.8 Correct fitted positions of piston seal and dust cover (Sec 13)

1   Piston seal   3   Piston
2   Dust cover

seating, ensuring that it is correctly fitted. Refit the dust cover into its special groove in the piston.
10   Release the bleed screw in the caliper one complete turn. Coat the piston with hydraulic fluid, and with it positioned squarely in the top of the cylinder bore, ease the piston in until 0.3 in (8 mm) is left protruding. Engage the outer lip of the dust cover in the piston groove and push the piston into the cylinder as far as it will go. Fit the dust cover retaining ring.
11   Repeat the operations in paragraphs 10 and 11 for the mounting half of the caliper.
12   Fit the pads and anti-squeal shims into the caliper and retain in position with the two pins and spring clips.
13   The caliper is now ready for refitting.

14 Pressure differential warning actuator (PDWA) valve – removal, overhaul and refitting

1   Disconnect the electrical lead plug from the top of the PDWA valve.
2   Clean the top of the brake hydraulic fluid reservoir and unscrew the cap. Place a piece of polythene over the top and refit the cap. This is to prevent fluid syphoning out when the pipes are disconnected from the PDWA valve.
3   Clean the area around the PDWA valve assembly and, using an open-ended spanner, unscrew the union nut that secures the rear brake fluid pipe to the valve, followed by the master cylinder-to-valve rear brake pipe, front brake fluid pipes and finally, the master cylinder-to-valve front brake pipe (photo).
4   Undo the PDWA valve securing screw and lift away the screw, spring washer and the valve.
5   Wipe down the outside of the valve and then unscrew and remove the switch from the top of the body.
6   Unscrew and remove the endplug and gasket; a new gasket must be fitted on reassembly.
7   Shake or tap out the piston components, noting the order in which they are fitted, and making sure the sleeve and O-ring are recovered from the bottom of the bore.
8   Carefully prise the C-clips from the piston grooves and discard them together with the O-rings.
9   Examine the bore of the valve carefully for any signs of scores, ridges or corrosion. If this is found to be smooth all over, new seals can be fitted. If there is any doubt of the condition of the bore, a new valve must be obtained. *Never re-use old seals as their condition will have deteriorated with use even though this may not be apparent during inspection.*
10   Before reassembly begins, thoroughly clean all the parts in

14.3 Hydraulic pipe connections at the PDWA valve

A   Rear brake pipe union, B   Master cylinder-to-valve rear brake pipe union, C   Front brake pipe unions, D   Master cylinder-to-valve front brake pipe union

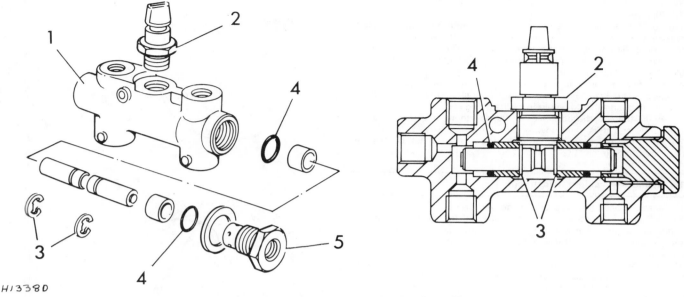

**Fig. 9.9 Pressure differential warning actuator valve components
(Sec 14)**

1 Valve body
2 Warning light switch
3 Circlips
4 O-ring seals
5 Endplug

methylated spirit or clean hydraulic fluid.

11 To reassemble the valve, first fit the piston C-clips into their grooves and the two sleeves and seals onto the piston, making sure that they slide freely on the piston.

12 Smear some fresh hydraulic fluid on the cylinder bore and the piston assembly, and then insert the piston fully into the bore.

13 Screw in the endplug so that the O-ring enters onto the piston, and then remove it and press the O-ring further down the bore until it contacts the sleeve.

14 Fit a new gasket to the endplug, then screw it into the valve body and tighten it to the specified torque.

15 Using a screwdriver through the switch aperture, move the piston to its central position, then screw in the switch and tighten it to the specified torque setting. Make sure that the piston is central, otherwise the switch may foul the two sleeves.

16 Refitting is a reversal of the removal procedure, but it will be necessary to bleed the complete hydraulic system as described in Section 3.

15 Hydraulic pipes and hoses – inspection, removal and refitting

1 The rigid metal brake pipes and the three flexible brake hoses, their connections, unions and mountings should periodically be carefully examined.

2 Examine first all the unions for signs of leaks. Then look at the flexible hoses for signs of fraying and chafing (as well as for leaks). This is only a preliminary inspection of the flexible hoses, as exterior condition does not necessarily indicate interior condition, which will be considered later.

3 The steel pipes must be examined equally carefully. They must be thoroughly cleaned and examined for signs of dents or other percussive damage, rust and corrosion. Rust and corrosion should be scraped off. If the depth of pitting in the pipes is significant, they will require renewal. This is most likely in those areas underneath the body where the pipes are exposed to the full force of road and weather conditions.

4 If any section of pipe is to be removed, plug or tape over the pipe unions when they are undone, to minimise hydraulic fluid loss. When removing a pipe which is 'downstream' from a flexible hose (ie rear axle or front caliper brake pipes) the hose may be compressed using a brake hose clamp. This will eliminate hydrauic fluid loss and simplify bleeding when the pipe is refitted.

5 Rigid pipe removal is usually quite straightforward. The unions at each end are undone and the pipe drawn out of the connection. The clips which may hold it to the car body are bent back, and it is then removed. Underneath the car, the exposed union can be particularly stubborn, defying the efforts of an open-ended spanner. As few people will have the special split ring spanner required, a self-grip wrench is the only answer. If the pipe is being renewed, new unions will be provided. If not, one will have to put up with the possibility of burring over the flats on the unions and of using a self-grip wrench for refitting also.

6 Flexible hoses are always fitted to a rigid support bracket where they join a rigid pipe. The rigid pipe unions must first be removed from the flexible union, which is then detached from its support bracket, after unscrewing the retaining nut (photo).

7 Once the flexible hose is removed, examine the internal bore. If clear of fluid, it should be possible to see through it. Any specks of rubber which come out, or signs of restriction in the bore, mean that

15.6 Flexible hose-to-support bracket and rigid pipe union

the inner lining is breaking up and the hose must be renewed.

8   Rigid pipes which need renewing can usually be purchased from your local dealer where they have the pipe, unions and special tools to make them up. All they need to know is the pipe length required and the type of flare used at the ends of the pipe. These may be different at each end of the same pipe. If possible, it is a good idea to take the old pipe along as a pattern.

9   Refitting of pipes is a straightforward reversal of the removal procedure. It is best to get all the sets (bends) made prior to refitting. Any acute bends should be put in by the garage on a bending machine, otherwise there is the possibility of kinking them, and restricting the bore area, and thus, fluid flow.

10 With the pipes refitted, the braking system must be bled as described in Section 3.

16 Handbrake cable – adjustment

1   Refer to Section 2 and adjust the rear brakes.

2   Pull up the handbrake lever four clicks of the ratchet. Check the handbrake adjustment by attempting to rotate the rear wheels, which should now be locked. If it is possible to turn the rear wheels, adjust the cable as follows.

3   Working underneath the car, slacken the locknut which secures the handbrake outer cable to the support bracket on the floor pan.

4   Now turn the adjustment nut clockwise, while the outer cable is held with a spanner, until the correct adjustment is obtained. Re-tighten the locknut.

5   Release the handbrake and check that the rear wheels can be rotated freely.

6   Lower the car to the ground.

17 Handbrake cable – removal and refitting

1   Chock the front wheels, jack up the rear of the car and support it on axle stands. Release the handbrake fully.

2   Working underneath the car, extract the split pin and remove the clevis pin and spring washer securing the inner cable yoke to the handbrake lever.

3   Unscrew fully the locknut that secures the outer handbrake cable to the support bracket on the floor pan.

4   At each rear wheel, extract the split pin and remove the clevis pin and washer securing the handbrake cable yokes to the wheel cylinder operating levers (photo).

5   Undo and remove the bolts and spring washers securing the handbrake cable support strap and retaining clip to the rear axle casing (photos). Lift out the handbrake cable assembly from under the car.

6   Refit the handbrake cable using the reverse sequence to removal, and then adjust its tension as described in the previous Section.

18 Handbrake lever assembly – removal and refitting

1   Jack up the front of the car and support it on axle stands.

2   From underneath the car, extract the split pin and remove the clevis pin and flat washer securing the handbrake cable yoke to the lever assembly.

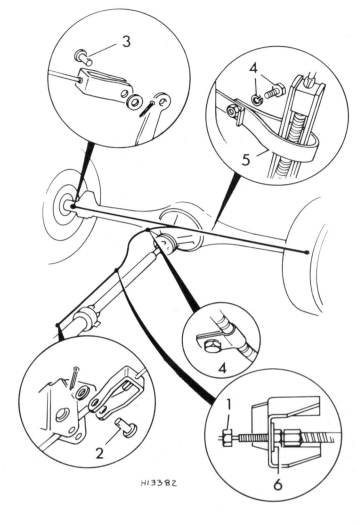

H13382

Fig. 9.10 Handbrake cable removal (Sec 17)

1 Locknut	4 Cable retaining clip and
2 Cable-to-handbrake lever	securing bolt
clevis pin	5 Support strap
3 Cable-to-operating lever	6 Adjustment nut
clevis pin	

17.4 Handbrake cable yoke-to-wheel cylinder operating lever attachment

17.5a Handbrake cable-to-rear axle support strap retaining bolt ...

17.5b ... and retaining clip bolt

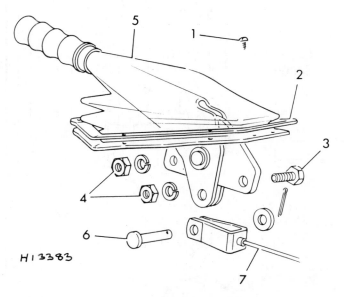

H13383

Fig. 9.11 Handbrake lever assembly removal (Sec 18)

1 Self-tapping screw
2 Rubber gaiter retaining plate
3 Mounting bolt
4 Nut and spring washer
5 Rubber gaiter
6 Clevis pin
7 Handbrake cable

3 Working inside the car, remove the centre console (if fitted) as described in Chapter 12.
4 Lift up the carpets sufficiently to provide access to the lever assembly.
5 Undo and remove the four screws securing the handbrake lever gaiter retaining plate to the floor. Lift off the plate and slide the gaiter up the lever.
6 Undo and remove the two nuts, bolts and spring washers securing the lever assembly to its mounting brackets. If a handbrake warning switch is fitted, disconnect the wiring from the switch.
7 Lift away the handbrake lever assembly.
8 Refitting is the reverse sequence to removal.

19 Brake pedal assembly – removal and refitting

1 Working inside the car, release the locking buttons and lift out the trim panel beneath the dashboard to provide access to the pedal assembly. Remove the face level vent hose, referring to Chapter 12 if necessary.
2 Refer to Chapter 3 and remove the throttle pedal.
3 Remove the split pin that retains the clutch master cylinder operating rod clevis pin and withdraw the clevis pin.
4 Undo and remove the clutch master cylinder securing nuts and move the cylinder to one side; then tap out the master cylinder lower securing stud.
5 Clean the top of the brake master cylinder and remove the fluid reservoir cap. Place a piece of polythene over the top of the reservoir and refit the cap. This is to prevent the hydraulic fluid syphoning out during subsequent operations.
6 Disconnect the brake master cylinder fluid pipes from the PDWA valve on the bulkhead.
7 Slacken the retaining clip and disconnect the vacuum hose from the servo unit connector.
8 Make a note of the cable connections on the ignition coil. Detach the cables and remove the ignition coil.
9 Undo and remove the nuts, bolts, spring and plain washers that secure the pedal mounting assembly to the bulkhead.
10 Partially withdraw the pedal assembly and disconnect the electrical connections at the stoplight switch, then remove the clevis pin from the brake pedal.
11 Carefully pull the the speedometer cable through the grommet in

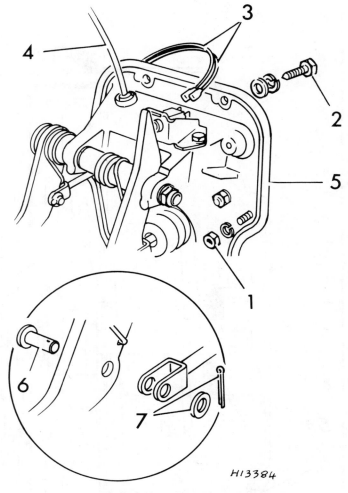

H13384

Fig. 9.12 Brake pedal assembly removal (Sec 19)

1 Nut
2 Bolt
3 Stoplight cables
4 Speedometer cable
5 Pedal mounting bracket
6 Clutch operating rod-to-clutch pedal clevis pin
7 Split pin and washer

the pedal mounting assembly after disconnecting it.
12 The pedal and mounting assembly may now be lifted away from inside the car.
13 Undo and remove the locknut and plain washer that retain the brake pedal pivot pin. Lift away the throttle pedal spring bracket, noting which way round it is fitted.
14 Withdraw the clutch pedal complete with pivot pin and remove the brake pedal and return springs.
15 Refitting is the reverse of the removal procedure. Ensure that the servo operating rod is connected to the lower hole in the brake pedal. Bleed the brake hydraulic system as described in Section 3.

20 Vacuum servo unit – description

The vacuum servo unit is fitted into the brake hydraulic circuit in series with the master cylinder to provide power assistance to the driver when the brake pedal is depressed.
The unit operates by vacuum 'obtained' from the induction manifold and comprises basically a booster diaphragm and a non-return valve.
The servo unit and hydraulic master cylinder are connected together so that the servo unit piston rod acts as the master cylinder pushrod. The driver's braking effort is transmitted through another pushrod to the servo unit piston and its built-in control system. The

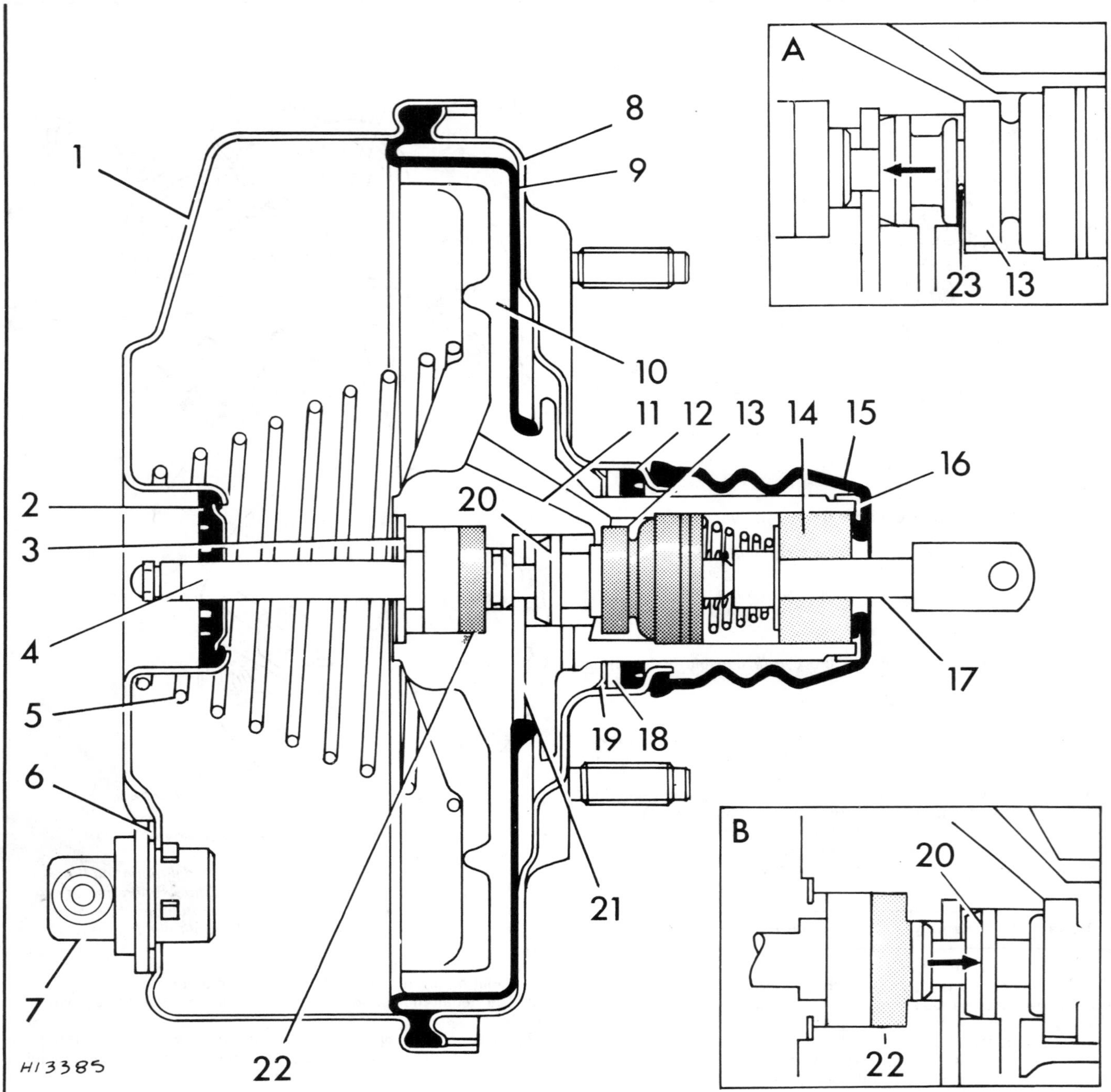

H13385

Fig. 9.13 Sectional view of brake vacuum servo unit (Sec 20)

1	Front shell	7	Non-return valve	13	Control valve	18 Bearing
2	Seal and plate assembly	8	Rear shell	14	Filter	19 Retainer
3	Retainer (sprag washer)	9	Diaphragm	15	Dust cover	20 Control piston
4	Pushrod (hydraulic)	10	Diaphragm plate	16	End cap	21 Valve retaining plate
5	Diaphragm return spring	11	Vacuum port	17	Valve operating rod	22 Reaction disc
6	O-ring	12	Seal		assembly	23 Atmospheric port

A Control valve closed, control piston moved forward, atmospheric port open

B Pressure from diaphragm plate causes reaction disc to extrude, presses back control piston and closes atmospheric port servo unit piston does not fit tightly into the cylinder but has a strong diaphragm to keep its edges in constant contact with the cylinder walls, so assuring an air-tight seal between the two parts. The forward chamber is held under vacuum conditions created in the inlet manifold of the engine and, during periods when the brake pedal is not in use, the controls open a passage to the rear chamber, so placing it under vacuum. When the brake pedal is depressed, the vacuum passage to the rear chamber is cut off and the chamber opened to atmospheric pressure. The consequent rush of air pushes the servo piston forward in the vacuum chamber and operates the main pushrod to the master cylinder. The controls are designed so that assistance is given under all conditions and, when the brakes are not required, vacuum in the rear chamber is established when the pedal is released. Air from the atmosphere entering the rear chamber is passed through a small air filter.

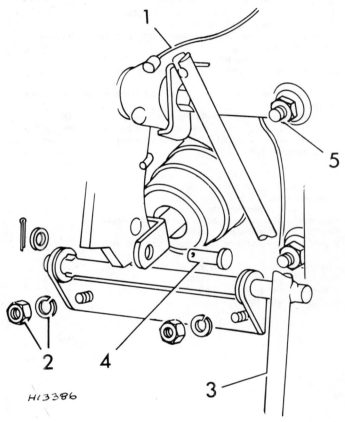

HI3386

Fig. 9.14 Vacuum servo unit attachments – car interior (Sec 21)

1   Throttle cable
2   Throttle pedal bracket securing nut and spring washer
3   Throttle pedal
4   Clevis pin with plain washer and split pin
5   Servo unit securing nut and spring washer

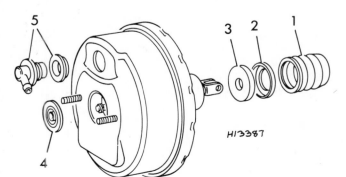

HI3387

21 Vacuum servo unit – removal and refitting

1   Refer to Section 9 and remove the brake master cylinder.
2   Slacken the hose clip and remove the vacuum hose from the servo connector.
3   Refer to Chapter 3 and remove the throttle pedal.
4   Extract the split pin and withdraw the clevis pin and flat washer securing the servo pushrod to the brake pedal (photo).
5   Undo and remove the four nuts and spring washers that secure the servo unit to the mounting bracket. Lift away the servo unit and gasket.
6   Refitting the servo unit is the reverse of the removal procedure. Always use a new gasket. It is important that the servo operating rod is attached to the lower of the two holes in the brake pedal lever.
7   Bleed the brake hydraulic system as described in Section 3.

22 Vacuum servo unit air filter – renewal

Under normal operating conditions, the vacuum servo unit is very reliable and does not require overhaul except possibly at very high mileages. In this case it is far better to obtain a service exchange unit, rather than repair the original. However, the air filter may be renewed and fitting details are given. This will not, however, repair any fault.
1   Remove the trim panel from below the dashboard, pull back the dust cover over the servo air filter and slide it up the pushrod.
2   Using a screwdriver, ease out the end cap and then, with a pair of scissors, cut off the old air filter.
3   Make a diagonal cut through the new air filter element and fit it over the pushrod. Hold it in position and refit the end cap.
4   Reposition the dust cover on the servo unit body.

21.4 Servo unit pushrod-to-brake pedal attachment

Fig. 9.15 Servo unit air filter renewal (Sec 22)

1   Dust cover
2   End cap
3   Filter
4   Front seal
5   Non-return valve and grommet

23 Fault diagnosis – braking system

Symptom	Reason(s)
Excessive brake pedal travel	Rear brakes out of adjustment Excessive front wheel bearing endfloat Air in hydraulic system
Brake pedal appears spongy	Air in hydraulic system Bulging in hydraulic flexible hose(s) Master cylinder mountings or servo unit mountings insecure Master cylinder faulty
Excessive effort required to stop car	Servo unit not functioning Excessively worn brake pads or linings One or more wheel cylinder or caliper pistons seized Incorrect linings or pads fitted Brake linings or pads contaminated with oil, grease or hydraulic fluid Failure of one braking circuit Rear brake shoes incorrectly fitted New brake pads or shoes not yet bedded in
Vehicle pulls to one side under braking	Brake linings or pads on one side contaminated with oil, grease or hydraulic fluid Disc caliper or wheel cylinder pistons seized on one side A mixture of friction lining materials fitted between sides Wear, incorrect or out of adjustment steering or suspension components, tyres or tyre pressures
Judder felt through pedal and/or steering wheel under braking	Excessive run-out of front discs Front discs worn, scored or grooved Excessively worn front brake pads Front caliper mountings loose Rear brake drums worn, scored or out-of-round Rear backplate mountings loose Wear in steering and/or suspension components
Brakes binding and/or overheating	Rear brake shoes adjusted too tightly Handbrake cable over-tightened Wheel cylinder or disc caliper pistons seized Master cylinder faulty

Chapter 10 Electrical system

Contents

Specifications

System	12 volt negative earth
Battery	12 volt 40 to 60 amp hour at 20 hour rate

Alternator
Type	Lucas 16ACR or 17ACR
Maximum output:	
16 ACR	34 amps
17 ACR	36 amps
Minimum brush length	0.2 in (5 mm) protruding beyond brush box moulding
Brush spring tension	9 to 13 oz (255 to 268g) with brush face flush with brush box

Starter motor
Type	Lucas M35J or 2M100 pre-engaged
Brush spring tension:	
M35J	28 oz (0.8 kg)
2M100	36 oz (1.02 kg)
Minimum brush length:	
M35J and 2M100	0.375 in (9.5 mm)

Wiper motor
Type	Lucas 14W, 2-speed
Armature endfloat	0.002 to 0.008 in (0.051 to 0.21 mm)
Light running current:	
Normal speed	1.5 amp
High speed	2.0 amp
Light running speed:	
Normal speed	46 to 52 rpm
High speed	60 to 70 rpm
Minimum brush length	0.187 in (4.76 mm)

Fuses

Fuse No	Rating	Circuit protected
1	17A	Direction indicators
		Stop lamps
		Reversing lamps
		Heated rear window and warning light
		Tailgate wiper and washer
2	8A	Side and tail lights
		Number plate lamp
		Panel lamps
		Glovebox light
		Automatic transmission selector light
		Rear fog guard lamps
3	17A	Windscreen wiper
		Windscreen washer
		Heater motor
4	8A	Hazard warning flashers
5	17A	Horn
		Headlight flasher
		Interior lamp
		Lighter
		Boot light
		Brake failure warning light
		Clock

Bulbs

	Wattage
Headlight bulb	60/55
Sidelight	4
Front and rear flashers	21
Stop/tail light	6/21
Number plate	4
Interior	6
Panel and warning	2.2
Reversing lights	21
Boot light	6
Automatic selector lever light	2
Heater backlight switch, brake failure light and hazard warning light	0.75
Glovebox light	6
Fog guard light	21
Front flasher repeaters	5
Engine compartment and clock light	5

1 General description

The electrical system is of the 12 volt type, and the major components comprise a 12 volt battery of which the negative terminal is earthed, a Lucas alternator which is fitted to the front right-hand side of the engine and is driven from the pulley on the front of the

2.1 When removing the battery, always disconnect the negative terminal first, and reconnect it last

crankshaft, and a starter motor which is mounted on the rear right-hand side of the engine.

The battery supplies a steady amount of current for the ignition, lighting and other electrical circuits, and provides a reserve of electricity when the current consumed by the electrical equipment exceeds that being produced by the alternator.

The battery is charged by a Lucas ACR alternator and information on this component will be found in Section 5.

When fitting electrical accessories to cars with a negative earth system, it is important, if they contain silicone diodes or transistors, that they are connected correctly, otherwise serious damage may result to the component concerned. Items such as radios, tape recorders, electronic tachometers etc, should all be checked for correct polarity.

It is important that the battery negative lead is always disconnected if the battery is to be boost charged, or if any body or mechanical repairs are to be carried out using electric arc welding equipment. Serious damage can be caused to the more delicate instruments, especially those containing semiconductors. It is equally important to ensure that neither battery lead is disconnected whilst the engine is running, and that the battery terminals are not inadvertently connected with the polarity reversed.

2 Battery – removal and refitting

1 The battery is in a special carrier fitted on the right-hand wing valance of the engine compartment. It should be removed once every three months for cleaning and testing. Disconnect the negative and then the positive leads from the battery terminals by slackening the clamp retaining nuts and bolts, or by unscrewing the retaining screws if terminal caps are fitted instead of clamps (photo).

2   Unscrew the clamp bar retaining nuts and lower the clamp bar to the side of the battery. Carefully lift the battery from its carrier. Hold the battery vertical to ensure that none of the electrolyte is spilled.

3   Refitting is a direct reversal of this procedure. Ensure that the positive lead is fitted before the negative lead and smear the terminals with petroleum jelly to prevent corrosion. Do not use an ordinary grease as applied to other parts of the car.

3   Battery – maintenance and inspection

1   Check the battery electrolyte level weekly, by lifting off the cover or removing the individual cell plugs. The tops of the plates should be just covered by the electrolyte. If not, add distilled water so that they are. *Do not add extra water with the idea of reducing the intervals of topping up.* This will merely dilute the electrolyte and reduce charging and current retention efficiency. On batteries fitted with patent covers, troughs, glass balls and so on, follow the instructions marked on the cover of the battery to ensure correct addition of water.

2   Keep the battery clean and dry all over by wiping it with a dry cloth. A damp top surface could cause tracking between the two terminal posts with consequent draining of power.

3   Every three months, remove the battery and check the support clamp and battery terminal connections for signs of corrosion – usually indicated by a whitish green crystalline deposit. Wash this off with clean water to which a little ammonia or washing soda has been added. Then treat the terminals with petroleum jelly and the battery clamp with suitable protective paint to prevent the metal being eaten away.

4   If the electrolyte level needs an excessive amount of replenishment but no leaks are apparent, it could be due to over-charging as a result of the battery having been run down and then left to recharge from the vehicle rather than an outside source. If the battery has been heavily discharged for one reason or another, it is best to have it continuously charged at a low amperage for a period of many hours. If it is charged from the car's system under such conditions, the charging will be intermittent and greatly varied in intensity. This does not do the battery any good at all. If the battery needs topping up frequently, even when it is known to be in good condition and not too old, then the voltage regulator should be checked to ensure that the charging output is being correctly controlled. An elderly battery, however, may need topping-up more than a new one, because it needs to take in more charging current. Do not worry about this, provided it gives satisfactory service.

5   When checking a battery's condition, a hydrometer should be used. On some batteries, where the terminals of each of the six cells are exposed, a discharge tester can be used to check the condition of any one cell. On modern batteries, the use of a discharge tester is no longer regarded as useful, as the renewal or repair of cells is not an economic proposition. The tables in the following Section give the hydrometer readings for various states or charge. A further check can be made when the battery is undergoing a charge. If, towards the end of the charge, when the cells are meant to be 'gassing' (bubbling), one cell appears not to be, this indicates the cell or cells in question are probably breaking down and the life of the battery is limited.

4   Battery – charging and electrolyte replenishment

1   It is possible that in winter, when the load on the battery cannot be recuperated during normal driving time, external charging is desirable. This is best done overnight at a 'trickle' rate of 1 to 1.5 amps. Alternatively, a 3 to 4 amp rate can be used over a period of four hours or so. Check the specific gravity in the latter case and stop the charge when the reading is correct. Most modern charging sets reduce the rate automatically when the fully charged state is neared. Rapid boost charges of 30 to 60 amps or more may get you out of trouble or can be used on a battery that has seen better days anyhow. They are *not* advised for a good battery that may have run flat for some reason.

2   Electrolyte replenishment should not normally be necessary unless an accident or some other cause, such as contamination, arises. If it is necessary then it is best first to discharge the battery completely and then tip out all the remaining liquid from all cells. Then acquire a quantity of mixed electrolyte from a battery shop or garage according to the specifications in the table given below. The quantity required

will depend on the type of battery but three or four pints should be more than enough for most. When the electrolyte has been put into the battery, a slow charge – not exceeding one amp – should be given for as long as is necessary to fully charge the battery. This could be up to thirty six hours. Specific gravities for hydrometer readings (check each cell) – 12 volt batteries are as follows:

	Climate below 80°F (26.7°C)	Climate above 80°F (26.7°C)
Fully charged	1.270 to 1.290	1.210 to 1.230
Half charged	1.190 to 1.210	1.120 to 1.150
Discharged completely	1.110 to 1.130	1.050 to 1.070

Note: *If the electrolyte temperature is significantly different from 60°F (15.6°C), then the specific gravity will be affected. For every 5°F (2.8°C) it will increase or decrease with the temperature by 0.002.* When the vehicle is being used in cold climates, it is essential to maintain the battery fully charged because the charge affects the freezing point of the electrolyte. The densities below have been corrected to suit measurement at 80°F (26.7°C)

| *Specific gravity* | *1.200 freezes* | –35°F |
| *Specific gravity* | *1.160 freezes* | 0°F |

5   Alternator – general description

A Lucas alternator is fitted as standard to the models covered by this manual. The alternator is of the rotating field ventilated design and comprises principally a laminated stator on which is wound a star connected 3-phase output winding, a twelve pole rotor carrying the field windings – each end of the rotor shaft runs in ball race bearings which are lubricated for life – natural finish aluminium die-cast end brackets incorporating the mounting lugs, a rectifier pack for converting the AC output of the machine to DC for battery charging, and an output control regulator.

The rotor is belt driven from the engine through a pulley keyed to the rotor shaft. A pressed steel fan adjacent to the pulley draws cooling air through the unit. This fan forms an integral part of the alternator specification. It has been designed to provide adequate air flow with a minimum of noise and to withstand the high stresses associated with maximum speed. Rotation is clockwise viewed on the drive end.

Rectification of alternator output is achieved by nine silicone diodes housed in a rectifier pack and connected as a 3-phase full wave bridge. The rectifier pack is attached to the outer face of the slip ring end bracket and contains also three 'field' diodes. At normal operating speeds rectified current from the stator output windings flow through these diodes to provide self-excitation of the rotor field via brushes bearing on face type slip rings.

The brushgear is housed in a moulding screwed to the outside of the slip ring end bracket. This moulding thus encloses the slip ring and brushgear assembly, and together with the shielded bearing, protects the assembly against the entry of dust and moisture.

The regulator is set during manufacture and requires no further attention.

6   Alternator – removal and refitting

1   Disconnect the battery negative terminal.

2   Loosen the pivot and adjustment bolts and swivel the alternator towards the engine to facilitate the removal of the fanbelt.

3   Disconnect the multi-connector from the alternator end cover.

4   Unscrew and remove the pivot and adjustment bolts and withdraw the alternator from the engine.

5   Refitting is a reversal of the removal procedure, but adjust the fanbelt as described in Chapter 2.

7   Alternator – fault diagnosis and repair

Due to the specialist knowledge and equipment required to test or service an alternator, it is recommended that if the performance is suspect, the car is taken to an automobile electrician who will have the facilities for such work. Because of this recommendation, information is limited to the inspection and renewal of the brushes. Should the

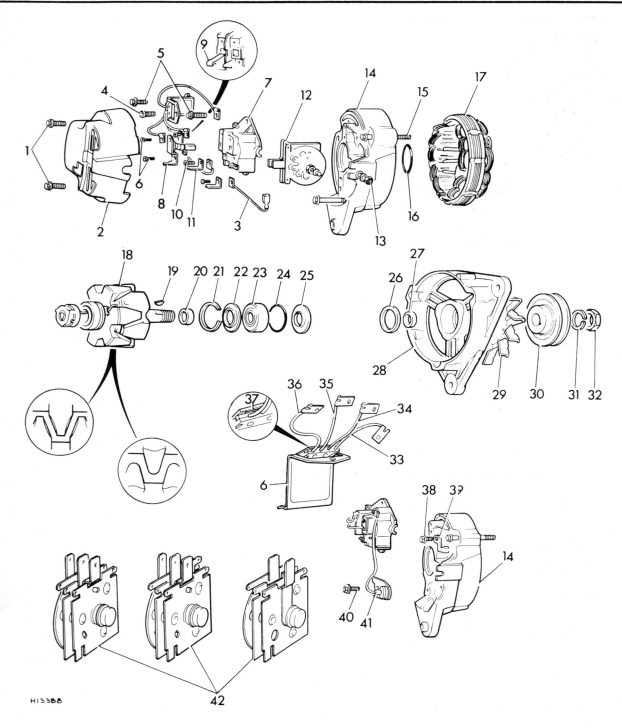

Fig. 10.1 Exploded view of the alternator (Sec 8)

1 Screw	13 Nut and washers	24 O-ring	36 B + red lead
2 End cover	14 Slip ring end bracket	25 Cover plate	37 Copper strip (alternative to item 33)
3 Lead (typical)	15 Through-bolts	26 Felt washer	38 Screw
4 Screw	16 O-ring	27 Distance piece	39 Earthing link
5 Screws	17 Stator lamination pack	28 Drive end bracket	40 Screw
6 Regulator screws	18 Rotor assembly with bearing and slip ring	29 Fan	41 Avalanche diode
7 Brush box mounting	19 Key	30 Pulley	42 Rectifiers (alternative types to item 12)
8 Brush assembly	20 Distance piece	31 Spring washer	
9 Brush spring	21 Circlip	32 Nut	
10 Screws	22 Cover plate	33 Black earth lead	
11 Terminals	23 Bearing	34 F green lead	
12 Rectifier assembly		35 + yellow lead	

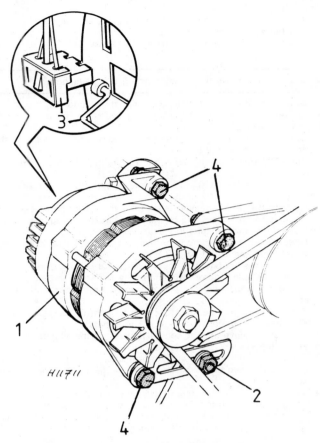

Fig. 10.2 Alternator removal (Sec 6)

1	Alternator	3	Wiring multi-plug connector
2	Adjusting arm nut	4	Pivot and adjustment bolts

alternator not charge, or the system be suspect, the following points should be checked before seeking further assistance:

1   *Check the fanbelt tension as described in Chapter 2*
2   *Check the battery as described in Section 3*
3   *Check the electrical cable connections for cleanliness and security*

8   Alternator brushes – inspection, removal and refitting

1   With the alternator removed from the car, undo and remove the two screws and lift off the end cover.
2   Make a note of the colour and location of the electrical leads connected to the rectifier spade terminals and disconnect them.
3   If a surge protection diode is fitted to the end bracket, undo and remove the retaining screw and lift it off.
4   Undo and remove the two screws securing the brush box to the end bracket, and the single screw securing the regulator to the end bracket, and lift away this assembly.
5   With the brush box removed and the brush assemblies still in position, check that they protrude from the face of the brush box by the dimension shown in the Specifications. Also check that when depressed the spring pressure is as specified. To be done with any accuracy a push type spring gauge is required.
6   If the brush length or spring pressure is not as specified, the brushes should be renewed as follows.
7   Undo and remove the screw securing the regulator to the brush box.
8   Make a note of the colour and location of the electrical leads and then undo and remove the retaining screws and terminal strips securing the brushes. Carefully lift out the brush assemblies, noting that there is a leaf spring fitted at the side of the inner brush.

9   When the brushes are refitted they should slide smoothly in their holders. Any sticking tendency may first be rectified by wiping with a petrol soaked cloth or, if this fails, by carefully polishing with a very fine file where any binding marks appear.
10   Before refitting the brush box, the slip rings on the end of the rotor should be cleaned with a petrol soaked cloth. Any signs of burning may be removed with fine glass paper. On no account should any other abrasive be used.
11   Reassembly of the brushes and brush box is the reverse of the dismantling sequence. Ensure that all the electrical leads are reconnected to the same positions as noted during dismantling.

9   Starter motor – general description

All Ital models covered by this manual are equipped with a Lucas pre-engaged starter motor. The motor is a 12 volt dc series wound unit, switched by a solenoid mounted on top of the motor casing.
The principle of operation of the starter motor is as follows: When the ignition is switched on and turned to the start position, current flows from the battery to the starter solenoid. The plunger in the solenoid moves inwards, so causing a centrally pivoted lever to move in such a manner that the forked end pushes the drive pinion into mesh with the starter ring gear. When the solenoid plunger reaches the end of its travel, it closes an internal contact and full starting current flows to the starter field coils. The armature is then able to rotate the crankshaft, so starting the engine.
A special one-way clutch is fitted to the starter drive pinion, so that when the engine fires and starts to operate on its own, it does not drive the starter motor.

10   Starter motor – testing on engine

1   If the starter motor fails to operate, first check the condition of the battery by turning on the headlights. If they glow brightly for several seconds and then gradually dim, or if they do not glow at all, the battery is in an uncharged condition or has developed an internal fault.
2   If the headlights glow brightly and it is obvious that the battery is in good condition, check the tightness of the battery terminals. Pay particular attention to the earth lead from the battery terminal to its connection on the bodyframe, and the engine earth lead at its engine and bodyframe attachments. If one of the battery terminals gets very hot or can be heard sizzling when attempting to operate the starter, remove the terminal and thoroughly clean it. Apply petroleum jelly to the terminal and battery post and then refit securely. Also check the tightness of the connections at the solenoid and starter motor.
3   If the wiring is in order, then check the operation of the solenoid as follows. At the rear of the solenoid it will be seen that there are two large threaded terminal studs and nuts, one of which contains the main feed cable from the battery, and the other the cable or strap from the starter motor itself. Connect one lead from a 12 volt test lamp or voltmeter to the solenoid terminal containing the cable or strap from the starter motor. Connect the other lead to a good earth. Turn the ignition to the 'start' position; if the lamp fails to illuminate or if there is no reading on the voltmeter, the fault lies with the solenoid or ignition switch. Remove the white and red lead from the solenoid and connect the test lamp or voltmeter between the lead and earth. An illuminated test lamp or voltmeter reading when the ignition switch is operated confirms a faulty solenoid. No reading indicates a fault in the ignition switch or associated wiring.
4   If a reading was obtained on the voltmeter or the test lamp illuminated when connected to the starter motor wiring terminal, then the fault lies with the motor, and it will have to be removed from the car for examination.

11   Starter motor – removal and refitting

1   Disconnect the battery earth terminal.
2   Undo and remove the terminal nut and washer securing the heavy duty battery cable to the solenoid and lift off the cable.
3   Make a note of the locations of the smaller cables secured to the rear of the solenoid by Lucar connectors and disconnect them.
4   Undo and remove the two bolts securing the starter motor to the bellhousing, noting that the engine earth strap is also secured by the

bottom bolt.

5   Undo and remove the two bolts securing the starter motor support strap to the engine and lift away the starter.

6   Refitting is the reverse sequence to removal.

12 Starter motor (M35J) – dismantling and reassembly

1   Detach the heavy duty cable that links the solenoid STA terminal to the starter motor terminal by undoing and removing the securing nuts and washers.

2   Undo and remove the two nuts and spring washers that secure the solenoid to the drive end bracket.

3   Carefully withdraw the solenoid coil unit from the drive end bracket.

4   Lift off the solenoid plunger and return spring from the engagement lever.

5   Remove the rubber sealing block from the drive end bracket.

6   Remove the retaining ring (spire nut) from the engagement lever pivot pin and withdraw the pin.

7   Unscrew and remove the two drive end bracket securing nuts and spring washers and withdraw the bracket.

8   Lift away the engagement lever from the drive operating plate.

9   Extract the split pin from the end of the armature and remove the shim washers and thrust plate from the commutator end of the armature shaft.

10 Remove the armature, together with its internal thrust washer.

11 Withdraw the thrust washer from the armature.

12 Undo and remove the two screws that secure the commutator end bracket to the starter motor body.

13 Carefully detach the end bracket from the yoke, at the same time disengaging the field brushes from the brush gear. Lift away the end bracket.

14 Move the thrust collar clear of the jump ring and then remove the jump ring. Withdraw the drive assembly from the armature shaft.

15 Inspection and renovation is basically the same as for the Lucas 2M100 starter motor and full information will be found in Section 13.

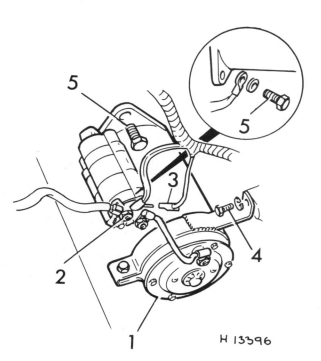

H 13396

Fig. 10.3 Starter motor removal (Sec 11)

1	Starter motor	4	Starter motor bracket securing bolt
2	Top heavy duty cable		
3	Lucar connectors	5	Starter motor-to-flywheel housing bolt

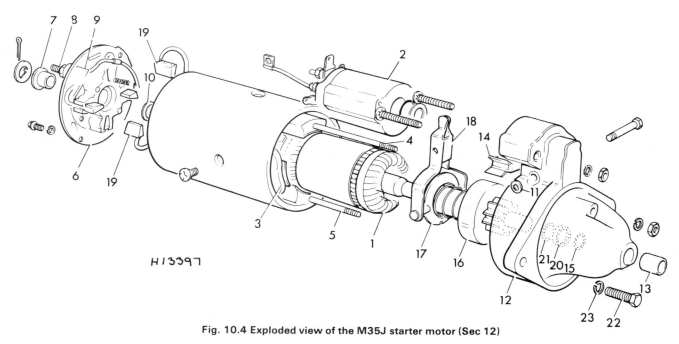

H 13397

Fig. 10.4 Exploded view of the M35J starter motor (Sec 12)

1	Armature	7	Commutator end bracket bush	12	Drive end bracket	18	Lever and pivot assembly
2	Solenoid			13	End bracket bush	19	Brush
3	Field coil	8	Field terminal	14	Grommet	20	Thrust collar
4	Pole piece and long stud	9	Terminal insulating bush	15	Jump ring	21	Shim
5	Pole piece and short stud	10	Thrust plate	16	Roller clutch drive	22	Fixing bolt
6	Commutator end bracket	11	Pivot pin retaining clip	17	Bearing bush	23	Lockwasher

The following necessitated by the fitting of the solenoid coil should be noted:

16 If a bush is worn, so allowing excessive side movement of the armature shaft, the bush must be renewed. Drift out the old bush with a piece of suitable diameter rod, preferably with a shoulder on it to stop the bush collapsing.

17 Soak a new bush in engine oil for 24 hours.

18 As new bushes must not be reamed after fitting they must be pressed into position using a small mandrel of the same diameter as the bush and with a shoulder on it. Place the bush on the mandrel and press into position using a bench vice.

19 Use a test light and battery to test the continuity of the coil windings between terminal STA and a good earth point on the solenoid body. If the light fails to come on, the solenoid should be renewed.

20 To test the solenoid contacts for correct opening and closing, connect a 12 volt battery and a 60 watt test light between the main unmarked Lucar terminal and the STA terminal. The light should not come on.

21 Energise the solenoid with a separate 12 volt supply connected to the small unmarked Lucar terminal and a good earth on the solenoid body.

22 As the coil is energised, the solenoid should be heard to operate and the test lamp should light with full brilliance.

23 The contacts may only be renewed as a set, ie moving and fixed contacts. The fixed contacts are part of the moulded cover.

24 To fit a new set of contacts, first undo and remove the moulded cover securing screws.

25 Unsolder the coil connections from the cover terminals.

26 Lift away the cover and moving contact assembly.

27 Fit a new cover and moving contact assembly, soldering the connections to the cover terminals.

28 Refit the moulded cover securing screws.

29 Whilst the motor is apart, check the operation of the drive clutch. It must provide instantaneous take-up of the drive in one direction and rotate easily and smoothly in the opposite direction.

30 Make sure that the drive moves smoothly on the armature shaft splines without binding or sticking.

31 Reassembly of the starter motor is the reverse sequence to dismantling. The following additional points should be noted:

32 When assembling the drive, always use a new retaining ring (spire nut) to secure the engagement lever pivot pin.

33 Make sure that the internal thrust washer is fitted to the commutator end of the armature shaft before the armature is fitted.

34 Make sure that the thrust washers and plate are assembled in the correct order and are prevented from rotating separately by engaging the collar pin with the locking piece on the thrust plate.

13 Starter motor (2M100) – dismantling and reassembly

1 Undo and remove the nut and spring washer that secure the connecting link between the solenoid and starter motor at the solenoid STA terminal. Carefully ease the connecting link out of engagement of the terminal post on the solenoid.

2 Undo and remove the two nuts and spring washers that secure the solenoid to the drive end bracket.

3 Carefully ease the solenoid back from the drive end bracket, lift the solenoid plunger and return spring from the engagement lever and completely remove the solenoid.

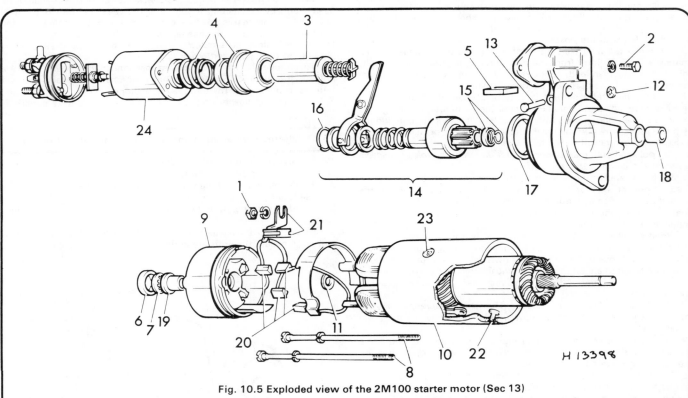

Fig. 10.5 Exploded view of the 2M100 starter motor (Sec 13)

1 Connecting link securing nut	6 Armature end cap seal	13 Engagement lever pivot pin	19 Commutator end cover armature shaft bush
2 Solenoid-to-drive end bracket securing setscrew	7 Armature shaft retaining ring (spire nut)	14 Armature and roller clutch drive assembly	20 Field coil brushes
3 Solenoid plunger	8 Through-bolts	15 Thrust collar and jump ring	21 Terminal and rubber grommet
4 Solenoid plunger return spring, spring seat and dust excluder	9 Commutator end cover	16 Spring ring	22 Rivet
5 Rubber grommet	10 Yoke	17 Dirt seal	23 Pole shoe retaining screw
	11 Thrust washer	18 Drive end bracket armature shaft bush	24 Solenoid
	12 Retaining ring (spire nut)		

4   Recover the shaped rubber block that is placed between the solenoid and starter motor body.

5   Carefully remove the end cap seal from the commutator end cover.

6   Ease the armature shaft retaining ring (spire nut) from the armature shaft. **Note:** *The retaining ring must not be reused, but a new one obtained ready for fitting.*

7   Undo and remove the two long through-bolts and spring washers.

8   Detach the commutator end cover from the yoke, at the same time disengaging the filed brushes from the brush box moulding.

9   Lift away the thrust washer from the armature shaft.

10 The starter motor body may now be lifted from the armature and drive end assembly.

11 Ease the retaining ring (spire nut) from the engagement lever pivot pin. **Note:** *The retaining ring must not be reused, but a new one obtained ready for fitting.*

12 Using a parallel pin punch of suitable size, remove the pivot pin from the engagement lever and drive end bracket.

13 Carefully move the thrust collar clear of the jump ring and slide the jump ring from the armature shaft.

14 Slide off the thrust collar and finally remove the roller clutch drive and engagement lever assembly from the armature shaft.

15 With the motor stripped, the brushes and brush gear may be inspected. To check the brush spring tension, fit a new brush into each holder in turn and, using an accurate spring balance, push the brush on the balance tray until the brush protrudes approximately $\frac{1}{16}$ in (1.5 mm) from the holder. Make a note of the reading which should be as shown in the Specifications. If the spring pressures vary considerably, the commutator end bracket must be renewed as a complete assembly.

16 Inspect the brushes for wear and fit new brushes if the ones fitted are nearing the minimum length as shown in the Specifications. To renew the end bracket brushes, cut the brush cables from the terminal posts and, with a small file or hacksaw, slot the head of the terminal posts to a sufficient depth to accommodate the new leads. Solder the new brush leads to the posts.

17 To renew the field winding brushes, cut the brush leads approximately $\frac{1}{4}$ in (6.35 mm) from the field winding junction and carefully solder the new brush leads to the remaining stumps, making sure that the insulation sleeves provide adequate cover.

18 If the commutator surface is dirty or blackened, clean it with a petrol dampened rag. Carefully examine the commutator for signs of excessive wear, burning or pitting. If evident, it may be reconditioned by having it skimmed at the local engineering works or BL dealer who possesses a centre lathe. For minor reconditioning, the commutator may be polished with glasspaper. *Do not undercut the mica insulators between the commutator segments.*

19 With the starter motor dismantled, test the field coils for open circuit. Connect a 12 volt battery with a 12 volt bulb in one of the leads between each of the field brushes and a clean part of the body. The lamp will light if continuity is satisfactory between the brushes, windings and body connection.

20 Renewal of the field coils calls for the use of a wheel operated screwdriver, a soldering iron, and caulking and riveting operations. This is beyond the scope of the majority of owners. The starter motor body should be taken to an automobile electrical engineering works for new field coils to be fitted. Alternatively, purchase an exchange Lucas starter motor.

21 Check the condition of the bushes. They should be renewed when they are sufficiently worn to allow visible side movement of the armature shaft.

22 To renew the commutator end bracket bush, drill out the rivets that secure the brush box moulding and remove the moulding, bearing seal retaining plate and felt washer seal.

23 Screw in a $\frac{1}{2}$ in tap and withdraw the bush with the tap.

24 As the bush is of the phosphor bronze type, it is essential that it is allowed to stand in engine oil for at least 24 hours before fitment.

25 Using a suitable diameter drift, drive the new bush into position. Do not ream the bush as its self-lubricating properties will be impaired.

26 To renew the drive end bracket bush, drive out the old bush with a suitable diameter drift and fit a new one as described in paragraphs 24 and 25.

27 Whilst the motor is apart, check the operation of the drive clutch. It must provide instantaneous take-up of the drive in one direction and rotate easily and smoothly in the opposite direction.

28 Make sure that the drive moves smoothly on the armature shaft splines without binding or sticking.

29 Reassembling the starter motor is the reverse sequence to

dismantling. The following additional points should be noted:

30 When assembling the drive end bracket, always use a new retaining ring (spire nut) to secure the engagement lever pivot pin.

31 Make sure that the internal thrust washer is fitted to the commutator end of the armature shaft before the armature end cover is fitted.

32 Always use a new retaining ring (spire nut) on the armature shaft. There should be a maximum clearance of 0.010 in (0.25 mm) between the retaining ring and the bearing shoulder. This will be the armature endfloat.

14 Flasher unit and circuit – fault tracing and rectification

The flasher unit is mounted in a holder located beneath the facia and attached to the steering column mounting bracket. The unit is operated only when the ignition is switched on by the left-hand stalk of the steering column combination switch. If the flasher unit fails to operate or works either very slowly or very rapidly, check out the flasher indicator circuit as described below before assuming there is a fault in the unit itself.

1   Examine the direction indicator bulbs (front and rear) for broken filaments.

2   If the external flashers are working but the internal flasher warning lights on one or both sides have ceased to function, check the internal bulb filaments and renew the bulbs as necessary.

3   With the aid of the wiring diagram, check all the flasher circuit connections if a flasher bulb is sound but does not work.

4   In the event of total indicator failure, check fuse No 1.

5   With the ignition switched on, check that current is reaching the flasher unit by connecting a voltmeter between the + or B terminal and earth. If this test is positive, connect the + or B terminal and the L terminal and operate the flasher switch. If the flasher bulb lights up, the flasher unit itself is defective and must be renewed as it is not possible to dismantle and repair it.

6   To remove the flasher unit, first disconnect the battery. Make a note of the electrical cable terminal positions and detach the two terminal connections. The unit may now be pulled out from its holder.

7   Refitting the flasher unit is the reverse sequence to removal.

15 Windscreen wiper arms and blades – removal and refitting

1   To remove a wiper blade, lift the blade away from the windscreen and lift the spring retainer away from the arm.

2   Tip the blade toward the windscreen to disengage the retainer and then slide the blade off the arm (photo).

3   To refit the blade, push it onto the arm until the retainer clicks into place.

4   Before removing a wiper arm, turn the windscreen wiper switch on and off to ensure the arms are in their normal parked position with the

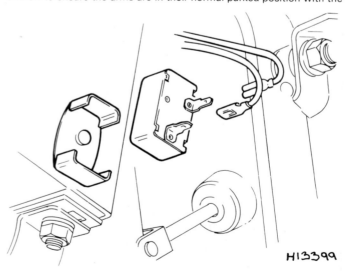

H13399

Fig. 10.6 Location of flasher unit (Sec 14)

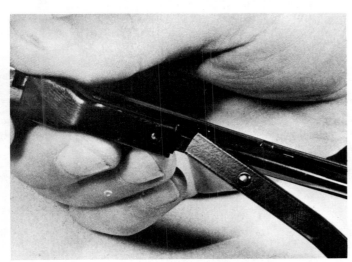

15.2 The wiper blade is removed by lifting the spring retainer and sliding the blade off the arm

15.5 The wiper arm head is a push fit on the splined drive

blades parallel with the bottom of the windscreen.
5   To remove the arm, pivot the arm back and pull the wiper arm head off the splined drive, at the same time easing back the clip with a screwdriver (photo).
6   When refitting an arm, place it so it is in the correct relative parked position, and then press the arm head onto the splined drive until the retaining clip clicks into place.

16 Windscreen wiper mechanism – fault tracing and rectification

1   Should the windscreen wipers fail or work very slowly, then check the terminals for loose connections and make sure the insulation of the external wiring is not broken or cracked. If this is in order, then check the current the motor is taking by connecting up an ammeter in the circuit and turning on the wiper switch. Consumption should be as shown in the Specifications.
2   If no current is passing, check the No 3 fuse. If the fuse has blown, renew it after having checked the wiring to the motor and other electrical circuits serviced by this fuse for short circuits. Further information will be found in Section 38. If the fuse is in good condition, check the wiper switch. Should the wiper take a very high current, check the wiper blades for freedom of movement. If this is satisfactory, check the wiper motor and drive cable for signs of damage. Measure

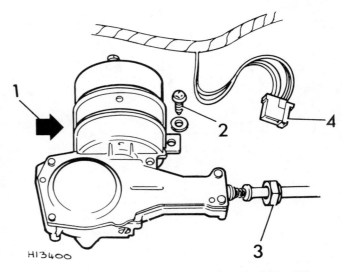

Fig. 10.7 Windscreen wiper motor removal (Sec 17)

| 1 | Wiper motor clamp | 3 | Drive tube retaining nut |
| 2 | Clamp retaining screw | 4 | Electrical plug |

the endfloat, which should also be as specified. The endfloat is set by the thrust screw. Check that excessive friction in the cable connecting tubes (caused by too small a curvature) is not the cause of the high current consumption.
3   If the motor takes a very low current, ensure that the battery is fully charged. Check the brushgear after removing the commutator yoke assembly, and ensure that the brushes are free to move. If necessary, renew the tension springs. If the brushes are very worn they should be replaced with new ones. The armature may be checked by substitution.

17 Windscreen wiper motor – removal and refitting

1   Refer to Section 15 and remove the wiper arms and blades.
2   Undo and remove the screw and plain washer that secure the wiper motor clamp to the body valance. Release the clamp and rubber moulding, by pressing the clamp band into the release slot.
3   Undo the wiper drive tube securing nut and slide the nut down the tube.
4   Next disconnect the electrical cable plug from the motor socket, and the earth lead under the cover screw.
5   Lift the motor clear of the body valance, whilst at the same time pulling the inner cable from the tube.
6   Refitting the wiper motor and inner cable is the reverse sequence to removal. Take care in feeding the inner cable through the outer tube and engaging the inner cable with each wiper wheelbox spindle. Lubricate the inner cable with general purpose grease.

18 Windscreen wiper motor – dismantling, inspection and re-assembly

The only repair which can be effectively undertaken by the do-it-yourself mechanic to a wiper motor is brush renewal. Anything more serious than this will mean either exchanging the complete motor or having a repair done by an auto electrician. Spare part availability is really the problem. Brush renewal is described as follows:
1   Undo and remove the four gearbox cover retaining screws and lift away the cover. Release the circlip and flat washer that secure the connecting rod to the crankpin on the shaft and gear. Lift away the connecting rod followed by the second flat washer.
2   Release the circlip and flat washer that secure the shaft and gear to the gearbox body.
3   De-burr the gear shaft and lift away the gear, making careful note of the location of the dished washer.
4   Scribe a mark on the yoke assembly and gearbox to ensure correct

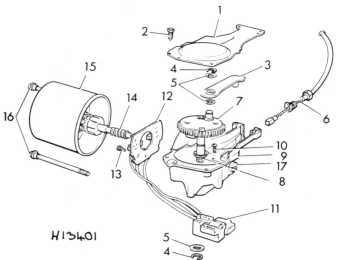

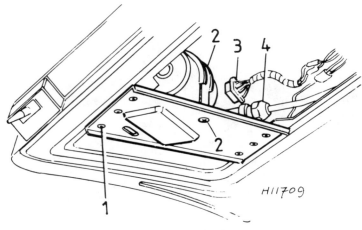

Fig. 10.8 Exploded view of windscreen wiper motor (Sec 18)

1	Gearbox cover	10	Screw for limit switch
2	Screw for cover	11	Limit switch assembly
3	Connecting rod	12	Brushgear
4	Circlip	13	Screw for brushgear
5	Plain washers	14	Armature
6	Cross head	15	Yoke assembly
7	Shaft and gear	16	Yoke bolts
8	Dished washer	17	Armature thrust screw
9	Gearbox		

reassembly and unscrew the two yoke bolts from the motor yoke assembly. Part the yoke assembly, including the armature, from the gearbox body. As the yoke assembly has residual magnetism, ensure that the yoke is kept well away from metallic dust.
5   Unscrew the two screws that secure the brushgear and the terminal and switch assembly and remove both the assemblies.
6   Inspect the brushes for excessive wear. If the main brushes are worn below the minimum specified thickness, or the narrow section of the third brush is worn to the full width of the brush, fit a new brushgear assembly. Ensure that the three brushes move freely in their boxes.
7   Reassembly at this stage is a straight reversal of disassembly.

19 Windscreen wiper wheelboxes and drive cable tubes – removal and refitting

1   Refer to Section 17 and remove the windscreen wiper motor.
2   Refer to Section 30 and remove the instrument panel.
3   Refer to Chapter 12 and remove the glovebox.
4   Refer to Section 15 and remove the windscreen wiper arms.
5   Undo and remove the nuts that secure the wheelboxes to the body. Lift away the shaped spacer from each wheelbox.
6   Slacken the two nuts that clamp the two wheelbox plates on the glovebox side. Carefully pull out the drive tube from the wheelbox.
7   Carefully remove the free drive tube and its grommet through the glovebox opening.
8   Lift away the two wheelbox units through the instrument panel opening.
9   Recover the spacer and washer from each wheelbox unit.
10 Refitting the wheelboxes and drive cable tubes is the reverse sequence to removal.

20 Tailgate wiper motor – removal and refitting

1   Remove the wiper arm as described in Section 15.
2   Remove the tailgate trim pad.
3   Disconnect the electrical cable plug from the motor socket.
4   Undo the wiper rack tube securing nut and slide the nut down the tube.

Fig. 10.9 Tailgate wiper motor removal (Sec 20)

1	Mounting plate securing screws	3	Electrical plug
2	Motor clamp and securing screw	4	Rack tube retaining nut

5   Undo and remove the six screws that secure the mounting plate to the tailgate and withdraw the cable rack from the tube.
6   Undo the motor clamp securing screw and lift away the motor assembly.
7   Refitting is the reverse of the removal procedure.

21 Horns – fault tracing and rectification

1   If a horn works badly or fails completely, first check the wiring leading to it for short circuits and loose connections. Also check that

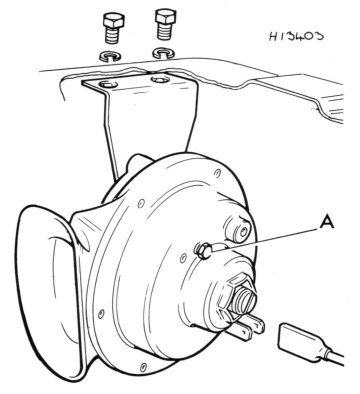

Fig. 10.10 Details of the horn (Sec 21)

A   Adjustment screw

the horn is firmly secured and that there is nothing lying on the horn body.

2   The horn is protected by the No 5 fuse and if this has blown, the circuit should be checked for short circuits.

3   The horn should never be dismantled, but it is possible to adjust it. This adjustment is to compensate for wear of the moving parts only and will not affect the tone. To adjust the horn proceed as follows:

(a)   *There is a small adjustment screw on the broad rim of the horn, nearly opposite the two terminals. Do not confuse this with the large screw in the centre*

(b)   *Turn the adjustment screw anti-clockwise until the horn just fails to sound. Then turn the screw a quarter of a turn clockwise, which is the optimum setting*

(c)   *It is recommended that if the horn has to be reset in the car, the No 5 fuse should be removed and temporarily replaced with a piece of wire, otherwise the fuse will continually blow due to the high current required for the horn in continual operation*

(d)   *Should twin horns be fitted, the horn which is not being adjusted should be disconnected while adjustments of the other takes place*

22 Headlight assembly – removal and refitting

Headlight unit

1   Open the bonnet and disconnect the headlight wiring at the multi-plug connector.

2   Undo and remove the nuts securing the headlight unit to the front body panel and carefully lift out the unit.

3   Refitting is the reverse sequence to removal.

Headlight bulb

4   Turn the protective cover at the rear of the light unit anti-clockwise and pull it away from the unit (photo).

5   Detach the three pin connector from the rear of the headlight bulb (photo).

6   Release the wire retaining clip and carefully lift out the bulb. **Note:** *Avoid touching the glass of the bulb with your fingers as this could cause premature failure (photos).*

7   To refit the bulb, position it in the light unit, ensuring that the flange of the bulb engages with the seat in the light unit.

8   Refit the wire retaining clip, reconnect the three pin connector and finally refit the protective cover.

Sidelight bulb

9   Remove the protective cover from the rear of the light unit.

10   Pull the sidelight bulb holder out of its location in the light unit and remove the bulb by pressing in and turning anti-clockwise (photo).

11   Refitting is the reverse sequence to removal.

23 Headlight beam – adjustment

1   The headlights may be adjusted for both vertical and horizontal beam positions by the two screws located on either side of the headlight unit (photo).

2   To set the headlights accurately it is necessary to use optical beam setting equipment, and it is recommended that this work is entrusted to your local BL dealer.

24 Front flasher bulb – renewal

1   Unscrew and remove the two lens securing screws and lift away the lens.

2   The bulb has a bayonet fitting and is removed by pressing in and turning anti-clockwise.

3   Refitting the bulb and lens is the reverse of the removal procedure.

4   To renew the flasher side repeater bulbs, remove the lens by turning anti-clockwise (photo).

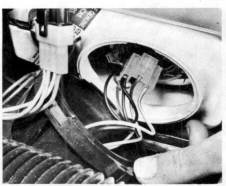

22.4 Turn the protective cover anti-clockwise and move it away from the light unit

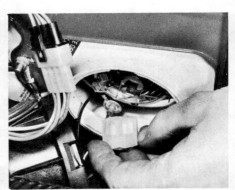

22.5 Detach the three-pin connector

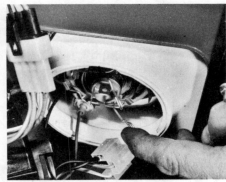

22.6a Release the wire retaining clip ...

22.6b ... and lift out the bulb. Avoid touching the glass

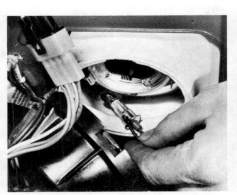

22.10 The sidelight bulb holder is a push fit in the light unit

23.1 Headlight beam adjustment screws (arrowed)

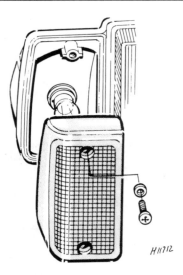

Fig. 10.11 Front flasher bulb renewal (Sec 24)

5   Withdraw the bulb by pressing it in and turning anti-clockwise.
6   Refitting is the reverse sequence to removal.

25 Stop, tail, flasher, reversing and rear fog guard light bulbs (Saloon) – renewal

1   Open the boot lid and lift away the protective cover from the rear of the light cluster (photo).
2   Using a coin, turn the two fasteners through 90° and withdraw the light cluster and bulbs (photos).
3   The bulbs all have bayonet fittings and are removed by pressing in and turning anti-clockwise.
4   Refitting is the reverse sequence to removal.

26 Stop, tail and flasher light bulbs (Estate) – renewal

1   *Right-hand side:* Remove the rear compartment trim pad.
2   *Left-hand side:* Remove the spare wheel cover and spare wheel.
3   Carefully pull the bulb holder from the light unit.
4   The bulbs have a bayonet fitting and are removed by pushing in and turning anti-clockwise. Note that the bayonet fitting pins on the stop/tail bulb are offset and the bulb will only fit in one position.
5   Refitting is the reverse sequence to removal, noting that the

24.4 Turn the side repeater lenses anti-clockwise to gain access to the bulb

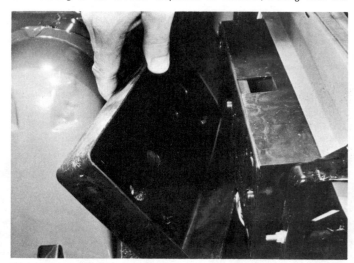

25.1 Lift away the protective cover

25.2a Release the light unit retainers by turning through 90° ...

25.2b ... and withdraw the light unit to gain access to the bulbs

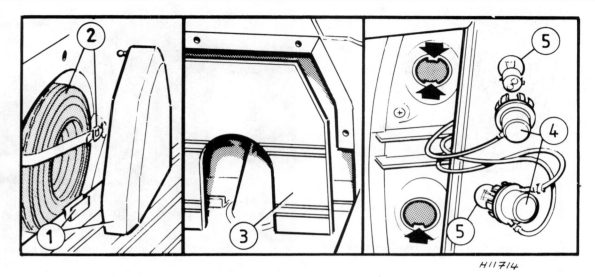

Fig. 10.12 Stop, tail and flasher light bulb renewal – Estate models
(Sec 26)

1 Spare wheel cover
2 Spare wheel and retaining strap
3 Trim panel
4 Bulb holders
5 Flasher light bulb

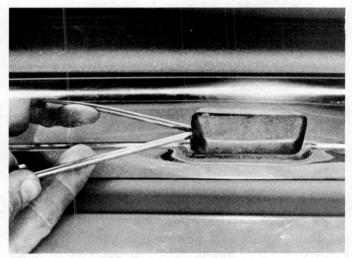

27.1 Press in the two retaining clips using a screwdriver ...

27.2 ... then lift out the number plate light and withdraw the lens cover

flasher light bulb holder has two locating slots and the stop/tail bulb holder has only one.

27 Rear number plate bulb – renewal

1 Using a thin screwdriver, press in the two retaining clips, one each side of the light unit (photo), and lift the unit out of the bumper.
2 Lift up the lens cover and release the bulb by pressing in and turning anti-clockwise (photo).
3 Refitting is the reverse sequence to removal.

28 Luggage compartment light bulb – renewal

1 Unscrew the two light unit securing screws.
2 Release the festoon type bulb from the retaining contacts.
3 Refitting is the reverse sequence to removal.

29 Interior light bulb – renewal

1 Gently squeeze the lens together and detach it from the light body.
2 Release the festoon type bulb from the retaining contacts.
3 Refitting is the reverse sequence to removal.

30 Instrument panel – removal and refitting

1 Disconnect the battery earth terminal.
2 Undo and remove the two instrument cowl securing screws and lift off the cowl (photos).
3 Undo and remove the screws securing the instrument panel to the facia (photo).
4 Pull the instrument panel forward and then, from the rear of the panel, depress the speedometer cable locking clip and release the cable (photo).

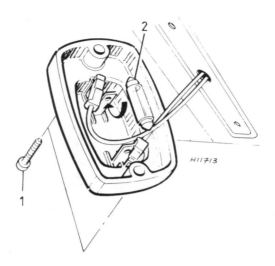

Fig. 10.13 Luggage compartment light bulb renewal (Sec 28)

1　*Light unit securing screws*　　　　2　*Bulb*

30.2a Undo and remove the instrument cowl securing screws ...

30.2b ... and lift away the cowl

30.3 Undo and remove the instrument panel retaining screws

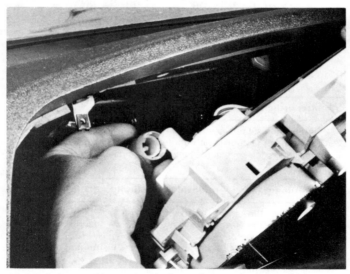

30.4 Pull the panel forward and release the speedometer cable ...

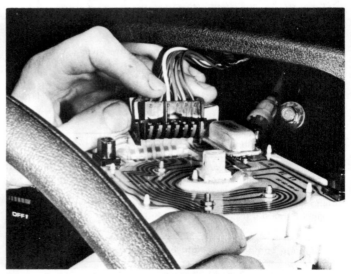

30.5 ... and then disconnect the multi-plug connector

31.1 The instrument panel and warning light bulb holders are a push fit in the panel ...

31.2 ... as is the voltage stabilizer

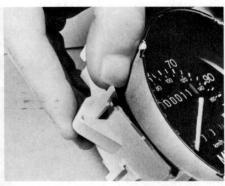
31.10 The speedometer and instrument lens is retained by plastic clips

5   Disconnect the wiring multi-plug from the printed circuit (photo) and any additional wires or bulb holders that may be fitted according to model. The instrument panel may now be lifted away.
6   Refitting is the reverse sequence to removal.

31 Instrument panel – dismantling and reassembly

Panel and warning light bulbs
1   The bulb holders are withdrawn by carefully pulling them out of their locations on the rear of the instrument panel (photo). The bulbs are a push fit in the holders.

Voltage stabilizer
2   The voltage stabilizer may be withdrawn by simply pulling it out of its locating contacts on the rear of the instrument panel (photo).

Printed circuit
3   Remove all the bulb holders and the voltage stabilizer.
4   Undo and remove the retaining screws and lift out the voltage stabilizer contacts.
5   If the instrument panel is of the four instrument type, undo and remove the retaining screw and lift off the main beam warning light connection. Also carefully release the plastic printed circuit retaining pegs.
6   Undo and remove the nuts and washers securing the printed circuit to the instruments, prise the printed circuit off the locating pegs (where fitted) and lift it off the instrument panel.

Instruments
7   Remove the bulb holders, voltage stabilizer and printed circuit as described previously.
8   On instrument panels of the four instrument type, the fuel and temperature gauges may be removed from the panel after unscrewing the two screws securing each gauge.
9   The remaining instruments on all panels are removed as follows:
10 Release the retaining clips securing the speedometer and instrument one piece lens to the instrument panel and lift away the lens (photo).
11 Withdraw the face plate.
12 Undo and remove the two screws securing the speedometer, tachometer, fuel gauge or temperature gauge and lift out the appropriate instrument.
13 Reassembly of the instrument panel is in all cases the reverse sequence to removal.

32 Ignition, starter and steering lock switch – removal and refitting

1   Disconnect the battery earth terminal.
2   Undo and remove the single securing screw and lift off the right-hand steering column cowl.
3   Undo and remove the two inner and one outer securing screws and lift off the left-hand steering column cowl. Allow the cowl to hang

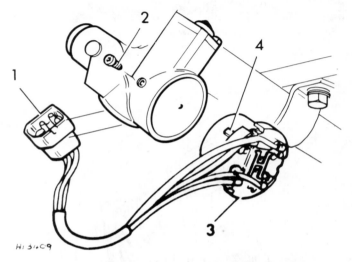
Fig. 10.14 Ignition, starter and steering lock switch (Sec 32)

1   Multi-pin plug   3   Switch assembly
2   Switch retaining screw   4   Locating peg

from the choke cable.
4   Disconnect the wiring harness multi-plug connector at the socket under the facia.
5   Undo and remove the single screw securing the switch assembly to the lock housing and slide out the switch. If it is wished to remove the complete lock housing, full information will be found in Chapter 11.
6   Refitting is the reverse sequence to removal. Make sure that the locating peg on the switch correctly engages with the notch in the lock housing.

33 Steering column combination switch – removal and refitting

1   Refer to Chapter 11 and remove the steering wheel.
2   Disconnect the battery earth terminal.
3   Undo and remove the single retaining screw and lift off the right-hand steering column cowl.
4   Undo and remove the two inner and one outer retaining screws and lift off the left-hand cowl. Allow the cowl to hang from the choke cable.
5   Disconnect the wiring harness multi-plug connector at the socket under the facia.
6   Slacken the switch retaining screw and slide the switch off the steering column (photos).
7   Refitting the switch is the reverse sequence to removal. Ensure that the lug on the inner diameter of the switch locates in the slot in the outer steering column.

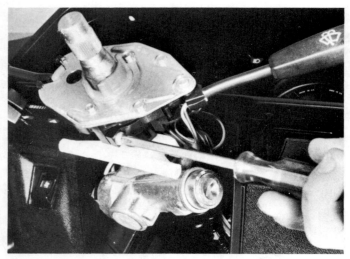

33.6a Slacken the combination switch securing screw ...

33.6b ... and withdraw the switch from the steering column

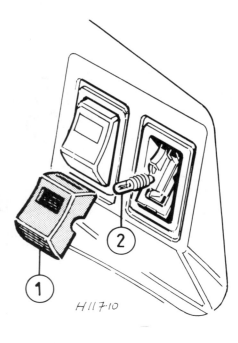

Fig. 10.15 Rocker switch bulb renewal (Sec 34)

1   Rocker cover   2   Bulb

34 Rocker switches – removal and refitting

1   If it is wished only to remove a switch warning/illuminatioon bulb, remove the switch rocker cover by levering the cover each side at the formed recess.
2   The bulb can now be unscrewed from the switch by using a piece of plastic or rubber tube which is a tight fit over the bulb glass.
3   Fit the new bulb and press the cover into position.
4   To remove the complete switch, compress the retaining spring clips at the top and bottom of the switch body.
5   Push the switch out of the panel and disconnect the wiring multi-plug at the rear of the switch.
6   Refitting is the reverse sequence to removal.

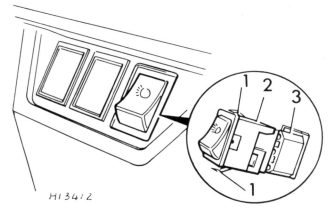

Fig. 10.16 Rocker switch removal (Sec 34)

1   Spring clip   3   Wiring multi-plug
2   Switch body

35 Stoplight switch – removal and refitting

1   Release the retainers and lift away the lower trim panel from under the facia.
2   Make a note of the two cable connections at the rear of the switch located on the top of the brake pedal mounting bracket. Detach the two terminals.
3   Undo and remove the two bolts and spring washers that secure the switch mounting bracket to the brake pedal mounting bracket. Lift away the switch and bracket.
4   Straighten the legs of the switch locking split pin and withdraw the split pin.
5   The switch may now be unscrewed from its mounting bracket.
6   Refitting the stoplight switch is the reverse sequence to removal. It is, however, necessary to adjust the position of the switch when refitting to its mounting bracket.
7   Screw the switch into its mounting bracket until one complete thread of the switch housing is visible on the pedal side of the bracket. Lock with a new split pin.

36 Handbrake warning light switch – removal and refitting

1   Remove the centre console as described in Chapter 12.

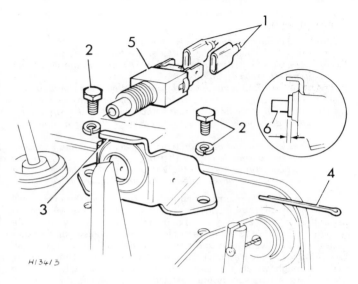

H13413

Fig. 10.17 Stoplight switch removal (Sec 35)

1	Cable connections	4	Split pin
2	Mounting bracket retaining bolts	5	Stoplight switch
3	Mounting bracket	6	Switch adjustment (see text)

2   Remove the gaiter retainer securing screws and pull the gaiter up the handbrake lever. To provide access to the retainer securing screws, it may be necessary to make a small cut in the carpet at each corner of the handbrake assembly aperture in the floor.
3   Disconnect the switch supply lead, unscrew the switch securing screw and remove the switch.
4   Refitting is the reverse of the removal procedure. To prevent entry of water from beneath the car, it is advisable to coat the gaiter securing screw holes with a suitable sealing compound.

37 Speedometer cable – removal and refitting

1   Disconnect the battery earth terminal.
2   Undo and remove the two screws securing the instrument panel cowl and lift off the cowl.
3   Undo and remove the screws securing the instrument panel to the facia and draw the panel forward slightly.
4   Depress the cable retaining clip and detach the cable from the rear of the speedometer.
5   The inner cable can be withdrawn from the outer cable at this stage if required. If, however, the inner cable is broken or it is wished to remove the complete inner and outer cable assembly, proceed as follows.
6   Jack up the front of the car and support it on axle stands.
7   Working underneath the car, undo and remove the bolt and spring washer securing the cable flange to the gearbox.
8   Pull the cable out of the drive pinion in the gearbox.
9   Release the outer cable from the support clips on the underbody.
10 Working in the engine compartment, pull the complete cable assembly through the aperture in the brake pedal housing, allowing the connector end to remove the grommet.
11 The speedometer cable can now be lifted away.
12 Refitting is the reverse sequence to removal, ensuring that the grommet is correctly located in the pedal housing.

38 Fuses

1   The fuse block is located inside the car at the back of the parcel shelf. Five fuses are used and protect the circuits as listed in the Specifications at the beginning of this Chapter (photo).
2   If any of the fuses should blow, check the circuits protected by that fuse, then trace and rectify the fault before renewing the fuse. Always fit a fuse of the correct rating.

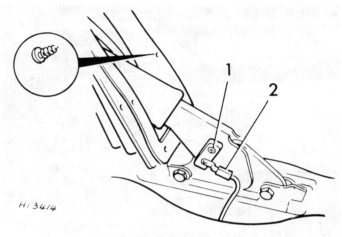

H13414

Fig. 10.18 Handbrake warning light switch (Sec 36)

1	Switch securing screw	2	Electrical lead

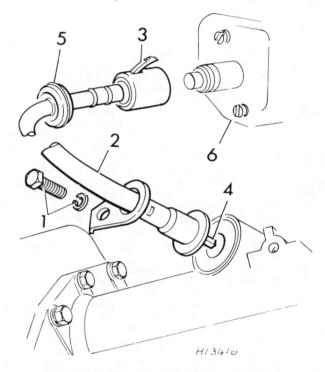

H13410

Fig. 10.19 Speedometer cable removal (Sec 37)

1	Locking flange securing screw and washer	4	Speedometer cable (inner)
2	Speedometer cable (outer)	5	Rubber grommet
3	Speedometer cable retaining clip	6	Speedometer

39 Radios and tape players – fitting (general)

A radio or tape player is an expensive item to buy, and will only give its best performance if fitted properly. It is useless to expect concert hall performance from a unit that is suspended from the dashpanel by string with its speaker resting on the back seat or parcel shelf! If you do not wish to do the fitting yourself, there are many in-car entertainment specialists who will do the fitting for you.

Make sure the unit purchased is of the same polarity as the vehicle. Ensure that units with adjustable polarity are correctly set before commencing the fitting operations.

38.1 The fuse block is located inside the car at the rear of the parcel shelf

It is difficult to give specific information with regard to fitting, as final positioning of the radio/tape player, speakers and aerial is entirely a matter of personal preference. However, the following paragraphs give guidelines to follow which are relevant to all fittings:

Radios

Most radios are a standardised size of 7 in wide by 2 in deep. This ensures that they will fit into the radio aperture provided in most cars. If your car does not have such an aperture, then the radio must be fitted in a suitable position either in or beneath the dashboard. Alternatively, a special console can be purchased which will fit between the dashpanel and the floor or on the transmission tunnel. These consoles can also be used for additional switches and instrumentation if required. Where no radio aperture is provided, the following points should be borne in mind before deciding exactly where to fit the unit:

(a) *The unit must be within easy reach of the driver wearing a seat belt*
(b) *The unit must not be mounted in close proximity to an electronic tachometer, the ignition switch and its wiring, or the flasher unit and associated wiring*
(c) *The unit must be mounted within reach of the aerial lead, and in such a place that the aerial lead will not have to be routed near the components detailed in the preceding paragraph (b)*
(d) *The unit should not be positioned in a place where it might cause injury to the car occupants in an accident; for instance under the dashpanel above the driver's or passenger's legs*
(e) *The unit must be fitted securely*

Some radios will have mounting brackets provided, together with instructions; others will need to be fitted using drilled and slotted metal strips, bent to form mounting brackets. These strips are available from most accessory shops. The unit must be properly earthed by fitting a separate earthing lead between the casing of the radio and the vehicle frame.

Use the radio manufacturers' instructions when wiring the radio into the vehicle's electrical system. If no instructions are available, refer to the relevant wiring diagram to find the location of the radio feed connection in the vehicle's wiring circuit. A 1 to 2 amp in-line fuse must be fitted in the radio's feed wire; a choke may also be necessary (see the following Section).

The type of aerial used, and its fitted position, is a matter of personal preference. In general, the taller the aerial the better the reception. It is best to fit a fully retractable aerial; especially if a mechanical car-wash is used or if you live in an area where cars tend to be vandalised. In this respect, electric aerials which are raised and lowered automatically when switching the radio on or off are convenient, but are more likely to give trouble than the manual type.

When choosing a position for the aerial, the following points should be considered:

(a) *The aerial lead should be as short as possible; this means that the aerial should be mounted at the front of the car*
(b) *The aerial must be mounted as far away from the distributor and HT leads as possible*
(c) *The part of the aerial which protrudes beneath the mounting point must not foul the roadwheels, or anything else*
(d) *If possible, the aerial should be positioned so that the coaxial lead does not have to be routed through the engine compartment*
(e) *The plane of the panel on which the aerial is mounted should not be so steeply angled that the aerial cannot be mounted vertically (in relation to the end-on aspect of the car). Most aerials have a small amount of adjustment available*

Having decided on a mounting position, a relatively large hole will have to be made in the panel. The exact size of the hole will depend upon the specific aerial being fitted, although generally, the hole required is of $\frac{3}{4}$ in (19 mm) diameter. On metal bodied cars, a tank-cutter of the relevant diameter is the best tool to use for making the hole. This tool needs a small diameter pilot hole drilled through the panel, through which the tool clamping bolt is inserted. On GRP bodied cars, a hole-saw is the best tool to use. Again, this tool will require the drilling of a small pilot hole. When the hole has been made, the raw edges should be de-burred with a file and then painted to prevent corrosion.

Fit the aerial according to the manufacturer's instructions. If the aerial is very tall, or if it protrudes beneath the mounting panel for a considerable distance, it is a good idea to fit a stay beneath the aerial and the vehicle frame. This stay can be manufactured from the slotted and drilled metal strips previously mentioned. The stay should be securely screwed or bolted in place. For best reception, it is advisable to fit an earth lead between the aerial and the vehicle frame; this is essential for GRP bodied cars.

It will probably be necessary to drill one or two holes through bodywork panels in order to feed the aerial lead into the interior of the car. Where this is the case, ensure that the holes are fitted with rubber grommets to protect the cable and to stop possible entry of water.

Positioning and fitting of the speaker depends mainly on its type. Generally, the speaker is designed to fit directly into the aperture already provided in the car. Where this is the case, fitting the speaker is just a matter of removing the protective grille from the aperture and screwing or bolting the speaker in place. Take great care not to damage the speaker diaphragm whilst doing this. It is a good idea to fit a gasket beneath the speaker frame and the mounting panel. In order to prevent vibration, some speakers will already have such a gasket fitted.

If a 'pod' type speaker was supplied with the radio, this can be secured to the mounting panel with self-tapping screws.

When connecting a rear mounted speaker to the radio, the wires should be routed through the vehicle beneath the carpets or floor mats, preferably along the side of the floorpan where they will not be trodden on by passengers. Make the relevant connections as directed by the radio manufacturer.

By now you will have several yards of additional wiring in the car; use PVC tape to secure this wiring out of harm's way. Do not leave electrical leads dangling. Ensure that all new electrical connections are properly made (wires twisted together will not do) and completely secure.

The radio should now be working, but before you pack away your tools it will be necessary to trim the radio to the aerial. If specific instructions are not provided by the radio manufacturer, proceed as follows: Find a station with a low signal strength on the medium-wave band, slowly turn the trim screw of the radio in or out until the loudest reception of the selected station is obtained. The set is then trimmed to the aerial.

Tape players

Fitting instructions for both cartridge and cassette stereo tape players are the same, and in general the same rules apply as when fitting a radio. Tape players are not usually prone to electrical interference like radios, although it can occur, so positioning is not so critical. If possible, the player should be mounted on an even-keel. Also it must be possible for a driver wearing a seat belt to reach the unit in order to change or turn over tapes.

For the best results from speakers designed to be recessed into a panel, mount them so that the back of the speaker protrudes into an enclosed chamber within the car (eg door interiors or the boot cavity).

To fit recessed type speakers in the front doors, first check that there is sufficient room to mount the speakers in each door without it fouling the latch or window winding mechanism. Hold the speaker against the skin of the door and draw a line around the periphery of the speaker. With the speaker removed, draw a second cutting line within the first to allow enough room for the entry of the speaker back, but at the same time providing a broad seat for the speaker flange. When you are sure that the cutting-line is correct, drill a series of holes around its periphery. Pass a hacksaw blade through one of the holes and then cut through the metal between the holes until the centre section of the panel falls out.

De-burr the edges of the hole and then paint the raw metal to prevent corrosion. Cut a corresponding hole in the door trim panel, ensuring that it will be completely covered by the speaker grille. Now drill a hole in the door edge and a corresponding hole in the door surround. These holes are to feed the speaker leads through, so fit grommets. Pass the speaker leads through the door trim, door skin and out through the holes in the side of the door and door surround. Refit the door trim panel and then secure the speaker to the door using self-tapping screws. **Note:** *If the speaker is fitted with a shield to prevent water dripping on it, ensure that this shield is at the top.*

Pod type speakers can be fastened anywhere offering a corresponding mounting point on each side of the car. Pod speakers sometimes offer a better reproduction quality if they face the rear window which then acts as a reflector so it is worthwhile to do a little experimenting before finally fixing the speaker.

40 Radios and tape players – suppression of interference (general)

To eliminate buzzes and other unwanted noises costs very little and is not as difficult as sometimes thought. With a modicum of common sense and patience, and following the instructions in the following paragraphs, interference can be virtually eliminated.

The first cause for concern is the generator. The noise this makes over the radio is like an electric mixer and the noise speeds up when the engine is revved. (To prove the point, remove the fanbelt and try it). The remedy for this is simple; connect a 1.0 to 3.0 mfd capacitor between earth (probably the bolt that holds down the generator base) and the positive (+) terminal on the alternator. This is most important for if it is connected to the small terminal, the generator will probably be damaged permanently (see Fig. 10.20).

A second common cause of electrical interference is the ignition system. Here a 1.0 mfd capacitor must be connected between earth and the SW or + terminal on the coil (see Fig. 10.21). This may stop the tick-tick sound that comes over the speaker. Next comes the spark itself.

There are several ways of curing interference from the ignition HT system. One is the use of carbon-cored HT leads as original equipment. Where copper cable is substituted then resistive spark plug caps must be used (see Fig. 10.22). These should be of about 10 000 to 15 000 ohm resistance. If due to lack of room these cannot be used, an alternative is to use in-line suppressors. If the interference is not too bad, it may be possible to get away with only one suppressor in the coil to distributor line. If the interference does continue (a clacking noise), then modify all HT leads.

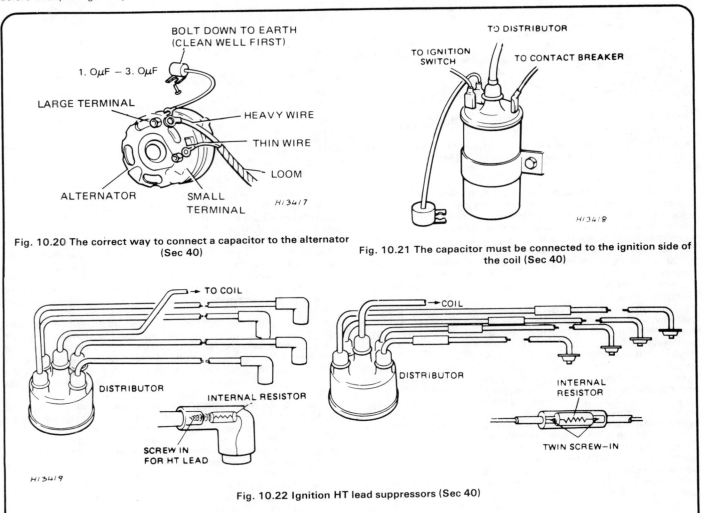

Fig. 10.20 The correct way to connect a capacitor to the alternator (Sec 40)

Fig. 10.21 The capacitor must be connected to the ignition side of the coil (Sec 40)

Fig. 10.22 Ignition HT lead suppressors (Sec 40)

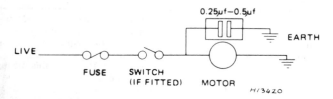

Fig. 10.23 Correct method of suppressing electric motors
(Sec 40)

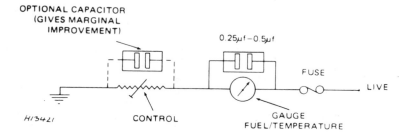

Fig. 10.24 Method of suppressing gauges and their control units (Sec 40)

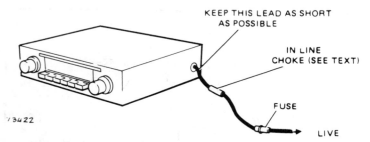

Fig. 10.25 An 'in-line' choke should be fitted with the live supply
lead as close to the unit as possible (Sec 40)

At this stage it is advisable to check that the radio is well earthed, also the aerial, and to see that the aerial plug is pushed well into the set and that the radio is properly trimmed (see preceding Section). In addition, check that the wire which supplies the power to the set is as short as possible. At this stage it is a good idea to check that the fuse is of the correct rating. For most sets this will be about 1 to 2 amps.

At this point, the more usual causes of interference have been suppressed. If the problem still exists, a look at the cause of interference may help to pinpoint the component generating the stray electrical discharges.

The radio picks up electromagnetic waves in the air. Some are made by regular broadcasters and some, which we do not want, are made by the car itself. The home made signals are produced by stray electrical discharges floating around in the car. Common producers of these signals are electrical motors, ie the windscreen wipers, electric screen washers, electric window winders, heater fan or an electric aerial, if fitted. Other sources of interference are flashing turn signals and instruments. The remedy for these cases is shown in Fig. 10.23 for an electric motor whose interference is not too bad and Fig. 10.24 for instrument suppression. Turn signals are not normally suppressed. In recent years, radio manufacturers have included in the live line of the radio, in addition to the fuse, an in-line choke. If your circuit lacks one of these, put one in as shown in Fig. 10.25.

All the foregoing components are available from radio stores or accessory stores. If you have an electric clock fitted, this should be suppressed by connecting a 0.5 mfd capacitor directly across it as shown for a motor in Fig. 10.23.

If after all this you are still experiencing radio interference, first assess how bad it is, for the human ear can filter out unobtrusive unwanted noises quite easily. But if you are still adamant about eradicating the noise, then continue.

As a first step, a few experts seem to favour a screen between the radio and the engine. This is OK as far as it goes, literally! The whole set is screened anyway and if interference can get past that then a small piece of aluminium is not going to stop it.

A more sensible way of screening is to discover if interference is coming down the wires. First, take the live lead; interference can get between the set and the choke (hence the reason for keeping the wires short). One remedy here is to screen the wire and this is done by buying screened wire and fitting that. The loudspeaker lead could be screened also to prevent pick-up getting back to the radio although this is unlikely.

Without doubt, the worst source of radio interference comes from the ignition HT leads, even if they have been suppressed. The ideal way of suppressing these is to slide screening tubes over the leads themselves. As this is impractical, we can place an aluminium shield over the majority of the lead areas. In a vee or twin-cam engine this is relatively easy but for a straight engine, the results are not particularly good.

Now for the really impossible cases, here are a few tips to try out. Where metal comes into contact with metal, an electrical disturbance is caused which is why good clean connections are essential. To remove interference due to overlapping or butting panels, you must bridge the join with a wide braided earth strap (like that from the frame to the engine/transmission). The most common moving parts that could create noise and should be strapped are, in order of importance:

(a) Silencer to frame
(b) Exhaust pipe to engine block and frame
(c) Air cleaner to frame
(d) Front and rear bumpers to frame
(e) Steering column to frame
(f) Bonnet and boot lids to frame

These faults are most pronounced when the engine is idling or labouring under load. Although the moving parts are already connected with nuts, bolts, etc, these do tend to rust and corrode, this creating a high resistance interference source.

If you have a ragged sounding pulse when mobile, this could be wheel or tyre static. This can be cured by buying some anti-static powder and sprinkling inside the tyres.

If the interference takes the shape of a high pitched screeching noise that changes its note when the car is in motion and only comes now and then, this could be related to the aerial, especially if it is of the telescopic or whip type. This source can be cured quite simply by pushing a small rubber ball on top of the aerial as this breaks the electric field before it can form; but it would be much better to buy yourself a new aerial of a reputable brand. If, on the other hand, you are getting a loud rushing sound every time you brake, then this is brake static. This effect is most prominent on hot dry days and is cured only by fitting a special kit, which is quite expensive.

In conclusion, it is pointed out that it is relatively easy, and therefore cheap, to eliminate 95 per cent of all noise, but to eliminate the final 5 per cent is time and money consuming. It is up to the individual to decide if it is worth it. Please remember, also, that you cannot get a concert hall performance out of a cheap radio.

Finally, players and eight track players are not usually affected by car noise but in a very bad case, the best remedies are the first three suggestions plus using a 3 to 5 amp choke in the live line, and in incurable cases, screening the live and speaker wires.

Note: *If your car is fitted with electronic ignition, then it is not recommended that either the spark plug resistors or the ignition coil capacitor be fitted as these may damage the system. Most electronic ignition units have built in suppression and should, therefore, not cause interference.*

41 Fault diagnosis – electrical system

Symptom	Reason(s)
No voltage at starter motor	Battery discharged Battery defective internally Battery terminal leads loose or earth lead not securely attached to body Loose or broken connections in starter motor circuit Starter motor switch or solenoid faulty
Voltage at starter motor: faulty motor	Starter motor pinion jammed in mesh with flywheel gear ring Starter brushes badly worn, sticking, or brush wires loose Commutator dirty, worn or burnt Starter motor armature faulty Field coils earthed
Electrical defects	Battery in discharged condition Starter brushes badly worn, sticking, or brush wires loose Loose wires in starter motor circuit
Mechanical damage	Pinion or flywheel gear teeth broken or worn
Lack of attention or mechanical damage	Pinion or flywheel gear teeth broken or worn Starter motor retaining bolts loose
Wear or damage	Battery defective internally Electrolye level too low or electrolyte too weak due to leakage Plate separators no longer fully effective Battery plates severely sulphated
Insufficient current flow to keep battery charged	Fanbelt slipping Battery terminal connections loose or corroded Alternator not charging properly Short in lighting circuit causing continual battery drain Regulator unit not working correctly
Alternator not charging*	Fanbelt loose and slipping, or broken Brushes worn, sticking, broken or dirty Brush springs weak or broken

* If all appears to be well but the alternator is still not charging, take the car to an automobile electrician for checking of the alternator and regulator.

Battery will not hold charge for more than a few days	Battery defective internally Electrolyte level too low or electrolyte too weak due to leakage Plate separators no longer fully effective Battery plates severely sulphated Fan/alternator belt slipping Battery terminal connections loose or corroded Alternator not charging properly Short in lighting circuit causing continual battery drain Regulator unit not working correctly
Ignition light fails to go out, battery runs flat in a few days	Fanbelt loose and slipping or broken Alternator faulty

Symptom	Reason(s)

Failure of individual electrical equipment to function correctly is dealt with alphabetically, below

Symptom	Reason(s)
Fuel gauge gives no reading	Fuel tank empty! Electric cable between tank sender unit and gauge disconnected Fuel gauge case not earthed Fuel gauge supply cable interrupted Fuel gauge unit broken
Fuel gauge registers full all the time	Electric cable between tank unit and gauge earthed
Horn emits intermittent or unsatisfactory noise	Cable connections loose Horn incorrectly adjusted
Horn fails to operate	Blown fuse Cable or cable connection loose, broken or disconnected Horn has an internal fault
Horn operates all the time	Horn push either earthed or stuck down Horn cable to horn push earthed
Instrument readings erratic	Voltage stabiliser faulty
Lights come on but fade out	If engine not running battery discharged
Lights do not come on	If engine not running, battery discharged Light bulb filament burnt out or bulbs broken Wire connections loose, disconnected or broken Light switch shorting or otherwise faulty
Lights give very poor illumination	Lamp glasses dirty Reflector tarnished or dirty Lamps badly out of adjustment Incorrect bulb with too low waggage fitted Exisiting bulbs old and badly discoloured
Wiper motor fails to work	Blown fuse Wire connections loose, disconnected or broken Brushes badly worn Armature worn or faulty Field coils faulty
Wiper motor works but wiper blades remain static	Linkage disengaged or faulty Drive spindle damaged or worn Wiper motor gearbox parts badly worn
Wiper motor works slowly and takes little current	Brushes badly worn Commutator dirty, greasy or burnt Armature badly worn or faulty
Wiper motor works very slowly and takes excessive current	Commutator dirty, greasy or burnt Drive to spindles too bent or unlubricated Drive spindle binding or damaged Armature bearings dry or unaligned Armature badly worn or faulty

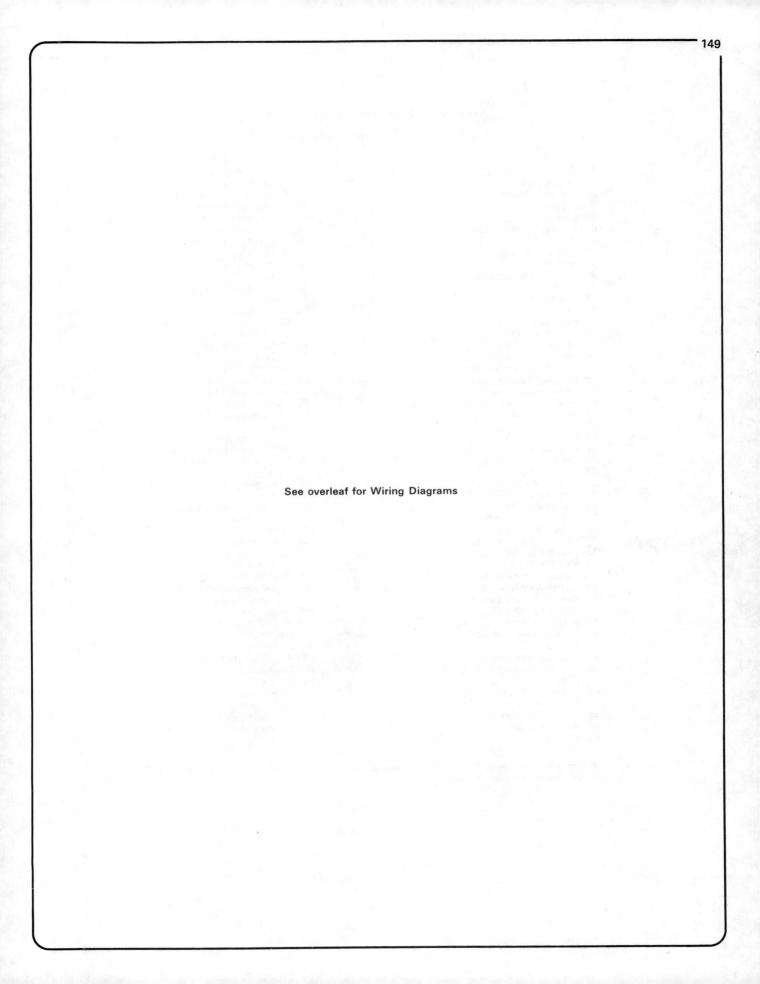

See overleaf for Wiring Diagrams

Key to wiring diagram for Saloon and Estate

Note: *Not all items listed are fitted to all models*

1   Battery
2   Starter motor
3   Starter solenoid
4   Fusebox
5   Line fuse
6   Ignition/starter switch
7   Not applicable
    (Van and Pick-up)
8   Ignition coil
9   Ignition warning lamp
10 Distributor
11 Alternator
12 Horn(s)
13 Horn switch
14 Ballast resistor
15 Lighting switch
16 Headlamp main beam
17 Main beam warning lamp
18 Headlamp dip switch
19 Headlamp dip beam
20 Headlamp flasher switch
21 Sidelamp (RH)
22 Sidelamp (LH)
23 Rear lamp (RH)
24 Rear lamp (LH)
25 Number plate lamp(s)
26 Stoplamp(s)
27 Stoplamp switch
28 Indicator unit
29 Indicator switch
30 Indicator warning lamp
31 Front RH indicator
32 Front LH indicator
33 Rear RH indicator
34 Rear LH indicator
35 Indicator repeater lamp
36 Hazard warning lamp
37 Hazard warning switch
38 Hazard warning unit
39 Reversing lamp
40 Reversing lamp switch
41 Rear fog lamp
42 Rear fog lamp switch
43 Rear fog lamp warning
    lamp
44 Voltage stabilizer
45 Panel lamps
46 Switch illumination
47 Blocking diode
48 Fuel gauge

49 Fuel gauge sender unit
50 Induction heater
51 Fuel pump (hot climate)
52 Choke warning switch
53 Choke warning lamp
54 Oil pressure switch
55 Oil pressure warning
    lamp
56 Water temperature
    gauge
57 Water temperature gauge
    sender unit
58 Tachometer
59 Clock
60 Handbrake warning switch
61 Handbrake warning lamp
62 Brake pressure
    differential switch
63 Brake failure switch
    and warning lamp
64 Dashpot heater
65 Windscreen wash/wipe
    switch
66 Windscreen wiper motor
67 Windscreen washer motor
68 Rear window demister
    switch
69 Rear window demister
    element
70 Rear window demister
    warning lamp
71 Heater switch
72 Heater motor
73 Heater control
    illumination
74 Selector illumination
    (automatic transmission)
75 Interior lamp(s)
76 Interior lamp switch
77 Interior lamp door
    switch(es)
78 Boot lamp
79 Boot lamp switch
80 Cigar lighter
81 Cigar lighter
    illumination
82 Radio
83 Glovebox lamp
84 Glovebox lamp switch

Note: *Where a cable is shown coded by two colours, the first indicates the main colour and the second indicates the tracer colour*

Colour code

BK	Black
RD	Red
YW	Yellow
BL	Blue
BR	Brown
SL	Slate
LGR	Light green
GR	Green
PI	Pink
OR	Orange
PU	Purple
WH	White

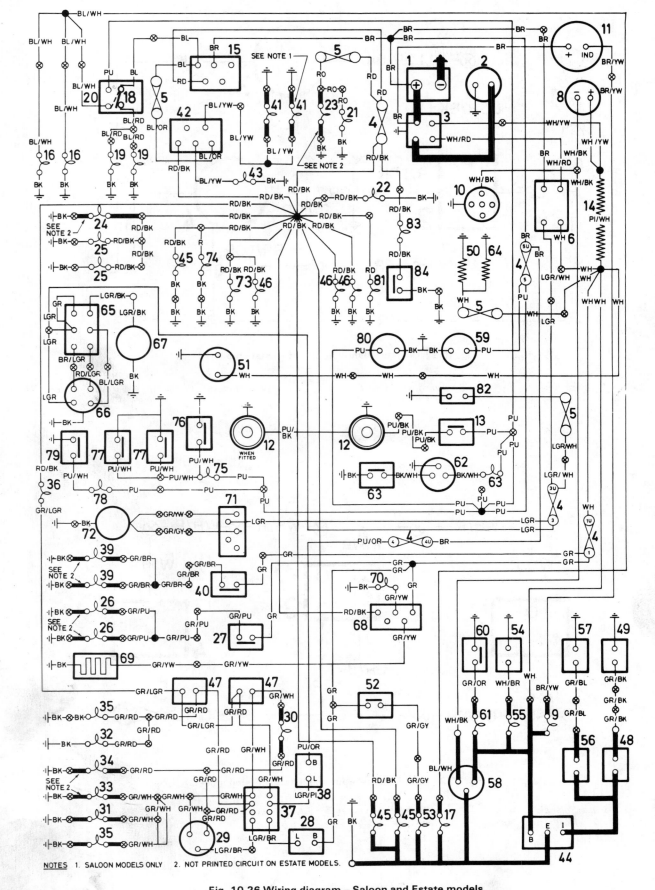

Fig. 10.26 Wiring diagram – Saloon and Estate models

NOTES 1. SALOON MODELS ONLY   2. NOT PRINTED CIRCUIT ON ESTATE MODELS.

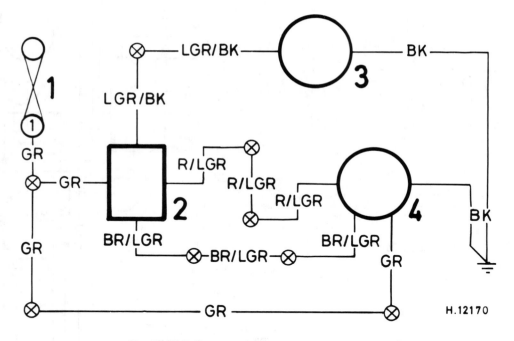

Fig. 10.27 Tailgate wash/wipe circuit – Estate models

| 1 | Fuse No 1 | 2 | Wash/wipe switch | 3 | Washer motor | 4 | Wiper motor |

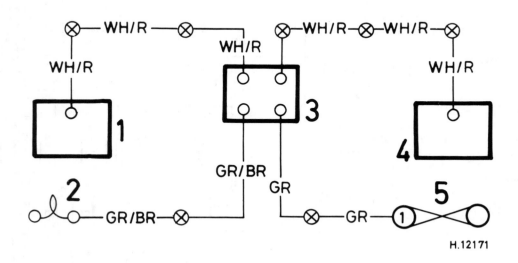

Fig. 10.28 Starter circuit – automatic transmission models

| 1 | Solenoid | 3 | Reverse and starter | 4 | Ignition switch | 5 | Fuse No 1 |
| 2 | Reversing lights | | inhibitor switch | | | | |

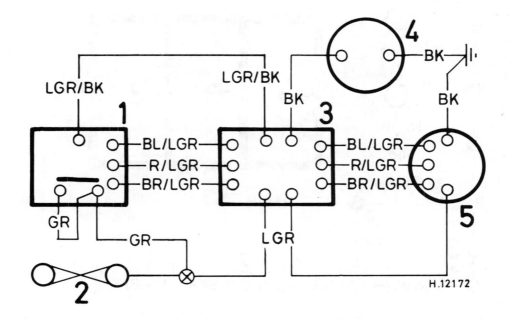

Fig. 10.29 Windscreen wiper delay circuit – HL models

| 1 | Wash/wipe switch | 3 | Wiper delay unit | 4 | Windscreen washer motor | 5 | Windscreen wiper motor |
| 2 | Fuse No 3 | | | | | | |

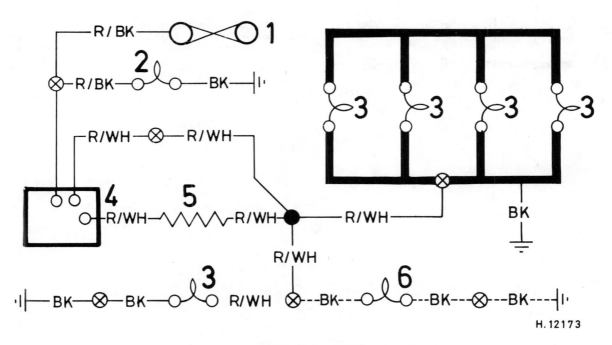

Fig. 10.30 Panel lamp circuit – Saloon models

| 1 | Fuse No 2 | 3 | Panel illumination lamps | 5 | Panel lamp resistor | 6 | Quadrant illumination lamp |
| 2 | Switch illumination lamps | 4 | Panel lamp switch | | | | |

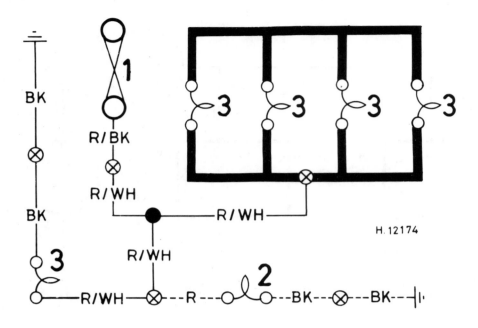

Fig. 10.31 Panel lamp circuit – Estate models

1 Fuse No 2

2 Quadrant illumination
   lamp

3 Panel illumination lamps

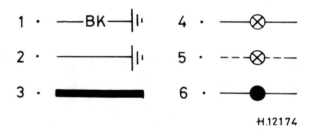

Fig. 10.32 Key to symbols used in wiring diagrams

1 Component earthed by
   cable
2 Component earthed by
   fixing

3 Printed circuit
4 Multi-way connector
5 When fitted
6 Sealed joint

H.12174

Chapter 11 Suspension and steering

Contents

Specifications

Front suspension

Type	Independent, by torsion bar with lever arm or telescopic type shock absorbers and anti-roll bar (on early models)
King pin inclination	$7\frac{1}{2}°$ positive $\pm$ 1°
Camber angle	$0°\ 50'$ positive $\begin{array}{l}+0°\ 15'\\-2°\ 00'\end{array}$
Castor angle:	
Saloon	$2°$ positive $\begin{array}{l}+0°\ 30'\\-1°\ 30'\end{array}$
Estate	$1°\ 18'$ positive $\begin{array}{l}+0°\ 30'\\-1°\ 30'\end{array}$
Hub bearing endfloat	0.001 to 0.005 in (0.025 to 0.127 mm)
Swivel pin link lower bush finished diameter	0.688 $\pm$ 0.0005 in (17.48 $\pm$ 0.013 mm)
Trim height	14.63 $\pm$ 0.25 in (371.6 $\pm$ 6.35 mm)

Rear suspension

Type	Semi-elliptic leaf spring with telescopic shock absorbers and anti-roll bar
Number of spring leaves:	
Saloon	2
Estate	4

Tyres

Size	155 x 13 radial ply	
Pressures (cold):	**lbf/in²**	**kgf/cm²**
Front (all models)	26	1.8
Rear (all models)	28	2.0
Front (laden Estate)	26	1.8
Rear (laden Estate)	32	2.3

Steering

Type	Rack-and-pinion
Steering wheel turns lock-to-lock	3.7
Pinion bearing preload	0.001 to 0.003 in (0.025 to 0.076 mm)
Cover gasket clearance	0.010 in (0.254 mm)
Yoke clearance	0.002 to 0.005 in (0.050 to 0.127 mm)
Cover gasket clearance	0.010 in (0.254 mm)
Balljoint ball-pin centre dimensions (balljoints screwed onto tie-rods by equal amounts)	43.7 in (1110 mm)
Steering rack-and-pinion lubricant:	
Type	BP Energrease FGL or equivalent
Capacity	7.32 in³ (120 cm³)
Front wheel alignment	0 to $\frac{1}{8}$ in (0 to 3.175 mm)/0° 30' toe-in

Torque wrench settings

Front suspension

	lbf ft	Nm
Swivel hub ball-pin retainer locknut	70 to 80	94 to 108
Eye bolt retaining nut	50 to 54	67 to 73
Tie-rod-to-body bracket nut	26 to 28	35 to 37
Torsion bar reaction lever lockbolt	22	29
Reaction pad nut	35 to 40	47 to 54
Shock absorber mounting retainer nuts	26 to 28	35 to 38
Shock absorber (telescopic) eye bolts	40	54
Tie-rod fork-to-suspension arm retaining nut	48 to 55	65 to 74
Tie-rod-to-tie-rod fork retaining nut	22	29
Caliper bracket and mud shield bolts	35 to 42	47 to 56
Roadwheels	38 to 41	51 to 55

Rear suspension

	lbf ft	Nm
Upper shackle pin nuts	28	38
Spring eye bolt nuts	40	54
Shock absorber to spring bracket	28	38
Shock absorber to body bracket	45	61
Anti-roll bar pivot bolt nut	63 to 67	85 to 91

Steering

	lbf ft	Nm
Rack U-bolt retaining nuts	15 to 18	20 to 24
Tie-rod ball-pin retaining nuts	20 to 24	27 to 32
Steering column universal joint coupling pinch bolts	17 to 20	23 to 27
Flexible rubber coupling retaining bolts	20 to 22	27 to 29
Flexible joint retaining bolts (shouldered)	4 to 7	5 to 9
Steering column retaining bolts	14 to 18	18 to 24
Pinion end cover retaining bolts	12 to 15	16 to 20
Rack yoke cover bolts	12 to 15	16 to 20
Steering wheel nut	43 to 50	58 to 67
Lower arm front and rear pivots and front-to-rear arm bolts	26 to 28	35 to 37

1   General description

The component parts of the right-hand side front suspension unit fitted to early models are shown in Fig. 11.1. Although the left-hand side front suspension is identical in principle, some parts are 'handed' and therefore not interchangeable.

Attached to the hub is the roadwheel as is also the brake disc, these being retained by bolts. The hub rotates on two opposed tapered roller bearings mounted on the swivel pin stub axle, and is retained on the stub axle by a nut. Also attached to the swivel pin is the disc brake dust shield.

The lever arm type shock absorber is attached to the body and its arm carries, at the outer end, the balljoint for the swivel pin top attachment. Its arm therefore acts as an upper suspension wishbone.

From VIN 701990 the lever arm type shock absorbers are replaced by a telescopic type. These are attached at the top to a bracket mounted in the place reserved for the main body of the lever arm shock absorbers used on earlier models. The lower mounting point is on the lower suspension arm. Eye bolts are used to secure the shock absorber, both top and bottom. The bottom end of the steering swivel screws into the lower link, which is mounted between the outer ends of the lower arms. This link is mounted on a pivot pin so that the suspension is able to move in a vertical manner. Horizontal movement of the suspension is controlled by a tie-rod assembly. The inner ends of the lower arms are free to pivot about an eye bolt, and the rear arm is spline-attached to the torsion bar. The rear of the torsion bar is attached to the body so that both the body weight and road shocks are taken by the torsion bar.

The anti-roll bar, if fitted, is attached to the lower suspension arm by balljoint swivel links.

Rear suspension is by semi-elliptic leaf springs, the springs being mounted on rubber bushed shackle pins. Double acting telescopic hydraulic shock absorbers are fitted to absorb road shocks and damp spring oscillations. An anti-roll bar is also fitted.

A rack-and-pinion steering is used. The steering wheel is splined to the upper inner column, which in turn is connected to the lower column by a flexible coupling. A second flexible coupling connects the lower column to the steering gear pinion. The pinion teeth mesh with those machined in the rack so that rotation of the pinion moves the rack from one side of the housing to the other. Located at either end of the rack are tie-rods and balljoints, which are attached to the suspension swivel hub steering levers.

2   Maintenance and inspection

1   At regular intervals, inspect the condition of all flexible gaiters, balljoint dust excluders and rubber suspension bushes. Renew any that have split or deteriorated, as described in the appropriate Sections of this Chapter.
2   At the same time, check for any wear or excess play in the suspension and steering balljoints and linkages. Ensure the hub bearings are correctly adjusted and check the torque of all nuts and bolts on the suspension and steering components are in accordance with those listed in the Specifications.
3   At the same intervals, on models equipped with telescopic type front shock absorbers, grease the top arm inner swivel shafts and roller bearings.
4   It is also a good idea to have the front wheel alignment (toe-in) checked, and if necessary, reset at regular intervals. Refer to Section 28.

3   Front hub bearings – adjustment

1   Jack up the front of the car and support it on firmly based axle stands.
2   Remove the wheel trim, roadwheel and grease cap.
3   Straighten the split pin legs and extract the split pin. Lift away the hub nut retainer.
4   Back off the hub nut and spin the hub. Whilst it is spinning, tighten the nut using a torque wrench set to 5 lbf ft (6.7 Nm).
5   Stop the hub spinning and slacken the nut. Tighten the nut again but this time finger-tight only.
6   Position the nut retainer so that the left-hand half of the split pin hole is covered by one of the arms of the retainer.
7   Slacken the nut and retainer until the split pin hole is fully uncovered.
8   Fit a new split pin and lock by opening the ears of the split pin and bending circumferentially around the nut retainer.

9 Fit the grease cap and refit the roadwheel and wheel trim.
10 It will be observed that the endfloat setting achieved can cause a considerable amount of movement when the tyre is rocked. Do not reduce the endfloat any further provided it has been set correctly as described. The bearings must not on any account be preloaded.
11 Finally lower the car to the ground.

4 Front hub bearings – removal and refitting

1 Jack up the front of the car and support it on axle stands. Remove the appropriate front roadwheel.
2 Refer to Chapter 9 and remove the disc brake caliper.

3 Using a wide-bladed screwdriver, carefully ease off the grease cap (photo).
4 Extract the split pin, lift away the nut retainer and then undo and remove the hub nut. Withdraw the splined washer. The hub complete with brake disc can now be slid off the stub axle. Take care not to allow the inner race of the outer bearing to fall out as the hub is withdrawn.
5 With the hub assembly on the bench, lift out the outer bearing inner race (photo).
6 Turn the hub over and ease out the oil seal using a large screwdriver. The inner bearing inner race can now be lifted out (photos).
7 Wipe away any surplus grease from the centre of the hub between the two bearing outer races.

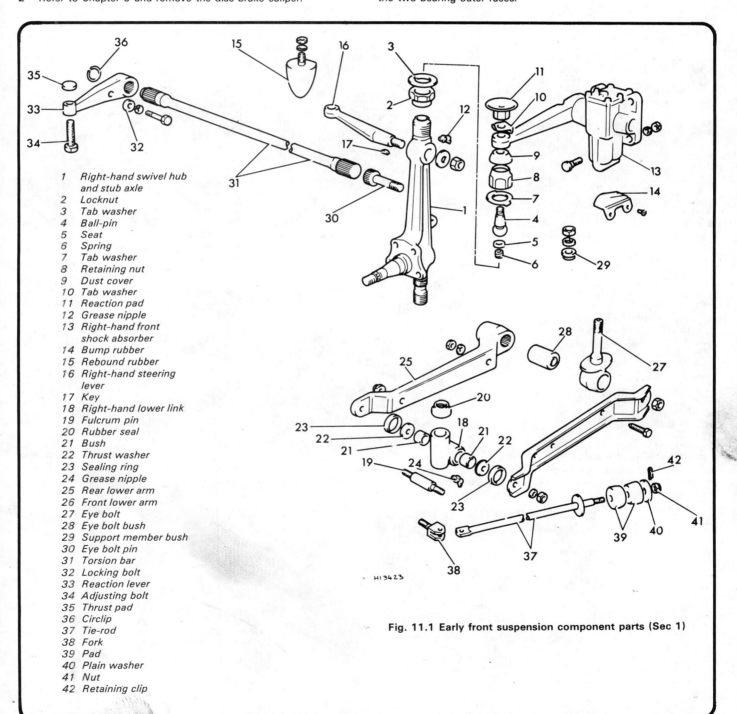

1   Right-hand swivel hub and stub axle
2   Locknut
3   Tab washer
4   Ball-pin
5   Seat
6   Spring
7   Tab washer
8   Retaining nut
9   Dust cover
10 Tab washer
11 Reaction pad
12 Grease nipple
13 Right-hand front shock absorber
14 Bump rubber
15 Rebound rubber
16 Right-hand steering lever
17 Key
18 Right-hand lower link
19 Fulcrum pin
20 Rubber seal
21 Bush
22 Thrust washer
23 Sealing ring
24 Grease nipple
25 Rear lower arm
26 Front lower arm
27 Eye bolt
28 Eye bolt bush
29 Support member bush
30 Eye bolt pin
31 Torsion bar
32 Locking bolt
33 Reaction lever
34 Adjusting bolt
35 Thrust pad
36 Circlip
37 Tie-rod
38 Fork
39 Pad
40 Plain washer
41 Nut
42 Retaining clip

H13423

Fig. 11.1 Early front suspension component parts (Sec 1)

4.3 Remove the grease cap with a wide-bladed screwdriver

4.5 Lift out the outer bearing inner race

4.6a Turn the hub over and extract the oil seal ...

4.6b ... then lift out the inner bearing inner race

4.8 The outer races can then be driven out using a suitable drift

4.12a Place the new outer race in position with the taper facing outward ...

4.12b ... and drift it into the hub using a tube of suitable diameter

4.13 Pack the inner bearing inner race with high melting point grease and position it in the outer race

4.14 Refit the oil seal with the lip towards the bearing

4.16 With the outer bearing inner race and the splined washer in place, refit the assembly to the stub axle

4.17 Screw on the hub nut finger tight, then adjust the bearing endfloat

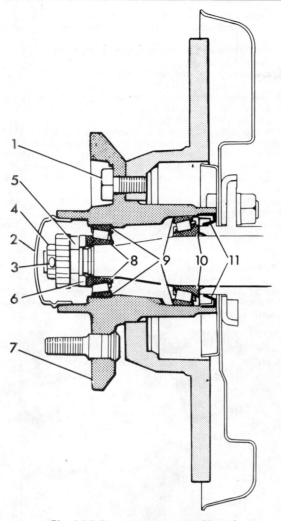

Fig. 11.2 Front hub assembly (Sec 4)

1	Disc-to-hub bolt	7	Hub
2	Grease cap	8	Outer bearing inner race
3	Split pin	9	Outer races
4	Nut retainer	10	Inner bearing inner race
5	Nut	11	Oil seal
6	Splined washer		

8 Using a suitable drift, and working from the inside of the hub, carefully drift out the bearing outer races (photo).

9 Thoroughly wash all the parts in paraffin and wipe dry using a lint-free cloth.

10 Inspect the bearing rollers and races for signs of scoring, pitting or overheating, and if evident renew the bearings. The oil seal must be renewed as a matter of course as it will have been damaged during removal.

11 Clean the oil seal journal face on the stub axle and remove any small burrs that may be present with fine emery paper.

12 To reassemble the hub, first drift in the new bearing outer races using a tube or socket of suitable diameter. Make sure that they are fitted with the tapers facing outwards and ensure that they enter the hub squarely (photos).

13 Pack the inner bearing inner race with multi-purpose lithium grease and place it in position on the outer race (photo).

14 Smear the lip of a new oil seal with engine oil and fit it to the hub with the lip innermost. Tap it into position with a block of wood until its face is flush with the hub flange (photo).

15 Pack the outer bearing inner race with multi-purpose lithium grease and position it in the outer race.

16 Place the splined washer over the bearing to hold it in the hub and

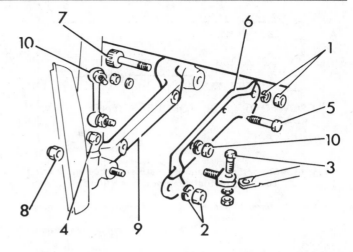

Fig. 11.3 Lower suspension arm removal – early models (Sec 5)

1	Eye bolt pin nut and washer	6	Front lower suspension arm
2	Lower link pin securing nut and washer	7	Eye bolt pin
3	Tie-rod securing bolt	8	Swivel lower link pin nut
4	Te-rod fork retaining nut	9	Lower suspension arm
5	Lower arm clamp bolt	10	Anti-roll bar link and securing nut

refit the assembly to the stub axle (photo).

17 Screw on the hub nut finger tight and then adjust the hub bearing endfloat as described in Section 3 (photo).

5 Lower suspension arm – removal and refitting

1 Jack up the front of the car and support it on firmly based axle stands. Suitably support the suspension unit under the rear lower arm.

2 Remove the wheel trim and the roadwheel.

3 Undo and remove the two anti-roll bar link securing nuts and washers, if fitted. Pull the link away from the lower suspension arm.

4 Undo and remove the nut and spring washer from the eye bolt pin.

5 Undo and remove the front nut and spring washers from the swivel lower link pin.

6 Undo and remove the nut, bolt and spring washer that retain the tie-rod to the tie-rod fork.

7 Undo and remove the nut that retains the tie-rod fork to the lower suspension arm. Lift away the fork.

8 Undo the nut, bolt and spring washer that clamp the front and rear lower arms together.

9 The front lower suspension arm may now be lifted away.

10 Refer to Section 11 and remove the torsion bar.

11 Withdraw the eye bolt pin and then undo and remove the rear nut and spring washer from the swivel lower link pin.

12 The rear lower suspension arm may now be lifted away.

13 Refitting the lower suspension arm assembly is the reverse sequence to removal. Ensure that the eye bolt pin retaining nut, the tie-rod fork-to-lower suspension arm retaining nut, and the tie-rod-to-fork retaining nut and bolt are tightened to the specified torque.

6 Front shock absorber – removal and refitting

Lever arm type

Note: *The torque figure given in paragraph 11(b) is the true (actual) torque for the reaction pad nut. To obtain this figure, a torque wrench has to be used with a special crowfoot adaptor (BL part No 18G 1237) and, because the torque is applied to the adaptor rather than the nut, a formula must be used so that the indicated (metered) torque can be related to the true torque. Referring to Fig. 11.4 the metered torque is calculated as follows:*

$$MT = \frac{AT \times Y}{Y + X}$$

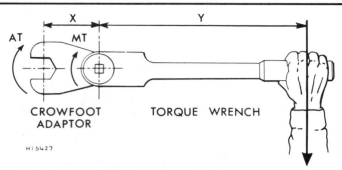

Fig. 11.4 Method of calculating metered torque when using special crowfoot adaptor (Secs 6 and 8)

MT = Metered torque   Y = Effective length of torque
AT = Actual torque   wrench
                         X = Effective length of adaptor

If you do not have this crowfoot adaptor, an open-ended spanner ($\frac{15}{16}$ in AF) can be used, but you should arrange for your BL dealer to check the tightness of the nut after fitting.

1   Jack up the front of the car and support on firmly based axle stands.

2   Remove the wheel trim and roadwheel.

3   Remove the grease nipple from the swivel pin lower link and place an axle stand beneath the lower suspension arm, and in contact with it.

4   Unlock the reaction pad nut and remove the nut (photo).

5   Lift away the lockwasher.

6   Free the arm from the swivel pin balljoint using a balljoint separator tool (photo).

7   Undo and remove the four nuts and plain washers that secure the shock absorber to its mounting (photo).

8   Lift away the shock absorber (photo).

9   Test the operation of the shock absorber by topping up the level if necessary and then moving the shock arm up and down. If the action is weak or jerky, then either the unit is worn or air has entered the operating cylinders. Move the arm up and down ten times and if the performance has not improved, a new shock absorber must be obtained.

10   Inspect the shock absorber arm bushes for wear. If evident, the shock absorber must be renewed.

11   Refitting the shock absorber is the reverse sequence to removal, but the following additional points should be noted:

(a)   Always use a new reaction pad lockwasher

(b)   Tighten the reaction pad nut to a torque of 35 to 40 lbf ft (47 to 54 Nm) using the crowfoot adaptor number 18G 1237

(c)   Tighten the shock absorber retaining nuts to a torque wrench setting of 26 to 28 lbf ft (35 to 38 Nm)

6.4 Undo and remove the reaction pad nut ...

6.6 ... and release the shock absorber arm with a balljoint separator

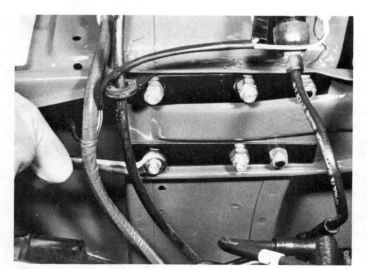

6.7 Working in the engine compartment, undo and remove the shock absorber retaining nuts ...

6.8 ... then lift away the shock absorber

Telescopic type

12 Jack up the front of the car and support it on firmly based stands.

13 Remove the wheel trim and roadwheel.

14 Remove the grease nipple from the swivel pin lower link. Place an axle stand beneath the lower suspension arm, and in contact with it to take its weight.

15 Remove the eye bolts at top and bottom of the shock absorber. Remove the shock absorber.

16 Refitting is a reversal of the removal procedure. Tighten the eye bolts to the specified torque.

---

7 Front swivel hub – removal and refitting

1 Refer to Section 6 and carry out the instructions given in paragraphs 1 to 6 inclusive (regardless of suspension type).

2 Wipe the top of the brake master cylinder reservoir. Remove the cap and place a thin piece of polythene over the top. Refit the cap. This will prevent hydraulic fluid syphoning out during subsequent operations.

3 Wipe the area around the flexible brake hose connection at the body mounted bracket. Hold the flexible hose metal end and undo and remove the metal pipe union nut. Undo and remove the flexible hose securing nut and washer and withdraw the hose from the bracket. Plug the pipe and hose ends to prevent dirt ingress.

4 Refer to Section 5 and carry out the instructions given in paragraphs 3 to 9 inclusive.

5 Undo and remove the lower link pin rear retaining nut. Mark the fitted position of the special overtravel nut and remove it.

6 The swivel hub assembly may now be lifted away.

7 Refitting is the reverse of the removal procedure. Ensure that the overtravel nut is refitted in the same position.

---

8 Swivel hub upper balljoint – removal and refitting

Note: *The torque figure given in paragraph 9 is the true (actual) torque for the ball retainer locknut. To obtain this figure, a torque wrench has to be used with a special crowfoot adaptor (BL part No 18G 1192) and, because the torque is applied to the adaptor rather than the nut, a formula must be used so that the indicated (metered) torque can be related to the true torque. Referring to Fig. 11.4 the metered torque is calculated as follows:*

$$MT = \frac{AT \times Y}{Y + X}$$

If you do not have this crowfoot adaptor, an open-ended spanner (1½ in AF) can be used, but you should arrange for your BL dealer to check the tightness of the nut after refitting.

1 Refer to Section 6 and carry out the instructions given in paragraphs 1 to 6 inclusive (regardless of suspension type).

2 Raise the arm until it is clear of the ball-pin.

3 Lift off the balljoint dust cover.

4 Unlock the tab washer and, using a large open-ended spanner, hold the locknut. With a ring spanner, undo the ball-pin retainer (photo).

5 Lift away the ball-pin, ball seat and spring. Finally remove the tab washer and locknut.

6 To reassemble the joint, first obtain a new tab washer. Smear the spherical surface of the ball-pin with Duckhams Q5648 grease or an equivalent molybdenum disulphide grease prior to assembly. Pack the ball-pin retainer with a general purpose grease.

7 Refit the locknut to the swivel hub and screw it down as far as it will go. Now refit the spring and ball seat followed by the tab washer. Enter the ball-pin into the retainer and screw this assembly onto the swivel hub (photos).

8 Tighten the ball-pin retainer until the torque required to produce articulation of the ball-pin is 32 to 52 lbf in (4.0 to 5.4 Nm). In practice the easiest way of doing this is to tighten the ball-pin retainer until the ball-pin is locked. Now slowly unscrew the retainer until the ball-pin can be moved to any position without binding (photo). A certain amount of resistance will be felt due to the spring under the ball seat, but the joint must not possess high spots or bind in any position.

9 Hold the ball retainer against rotation and tighten the locknut

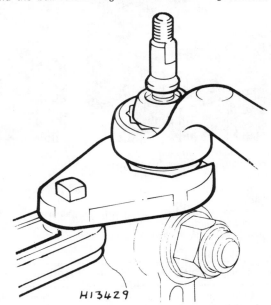

H13429

Fig. 11.5 Using the crowfoot adaptor (Sec 8)

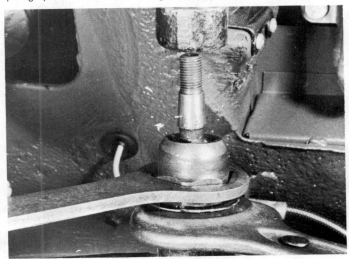

8.4 Using an open-ended spanner to hold the locknut, unscrew the ball-pin retainer with a ring spanner

8.7a Refit the spring ...

8.7b ... ball seat ...

8.7c ... and tab washer ...

8.7d ... then screw the ball-pin and retainer assembly onto the swivel hub

8.8 With the retainer tightened the ball-pin must move to any position without binding

8.10a Lock the ball-pin retainer and locknut with the tab washer ...

8.10b ... and refit the dust cover

against it to a torque of 70 to 80 lbf ft (94 to 108 Nm) using the crowfoot adaptor.

10 Lock the retainer and the locknut with the tab washer, and then refit the dust cover (photos).

11 Refitting is now the reverse sequence to removal.

9 Lower swivel link and pin – removal and refitting

1 Jack up the front of the car and support it on axle stands. Place a jack or suitable blocks under the lower suspension arm and *just* take the weight of the suspension.

2 Remove the wheel trim and roadwheel.

3 Refer to Chapter 9 and remove the disc brake caliper.

4 Using a wide-bladed screwdriver, carefully ease off the grease cap from the centre of the hub.

5 Extract the split pin, lift off the nut retainer and then undo and remove the hub nut. The hub assembly and brake disc can now be withdrawn from the stub axle. Take care not to allow the splined washer and outer bearing inner race to fall out as the hub is removed.

6 Undo and remove the nut and washer securing the front brake hose to the bracket on the swivel hub. Slide the hose out of the bracket.

7 Undo and remove the four nuts, bolts and spring washers securing the disc brake mud shield and caliper mounting bracket to the swivel hub. Lift away the mud shield and bracket.

8 Refer to Section 5 and carry out the instructions in paragraphs 3 to 9 inclusive.

9 Undo and remove the remaining nut and washer securing the link pin to the rear lower suspension arm.

10 Swing the swivel hub forwards and remove the rubber sealing washers and thrust washers from the lower link.

11 Withdraw the lower link pin and then unscrew the lower link from the swivel hub.

12 Thoroughly wash all the parts in paraffin, and dry with a lint-free rag.

13 Check for excessive wear across the thrust faces of the lower link,

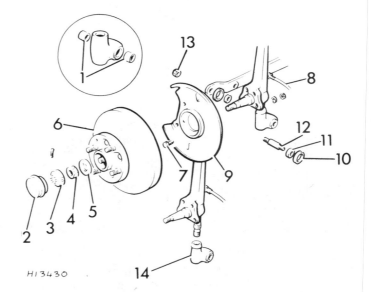

H13430

Fig. 11.6 Lower swivel link and pin removal (Sec 9)

1	Lower link bushes	8	Brake hydraulic hose
2	Grease cap	9	Disc brake mud shield
3	Nut retainer and split pin	10	Sealing ring
4	Nut	11	Thrust washer
5	Splined washer	12	Lower link pin
6	Hub	13	Link pin securing nut
7	Mud shield retaining bolt		and spring washer
	and spring washer	14	Lower link

and in the threaded bore. Check also for wear on the threads of the swivel hub. If the wear is excessive both these components must be renewed.

14 Check the bushes in the lower link, and also the link pin, for wear or ridging. If wear is excessive, new bushes and link pin should be obtained. The bushes must be reamed to a specified dimension after fitting, and it is advisable to entrust the work of removing, refitting and reaming the bushes to a BL dealer who will have the necessary equipment to do this work. If an expanding reamer and micrometer are available, however, the old bushes may be drifted out and new ones fitted as described in paragraphs 18 and 19.

15 Inspect the thrust washers for signs of damage or wear; if evident, new thrust washers must be obtained.

16 Remove the grease nipple and ensure that both it and its hole are free from obstructions.

17 Obtain a new set of rubber sealing rings.

18 If new bushes are to be fitted, these should be drifted or pressed in so that the oil groove is located as shown in Fig. 11.7. The bush oil groove blank ends should be towards the outside edge of the link.

19 Using the expanding reamer, line ream the new bushes to a finished size of 0.688 in ± 0.0005 in (17.48 mm ± 0.013 mm).

20 Pack the area between the lower link bushes and the swivel hub threads with approximately 2.5 cc of Duckhams Q5648 grease or an equivalent molybdenum disulphide grease.

21 Place the lower link and seal on the swivel hub and screw on the link. Engage the seal on the recessed shoulder of the link and screw the link fully onto the swivel hub.

22 Unscrew the link one complete turn.

23 Reassembly is now the reverse sequence to removal, but the following additional points should be noted:

(a) The caliper mounting bracket and mud shield retaining bolts should be tightened to the specified torque as shown in the Specifications

(b) Adjust the front hub bearing endfloat as described in Section 3

(c) Bleed the brake hydraulic system as described in Chapter 9

10 Eye bolt bush – removal and refitting

1 Refer to Section 11 and remove the torsion bar.

2 Undo and remove the eye bolt pin retaining nut and spring washer.

3 Withdraw the eye bolt pin from the rear lower suspension arm.

4 Ease the lower suspension arm away from the eye bolt and withdraw the eye bolt from its location in the chassis member.

5 The eye bolt bush may be removed by pressing it out on a bench vice using pieces of suitable diameter tube.

6 To fit a new bush, lubricate its outer surface with soapy water and press it into the eye bolt using the bench vice and tubing.

7 Refitting the eye bolt is the reverse sequence to removal. Tighten the eye bolt retaining nut to the specified torque after refitting the torsion bar.

11 Torsion bar – removal and refitting

1 Unscrew and remove the grease nipple from the swivel pin lower link.

2 Place a wooden block 8 in (200 mm) thick on the floor under the lower suspension arm as near as possible to the disc brake dust shield as shown in Fig. 11.9.

3 Jack up the front of the car. Remove the wheel trim and roadwheel.

4 Carefully lower the car until the weight of the suspension is placed on the wooden block.

5 Undo and remove the two anti-roll bar link retaining nuts and washers, if fitted, and pull the link away from the anti-roll bar and lower suspension arm.

6 On models with a lever arm shock absorber unlock and remove the reaction pad nut. Free the shock absorber from the swivel pin balljoint using a balljoint separator tool.

7 On models with a telescopic shock absorber undo and remove the eye bolt securing the lower suspension to the shock absorber.

8 On all models undo and remove the steering tie-rod ball-pin nut.

9 Using a universal balljoint separator, release the ball-pin from the steering lever.

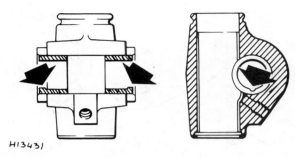

H13431

Fig. 11.7 Correct position of lower swivel link bush oil groove (Sec 9)

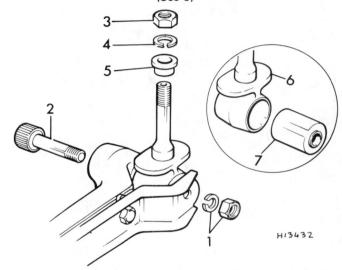

H13432

Fig. 11.8 Eye bolt bush removal (Sec 10)

1	Eye bolt pin nut and spring washer	4	Spring washer
2	Eye bolt pin	5	Spacer
3	Nut	6	Eye bolt
		7	Bush

10 Jack up the front of the car so as to relieve the torsion bar load. Ensure the lower suspension arm is still just resting on the wooden block.

11 Undo and remove the bolt, spring washer and special washer that secure the torsion bar reaction lever onto the chassis member.

12 Remove the reaction lever from the chassis member and move the lever forwards along the torsion bar.

13 Release the nut that retains the eye bolt through the chassis member and make sure that the suspension lowers itself by ½ in (12 mm).

14 Ease the torsion bar forwards until it clears the shoulder from the chassis housing. Lower the torsion bar and remove it in a rearwards direction.

15 Using a pair of circlip pliers, remove the torsion bar circlip.

16 Slide off the reaction lever from the torsion bar.

17 Refitting the torsion bar is the reverse sequence to removal but the following additional points should be noted:

(a) Once a torsion bar has been fitted and used on one side of the car it must not under any circumstances be used on the other side. This is because a torsion bar becomes 'handed' once it has been in use. Torsion bars are only interchangeable when new

(b) Do not fit a torsion bar that is corroded or deeply scored as this will affect its reliability and in bad cases cause premature failure

18 When refitting a torsion bar that has been removed without using a wooden block of the correct size, or when fitting a new torsion bar, it should be initially set up using the following procedure before fitting the reaction lever:

19 First measure the height of the eye bolt centre above the floor (dimension A in Fig. 11.10). Then deduct the dimension given in the following table to obtain the dimension C in Fig. 11.10.

Torsion bar settled – 7.37 in (187.20 mm)
New unsettled bar – 7.66 in (194.56 mm)

20 Adjust the swivel link pin centre to dimension C and retain it in this position. Fit the reaction lever with the adjusting screw set in the mid-way position, making sure that the eye bolt centre to floor dimension is not altered.
21 Tighten all retaining nuts and bolts to the specified torque as shown in the Specifications (see also Section 6).
22 Refer to Section 14 and adjust the front suspension trim height if necessary.

12 Tie-rod – removal and refitting

1 Jack up the front of the car and support it on axle stands. Remove the wheel trim and roadwheel.
2 Using a pair of pliers, extract the tie-rod spring clip from the end of the tie-rod (photo).
3 Undo and remove the locknut and plain washer, then slide off the outer rubber pad.
4 Undo and remove the nut, bolt and spring washer securing the tie-rod to the tie-rod fork on the lower suspension arm (photo).

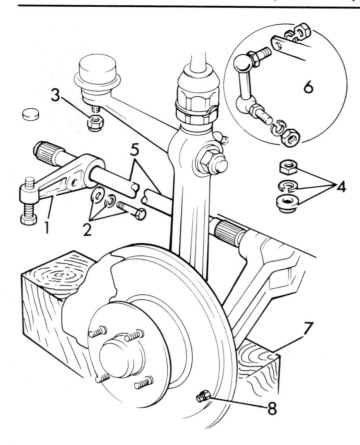

Fig. 11.9 Torsion bar removal (Sec 11)

1	Reaction lever	5	Torsion bar
2	Bolt, spring and special washer	6	Anti-roll bar link
3	Tie-rod ball-pin nut	7	Wooden block
4	Eye bolt retaining nut, washer and bush	8	Grease nipple

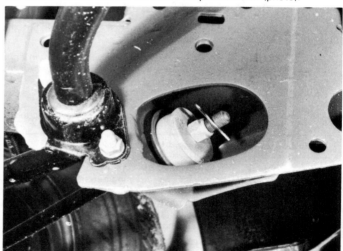

12.2 Tie-rod retaining spring clip and front mounting

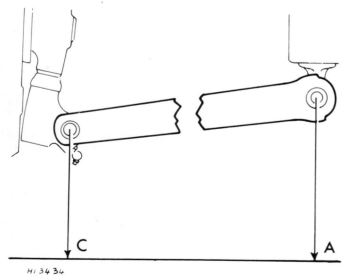

Fig. 11.10 Torsion bar setting dimensions – see text (Sec 11)

12.4 Tie rod and anti-roll bar attachments on lower suspension arm; (A) tie-rod-to-fork attachments and (B) anti-roll bar link nuts (early models)

5   Slide the tie-rod out of the fork and withdraw it rearwards from the car. Remove the inner rubber pad from the front of the tie-bar.
6   Refitting the tie-rod is the reverse sequence to removal, but the following additional points should be noted:

(a) Inspect the two rubber pads, and if they show signs of cracking, perishing or other damage, obtain a new set of pads
(b) Tighten the retaining nuts and bolts to the specified torque as shown in the Specifications

13 Front anti-roll bar – removal and refitting

1   Jack up the front of the car and support it on firmly based axle stands.
2   Unscrew and remove the link retaining nuts and spring washers from both ends of the anti-roll bar and detach the link ends.
3   Mark the anti-roll bar mounting carriers 'left' and 'right' so that they can be refitted in their original positions, then unscrew and remove the four retaining screws (photo).
4   Note that the front left-hand face of the anti-roll bar, near the link position, is marked L and then lower the complete bar.
5   Detach the rubber bushes from the anti-roll bar and unscrew and remove the anti-roll bar links from the lower suspension arms.
6   Renew any bushes or links which show any indication of wear or deterioration.
7   Refitting is a reversal of the removal procedure, but soak the rubber bushes in soapy water prior to tightening the retaining carriers.

13.3 Anti-roll bar carrier-to-chassis attachment (left-hand side)

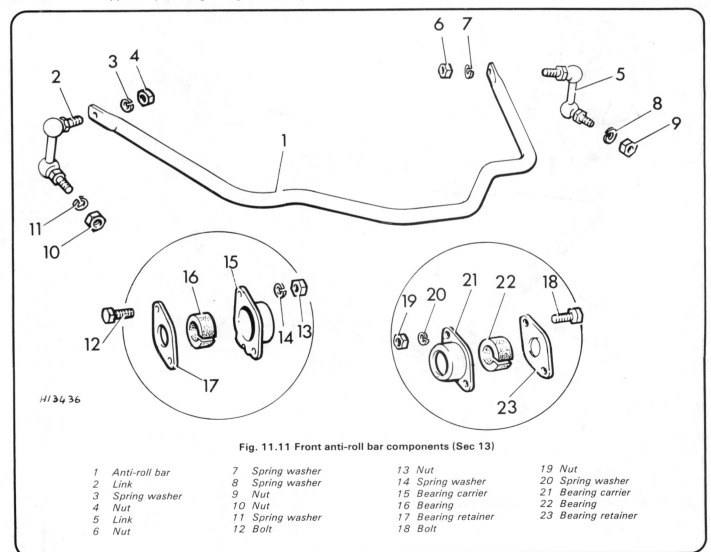

H13436

Fig. 11.11 Front anti-roll bar components (Sec 13)

1 Anti-roll bar	7 Spring washer	13 Nut	19 Nut
2 Link	8 Spring washer	14 Spring washer	20 Spring washer
3 Spring washer	9 Nut	15 Bearing carrier	21 Bearing carrier
4 Nut	10 Nut	16 Bearing	22 Bearing
5 Link	11 Spring washer	17 Bearing retainer	23 Bearing retainer
6 Nut	12 Bolt	18 Bolt	

14 Front suspension trim height – checking and adjustment

1   Before checking the front trim height of the car, it must be prepared by removing the contents of the boot with the exception of the spare wheel. Ideally there should be two gallons of petrol in the tank. Check and, if necessary, adjust the tyre pressures.
2   Stand the car on a level surface and measure the vertical distance from the centre of the hub to the underside of the front wheel arch. This measurement should be as shown in the Specifications.
3   To adjust the trim height, slacken the reaction lever lockbolt at the rear of the torsion bar and turn the adjuster bolt as necessary to obtain the correct height (photo). Turning the adjuster bolt clockwise increases the trim height and turning it anti-clockwise decreases the height. Maximum movement of the adjuster bolt from the mid-way position increases the trim height by 0.75 in (19.05 mm) or decreases the height by 1.25 in (31.75 mm).
4   When the height is correct, tighten the reaction lever lockbolt.
5   Repeat this procedure on the other side of the car.

15 Rear anti-roll bar – removal and refitting

1   Chock the front wheels, jack up the rear of the car and support it on axle stands. Remove the rear roadwheels.
2   Undo and remove the two lower retaining nuts, washer and lower bush from each rear shock absorber. Push the shock absorber lower

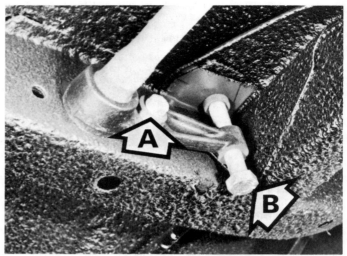

14.3 Reaction lever lockbolt (A) and adjuster bolt (B)

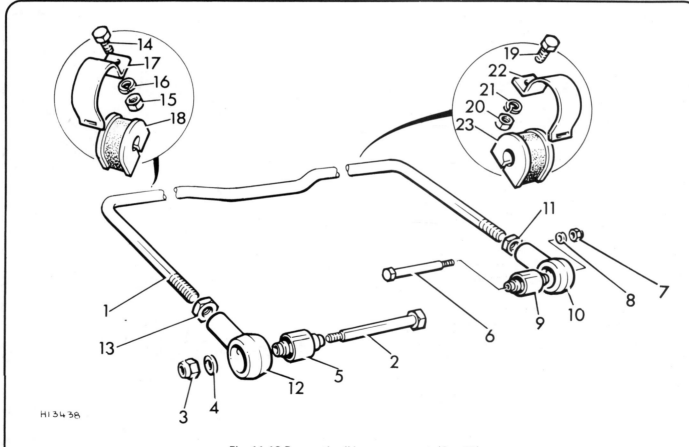

H13438

Fig. 11.12 Rear anti-roll bar components (Sec 15)

1 Rear anti-roll bar	7 Locknut	13 Locknut	19 Bolt
2 Bolt	8 Washer	14 Bolt	20 Nut
3 Locknut	9 Slotted bush	15 Nut	21 Spring washer
4 Washer	10 End fitting	16 Spring washer	22 Clamp
5 Slotted bush	11 Locknut	17 Clamp	23 Bearing
6 Bolt	12 End fitting	18 Bearing	

cylinders upwards until their lower ends are clear of the mounting plates. Now swing the shock absorbers towards the centre of the car.

3 Undo and remove the nut, bolt and spring washer securing each anti-roll bar clamp to the rear axle casing. Unclip the clamps from their mounting lugs and lift them away.

4 Undo and remove the two end pivot bolts and lock washers and withdraw the anti-roll bar from under the car (photo).

5 With the anti-roll bar removed, the two rubber bushes can be eased off the bar for renewal if necessary.

6 If the end fittings are to be removed, first mark their locations, slacken the locknuts, then unscrew them from the anti-roll bar.

7 Refitting the anti-roll bar is the reverse sequence to removal bearing in mind the following points:

(a) *Ensure that the end fitting bushes line up with the chassis member holes, and adjust them on the anti-roll bar if necessary. It is important not to distort the rubber bushes when inserting the pivot bolts*

(b) *Tighten the pivot bolts to the specified torque as shown in the Specifications*

16 Rear road spring – removal and refitting

1 Refer to Section 17 and remove the rear shackles.

2 Support the rear axle with a jack on the side from which the spring is to be removed, and *just* take the weight of the axle.

3 Undo and remove the shock absorber locknut, plain nut and plain washer. Note the location of the lower bush in the shock absorber lower mounting plate and remove the lower bush.

4 Undo and remove the nut, spring washer and bolt that secure the front spring eye to the body mounted brackets.

5 Undo and remove the four nuts from the two U-bolts.

6 Carefully lower the spring and its mountings.

7 Remove the shock absorber mounting plate followed by the spring mounting plates and mounting rubbers. Note the fitted location of the spring mounting wedge.

8 Lift away the two U-bolts and packing plate (if fitted).

9 If the spring bushes are worn or have deteriorated, they should be pressed out using suitable diameter tubes and a large bench vice.

10 Should the spring have considerably weakened or failed, necessitating the fitting of a new one, rear springs must be renewed in pairs and not singly, as the remaining spring will have settled slightly. Unless the springs have the same performance and characteristics, road holding can be adversely affected.

11 Refitting is the reverse of the removal sequence. Ensure that all nuts and bolts are tightened to the specified torque.

17 Rear road spring shackles – removal and refitting

1 Chock the front wheels, jack up the rear of the car and place it on firmly based axle stands located under the main longitudinal chassis members.

2 Remove the wheel trim and roadwheel.

3 Undo and remove the nut and spring washer on each side of the upper shackle pin.

4 Undo and remove the nut and spring washer from the spring bush bolt.

5 Lift away the inner shackle plate.

6 Using a suitable diameter parallel pin punch, partially drift out the spring bolt and then release the outer plate from the upper pin.

7 Remove the upper shackle pin and lift away the two half bushes.

8 Inspect the bushes for signs of deterioration or oil contamination; if evident, new bushes should be obtained.

9 Refitting is the reverse sequence to removal. Tighten the shackle pin and bolt retaining nuts to the specified torque.

18 Rear shock absorber – removal and refitting

1 Undo and remove the shock absorber lower locknut and retaining nut (photo).

2 Lift away the plain washer and note the position of the lower bush. Lift away the lower bush (photos).

3 Contract the shock absorber, thereby detaching it from the

15.4 Rear anti-roll bar end pivot and retaining bolt

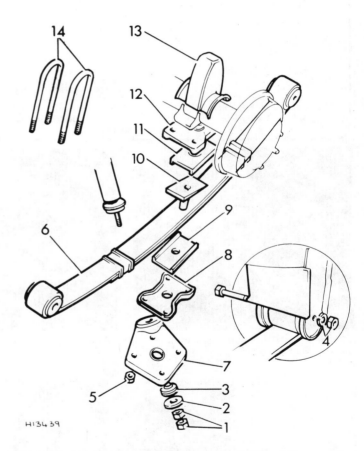

H13439

Fig. 11.13 Rear road spring removal (Sec 16)

1 Shock absorber retaining nut and locknut	8 Spring mounting plate (lower)
2 Plate washer	9 Rubber pad
3 Lower bush	10 Wedge
4 Forward spring eye bolt securing nut and spring washer	11 Rubber pad
5 U-bolt nut	12 Spring mounting plate (upper)
6 Spring assembly	13 Rubber bump stop
7 Shock absorber mounting plate	14 U-bolts

Fig. 11.14 Rear spring shackle removal (Sec 17)

1	Upper shackle pin securing nut and spring washer	2	Lower spring shackle bolt securing nut and spring washer	3	Inner shackle plate	5	Upper shackle bushes
				4	Shackle bolt	6	Upper shackle pin

18.1 Undo and remove the shock absorber lower locknut and retaining nut

18.2a Lift away the plain washer ...

18.2b ... and lower bush

18.3 Contract the shock absorber until it is clear of the mounting bracket

18.5 Undo and remove the upper mounting bolt and withdraw the shock absorber

19.1 Remove the centre motif pad

19.2 Undo and remove the retaining nut ...

19.3 ... and withdraw the steering wheel

mounting bracket (photo).

4 Note the position of the upper bush and then lift it away followed by the plain washer.

5 Undo and remove the bolt and washer securing the upper part of the shock absorber to the body bracket. Lift away the shock absorber (photo).

6 To test the shock absorber, alternatively compress and extend it throughout its full movement. If the action is jerky or weak, it is an indication that either it is worn or there is air in the hydraulic cylinder. Continue to compress and extend it; if the action does not become more positive a new shock absorber should be obtained. If the shock absorber is showing signs of leaking it should be discarded as it is not possible to overhaul it.

7 Check the bushes; if they show signs of deterioration a new set of rubbers should be obtained.

8 Refitting the shock absorber is the reverse sequence to removal. Tighten the mounting nuts and bolt to the specified torque.

19 Steering wheel – removal and refitting

1 Prise the motif pad from the centre of the steering wheel (photo).

2 Undo and remove the steering wheel retaining nut and washer (photo).

3 With the palms of the hands behind the spokes, and near to the centre hub, knock the steering wheel from the inner column splines and lift away (photo). Take care to avoid injury if the wheel is released suddenly from the column.

4 Refitting the steering wheel is the reverse sequence to removal, but the following additional points should be noted:

(a) Make sure that the arrow on the cancelling ring is facing the indicator switch when fitting the steering wheel

(b) With the roadwheels in the straight-ahead position, fit the steering wheel on the inner column so that the spokes are in a horizontal plane

(c) Tighten the steering wheel retaining nut to the specified torque

20 Steering column cowl – removal and refitting

1 Unscrew the single screw securing the right-hand cowl to the steering column and lift away the cowl.

2 Unscrew the two inner screws and single outer screw securing the left-hand cowl to the column.

3 Slide the left-hand cowl over the combination switch arm and allow it to hang from the choke cable. If it is wished to remove the left-hand cowl completely, refer to Chapter 3 and remove the choke cable.

4 Refitting is the reverse sequence to removal.

21 Steering column lock and ignition/starter switch housing – removal and refitting

1 Disconnect the battery earth terminal.

2 Remove the steering wheel as described in Section 19, and the steering column cowl as described in Section 20.

3 Release the retainers and lift out the trim panel under the facia.

4 Disconnect the ignition switch and combination switch wiring harness at the multi-plug connectors under the facia.

5 Undo and remove the four steering outer column retaining bolts and carefully slide the outer column up and off the inner column. Slide out the felt bush from the lower end of the outer column.

6 Using a drill and suitable stud extractor, remove the two shear bolts securing the clamp plate to the steering column lock. The lock assembly can now be lifted away.

7 To refit the lock assembly, place it in position on the outer column and refit the clamp plate and two new shear bolts. Tighten the shear bolts finger tight only at this stage.

8 Refit the felt bush to the base of the column ensuring that its ends are butted together.

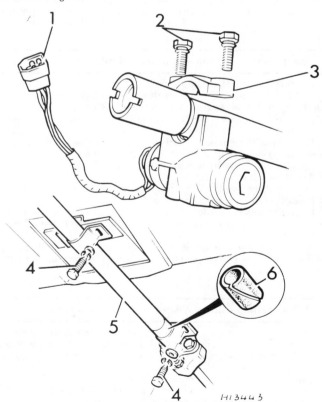

Fig. 11.15 Steering column lock and ignition/starter switch housing removal (Sec 21)

1 Multi-pin connector	4 Mounting bolts
2 Shear bolts	5 Outer column
3 Clamp plate	6 Felt bush

9   Carefully slide the outer column over the inner column taking care not to dislodge the felt bush. Refit the four outer column securing bolts and tighten them fully.
10 Check the operation of the steering column lock, and if satisfactory tighten the two shear bolts progressively until the heads shear off.
11 The remainder of the refitting is the reverse sequence to removal.

22 Steering column universal joint couplings – removal and refitting

1   Release the retainers and lift out the lower trim panel from beneath the facia.
2   Undo and remove the bolts securing the flexible rubber coupling to the upper column and lower column.
3   Undo and remove the lower column pinch bolt and then lift out the flexible rubber coupling.
4   Undo and remove the pinch bolt securing the lower flexible joint to the steering gear pinion. The lower column and lower flexible joint can now be withdrawn from the pinion.
5   If the flexible joint retaining bolts are not peened, cut the retaining wire and unscrew the bolts. Remove the conical rubbers, noting that they locate in the countersunk holes in the joint plate. Remove the plain washers.
6   Examine the couplings for wear and damage and renew the components as necessary.
7   When refitting the lower coupling, first reassemble half the joint using the two hexagon-headed bolts. After tightening them, re-assemble the remaining half using the two slotted or cross-headed bolts.
8   When all the bolts have been tightened, lock them with new retaining wire.
9   Refitting is now the reverse of the removal procedure. Ensure that the bolts securing the flexible rubber coupling to the lower column are fitted with their bolt heads facing downwards, and the bolts securing the coupling to the upper column with their bolt heads upwards. Tighten the retaining bolts and pinch bolts to the specified torque.

23 Upper steering column – removal and refitting

1   Disconnect the battery earth terminal.
2   Remove the steering wheel as described in Section 19, and the steering column cowl as described in Section 20.
3   Release the retainers and lift out the lower trim panel from under the facia.
4   Disconnect the ignition switch wiring harness and combination switch wiring harness at the multi-plug connectors.
5   Slacken the clamping screw and slide the combination switch off the top of the steering column.
6   Undo and remove the two bolts securing the steering column to the flexible rubber coupling.
7   Undo and remove the four bolts securing the upper column to the underside of the facia, and withdraw the upper column assembly from the car.
8   Refitting is the reverse of the removal procedure. Tighten the steering column and flexible rubber coupling retaining bolts to the specified torque.

24 Upper steering column bushes – removal and refitting

1   The inner steering column is supported within the outer column by a nylon bush at the top and a felt bush at the bottom. To renew these bushes it is first necessary to remove the outer column from the car as follows.
2   First disconnect the battery earth terminal.
3   Remove the steering wheel as described in Section 19, and the steering column cowl as described in Section 20.
4   Slacken the clamp screw and slide the combination switch off the top of the column.
5   Release the retainers and lift out the trim panel under the facia.
6   Disconnect the ignition switch wiring harness at the multi-plug connector under the facia.
7   Undo and remove the four steering outer column retaining bolts

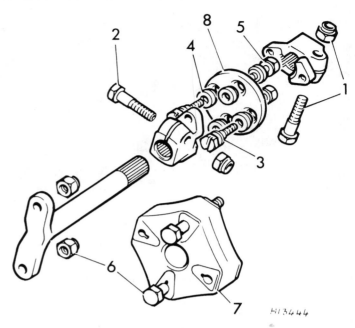

Fig. 11.16 Steering column universal joint couplings (Sec 22)

1   Flexible joint-to-steering gear pinion pinch bolt and locknut
2   Flexible joint-to-lower column pinch bolt and locknut
3   Slotted-head or cross-head bolts
4   Conical rubber washers
5   Hexagon-headed bolts
6   Flexible rubber coupling retaining nut and bolt
7   Flexible rubber coupling
8   Joint plate

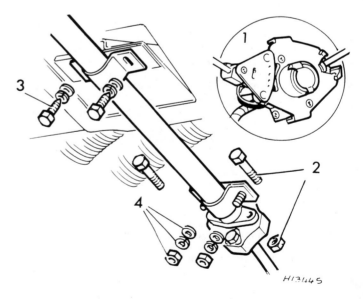

Fig. 11.17 Upper steering column removal (Sec 23)

1   Combination switch
2   Upper column-to-flexible coupling bolt and locknut
3   Column-to-upper support bracket, bolt, plain and spring washer
4   Column-to-lower support bracket securing nut spring and plain washer (bolts on later models)

and carefully slide the outer column up and off the inner column.

8 With the outer column removed from the car, withdraw the felt bush from the base of the column.

9 Using a screwdriver, ease the nylon top bush from the inside of the outer column.

10 To refit the top bush, first align the slits in the bush with the depression in the outer column and ensure that the chamfered end of the bush enters the column first. Drive the top bush fully into position using a drift of suitable diameter.

11 Position the felt bush in the base of the column, ensuring that the ends are butted together. If a new felt bush has been fitted, lubricate it thoroughly with engine oil.

12 The steering column can now be refitted using the reverse of the removal procedure. Take care not to dislodge the felt bush as the column is refitted.

25 Steering rack-and-pinion assembly – removal and refitting

1 Jack up the front of the car and support it on axle stands. Remove the front roadwheels.

2 Undo and remove the nut securing each tie-rod end ball-pin to the steering levers. Release the ball-pin tapers from the steering levers using a universal balljoint separator.

3 Release the retainers and lift out the lower trim panel from under the facia.

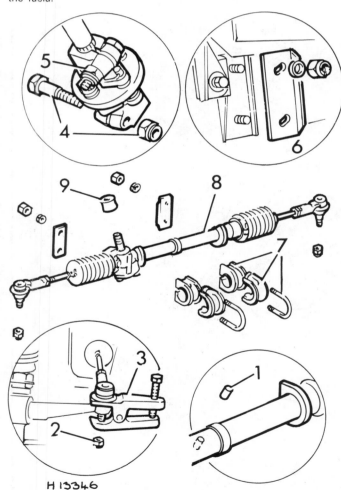

H 13346

Fig. 11.18 Steering rack-and-pinion assembly removal (Sec 25)

1 Rubber sealing plug	6 Rack clamp plate
2 Tie-rod ball-pin nut	7 Rack clamps, rubber inserts
3 Balljoint separator tool	and U-bolts
4 Lower pinch bolt and locknut	8 Rack-and-pinion assembly
5 Upper pinch bolt	9 Pinion seal

4 Undo and remove the pinch bolt that secures the lower flexible joint to the steering gear pinion. Slacken the pinch bolt that secures the lower column to the flexible joint and move the joint upwards away from the pinion.

5 Undo and remove the four rack U-bolt retaining nuts and washers, and then withdraw the U-bolts, clamp brackets, and rubbers from the bulkhead.

6 The rack assembly may now be withdrawn from the car through the wheel arch opening.

7 Lift away the pinion seal from over the end of the pinion.

8 Before refitting the rack-and-pinion assembly, inspect the condition of the pinion seal and the two clamp bracket rubber inserts for signs of deterioration. If evident renew the rubbers.

9 Refitting the rack-and-pinion assembly is the reverse of the removal sequence. Ensure that all nuts and bolts are tightened to the specified torque.

26 Steering rack-and-pinion assembly – dismantling, overhaul and reassembly

1 Wash the outside of the rack-and-pinion assembly in paraffin and wipe dry with a non-fluffy rag.

2 Slacken off the two tie-rod end locknuts and unscrew the two tie-rod ends as complete assemblies.

3 Unscrew and remove the two locknuts from the ends of the tie-rods.

4 Slacken the rack seal clips at either end of the rack assembly body. Remove the clips and two rack seals.

5 Using a small chisel, carefully ease out the locknut indent from each of the balljoint housings.

6 Using two self-gripping wrenches or one self-gripping wrench and a soft metal drift, hold the locknut and unscrew the balljoint housing from each end of the rack. Lift away the tie-rods.

7 Recover the ball cup and spring from each end of the rack.

8 Using a small chisel, carefully ease out the locknut indent from the rack. Unscrew the locknuts.

9 Undo and remove the rack bearing pan-head retaining screw located in the rack tube end as opposed to the pinion housing.

10 The bearing may now be removed from the rack housing.

11 Undo and remove the two bolts and spring washers that secure the rack yoke cover plate.

12 Lift away the cover plate, shims and joint washer.

13 Recover the rack support yoke from the pinion housing.

14 Remove the O-ring and thrust spring from the support yoke.

15 Undo and remove the two bolts and spring washers that secure the pinion end cover plate. Lift away the cover plate, shims and joint washers.

16 Carefully push out the pinion and the lower bearing. Note which way round the bearing is fitted.

17 The steering rack may now be withdrawn from the rack tube. Note which way round the rack is fitted in the rack tube.

18 Using a soft metal drift, tap out the upper pinion bearing and its washer. Note which way round the bearing is fitted.

19 Recover the pinion shaft oil seal from the pinion housing.

20 The steering rack assembly is now fully dismantled. Clean all parts in paraffin and wipe dry with a non-fluffy rag.

21 Thoroughly inspect the rack and pinion teeth for signs of wear, cracks or damage. Check the ends of the rack for wear, especially where it moves in the bushes.

22 Examine the rubber gaiters for signs of cracking, perishing or other damage which if evident, new gaiters must be obtained.

23 Inspect the ball ends and housing for wear; if evident, new parts will be necessary. Any other parts that show wear or damage must be renewed.

24 During reassembly, liberally lubricate all the parts using the measured quantity of the specified grease as shown in the Specifications.

25 To reassemble, first fit a new rack bearing into the rack housing so that the flats of the bearing are positioned offset to the bearing retaining screw hole.

26 Using a 0.119 in (3.00 mm) diameter drill located in the retaining screw hole, drill through the bearing. Clear away any swarf from the bearing and the housing.

27 Apply some non-hardening oil resistant sealing compound to the

H15447

bush retaining screw and refit the screw.

28 It is very important that the screw does not protrude into the bore of the bearing. Should this condition exist, the end of the screw must be filed flat.

29 Fit the pinion washer to the pinion followed by the upper bearing. The thrust face must face towards the pinion washer.

30 Carefully fit the rack into the rack housing the correct way round as noted during dismantling.

31 Insert the pinion into the housing and then centralise the rack relative to the rack housing. Fit a peg into the centre locating hole.

32 Position the pinion, making sure the groove in the pinion serrations is facing and also parallel with the rack teeth. Remove the centralising peg.

33 Refit the lower bearing with the thrust face facing towards the pinion.

34 Refit the bearing shims and make sure that the bearing shim pack stands proud of the pinion housing. If necessary, add new shims to achieve this condition.

35 Refit the pinion housing end cover but without the paper gasket. Secure in position with the two bolts and spring washers. The two bolts should only be tightened sufficiently to nip the end cover.

36 Using feeler gauges, measure the gap between the pinion housing and the end cover. Make a note of the measurement.

37 Undo and remove the two pinion housing end cover securing bolts and spring washers. Lift away the end cover.

38 Adjust the number of shims in the end pack so as to obtain a 0.011 to 0.013 in (0.279 to 0.330 mm) gap. A range of shims is available for this adjustment.

39 It is important that the 0.060 in (1.524 mm) shim is positioned next to the joint washer. Refit the shim pack, joint washer and end cover.

40 Apply a little non-hardening oil resistant sealing compound to the end cover securing bolts. Fit the two bolts and spring washers and tighten to the specified torque.

41 Carefully fit a new pinion oil seal.

Fig. 11.19 Exploded view of the steering mechanism (Sec 26)

1 Steering wheel	15 Rack gaiter	29 Bolt	43 Shim – 0.060 in (1.524 mm)	57 Joint gasket
2 Motif	16 Clip	30 Pinion oil seal	44 Shim gasket – 0.010 in (0.254 mm)	58 End cover
3 Nut	17 Locknut	31 Sealing washer	45 End cover	59 Bolt and spring washer
4 Shakeproof washer	18 Ball housing	32 Nut and washer	46 Bolt and spring washer	60 Pinch bolt
5 Bush	19 Tie-rod	33 Locating plate	47 Pinch bolt	61 Flexible joint (half)
6 Shear bolt	20 Ball seat	34 Rack bearing	48 Flexible joint (half)	62 Nut
7 Clamp plate	21 Locknut (tie-rod end)	35 Rack bearing screw	49 Nut	63 Rack mounting rubbers
8 Steering lock	22 Thrust spring	36 Sealing rubber	50 Shouldered bolt	64 Rack clamps
9 Column outer	23 Rack	37 Pinion housing	51 Rubber bush	65 Rack U-bolts
10 Column inner	24 Bolt	38 Pinion bearing	52 Joint plate	
11 Screw	25 Lower bush	39 Washer	53 Support yoke	
12 Tie-rod end balljoint	26 Nut	40 Pinion	54 O-ring	
13 Locknut	27 Flexible coupling	41 Pinion bearing	55 Shims	
14 Clip	28 Column (lower)	42 Shims	56 Thrust spring	

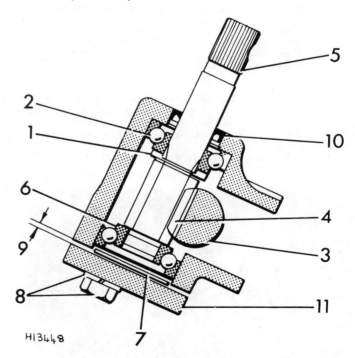

H13448

Fig. 11.20 Sectional view of the pinion end housing (Sec 26)

1 Pinion washer	7 Shims
2 Upper bearing	8 Bolt and spring washer
3 Rack	9 Gap measurement
4 Pinion teeth	10 Pinion shaft oil seal
5 Pinion	11 End cover
6 Lower bearing	

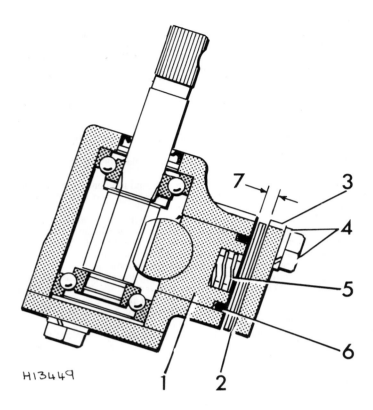

H13449

Fig. 11.21 Damper cover shim thickness (Sec 26)

1	Damper yoke	5	Damper spring
2	Shims and gasket	6	O-ring seal
3	Cover plate	7	Gap measurement
4	Bolt and spring washer		

42 Refit the damper yoke, cover plate gasket and cover plate.
43 Refit the cover bolts and spring washers and gradually tighten these in a progressive manner whilst turning the pinion to and fro through 180° until it is just possible to rotate the pinion between the finger and thumb.
44 Using feeler gauges, measure the gap between the cover and the housing.

45 Remove the cover and reassemble, this time including the damper spring, a new O-ring oil seal and shims to the previous determined measurement plus 0.002 to 0.005 in (0.05 to 0.13 mm).
46 Tighten the bolts that secure the yoke cover to the specified torque.
47 Screw a new ball housing locknut onto each end of the rack to the limits of the thread.
48 Insert the two thrust springs into the ends of the rack.
49 Fit each tie-rod into its ball housing and locate the ball cup against the thrust spring.
50 Slowly tighten the two ball housings until the tie-rod is just nipped.
51 Using a self-gripping wrench and a soft metal drift, carefully tighten the locknut onto the ball housing. Again check that the tie-rod is still pinched.
52 Next slacken the ball housing back by $\frac{1}{8}$ turn to allow full articulation of the tie-rods.
53 Fully tighten the locking ring to the housing. Whilst this is being done, make sure the housing does not turn.
54 Using a centre punch or blunt chisel, drive the ball housing edge of the locking ring into the locking slots of the ball housing and the opposite edge into the locking slot of the rack.
55 Refit the two rack rubber seals and secure with the large clips to the housing and small clips to the tie-rods.
56 Refit the tie-rod locknuts and then screw on each tie-rod end by an equal amount until the dimension between the two ball-pin centres is 43.7 in (1109 mm). Tighten the locknuts sufficiently to prevent this initial setting being lost during refitting.
57 The rack-and-pinion assembly can now be refitted to the car as described in Section 25. After refitting it will be necessary to adjust the front wheel alignment as described in Section 28.

27 Steering tie-rod end balljoint – removal and refitting

1   Jack up the front of the car and support it on axle stands. Remove the wheel trim and the front roadwheel.
2   Inspect the condition of the balljoint dust excluding rubber boots. If they are damaged or split the complete balljoint will have to be renewed; the boots are not supplied separately.
3   If any free movement can be felt or seen when the tie-rod is gripped and moved up and down, or from side to side, then the balljoint is worn and must be renewed.
4   To remove the tie-rod end balljoint, first slacken the nut that locks the balljoint to the tie-rod by half a turn (photo).
5   Undo and remove the locknut securing the balljoint ball-pin to the steering lever. Using a universal balljoint separator, release the ball-pin from the steering lever (photo).
6   Finally unscrew the balljoint from the tie-rod.
7   Refitting is the reverse sequence to removal. Tighten the ball-pin

27.4 Slacken the balljoint-to-tie-rod locknut (A) half a turn

27.5 With the ball-pin-to-steering lever retaining nut removed, release the ball-pin with a balljoint separator

retaining locknut to the specified torque and adjust the front wheel alignment as described in Section 28 after the balljoint has been refitted.

28 Front wheel alignment – checking and adjustment

1   The front wheels are correctly aligned when they are turning in at the front $\frac{1}{8}$ in (3.175 mm). It is important that this measurement is taken on a centre line drawn horizontally and parallel to the ground through the centre line of the hub. The exact point should be in the centre of the sidewall of the tyre, and not on the wheel rim which could be distorted and therefore give inaccurate readings.
2   The adjustment is effected by loosening the locknut on each tie-rod balljoint and also slackening the rubber gaiter clip holding it to the tie-rod; both tie-rods then being turned equally until the adjustment is correct.
3   This is a job best left to a BL garage as accurate alignment requires the use of special equipment. If the wheels are not in alignment, tyre wear will be heavy and uneven and the steering stiff and unresponsive.

29 Wheels and tyres

1   Check the tyre pressures weekly (when they are cold).
2   Frequently inspect the tyre walls and treads for damage and pick out any large stones which have become trapped in the tread pattern.
3   If the wheels and tyres have been balanced on the car, then they should not be moved to a different axle position. If they have been balanced off the car then, in the interests of extending tread life, they can be moved between front and rear on the same side of the car and the spare incorporated in the rotational pattern.
4   Never mix tyres of different construction or very dissimilar tread patterns.
5   Always keep the roadwheels tightened to the specified torque, and if the bolt holes become elongated or flattened, renew the wheel.
6   Occasionally clean the inner faces of the roadwheels, and if there is any sign of rust or corrosion, paint them with metal preservative paint.
7   Before removing a roadwheel which has been balanced on the car, always mark one wheel and hub bolt hole so that the roadwheel may be refitted in the same relative position to maintain the balance.

30 Fault diagnosis – suspension and steering

Symptom	Reason(s)
Excessive free play felt at steering wheel	Excessive wear in steering and suspension linkages or balljoints Steering upper column universal couplings worn Incorrect adjustment of steering rack-and-pinion assembly
Vehicle difficult to steer in a consistent straight line – wandering	As above Wheel alignment incorrect Front hub bearings worn or incorrectly adjusted
Steering stiff and heavy	Wheel alignment incorrect Insufficient lubricant in rack-and-pinion assembly Bent or distorted upper steering column Partial seizure of one or more steering or suspension joints Incorrect tyre pressures
Wheel wobble and vibration	Roadwheels out of balance Roadwheels buckled or distorted Faulty or defective tyre *See also 'Fault diagnosis – propeller shaft' (Chapter 7), and 'Fault diagnosis – rear axle' (Chapter 8)*
Excessive pitching and rolling on corners and during braking	Weak or ineffective shock absorbers Broken or worn anti-roll bar mountings Broken rear spring leaf
Excessive tyre wear	Incorrect tyre pressures Incorrect front wheel alignment Wear in suspension or steering linkages Incorrect vehicle trim height Bent or damaged steering or suspension component

Chapter 12 Bodywork and fittings

Contents

1 General description

The vehicle body structure is a welded fabrication of many individual shaped panels which form a 'monocoque' bodyshell. Certain areas are strengthened locally to provide for suspension system, steering system, engine support anchorages and transmission. The resultant structure is very strong and rigid.

It is as well to remember that monocoque structures have no discreet load paths and all metal is stressed to an extent. It is essential therefore to maintain the whole bodyshell both top and underside., inside and outside, clean and corrosion free. Every effort should be made to keep the underside of the car as clear of mud and dirt accumulations as possible. If you were fortunate enough to acquire a new car then it is advisable to have it rustproofed and undersealed at one of the specialist workshops who guarantee their work.

2 Maintenance – bodywork and underframe

1   The general condition of a car's bodywork is the thing that significantly affects its value. Maintenance is easy but needs to be regular. Neglect, particularly after minor damage, can lead quickly to further deterioration and costly repair bills. It is important also to keep watch on those parts of the car not immediately visible, for instance the underside, inside all the wheel arches and the lower part of the engine compartment.
2   The basic maintenance routine for the bodywork is washing – preferably with a lot of water, from a hose. This will remove all the loose solids which may have stuck to the car. It is important to flush these off in such a way as to prevent grit from scratching the finish. The wheel arches and underframe need washing in the same way to remove any accumulated mud which will retain moisture and tend to encourage rust. Paradoxically enough, the best time to clean the underframe and wheel arches is in wet weather when the mud is thoroughly wet and soft. In very wet weather the underframe is usually cleaned of large accumulations automatically and this is a good time for inspection.

3   Periodically, it is a good idea to have the whole of the underframe of the car steam cleaned, engine compartment included, so that a thorough inspection can be carried out to see what minor repairs and renovations are necessary. Steam cleaning is available at many garages and is necessary for removal of the accumulation of oily grime which sometimes is allowed to become thick in certain areas. If steam cleaning facilities are not available, there are one or two excellent grease solvents available which can be brush applied. The dirt can then be simply hosed off.
4   After washing paintwork, wipe off with a chamois leather to give an unspotted clear finish. A coat of clear protective wax polish will give added protection against chemical pollutants in the air. If the paintwork sheen has dulled or oxidised, use a cleaner/polisher combination to restore the brilliance of the shine. This requires a little effort, but such dulling is usually caused because regular washing has been neglected. Always check that the door and ventilator opening drain holes and pipes are completely clear so that water can be drained out. Bright work should be treated in the same way as paintwork. Windscreens and windows can be kept clear of the smeary film which often appears, by adding a little ammonia to the water. If they are scratched, a good rub with a proprietary metal polish will often clear them. Never use any form of wax or other body or chromium polish on glass.

3 Maintenance – upholstery and carpets

1   Mats and carpets should be brushed or vacuum cleaned regularly to keep them free of grit. If they are badly stained remove them from the car for scrubbing or sponging and make quite sure they are dry before refitting. Seats and interior trim panels can be kept clean by a wipe over with a damp cloth. If they do become stained (which can be more apparent on light coloured upholstery) use a little liquid detergent and a soft nail brush to scour the grime out of the grain of the material. Do not forget to keep the head lining clean in the same way as the upholstery. When using liquid cleaners inside the car do not over-wet the surfaces being cleaned. Excessive damp could get into the seams and padded interior causing stains, offensive odours or even

rot. If the inside of the car gets wet accidentally it is worthwhile taking some trouble to dry it out properly, particularly where carpets are involved. *Do not leave oil or electric heaters inside the car for this purpose.*

---

4 Minor body damage – repair

The photographic sequences on pages 182 and 183 illustrate the operations detailed in the following sub-sections.

Repair of minor scratches in the car's bodywork

If the scratch is very superficial, and does not penetrate to the metal of the bodywork, repair is very simple. Lightly rub the area of the scratch with a paintwork renovator, or a very fine cutting paste, to remove loose paint from the scratch and to clear the surrounding bodywork of wax polish. Rinse the area with clean water.

Apply touch-up paint to the scratch using a thin paint brush; continue to apply thin layers of paint until the surface of the paint in the scratch is level with the surrounding paintwork. Allow the new paint at least two weeks to harden: then blend it into the surrounding paintwork by rubbing the paintwork, in the scratch area, with a paintwork renovator or a very fine cutting paste. Finally, apply wax polish.

Where the scratch has penetrated right through to the metal of the bodywork, causing the metal to rust, a different repair technique is required. Remove any loose rust from the bottom of the scratch with a penknife, then apply rust inhibiting paint to prevent the formation of rust in the future. Using a rubber or nylon applicator fill the scratch with bodystopper paste. If required, this paste can be mixed with cellulose thinners to provide a very thin paste which is ideal for filling narrow scratches. Before the stopper-paste in the scratch hardens, wrap a piece of smooth cotton rag around the top of a finger. Dip the finger in cellulose thinners and then quickly sweep it across the surface of the stopper-paste in the scratch; this will ensure that the surface of the stopper-paste is slightly hollowed. The scratch can now be painted over as described earlier in this Section.

Bodywork repairs – filling and re-spraying

Before using this Section, see the Sections on dent, deep scratch, rust holes and gash repairs.

Many types of bodyfiller are available, but generally speaking those proprietary kits which contain a tin of filler paste and a tube of resin hardener are best for this type of repair. A wide, flexible plastic or nylon applicator will be found invaluable for imparting a smooth and well contoured finish to the surface of the filler.

Mix up a little filler on a clean piece of card or board – measure the hardener carefully (follow the maker's instructions on the pack) otherwise the filler will set too rapidly or too slowly.

Using the applicator apply the filler paste to the prepared area; draw the applicator across the surface of the filler to achieve the correct contour and to level the filler surface. As soon as a contour that approximates the correct one is achieved, stop working the paste – if you carry on too long the paste will become sticky and begin to 'pick up' on the applicator. Continue to add thin layers of filler paste at twenty-minute intervals until the level of the filler is just proud of the surrounding bodywork.

Once the filler has hardened, excess can be removed using a metal plane or file. From then on, progressively finer grades of sandpaper should be used, starting with a 40 grade production paper and finishing with 400 grade wet-and-dry paper. Always wrap the abrasive paper around a flat rubber, cork, or wooden block – otherwise the surface of the filler will not be completely flat. During the smoothing of the filler surface the wet-and-dry paper should be periodically rinsed in water. This will ensure that a very smooth finish is imparted to the filler at the final stage.

At this stage the dent should be surrounded by a ring of bare metal, which in turn should be encircled by the finely 'feathered' edge of the good paintwork. Rinse the repair area with clean water, until all of the dust produced by the rubbing-down operation has gone.

Spray the whole repair area with a light coat of primer – this will show up any imperfections in the surface of the filler. Repair these imperfections with fresh filler paste or bodystopper, and once more smooth the surface with abrasive paper. If bodystopper is used, it can be mixed with cellulose thinners to form a really thin paste which is ideal for filling small holes. Repeat this spray and repair procedure until you are satisfied that the surface of the filler, and the feathered edge of the paintwork are perfect. Clean the repair area with clean water and allow to dry fully.

The repair area is now ready for final spraying. Paint spraying must be carried out in a warm, dry, windless and dust free atmosphere. This condition can be created artificially if you have access to a large indoor working area, but if you are forced to work in the open, you will have to pick your day very carefully. If you are working indoors, dousing the floor in the work area with water will help to settle the dust which would otherwise be in the atmosphere. If the repair area is confined to one body panel, mask off the surrounding panels; this will help to minimise the effects of a slight mis-match in paint colours. Bodywork fittings (eg chrome strips, door handles etc) will also need to be masked off. Use genuine masking tape and several thicknesses of newspaper for the masking operations.

Before commencing to spray, agitate the aerosol can thoroughly, then spray a test area (an old tin, or similar) until the technique is mastered. Cover the repair area with a thick coat of primer; the thickness should be built up using several thin layers of paint rather than one thick one. Using 400 grade wet-and-dry paper, rub down the surface of the primer until it is really smooth. While doing this, the work area should be thoroughly doused with water, and the wet-and-dry paper periodically rinsed in water. Allow to dry before spraying on more paint.

Spray on the top coat, again building up the thickness by using several thin layers of paint. Start spraying in the centre of the repair area and then, using a circular motion, work outwards until the whole repair area and about 2 inches of the surrounding original paintwork is covered. Remove all masking material 10 to 15 minutes after spraying on the final coat of paint.

Allow the new paint at least two weeks to harden, then, using a paintwork renovator or a very fine cutting paste, blend the edges of the paint into the existing paintwork. Finally, apply wax polish.

Repair of dents in the car's bodywork

When deep denting of the car's bodywork has taken place, the first task is to pull the dent out, until the affected bodywork almost attains its original shape. There is little point in trying to restore the original shape completely, as the metal in the damaged area will have stretched on impact and cannot be reshaped fully to its original contour. It is better to bring the level of the dent up to a point which is about $\frac{1}{8}$ in (3 mm) below the level of the surrounding bodywork. In cases where the dent is very shallow anyway, it is not worth trying to pull it out at all. If the underside of the dent is accessible, it can be hammered out gently from behind, using a mallet with a wooden or plastic head. Whilst doing this, hold a suitable block of wood firmly against the outside of the panel to absorb the impact from the hammer blows and thus prevent a large area of the bodywork from being 'belled-out'.

Should the dent be in a section of the bodywork which has double skin or some other factor making it inaccessible from behind, a different technique is called for. Drill several small holes through the metal inside the area – particularly in the deeper section. Then screw long self-tapping screws into the holes just sufficiently for them to gain a good purchase in the metal. Now the dent can be pulled out by pulling on the protruding heads of the screws with a pair of pliers.

The next stage of the repair is the removal of the paint from the damaged area, and from an inch or so of the surrounding 'sound' bodywork. This is accomplished most easily by using a wire brush or abrasive pad on a power drill, although it can be done just as effectively by hand using sheets of abrasive paper. To complete the preparation for filling, score the surface of the bare metal with a screwdriver or the tang of a file, or alternatively, drill small holes in the affected area. This will provide a really good 'key' for the filler paste.

To complete the repair see the Section on filling and re-spraying.

Repair of rust holes or gashes in the car's bodywork

Remove all paint from the affected area and from an inch or so of the surrounding 'sound' bodywork, using an abrasive pad or a wire brush on a power drill. If these are not available a few sheets of abrasive paper will do the job just as effectively. With the paint removed you will be able to gauge the severity of the corrosion and therefore decide whether to renew the whole panel (if this is possible) or to repair the affected area. New body panels are not as expensive as most people think and it is often quicker and more satisfactory to fit a new panel than to attempt to repair large areas of corrosion.

Remove all fittings from the affected area except those which will act as a guide to the original shape of the damaged bodywork (eg headlamp shells etc). Then, using tin snips or a hacksaw blade, remove all loose metal and any other metal badly affected by corrosion. Hammer the edges of the hole inwards in order to create a slight depression for the filler paste.

Wire brush the affected area to remove the powdery rust from the surface of the remaining metal. Paint the affected area with rust inhibiting paint; if the back of the rusted area is accessible treat this also.

Before filling can take place it will be necessary to block the hole in some way. This can be achieved by the use of zinc gauze or aluminium tape.

Zinc gauze is probably the best material to use for a large hole. Cut a piece to the approximate size and shape of the hole to be filled, then position it in the hole so that its edges are below the level of the surrounding bodywork. It can be retained in position by several blobs of filler paste around its periphery.

Aluminium tape should be used for small or very narrow holes. Pull a piece off the roll and trim it to the approximate size and shape required, then pull off the backing paper (if used) and stick the tape over the hole; it can be overlapped if the thickness of one piece is insufficient. Burnish down the edges of the tape with the handle of a screwdriver or similar, to ensure that the tape is securely attached to the metal underneath.

5 Major body damage – repair

Because the body is built on the monocoque principle and is integral with the underframe, major damage must be repaired by specialists with the necessary welding and hydraulic straightening equipment.

If the damage is serious, it is vital that on completion of the repair the chassis is in correct alignment. Less severe damage may also have twisted or distorted the chassis, although this may not be visible immediately. It is therefore always best on completion of repair to check for twist and squareness to make sure all is well.

To check for twist, position the car on a clean level floor, place a jack under each jacking point, raise the car and take off the wheels. Raise or lower the jack until the sills are parallel with the ground. Depending where the damage occurred, using an accurate scale, take measurements at the suspension mounting points; if comparable readings are not obtained, it is an indication that the body is twisted.

After checking for twist, check for squareness by taking a series of measurements on the floor. Drop a plumb line and bob weight from various mounting points on the underside of the body and mark these points on the floor with chalk. Draw a straight line between each point and measure and mark the middle of each line. A line drawn on the floor starting at the front and finishing at the rear should be quite straight and pass through the centres of the other lines. Diagonal measurement can also be made as a check for squareness.

6 Maintenance – locks and hinges

Once every 6000 miles (10 000 km) or 6 months, the door, bonnet, and boot or tailgate hinges should be oiled with a few drops of engine oil from an oil can. The door striker plate can be given a thin smear of grease to reduce wear and ensure free movement.

7 Door rattles – tracing and rectification

1   The most common cause of door rattles is a misaligned, loose or worn striker plate, but other causes may be:

   (a) *Loose door handles, window winder handles or door hinges*
   (b) *Loose, worn or misaligned door lock components*
   (c) *Loose or worn remote control mechanism*

2   If the striker catch is worn as a result of door rattles, renew it and adjust as described later in this Chapter.
3   Should the hinges be badly worn then they must be renewed.

8.3 The door hinge retaining locknuts are accessible through the door panel aperture

8 Doors – removal and refitting

1   Refer to Section 10 and remove the door trim panel.
2   Working inside the door, mark the outline of the stiffener plate at each hinge position. An assistant should now take the weight of the door.
3   Undo and remove the locknuts and plain washers that secure the door to the hinge (photo).
4   Lift away the stiffener plates and finally the door.
5   Refitting the door is the reverse sequence to removal. Should it be necessary to adjust the position of the door in the aperture, leave the locknuts slightly loose and reposition the door by trial and error. Fully tighten the locknuts.

9 Door hinges – removal and refitting

1   Remove the door as described in Section 8.
2   Using a wide-bladed screwdriver or similar tool, carefully ease back the side trim panel door seal and then the trim panel.
3   If the rear door hinges are to be removed, use a wide-bladed screwdriver to ease back the B-post door seals. Undo and remove the carpet finisher retaining screw, slide the front seal forward and ease the trim panel retaining clips from the B-post. Hinge the trim panel up at the PVC lining crease. This will provide access to the door hinge securing nuts.
4   Undo and remove the locknuts and plain washers that secure each hinge. Lift away the stiffener plates and finally the door hinges.
5   Refitting the door hinges is the reverse of the removal procedure.

10 Door inner trim panel – removal and refitting

1   Wind the window up fully and note the position of the handle.
2   Undo and remove the screw that secures the handle to the window regulator, and then lift off the handle and washer (photos).
3   Undo and remove the two retaining screws and lift away the arm rest (photo).
4   Unscrew the remote control handle bezel retaining screw and lift off the bezel (photos).
5   Unscrew the locking button (photo).
6   If a storage bin is fitted, undo and remove the retaining screws and withdraw the bin.
7   Using a wide-bladed screwdriver inserted between the trim panel and the door, carefully ease the trim panel clips from the door. When all the clips are released, lift away the panel (photos).
8   Refitting the trim panel is the reverse sequence to removal.

10.2a Undo and remove the window regulator handle retaining screw ...

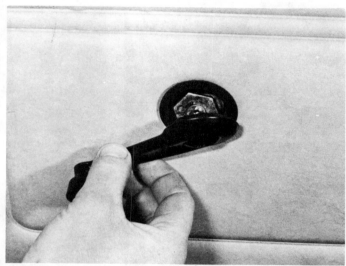

10.2b ... and lift off the handle and washer

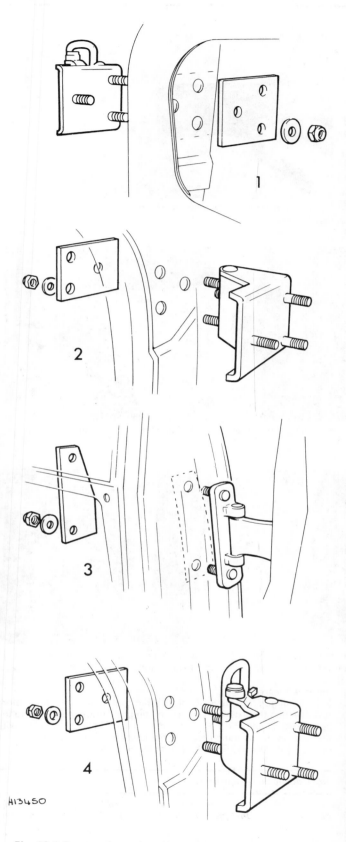

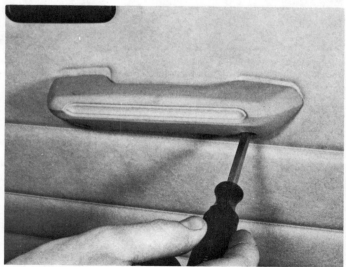

10.3 Undo and remove the armrest retaining screws and lift off the armrest

H13450

Fig. 12.1 Front and rear door hinge assemblies (Secs 8 and 9)

1	Top, front door	3	Top, rear door
2	Bottom, front door	4	Bottom, rear door

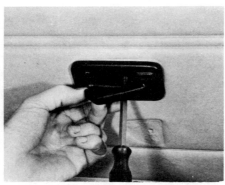

10.4a Undo and remove the retaining screw ...

10.4b ... and withdraw the remote control handle bezel

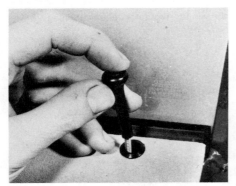

10.5 Unscrew the locking button

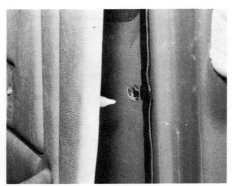

10.7a Prise the trim panel retaining clips out of the door ...

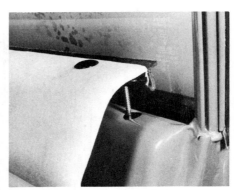

10.7b ... and lift away the panel

11.2 Peel back the polythene covering to gain access to the door internal components

11.3 The door lock remote control operating link and retaining clip (arrowed)

11.6 The external part of the door lock mechanism and retaining screws

11 Door lock – removal and refitting

1   Remove the door trim panel as described in Section 10.
2   Peel back the polythene covering from the inside door panel (photo). With the door glass in the fully raised position, remove the screw that secures the door glass rear channel to the door panel (front doors).
3   Prise off the retaining clip and detach the remote control operating link from the lock mechanism (photo).
4   Remove the retainer and detach the exterior handle link from the lock mechanism (front door). On rear doors, screw the knob from the end of the child safety operating link.
5   Using a pencil, mark the position of the lock on the door.
6   Undo the four screws that secure the lock and lock mechanism to the door, and then remove the locking mechanism and locking link through the opening in the door panel (photo). On rear doors, release the retaining clip and disconnect the child safety operating link from

the lock mechanism.
7   Refitting is the reverse of the removal procedure, but before reconnecting the exterior handle operating link, move the handle to the open position and check that the cranked end of the link is in line with the bush in the operating lever of the lock mechanism; screw it up or down, as necessary, until the alignment is correct.

12 Door lock – adjustment

Four adjustments may be made to the door locks and it will usually be found that any malfunction of a lock is caused by incorrect adjustment.

Exterior handle

1   Refer to Section 10 and remove the trim panel.
2   Close the door and partially operate the exterior release lever. Check that there is free movement of the lever before the point is

reached where the transfer lever and its screwed rod move.
3 Operate the exterior release lever fully and check that the latch disc is released from the door striker before the lever is fully open.
4 To adjust, disconnect the screwed rod and screw in or out to achieve the correct setting.

Remote control
5 Refer to Section 10 and remove the trim panel.
6 Undo and remove the screw and slacken the control retaining screws.
7 Move the remote control assembly towards the latch unit. Retighten the retaining screws and make sure that the operating lever is against its stop A (Fig. 12.2 or 12.3).

Safety locking lever (front)
8 Refer to Section 10 and remove the trim panel.
9 Disconnect the long lockrod from the safety locking lever and then the short rod from the locking bar. Push the locking bar against its stop B (Fig. 12.2) and move the safety locking lever to the locked position.
10 Refit the long rod in the safety locking lever and then press in the legs of the clip. Adjust the short rod so as to fit into the rod bush in the locking bar.
11 Release the safety locking lever and make sure that the operating lever is quite free to operate.

Safety locking lever (rear)
12 Refer to Section 10 and remove the trim panel.
13 Disconnect the long lockrod from the safety locking lever and then the short lockrod from the locking lever.
14 Press the free wheeling operating lever against the stop D (Fig. 12.3) and position the safety locking lever in the locked position.

15 Reconnect the long lockrod to the safety locking lever. Push in the legs of the clip and adjust the short rod to fit into the rod bush in the locking lever.
16 Release the safety locking lever and ensure that the operating tab aligns with the striker pin of the latch disc release lever.

Door striker
17 It is very important that the latch disc is in the open position.
Note: *Do not slam the door whilst any adjustment is being made, otherwise damage may result.*
18 Slacken the striker plate retaining screws until it is just sufficient to allow the door to close and latch.
19 Push the door inwards or pull it outwards without operating the release lever until the door is level with the body and aperture.
20 Open the door carefully and mark with a pencil round the striker plate to act as a datum.
21 Place the striker accurately by trial and error until the door can be closed easily without signs of lifting, dropping or rattling.
22 Close the door and make sure that the striker is not positioned too far in by pressing on the door. It should be possible to press the door in slightly as the seals are compressed.
23 Finally tighten the striker plate retaining screws.

---

13 Door lock remote control – removal and refitting

1 Remove the door trim panel as described in Section 10.
2 Undo the screw that secures the remote control handle to the door inner panel.
3 Release the remote control by sliding it rearwards against the spring pressure to release it from the door inner panel.
4 Disconnect the operating link from the remote control handle by compressing the retaining spring and detaching the link bush from the remote control handle.
5 Refitting is the reverse of the removal procedure.

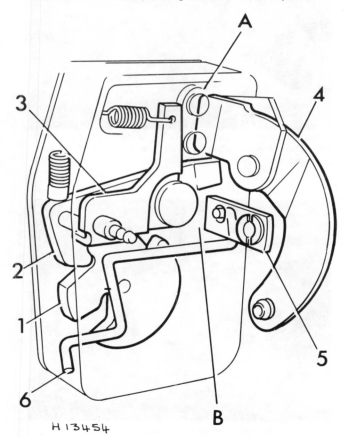

H13454

Fig. 12.2 Front door lock adjustment (Sec 12)

1 Latch disc	5 Locking bar
2 Latch disc release lever	6 Locking bar cross-shaft
3 Cross control lever	Positive stop A
4 Operating lever	Positive stop B

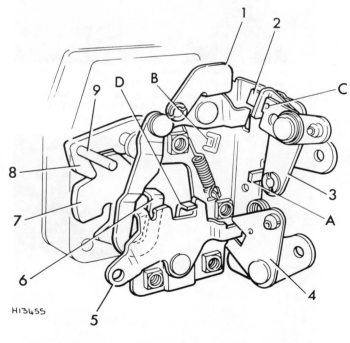

H13455

Fig. 12.3 Rear door lock adjustment (Sec 12)

1 Cross lever	7 Latch disc
2 Child safety intermediate lever	8 Latch disc release lever
3 Operating lever	9 Striker pin
4 Locking lever	Positive stop A
5 Freewheel actuating lever	Positive stop B
6 Operating tab	Positive stop C
	Positive stop D

This sequence of photographs deals with the repair of the dent and paintwork damage shown in this photo. The procedure will be similar for the repair of a hole. It should be noted that the procedures given here are simplified – more explicit instructions will be found in the text

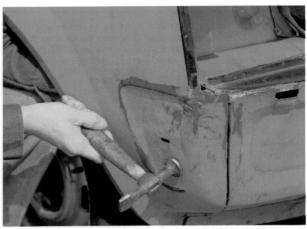

In the case of a dent the first job – after removing surrounding trim – is to hammer out the dent where access is possible. This will minimise filling. Here, the large dent having been hammered out, the damaged area is being made slightly concave

Now all paint must be removed from the damaged area, by rubbing with coarse abrasive paper. Alternatively, a wire brush or abrasive pad can be used in a power drill. Where the repair area meets good paintwork, the edge of the paintwork should be 'feathered', using a finer grade of abrasive paper

In the case of a hole caused by rusting, all damaged sheet-metal should be cut away before proceeding to this stage. Here, the damaged area is being treated with rust remover and inhibitor before being filled

Mix the body filler according to its manufacturer's instructions. In the case of corrosion damage, it will be necessary to block off any large holes before filling – this can be done with aluminium or plastic mesh, or aluminium tape. Make sure the area is absolutely clean before ...

... applying the filler. Filler should be applied with a flexible applicator, as shown, for best results; the wooden spatula being used for confined areas. Apply thin layers of filler at 20-minute intervals, until the surface of the filler is slightly proud of the surrounding bodywork

Initial shaping can be done with a Surform plane or Dreadnought file. Then, using progressively finer grades of wet-and-dry paper, wrapped around a sanding block, and copious amounts of clean water, rub down the filler until really smooth and flat. Again, feather the edges of adjoining paintwork

The whole repair area can now be sprayed or brush-painted with primer. If spraying, ensure adjoining areas are protected from over-spray. Note that at least one inch of the surrounding sound paintwork should be coated with primer. Primer has a 'thick' consistency, so will find small imperfections

Again, using plenty of water, rub down the primer with a fine grade wet-and-dry paper (400 grade is probably best) until it is really smooth and well blended into the surrounding paintwork. Any remaining imperfections can now be filled by carefully applied knifing stopper paste

When the stopper has hardened, rub down the repair area again before applying the final coat of primer. Before rubbing down this last coat of primer, ensure the repair area is blemish-free – use more stopper if necessary. To ensure that the surface of the primer is really smooth use some finishing compound

The top coat can now be applied. When working out of doors, pick a dry, warm and wind-free day. Ensure surrounding areas are protected from over-spray. Agitate the aerosol thoroughly, then spray the centre of the repair area, working outwards with a circular motion. Apply the paint as several thin coats

After a period of about two weeks, which the paint needs to harden fully, the surface of the repaired area can be 'cut' with a mild cutting compound prior to wax polishing. When carrying out bodywork repairs, remember that the quality of the finished job is proportional to the time and effort expended

14 Door private lock – removal and refitting

1   Wind up the window to the fully raised position.
2   Remove the door trim panel as described in Section 10.
3   Peel back the polythene sheeting as necessary to provide access to the private lock.
4   Prise the retaining clip from the body of the lock and withdraw the lock from the outside of the door (photo).
5   Using a screwdriver, carefully remove the circlip and lift away the spring and special washers.
6   The lock barrel may now be removed.
7   Refitting is the reverse sequence to removal.

15 Door exterior handle – removal and refitting

Front door

1   Remove the door trim panel as described in Section 10.
2   Peel back the polythene sheeting from the area around the lock and handle assemblies.
3   Release the retainer and detach the handle control rod from the lock assembly.
4   Undo and remove the two nuts and washers securing the handle to the door (photo).

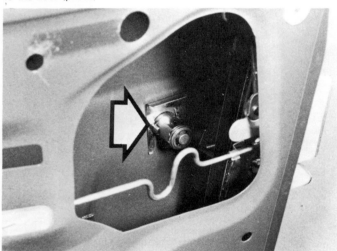

14.4 The door private lock retaining clip (arrowed)

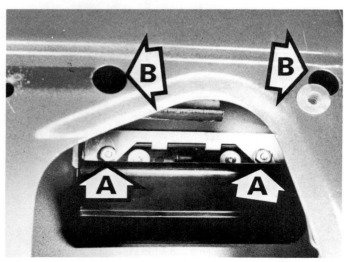

15.4 The door exterior handle retaining nuts (A) are accessible through the holes in the door (B) using a socket and extension

5   Lift off the retaining bracket and then withdraw the handle and sealing washer. Detach the operating link from the handle.
6   Refitting is the reverse sequence to removal. Adjust the handle if necessary as described in Section 12.

Rear door

7   Remove the door trim panel as described in Section 10.
8   Peel back the polythene sheeting from the area around the lock and handle assemblies.
9   Undo and remove the two nuts and washers securing the handle to the door.
10 Lift off the retaining bracket and then withdraw the handle and sealing washer.
11 Detach the control rod from the lock, and then unscrew the control rod and trunnion from the handle.
12 Refitting is the reverse sequence to removal. Adjust the handle if necessary as described in Section 12.

16 Door glass – removal and refitting

1   Remove the door trim as described in Section 10 and the glass regulator as described in Section 17.
2   Release the outer weatherstrip by undoing the five retaining clips and then remove the weatherstrip.
3   The window glass may now be lifted out of the door.
4   After noting the position of the glass channel, remove the channel and channel rubber.
5   Refitting is the reverse of the removal procedure. When positioning the glass, make sure that dimension X in Fig. 12.4 is 6 in (152 mm).

17 Door glass regulator – removal and refitting

1   Remove the door trim panel as described in Section 10.
2   Peel back the polythene sheet from the door inner panel.
3   Raise the door glass and wedge it in the closed position.
4   Undo and remove the three screws, spring washers and flat

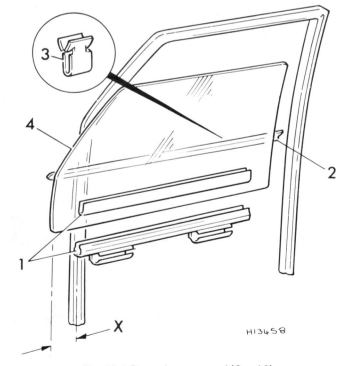

Fig. 12.4 Door glass removal (Sec 16)

1   *Channel and rubber*   4   *Door glass*
2   *Weatherstrip*   *Dimension X = 6 in (152 mm)*
3   *Clip*

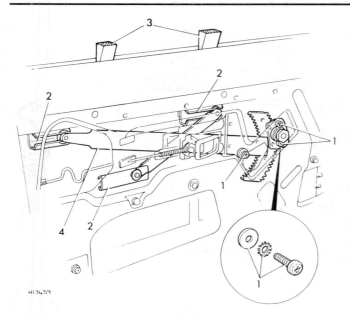

17.4 The door glass regulator retaining screws (arrowed)

Fig. 12.5 Door glass regulator removal (Sec 17)

1 Securing screws
2 Door glass channel and
   door channel
3 Wedges
4 Regulator assembly

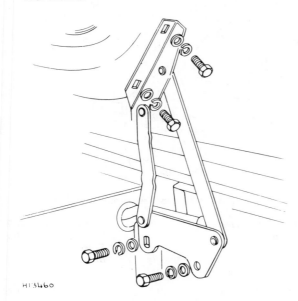

Fig. 12.6 Bonnet hinge assembly (Sec 18)

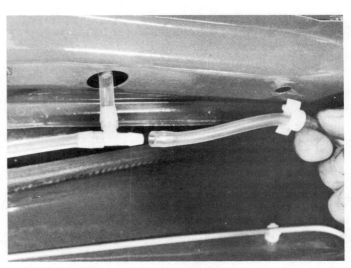

18.2 Detach the windscreen washer hose and clip before removing the bonnet

remove the bonnet-to-hinge retaining bolts, spring washers and plain washers at both hinges. Carefully lift away the bonnet over the front of the car.
5   Refitting is the reverse sequence to removal. Align the previously made pencil marks before finally tightening the bonnet-to-hinge retaining bolts.

washers securing the regulator to the door (photo).
5   Disengage the regulator arms from the door glass channel and the channel on the inner door casing. The regulator can now be withdrawn through the door aperture.
6   Refitting is the reverse sequence to removal.

18 Bonnet – removal and refitting

1   Open the bonnet and support it on its stay.
2   Detach the windscreen washer supply hose at the T-piece and also from the bonnet clip (photo).
3   With a pencil, mark the outline of the hinge on the bonnet to assist correct refitting. If the hinge is to be removed, also mark the inner panel.
4   An assistant should now take the weight of the bonnet. Undo and

19 Bonnet lock – removal and refitting

1   Open the bonnet and support it on its stay. Remove the radiator grille as described in Section 38.
2   Slacken the nut and detach the release cable from the trunnion located at the lock lever.
3   Detach the release cable and its clip from the bonnet lock.
4   Undo and remove the three bolts, plain washers and shakeproof washers that secure the bonnet lock. Lift away the bonnet lock.
5   Undo and remove the two bolts, plain washers and shakeproof washers that secure the locking pin assembly to the underside of the bonnet.
6   Detach the return spring and remove the rivet that secures the safety catch.
7   Refitting is the reverse sequence to removal. It is now necessary to adjust the lock pin assembly until a clearance of 2 in (50.8 mm)

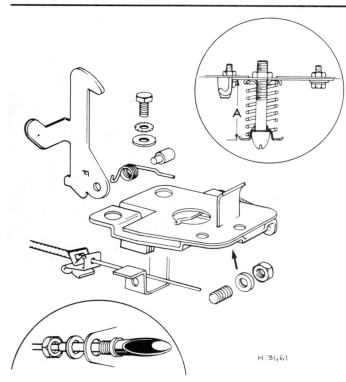

H13161

Fig. 12.7 Bonnet lock and control cable – see text
(Secs 19 and 20)

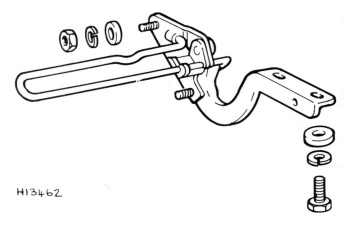

H13462

Fig. 12.8 Boot hinge assembly (Sec 21)

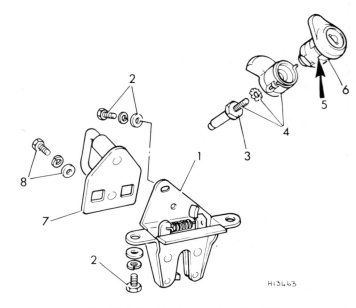

H13463

Fig. 12.9 Boot lock assembly (Sec 22)

1	Lock catch plate	5	Barrel housing spring
2	Bolt	6	Lock barrel assembly
3	Locknut	7	Striker
4	Shakeproof washer, spindle and spring	8	Bolt

exists (A, Fig. 12.7) between the thimble and bonnet panel.
8   Carefully lower the bonnet and check the alignment of the pin thimble with the lock hole. If misaligned, slacken the fixing bolts and move the assembly slightly. Retighten the fixing bolts.
9   Close the bonnet and check its alignment with the body wing panels. If necessary, reposition the locking pin assembly.
10 The bonnet must contact the rubber stops. To adjust the position of the stops, screw in or out as necessary.
11 Lubricate all moving parts and finally check the bonnet release operations.

20 Bonnet lock control cable – removal and refitting

1   Open the bonnet and support it on its stay. Remove the radiator grille as described in Section 38.
2   Slacken the nut and detach the release cable from the trunnion located at the lock lever.
3   Detach the release cable and its clip from the bonnet lock.
4   Release the outer control cable from its snap clamp, and then unscrew and remove the screw that secures each clip to the wing valance. Lift away the two clips.
5   Undo and remove the nut and shakeproof washer that secure the outer cable to the body side bracket mounted below the facia panel.
6   Carefully withdraw the control cable assembly through the body grommet.
7   Refitting is the reverse sequence to removal. It is, however, necessary to adjust the inner cable. Push the release knob in fully and make sure that the lock release lever is not preloaded by the release cable.
8   There must be a minimum movement of 0.5 in (12.7 mm) prior to the release of the bonnet. To adjust, slacken the cable trunnion nut and readjust the cable so that the bonnet is released with 0.5 to 2.0 in (12.7 to 50.8 mm) of cable movement.

21 Boot lid and hinge – removal and refitting

1   Open the lid and, using a pencil, mark the position of the hinge relative to the luggage compartment lid.
2   Undo and remove the four bolts, spring washers and plain washers

that secure the hinges to the lid. Lift away the lid over the back of the car. For this operation, it is desirable to have the assistance of a second person.
3   To remove the hinge, undo and remove the two nuts, plain washers and spring washers that secure each hinge to the body bracket. Lift away the hinge.
4   Refitting is the reverse sequence to removal, but if adjustment is necessary, leave the bolts that secure the hinge to the lid slack.
5   Close the lid and adjust the position to ensure correct trim spacing. Open the lid and tighten the hinge bolts. Do not overtighten as they could damage the outer lid panel.

22 Boot lid lock – removal and refitting

1   Using a pencil, mark the outline of the lock catch plate on the lid under the panel.
2   Undo and remove the three bolts, spring washers and plain washers that secure the lock catch (photo).
3   Slacken the locknut and unscrew the spindle. Lift away the

22.2 The boot lid lock ...

22.6 ... and striker plate

shakeproof washer, spindle striker and spring.
4   Using a screwdriver, break off the two retaining ears of the barrel housing spring retaining clip, and withdraw the barrel assembly and sealing gasket from outside the lid. A new clip will be necessary during assembly.
5   Using a pencil, mark the outline of the striker on the body panel.
6   Undo and remove the two bolts, spring washers and plain washers that retain the striker. Lift away the striker (photo).
7   Refitting is the reverse sequence to removal. Lubricate all moving parts with engine oil.

23 Tailgate and tailgate hinges (Estate) – removal and refitting

Tailgate
1   The tailgate of the Estate is removed by undoing the hinge bolts on the tailgate itself. Have an assistant hold the tailgate in the open position so that as the bolts are removed it will still remain supported. Do not forget to scribe round the hinges so that they can be refitted in a similar position. Refitting a new tailgate will mean that the exact positioning when closed will have to be adjusted using the same method as for a side door.

Tailgate hinges
2   Remove the rear interior light; note the earth wire secured beneath one fixing screw.
3   Carefully detach the rear compartment rear headlining and collect the press fasteners.
4   Detach the courtesy light switch from the right-hand hinge bracket. Disconnect the wire from the rear of the switch.
5   Using a pencil, mark the position of the hinges relative to the body to act as a datum for refitting.
6   Undo and remove the four screws, spring washers and plain washers that secure the hinge and torsion bar to each side of the body.
7   Lift away the hinge and torsion bar assembly.
8   Refitting the hinge and torsion bar assembly is the reverse sequence to removal.

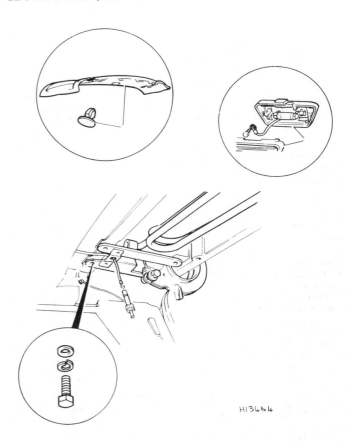

H13464

Fig. 12.10 Tailgate hinge removal (Sec 23)

24 Tailgate lock (Estate) – removal and refitting

1   Remove the tailgate trim panel.
2   Carefully unclip the retainer and detach the operating rod from the outside handle assembly.
3   Undo and remove the three screws and spring washers that secure the lock to the tailgate.
4   Lift away the tailgate lock assembly.
5   Refitting the tailgate lock assembly is the reverse sequence to removal. Lubricate all moving parts.

25 Tailgate lock striker plate (Estate) – removal and refitting

1   Lift up the tailgate.
2   Using a pencil, mark the position of the striker plate relative to the body to act as a datum for refitting.
3   Undo and remove the three screws, spring washers and plain washers that secure the striker plate to the body.
4   Lift away the striker plate.
5   Refitting the striker plate is the reverse sequence to removal.

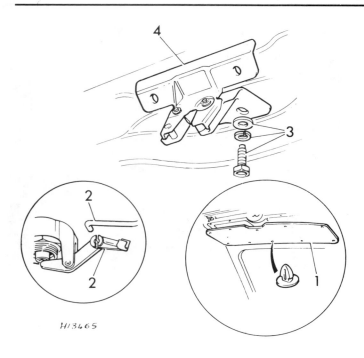

Fig. 12.11 Tailgate lock assembly (Sec 24)

1   Trim panel   3   Screw and washer
2   Operating rod and retainer   4   Lock assembly

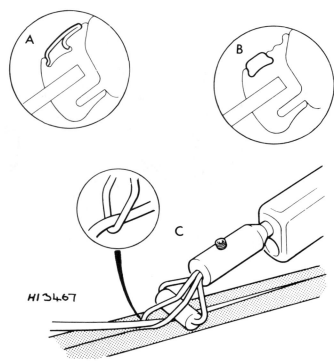

Fig. 12.12 Glass removal and refitting (Sec 27)

A and B Profiles of two types of finisher strip in place
C Type of tool necessary to fit finisher

26 Tailgate exterior handle and lock (Estate) – removal and refitting

1   Lift up the tailgate and remove the trim pad.
2   Carefully unclip the retainer and detach the lock operating rod from the operating lever.
3   Undo and remove the nut that secures the handle assembly to the tailgate.
4   Detach the operating lever assembly and remove the handle assembly and seal.
5   To remove the lock cylinder from the outside handle, first detach the retaining circlip.
6   Lift away the plain washer and coil spring and withdraw the cylinder assembly.
7   Refitting the lock cylinder and exterior handle is the reverse sequence to removal, but the following additional points should be noted:

   (a)   Lubricate all moving parts
   (b)   The handle grip should face downwards when fitted

27 Windscreen and rear window glass – removal and refitting

If you are unfortunate enough to have a windscreen shatter, fitting a replacement windscreen is one of the few jobs which the average owner is advised to leave to a professional. For the owner who wishes to do the job himself the following instructions are given:
1   Remove the wiper arms from their spindles, using a screwdriver to lift the retaining clip from the spindle end, and pull away.
2   Using a screwdriver, very carefully prise up the end of the finisher strip and withdraw it from its slot in the rubber moulding (Fig. 12.12).
3   The assistance of a second person should now be enlisted, ready to catch the glass when it is released from its aperture.
4   Working inside the car, commencing at one top corner, press the glass and ease it from its rubber moulding.
5   Remove the rubber moulding from the windscreen aperture.
6   Now is the time to remove all pieces of glass if the screen has shattered. Use a vacuum cleaner to extract as much as possible. Switch on the heater boost motor and adjust the controls to 'screen

defrost'. *Watch out for flying pieces of glass which might be blown out of the ducting.*
7   Carefully inspect the rubber moulding for signs of splitting or deterioration. Clean all trace of sealing compound from the rubber moulding and windscreen aperture flange.
8   To refit the glass, first apply sealer between the rubber and glass.
9   Press a little general purpose grease onto 4 or 5 in of the body flange on either side of each corner.
10 Apply some mastic sealer to the body flange.
11 With the rubber moulding correctly positioned on the glass, it is now necessary to insert a piece of cord about 16 ft long all round the outer channel in the rubber surround which fits over the windscreen aperture flange. The two free ends of the cord should finish at either top or bottom centre and overlap each other by a minimum of 1 ft.
12 Offer the screen up to the aperture and get an assistant to press the rubber surround hard against the body flange. Slowly pull one end of the cord, moving round the windscreen so drawing the lip over the windscreen flange on the body. If necessary, use a piece of plastic or tapered wood to assist in locating the lip on the windscreen flange.
13 The finisher strip must next be fitted to the moulding and for this a special tool is required. An illustration of this tool is shown in Fig. 12.12 and a handyman should be able to make up an equivalent using netting wire and a wooden file handle.
14 Fit the eye of the tool into the groove and feed in the finisher strip.
15 Push the tool around the complete length of the moulding, feeding the finisher into the channel as the eyelet opens it. The back half beds the finisher into the moulding.
16 Clean off all traces of sealer using turpentine.

28 Rear body side glass (Estate) – removal and refitting

1   With an assistant ready to catch the glass and rubber surround assembly, push outwards on the glass to release it from the aperture flange.
2   Carefully remove the finisher from the rubber surround.
3   Remove the rubber surround from the glass.
4   If the original glass and/or rubber surround are to be used again, all traces of old sealer should be removed.

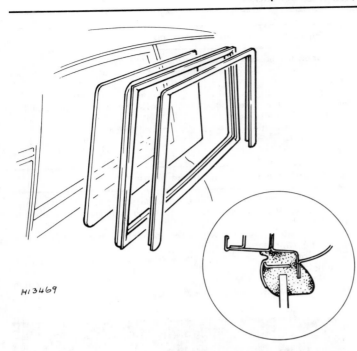

H13469

Fig. 12.13 Body side glass assembly (Sec 28)

5 Refit the rubber surround to the glass.
6 Using a suitable sealer, seal the rubber surround to the glass at the outside face.
7 Lubricate the finisher channel in the rubber surround with a soapy solution or washing up liquid.
8 Fit the finisher to the rubber surround.
9 Apply some sealer to the middle groove around the outside edge of the rubber surround.
10 Apply some sealer to the outside face of the window aperture in the body.
11 Fit some cord around the locating groove in the rubber surround, and with the ends inside the body, position the assembly up in the aperture.
12 Pull on the cord whilst an assistant pushes hard on the glass. The retaining lip should now move over the aperture flange and hold the glass and surround assembly in position. Clean off any surplus sealer.

29 Tailgate glass (Estate) – removal and refitting

The procedure is the same as described in Section 27, except that it will be necessary to disconnect the supply leads to the heated rear glass.

30 Facia panel – removal and refitting

1 Disconnect the battery earth terminal.
2 Refer to Chapter 11 and remove the steering wheel.
3 Refer to Chapter 10 and remove the instrument panel.

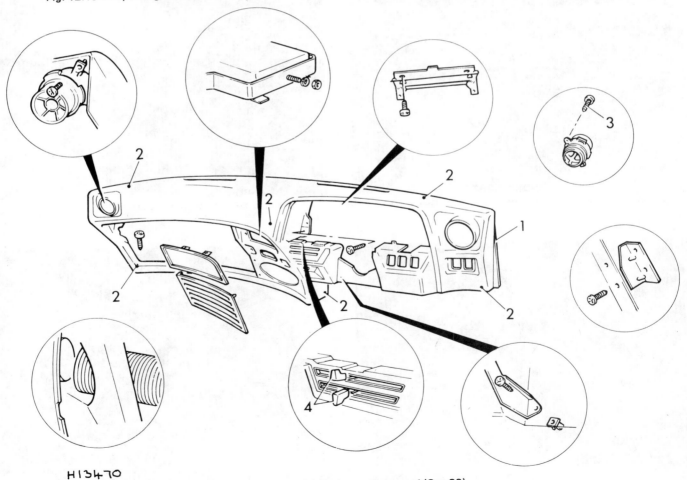

H13470

Fig. 12.14 Facia panel removal (Sec 30)

1 Facia panel   2 Retaining screw locations   3 Vent retaining screw   4 Heater controls

4   Refer to Section 31 and remove the glovebox.
5   Remove the parcel shelf by undoing the two securing nuts and washers, the screws and the clip.
6   Disconnect the face level vent tubes and detach the steering column bridge bracket.
7   Carefully pull off the heater control knobs.
8   Unscrew and remove the heater control retaining screws and secure the heater control to one side.
9   Note the position of all the switches and multi-plug connectors and then disconnect them from the facia panel.
10 Unscrew and remove the five facia panel securing screws and the three panel retaining nuts, then press the centre of the panel downwards to release it from the retaining clip.
11 The facia panel assembly can now be removed.
12 If further dismantling is necessary, unscrew the retaining screws and detach the two face level vents and glovebox hinge brackets.
13 Remove the ashtray and cigar lighter (if fitted).
14 Remove the speaker grille and prise out the radio blank.
15 Unscrew and remove the two retaining screws that secure the instrument pack support bracket to the facia panel.
16 Finally drill out the rivets to release the facia panel stud clip fasteners and remove the vent, glovebox and steering column bracket fixing.
17 Refitting is the reverse of the removal procedure.

31 Glovebox – removal and refitting

1   Open the lid and disconnect the hinge stay.
2   Remove the lower hinge bracket screws and loosen the upper ones.
3   Ease the lid from the right-hand hinge and remove it.
4   Remove the striker plate (two screws) followed by the glovebox itself (two more screws).
5   Refitting is the reverse of the removal procedure.

32 Centre console – removal and refitting

1   Unscrew the gear lever knob from the end of the gear lever.
2   Prise up the rear edge and remove the gear lever aperture trim panel and boot.
3   Undo and remove the two screws securing the front of the console to the floor (photo).
4   Disconnect the clock electrical lead and withdraw the illuminating bulb holder from the rear of the clock (photo).
5   Carefully prise up the rear cover plate and then undo and remove the console rear retaining screws (photos).

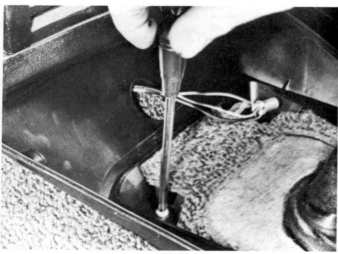

32.3 Undo and remove the two centre console front securing screws

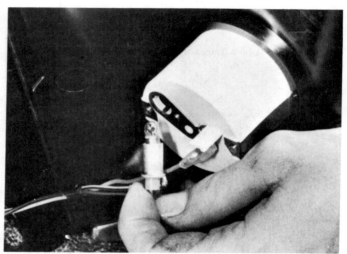

32.4 Detach the clock electrical lead and bulb holder

32.5a Prise up the rear cover plate ...

32.5b ... and then undo and remove the rear securing screws

6 Lift the centre console up over the gear lever and lift it off the car.
7 Refitting is the reverse sequence to removal.

33 Windscreen demister ducts – removal and refitting

1 Remove the instrument panel as described in Chapter 10, and the facia panel as described in Section 30.
2 Detach the hoses from the ducts, undo and remove the duct retaining screws or nuts, and lift away the ducts.
3 Refitting is the reverse sequence to removal.

34 Front seats – removal and refitting

1 Remove the two screws that secure the outer seat runner.
2 Unscrew the two locknuts that secure the inner seat runner to the car floor. Lift out the seat and lock bar assembly.
3 Refitting is the reverse of the removal procedure.

35 Rear seat squab and cushion (Saloon) – removal and refitting

1 Release the two cushion retaining clips and lift away the seat cushion.
2 Slacken the two screws and remove the arm rest.
3 Using a drill, remove the two rivet heads that secure the squab brackets. **Caution:** *Do not pass the drill through the body as it may damage or even puncture the brake pipes.*
4 Raise the squab to release the back panel from the three retaining hooks and lift away the squab.
5 Refitting the seat squab and cushion is the reverse sequence to removal. Always use pop rivets to retain the squab brackets. Do not use self-tapping screws.

36 Rear seat cushion (Estate) – removal and refitting

1 Pivot the cushion assembly forwards.
2 Using a pencil, mark the position of the hinges on the seat to act

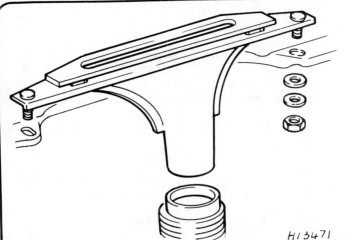

H13471

Fig. 12.15 Windscreen demister duct attachments (Sec 33)

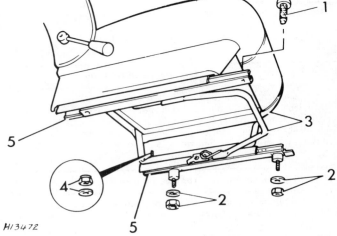

H13472

Fig. 12.16 Front seat removal (Sec 34)

1 Securing screws
2 Locknuts
3 Seat and lockbar
4 Seat runner securing nut
5 Seat runners

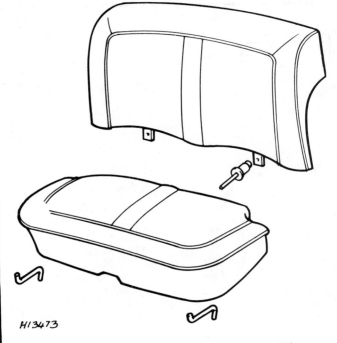

H13473

Fig. 12.17 Rear seat squab and cushion (Sec 35)

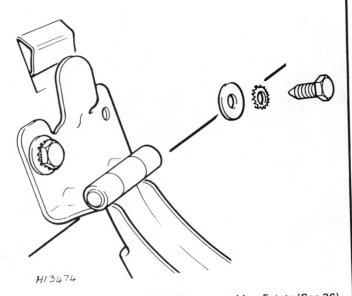

H13474

Fig. 12.18 Rear seat cushion hinge assembly – Estate (Sec 36)

as a datum for refitting.

3   Undo and remove the two screws, shakeproof washers and plain washers that secure the hinges to the seat.

4   Lift the cushion from the hinges.

5   Refitting the rear seat cushion is the reverse of the removal procedure.

37 Rear seat squab (Estate) – removal and refitting

1   Release the squab from its retaining catches and pivot the squab forwards.

2   Undo and remove the two countersunk screws that secure the squab pivots to the body at each side.

3   The squab may now be lifted away.

4   Refitting the rear seat squab is the reverse sequence to removal.

38 Radiator grille – removal and refitting

1   Refer to Chapter 10 and remove the two headlight assemblies.

2   Undo and remove the screws and plain washers securing the top and sides of the radiator grille to the front body panel.

3   Slacken the radiator grille lower retaining screws and lift off the grille.

4   Refitting is the reverse sequence to removal.

39 Front bumper assembly – removal and refitting

1   Undo and remove the bumper end securing bolts.

2   Undo and remove the nuts and bolts securing the bumper brackets to the front chassis members.

3   Carefully draw the front bumper forward and lift it off the car.

4   Refitting is the reverse sequence to removal.

40 Rear bumper assembly – removal and refitting

1   Open the boot lid and disconnect the number plate light leads at the wiring connectors. On Estate models, also disconnect the reversing light leads.

2   Remove the spare wheel from the luggage compartment.

3   Undo and remove the bumper end securing bolts.

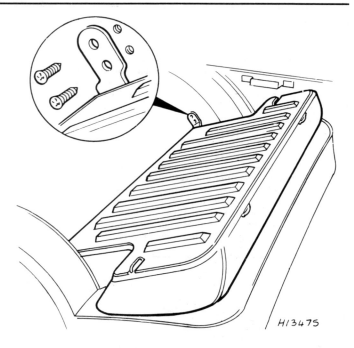

Fig. 12.19 Rear seat squab pivot attachment – Estate (Sec 37)

4   Undo and remove the bumper bracket retaining bolts and lift off the bumper.

5   Refitting is the reverse sequence to removal.

41 Heater unit – removal and refitting

1   Disconnect the battery earth terminal.

2   Refer to Chapter 2 and drain the cooling system.

3   Refer to Chapter 10 and remove the instrument panel. Remove the facia panel as described in Section 30.

4   Disconnect the demister and heating duct tubes from the heater and detach the fuse box from the parcel shelf.

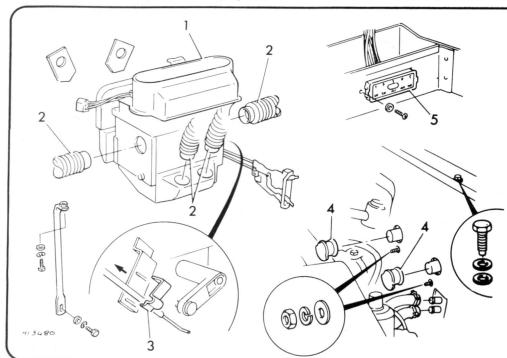

Fig. 12.20 Heater unit removal (Sec 41)

1   Heater assembly
2   Air ducts
3   Outer control cable clamp
4   Plenum drain point caps
5   Fuse box (on parcel shelf)

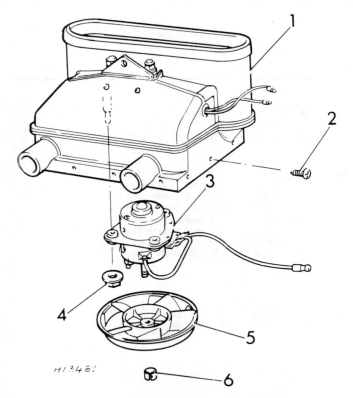

Fig. 12.21 Heater fan and motor assembly (Sec 42)

1	Plenum chamber	4	Nut
2	Screws	5	Fan
3	Motor	6	Fan retainer

5   Undo the securing screws and remove the parcel shelf.
6   Note the location of the heater motor supply leads and then disconnect them at their connectors.
7   Remove the centre console as described in Section 32.
8   Detach the passenger side facia support stay.
9   Loosen the clips and disconnect the two water hoses from the heater.
10 Pull off the two plenum drain point caps at the front of the bulkhead.
11 Unscrew and remove the two nuts and four washers that retain the heater side brackets to the bulkhead, then remove the upper windscreen panel heater retaining bolt.
12 Carefully pull the bottom of the heater rearwards and out of its location.
13 Detach the inner and outer control cables from the heater unit, withdraw the heater and remove the insulation and seal pads.
14 Refitting follows a reversal of the removal procedure, but before connecting the outer control cable clamp, hold the control levers in the 'OFF' position and slightly pull the outer cable away from the operating arm.

42 Heater fan and motor – removal and refitting

1   Refer to Section 41 and remove the heater unit.
2   Undo and remove the heater plenum chamber securing self-

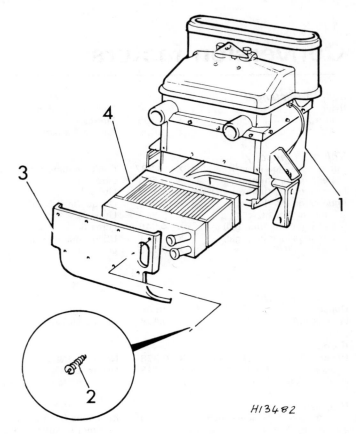

Fig. 12.22 Heater matrix removal (Sec 43)

1	Heater casing	3	Cover plate
2	Screw	4	Matrix

tapping screws and lift away the plenum chamber.
3   Undo and remove the three nuts and plain washers that secure the motor and fan assembly to the heater body. Lift away the motor.
4   If it is necessary to remove the fan, note which way round on the motor spindle it is fitted and remove the spring clip on the fan boss. Lift away the fan.
5   Refitting the heater fan and motor is the reverse sequence to removal. Before fitting a new motor, always test it by placing the cable terminals on the battery terminals.

43 Heater matrix – removal and refitting

1   Refer to Section 41 and remove the heater unit.
2   Carefully remove the packing rubber from the forward end of the heater unit.
3   Undo and remove the screws that secure the matrix cover plate to the heater body. Lift away the cover plate.
4   The heater matrix may now be slid out from its location in the heater body.
5   If the matrix is leaking or blocked, renewal is recommended.
6   Refitting the heater matrix is the reverse sequence to removal.

Conversion factors

Length (distance)

Inches (in)	X	25.4	= Millimetres (mm)	X	0.0394	= Inches (in)
Feet (ft)	X	0.305	= Metres (m)	X	3.281	= Feet (ft)
Miles	X	1.609	= Kilometres (km)	X	0.621	= Miles

Volume (capacity)

Cubic inches (cu in; in^3)	X	16.387	= Cubic centimetres (cc; cm^3)	X	0.061	= Cubic inches (cu in; in^3)
Imperial pints (Imp pt)	X	0.568	= Litres (l)	X	1.76	= Imperial pints (Imp pt)
Imperial quarts (Imp qt)	X	1.137	= Litres (l)	X	0.88	= Imperial quarts (Imp qt)
Imperial quarts (Imp qt)	X	1.201	= US quarts (US qt)	X	0.833	= Imperial quarts (Imp qt)
US quarts (US qt)	X	0.946	= Litres (l)	X	1.057	= US quarts (US qt)
Imperial gallons (Imp gal)	X	4.546	= Litres (l)	X	0.22	= Imperial gallons (Imp gal)
Imperial gallons (Imp gal)	X	1.201	= US gallons (US gal)	X	0.833	= Imperial gallons (Imp gal)
US gallons (US gal)	X	3.785	= Litres (l)	X	0.264	= US gallons (US gal)

Mass (weight)

Ounces (oz)	X	28.35	= Grams (g)	X	0.035	= Ounces (oz)
Pounds (lb)	X	0.454	= Kilograms (kg)	X	2.205	= Pounds (lb)

Force

Ounces-force (ozf; oz)	X	0.278	= Newtons (N)	X	3.6	= Ounces-force (ozf; oz)
Pounds-force (lbf; lb)	X	4.448	= Newtons (N)	X	0.225	= Pounds-force (lbf; lb)
Newtons (N)	X	0.1	= Kilograms-force (kgf; kg)	X	9.81	= Newtons (N)

Pressure

Pounds-force per square inch (psi; lbf/in^2; lb/in^2)	X	0.070	= Kilograms-force per square centimetre (kgf/cm^2; kg/cm^2)	X	14.223	= Pounds-force per square inch (psi; lbf/in^2; lb/in^2)
Pounds-force per square inch (psi; lbf/in^2; lb/in^2)	X	0.068	= Atmospheres (atm)	X	14.696	= Pounds-force per square inch (psi; lbf/in^2; lb/in^2)
Pounds-force per square inch (psi; lbf/in^2; lb/in^2)	X	0.069	= Bars	X	14.5	= Pounds-force per square inch (psi; lbf/in^2; lb/in^2)
Pounds-force per square inch (psi; lbf/in^2; lb/in^2)	X	6.895	= Kilopascals (kPa)	X	0.145	= Pounds-force per square inch (psi; lbf/in^2; lb/in^2)
Kilopascals (kPa)	X	0.01	= Kilograms-force per square centimetre (kgf/cm^2; kg/cm^2)	X	98.1	= Kilopascals (kPa)

Torque (moment of force)

Pounds-force inches (lbf in; lb in)	X	1.152	= Kilograms-force centimetre (kgf cm; kg cm)	X	0.868	= Pounds-force inches (lbf in; lb in)
Pounds-force inches (lbf in; lb in)	X	0.113	= Newton metres (Nm)	X	8.85	= Pounds-force inches (lbf in; lb in)
Pounds-force inches (lbf in; lb in)	X	0.083	= Pounds-force feet (lbf ft; lb ft)	X	12	= Pounds-force inches (lbf in; lb in)
Pounds-force feet (lbf ft; lb ft)	X	0.138	= Kilograms-force metres (kgf m; kg m)	X	7.233	= Pounds-force feet (lbf ft; lb ft)
Pounds-force feet (lbf ft; lb ft)	X	1.356	= Newton metres (Nm)	X	0.738	= Pounds-force feet (lbf ft; lb ft)
Newton metres (Nm)	X	0.102	= Kilograms-force metres (kgf m; kg m)	X	9.804	= Newton metres (Nm)

Power

Horsepower (hp)	X	745.7	= Watts (W)	X	0.0013	= Horsepower (hp)

Velocity (speed)

Miles per hour (miles/hr; mph)	X	1.609	= Kilometres per hour (km/hr; kph)	X	0.621	= Miles per hour (miles/hr; mph)

Fuel consumption*

Miles per gallon, Imperial (mpg)	X	0.354	= Kilometres per litre (km/l)	X	2.825	= Miles per gallon, Imperial (mpg)
Miles per gallon, US (mpg)	X	0.425	= Kilometres per litre (km/l)	X	2.352	= Miles per gallon, US (mpg)

Temperature

Degrees Fahrenheit = (°C x 1.8) + 32

Degrees Celsius (Degrees Centigrade; °C) = (°F - 32) x 0.56

*It is common practice to convert from miles per gallon (mpg) to litres/100 kilometres (l/100km), where mpg (Imperial) x l/100 km = 282 and mpg (US) x l/100 km = 235

Index

**Printed by
Haynes Publishing Group
Sparkford Yeovil Somerset
England**